W9-BSR-072

Learning Web Design

A Beginner's Guide to HTML, Graphics, and Beyond

Jennifer Niederst

O'REILLY®

Beijing • Cambridge • Farnham • Köln • Paris • Sebastopol • Taipei • Tokyo

Learning Web Design

by Jennifer Niederst

Copyright © 2001 O'Reilly & Associates, Inc. All rights reserved.
Printed in the United States of America.

Published by O'Reilly & Associates, Inc., 101 Morris Street, Sebastopol, CA 95472.

Print History:		**Editors:**	Richard Koman and Paula Ferguson
March 2001:	First edition.	**Production Editor:**	Colleen Gorman
		Cover Designer:	Edie Freedman
		Interior Designer:	David Futato

Nutshell Handbook, the Nutshell Handbook logo, and the O'Reilly logo are registered trademarks and the O'Reilly Web Studio logo is a trademark of O'Reilly & Associates, Inc. Many of the designations used by manufacturers and sellers to distinguish their products are claimed as trademarks. Where those designations appear in this book, and O'Reilly & Associates, Inc. was aware of a trademark claim, the designations have been printed in caps or initial caps.

While every precaution has been taken in the preparation of this book, the publisher assumes no responsibility for errors or omissions, or for damages resulting from the use of the information contained herein.

0-596-00036-7
[C]

Learning Web Design

Contents

Part II: Learning HTML

Preface

Over the past few years, I've had the opportunity to teach web design to hundreds of absolute beginners. My classes and workshops have been filled to capacity with seasoned graphic designers, office assistants, recent college graduates, programmers looking for a more creative outlet, work-at-home moms, and anyone else looking to get a start in web design. Despite the variety of backgrounds, I find that I keep hearing the same questions and concerns over and over. Similarly, I've noticed that there are certain concepts that regularly trip up my students and other topics that they master with ease.

Through a certain amount of trial and error, I've developed a successful method for teaching beginning web design, and that method forms the structure for this book. Reading this book is a lot like sitting in my classroom!

I wrote my last book, *Web Design in a Nutshell* (O'Reilly, 1999), because it was the book I needed to do my job as a web designer. I've written this book because it is the book I wish I had been able to give my students. While *Web Design in a Nutshell* is comprehensive and contains detailed explanations, it is most appropriate for intermediate-level and professional web designers. *Learning Web Design* addresses the specific needs and concerns of beginners. I like to think of it as the "prequel" to the Nutshell book.

Although this book is for newcomers, I haven't "dumbed down" or glossed over anything. I dig deep into HTML coding and web graphics production. You will certainly find plenty of technical information, as you'd expect in a book from O'Reilly.

However, I do assume you have a certain level of knowledge. Obviously, you'll need to know your way around a computer and have a basic familiarity with the Web, even if you've just surfed a little. Also, this book doesn't teach basic principles of graphic design such as color theory, type design, or balance and proportion. However, I do provide some design tips in Chapter 19, Web Design Dos and Don'ts. Finally, I assume that you know how to use an image editing software package to create graphics; I'll teach you how to make them appropriate for the Web.

TIP

Be sure to visit the companion web site for this book at *www.learningwebdesign.com*. It features color charts, lists of links from the book, updates, and other good stuff.

Whenever possible, I provide pointers on how current web design tools, both for authoring web pages and creating web graphics, can help you create web sites more quickly and easily. These tools have come a long way in the past few years, and I wholeheartedly recommend that you take advantage of them, even for professional-level work. Unfortunately, I can't include every available web-related product in this book, so I've stuck with the most popular tools: Dreamweaver, GoLive, and FrontPage for web authoring, and Photoshop, Fireworks, and Paint Shop Pro for creating web graphics. In most cases, the general principles apply to whichever tool you prefer, so don't be dismayed if your favorite tool isn't featured here. If it works for you, that's all that matters.

Whether you are reading this book on your own or using it as a companion to a web design course, I hope it gives you a good head start toward becoming a web designer. And more importantly, I hope you have fun!

Contents

The book is divided into four parts, each covering a general subject area.

Part I: Getting Started

Part I provides answers to the common questions people have when getting started in web design. It lays a foundation for understanding the medium, before jumping into the nitty-gritty of tags and file formats.

Chapter 1, Where Do I Start?, answers the big questions: where to start, what you need to learn, what you need to buy, and so on.

Chapter 2, How the Web Works, introduces the Web, URLs, servers, browsers, and the anatomy of basic web pages.

Chapter 3, Getting Your Pages on the Web, provides a step-by-step demonstration of how to upload a web page. This chapter also addresses finding a hosting service and registering domain names.

Chapter 4, Why Web Design Isn't Like Print Design, is a summary of the unknown factors that affect the web design process, as well as tips for coping with them.

Chapter 5, The Web Design Process, takes you through the steps of creating a web site, from conceptualization through final testing.

Part II: Learning HTML

Part II focuses on HTML tags and their uses. I provide complete instructions for tagging by hand, and also offer tips on using popular web authoring tools that can do the job for you.

Chapter 6, Creating a Simple Page, shows how to create a basic web page, and includes explanations of how HTML works and the tags necessary to structure a document.

Chapter 7, Formatting Text, explains all the tags and attributes used to control the display of type in web pages.

Chapter 8, Adding Graphic Elements, explores the HTML tags related to adding graphics and horizontal rules to the page.

Chapter 9, Adding Links, focuses on the tags used for adding hypertext links to a page.

Chapter 10, Tables, provides a thorough introduction to tables: how they're used, how they're tagged, and how they can go wrong.

Chapter 11, Frames, covers the structure and creation of framed documents, including explanations of frame-related HTML tags as well as tips and tricks for using frames effectively.

Chapter 12, Color on the Web, explains the options for specifying colors for HTML elements.

Part III: Creating Web Graphics

Part III covers what you need to know about creating graphics for the Web. I provide background information on web graphics file formats, overviews of available tools, and practical tips for graphics production and optimization.

Chapter 13, All About Web Graphics, introduces important concepts that apply to all web graphics: appropriate file formats, image resolutions, production tips, and more.

Chapter 14, Creating GIFs, discusses all aspects of creating graphics in the GIF format, including transparency, optimization tips, and the web palette.

Chapter 15, Creating JPEGs, describes the process of creating and optimizing JPEGs.

Chapter 16, Animated GIFs, looks at the creation and optimization of animated GIFs.

Part IV: Form and Function

Part IV returns to the big-picture issues of what makes a web site work well and look professional.

Chapter 17, Web Design Techniques, uses a combination of the skills established in Parts II and III to create a number of common web design elements.

Chapter 18, Building Usable Web Sites, introduces the basic principles of information design, interface design, and navigation.

Chapter 19, Web Design Dos and Don'ts, provides a rapid-fire list of tips for what to do and what *not* to do in web design.

Chapter 20, How'd They Do That: An Introduction to Advanced Techniques, introduces advanced techniques and technologies, so you can recognize them when you see them.

Conventions Used in This Book

The following typographic conventions are used in this book:

Italic

> Used to indicate URLs, email addresses, filenames, and directory names, as well as for emphasis.

Colored roman text

> Used for special terms that are being defined and for cross-references.

`Constant width`

> Used to indicate code examples and keyboard commands.

`Colored constant width`

> Used to indicate HTML tags and attributes, and used for emphasis in code examples.

`Constant width italic`

> Used to indicate placeholders for values in HTML attributes.

G Used to indicate a figure that appears in full color in the gallery insert.

Acknowledgments

Once again, thanks go to my editor, Richard Koman, for believing in a beginner's book and making it happen. I want to thank Edie Freedman for her diligence with the series cover design and David Futato for his patience in creating the series interior design. Thanks also to the others who have contributed hands-on time to the project: Chris Reilley for his top-notch figures and information design, Colleen Gorman for copyediting, Paula Ferguson for jumping in on the editing in the ninth inning, Bruce Tracy for writing the index, Rachel Wheeler for proofreading the manuscript, and everyone else who contributed to the construction of this book.

As always, I want to thank my Mom and Dad for their unending encouragement, optimism, and humor. Warm thanks go to my brother, Liam, for being an inspiration and for happily contributing images for several figures in this book. Thanks also go to the whole Robbins clan for their interest in my writing endeavors and for making me feel like one of the family. And last, but certainly not least, my love and appreciation go to Jeff, my favorite distraction.

Getting Started

There's a lot more to the art of web design than HTML and GIF files. If you're just getting started, chances are you have some big questions. Where do I start? How does it all work? How do I actually get my stuff on the Web? How is web design different from print design?

Part I answers all of these questions and more. Before we get into the nitty-gritty of tags and file formats, it is important that you have a good feel for the web design environment. Once you understand the medium and its quirks, you'll have a good head start toward using your tools and making design decisions. All the rest will fall into place.

Chapter 1

Where Do I Start?

The buzz about the Web has been so loud it is impossible to ignore. For many people, it's a call to action—a new career opportunity, an incentive to keep up with competitors, or just a chance to get stuff out there for the world to see. But the Web can also seem overwhelming.

Through my experience teaching web design courses and workshops, I've had the opportunity to meet people of all backgrounds who are interested in learning how to build web pages. Allow me to introduce you to just a few:

> "I've been a print designer for 17 years, and now all my clients want web sites."

> "I work as a secretary in a small office. My boss has asked me to put together a small internal web site to share company information among employees."

> "I've been a programmer for years, but I want to try my hand at more visual design. I feel like the Web is a good opportunity to explore new skills."

> "I am an artist and I want to know how to get samples of my paintings and sculpture online."

> "I'm right out of college and I heard that there are lots of jobs in the web design field."

> "I'm a designer who has watched all my colleagues switch to web design in the last few years. I'm curious about it, but I feel like I'm too late."

Whatever the motivation, the first question is always the same: "Where do I start?" With something as seemingly vast and fast-moving as the Web, it's not easy to know where to jump in. But you have to start somewhere.

In this chapter, I will answer the most frequently asked questions from people who are ready to make the leap into web design.

IN THIS CHAPTER

Am I too late?

Where do I start?

What do I need to learn?

Do I need to learn Java? What other languages do I need to know?

What software and equipment do I need to buy?

Am I Too Late?

That's an easy one—absolutely not! Although it may seem that everyone in the whole world has a personal web page, or that your colleagues are all light years ahead of you in web experience, I can assure you that you're not too late. Furthermore, there is plenty of room for you in the business. The industry as a whole is thirsty for folks who know how to make web pages (even at an entry level) and the opportunities continue to expand.

Keep in mind that this is a medium and an industry in its infancy. You're still in time to be a pioneer!

Where Do I Start?

The first step is understanding the fundamentals of how the Web works, including a working knowledge of HTML, the role of the server, and the importance of the browser.

The first step is understanding the fundamentals of how the Web works, including a working knowledge of HTML, the role of the server, and the importance of the browser. This book has been written specifically to address these topics, so you are certainly on the right track. Once you learn the fundamentals, there are plenty of resources on the Web and in bookstores for you to further your learning in specific areas.

One way to get up to speed quickly is to take an introductory web design class. If you don't have the luxury of a full-semester course, even a weekend or one-day seminar can be extremely useful in getting over that first hump.

If your involvement in web design is purely at the hobbyist level, or if you have just one or two web projects you'd like to publish, you may find that a combination of personal research (like reading this book) and solid web-design tools (such as Macromedia Dreamweaver) may be all you need to accomplish the task at hand.

If you are interested in pursuing web design as a career, I recommend learning enough to put together some sample web sites for yourself or your friends, just to show your stuff to potential employers. Getting an entry-level job and working as part of a team is a great way to learn how larger sites are constructed and can help you decide which specific area of web design you would like to pursue.

What Do I Need to Learn?

This one's a big question. The answer depends on where you are starting and what you want to do. I know, I know, that answer sounds like a cop-out, but it really is true, given the wide variety of tasks involved in web design.

The term "web design" has become a catch-all for a process that actually encompasses a number of different disciplines, from graphic design to programming. We'll take a look at each of them.

If you are designing a small web site on your own, you will need to wear many hats. The good news is that you probably won't notice. Consider that the day-to-day upkeep of your household requires you to be part-time chef, housecleaner, accountant, diplomat, gardener, and construction worker—but to you it's just the stuff you do around the house. In the same way, as a solo web designer, you'll be part-time graphic designer, writer, producer, and information architect, but to you, it'll just feel like "making web pages." Nothing to worry about.

Large-scale web sites are almost always created by a team of people, numbering from a handful to hundreds. In this scenario, each member of the team focuses on just one facet of the design process. If you are not interested in becoming a jack-of-all-trades solo web designer, you may choose to specialize and work as part of a team. If that is the case, you may be able to simply adapt your current set of skills and interests to the new medium.

The following are some of the core disciplines involved in the web design process, along with brief descriptions of the skills required in each area.

Graphic Design

Because the Web is a visual medium, web pages require attention to presentation and design. The graphic designer makes decisions regarding everything you see on a web page: graphics, type, colors, layout, etc. As in the print world, graphic designers play an important role in the success of the final product. If you work as a graphic designer in the web design process, you may never need to learn any programming. (I didn't!)

If you are interested in designing commercial sites professionally, I strongly recommend formal graphic design training as well as a strong proficiency in Adobe Photoshop (the industry standard). If you are already a graphic designer, you will be able to adapt your skills to the Web easily.

Because graphics are a big part of web design, hobbyist web designers will need to know how to use some image editing software, at minimum. In addition, you may also want to do some personal research on the fundamentals of good design. I recommend *The Non-Designer's Web Book* by Robin Williams (well-known for her popular *The Non-Designer's Design Book*) and John Tollett (Peachpit Press, 1998). It provides sound graphic design advice as applied to the web medium. For more general background on design principles, check out *Design Basics, Fifth Edition* by David Lauer and Stephen Pentak (Harcourt College Publishers, 2000).

AT A GLANCE

"Web design" actually combines a number of disciplines, including:

- Graphic design
- Interface design
- Information design
- HTML production
- Programming
- Multimedia

Web Design Skills of Working Web Designers

Adam Gibbons

Senior Designer at a large web marketing firm

DOES:

- Information architecture
- Interface design
- Graphic production
- HTML production (with authoring tool)

DOESN'T DO:

- JavaScript
- DHTML
- Programming

Jennifer Niederst

Freelance web designer
www.littlechair.com

DOES:

- Graphic design and production
- Interface design
- Information design
- Writing/content development
- Basic HTML production
- Style sheet creation

DOESN'T DO:

- JavaScript
- Back-end programming (CGI, XML)

Jason Warne

Senior Designer at a large web development company

DOES:

- Interface design
- Graphic production
- Multimedia production (Flash)

DOESN'T DO:

- HTML production
- JavaScript
- Programming

Interface Design

If graphic design is concerned with how the page looks, interface design focuses on how the page works. The interface of a web site includes the methods for doing things on a site: buttons, links, navigation devices, etc., as well as the functional organization of the page. In most cases, the interface and graphic design of a site are inextricably entwined. I discuss interface design further in Chapter 18, Building Usable Web Sites.

Often, the interface design falls into the hands of a graphic designer by default; in other cases, it is handled by an interface design specialist. Many interface designers have backgrounds in software design. It is possible to find courses on interface design; however, this is an area that you can build expertise in by a combination of personal research, experience in the field, and common sense.

Information Design

One easily overlooked aspect of web design is information design—the organization of content and how you get to it. Information designers (also called "information architects") deal with flow-charts and diagrams and may never touch a graphic or text file; however, they are a crucial part of the creation of the site.

Some information designers have a background in the Library Sciences. It is possible (but not simple) to find courses specifically about information design, although they are likely to be at the graduate level. Again, some personal research and experience working on a team will go a long way toward rounding out this skill. We will look at some basic principles of information design in Chapter 18.

HTML Production

A fair amount of the web design process involves the creation and troubleshooting of the HTML documents that make up a site. Production people need to have an intricate knowledge of HTML (the tagging language used to make web documents), and usually some additional scripting or programming skills. At large web design firms, the team that handles HTML and coding is sometimes called the "development" department.

Fortunately basic HTML is easy to learn on your own, and there are new and powerful tools that can reduce errors and speed up the production process.

Programming

Advanced web functionality (such as forms and interactivity) requires traditional programming skills for writing scripts, programs, and applications, and for working with databases, servers, and so on. The stuff behind the scenes makes web pages work their real magic, and there is a huge demand for programmers. Professional programmers may never touch a graphic file or have input on how the pages look. If you want to become a programmer, definitely pursue a degree in Computer Science. Although some programmers are self-taught, formal training is beneficial.

It is possible to turn out competent, content-rich, well-designed sites without the need for programming, so hobbyist web designers should not be discouraged. However, once you get into collecting complex information via forms, or serving information on demand, it is necessary to have a programmer on the team.

Multimedia

One of the cool things about the Web is that you can add multimedia elements to your site, including sound, video, animation, and interactivity. If you are interested in specializing in multimedia for the Web, I recommend becoming a power-user of multimedia tools such as Macromedia Flash and/or Director. A background in sound and video production is also beneficial. Web development companies usually look for people who have mastered the standard multimedia tools, and have a good visual sensibility and an instinct for intuitive and creative multimedia design.

Do I Need to Learn Java?

You'd be surprised at the number of times I've heard the following: "I want to get into web design so I went out and bought a book on Java." I usually respond, "Well, go return it!" Before you spend money on a big Java book, I'm here to tell you that you won't ever need to know Java programming to be a web designer.

The following is a list of "languages" associated with the creation of web sites. They are listed in general order of complexity and in the order that you might want to learn them. Bear in mind, the only *requirement* is HTML. Where you draw the line after that is up to you.

HTML (HyperText Markup Language)

This is the language used to write web page documents (we'll discuss it further in the next part and throughout this book). Writing HTML is not programming, it's more like word processing in longhand.

Everyone involved with the Web needs a basic understanding of how HTML works. Its limitations and quirks define what can be done on the Web. If you're in web production, you'll live it and breathe it. The good news is that it's simple to learn the basics. Plus, there are HTML editing tools that will make the work even easier for you.

AT A GLANCE
Web-related programming "languages" in order of increasing complexity: · HTML · Style sheets · JavaScript · DHTML · CGI scripting · XML · Java

Style Sheets

Once you've mastered HTML, you may want to try your hand at Cascading Style Sheets (CSS). Style sheets give you extended control over the text and page formatting, and are great for automating production. Style sheets for the Web are still relatively new, so they won't work on all browsers. However, the current browser developments suggest that style sheets will become increasingly important in the next several years. Style sheets are discussed further in Chapter 20, How'd They Do That?.

JavaScript

Despite its name, JavaScript is not at all related to Java. JavaScript is a web-specific scripting language; special instructions can be inserted in web pages to add functionality, like popping up new windows or making something change when the mouse is passed over it. Learning JavaScript means learning a programming language, so the learning curve is steep. Depending on your role in the web design process, the tools you use, and the people you hire or work with, you may never need to learn to write JavaScript yourself. JavaScript is discussed a little more in Chapter 20.

DHTML (Dynamic HTML)

DHTML is not a separate programming language; it refers to the use of a combination of HTML, JavaScript, and CSS in a way that makes page elements move or change (thus the term "dynamic"). Because browsers have different ways of handling DHTML content, making DHTML work correctly is tricky. Writing DHTML code is an advanced web-production skill—useful to learn if you want to specialize in web production and programming, but not essential for everyone. Fortunately, tools like Macromedia Dreamweaver provide an easy interface for adding basic DHTML tricks animation to your pages. For a more thorough introduction, see Chapter 20.

CGI Programming

Some web pages, including those that use forms and databases, rely on special programs to send information to and from the user. These programs are sometimes called CGI (Common Gateway Interface) scripts, and can be written in a number of programming languages. Writing CGI scripts is typically programmer territory and is not expected of web designers.

XML

XML (which stands for eXtensible Markup Language) is a tagging language like HTML, only on a much larger, more robust scale. Whereas

HTML concerns itself mainly with the elements on a page (headings, paragraphs, quotes, etc.), XML is used to define the types of content within the document (author, creation date, account number, etc.). The cool thing about XML is that you can create sets of tags appropriate for your information. To use a classic example, if you were publishing recipes, you might create a set of XML tags that included `<ingredient>`, `<instructions>`, and `<servings>`. A bank might use a set of XML tags to identify the `<account>`, `<balance>`, `<date>`, etc. This makes XML a powerful tool for transferring data between applications and handling the data in complex databases, as well as displaying it on a web page. Since most of this happens on the "back end" (rather than in the browser window), the responsibility for XML development usually falls in the hands of programmers.

Java

Although Java can be used for creating small applications for the Web (known as "applets"), it is a complete and complex programming language that is typically used for developing large, enterprise-scale applications. Learn Java only if you want to become a Java programmer. You can live your life as a web designer without knowing a stitch of Java (as I do).

What Do I Need to Buy?

It should come as no surprise that professional web designers require a fair amount of gear, both hardware and software. One of the most common questions I'm asked by my students is, "What should I get?" I can't tell you specifically what to buy, but I will provide an overview of the typical tools of the trade.

Equipment

For a comfortable web site–creation environment, I recommend the following equipment:

A solid, up-to-date computer. Either Windows or Macintosh is fine, but most creative departments in professional web development companies tend to be Mac-based. Although it is nice to have a super-fast machine, the files that make up web pages are very small and tend not to be too taxing on computers. Unless you're getting into sound and video editing, don't worry if your current setup is not absolute state-of-the-art.

Extra memory. Because you'll tend to bounce between a number of software programs, it's a good idea to have enough RAM installed on your computer to be able to leave those programs running at the same time. It depends on the programs you're running, but as a ballpark figure, 32 MB is an absolute minimum; 64 MB is more comfortable; and 128 MB and up is preferable.

A large monitor. While not a requirement, a large or high-resolution monitor (1024 × 768 pixels and up) makes life easier. The more monitor real estate you have, the more windows and control panels you can have open at the same time. You can also see more of your page to make design decisions.

A second computer. Many web designers find it useful to have test computers that are different platforms than their primary computers (i.e., if you design on a Mac, test on a PC). Because browsers work differently on Macs than on Windows machines, it's critical to test your pages in as many environments as possible. If you are a hobbyist web designer working at home, check your pages on a friend's machine.

A scanner. Scanners come in handy for creating images or textures. I know a designer who has two scanners: one is the "good" scanner, and the other he uses to scan things like dead fish and rusty pans. I sometimes use my digital camera to collect images as well.

Software

There's no shortage of software available for creating web pages. In the early days, we just made do with tools originally designed for print. Today, there are wonderful tools designed with web design specifically in mind. Now in their third- and fourth-version releases, they have become very savvy at making the web design process more efficient. Although I can't list every available software release (you can find other offerings as well as the current version numbers of the following programs in software catalogs), I'd like to introduce you to the most common and proven tools for web design.

Web page authoring

Web-authoring tools are similar to desktop publishing tools, but the end product is a web page document (an HTML file). These tools provide a visual "WYSIWYG" (What You See Is What You Get) interface and shortcuts that save you from typing repetitive HTML code. Some of the more powerful packages also generate JavaScript and DHTML. The following are the names of some popular web-authoring programs:

Macromedia Dreamweaver. This is the industry standard due to its clean code and advanced features.

Adobe GoLive. GoLive is another top-of-the-line tool with advanced features.

Microsoft FrontPage. This program is quite popular in the business world, but notorious for adding extra proprietary code to its files, so it tends to be shunned by professional web designers. Another drawback is that some functions require special Microsoft software on the server, so check with your server administrator if you are planning on using FrontPage.

HTML editors

HTML editors (as opposed to authoring tools) are designed to speed up the process of writing HTML by hand. They do not allow you edit the page visually like WYSIWYG authoring tools (listed previously) do. Many professional web designers actually prefer to create HTML documents by hand, and they overwhelmingly recommend the following two tools:

Allaire HomeSite (Windows only). This inexpensive tool includes shortcuts, templates, and even wizards for more complex elements.

BBEdit by Bare Bones Software (Macintosh only). Lots of great features make this the editor of choice for Mac-based web developers.

Graphics software

You'll probably want to add pictures to your pages (that's part of the fun of the Web), so you will need an image-editing program. We'll look at some of the more popular programs in greater detail in Part III: Creating Web Graphics. In the meantime, you may want to look into the following popular web graphics–creation tools:

Adobe Photoshop. Photoshop is undeniably the industry standard for graphics creation in both the print and web worlds. Version 5.5 added many advanced features tailored specifically for creating efficient and high-quality web graphics. If you want to be a professional designer, you'll need to learn Photoshop inside and out.

Adobe ImageReady. Bundled with Adobe Photoshop, this web graphics program helps make smaller, better graphics and also provides special functions such as animation and "rollover" effects.

Macromedia Fireworks. This web graphics–creation program combines a drawing program (similar to Macromedia Freehand or Adobe Illustrator) with an image editor. Its real power lies in its web-specific functions for creating optimized graphics, animated graphics, and interactive buttons.

Adobe Illustrator. This drawing program is often used to create graphics, which are then brought into Photoshop for fine-tuning.

JASC Paint Shop Pro (Windows only). This full-featured image editor is very popular with the Windows crowd, primarily due to its low price (only $99 at the time of this printing).

Where Do I Start?

AT A GLANCE

Popular Web Design Software

Web Page Authoring

Macromedia Dreamweaver
www.macromedia.com

Adobe GoLive
www.adobe.com

Microsoft FrontPage
www.microsoft.com/catalog/

HTML Editing

Allaire HomeSite
www.allaire.com

BBEdit by Bare Bones Software
www.barebones.com

Graphics

Adobe Photoshop

Adobe ImageReady

Macromedia Fireworks

JASC Paint Shop Pro
www.jasc.com

Adobe Illustrator

Macromedia Freehand

Multimedia

Macromedia Flash

Macromedia Director

Adobe Premier

Adobe After Effects

Macromedia SoundEdit

Internet Tools

Netscape Navigator (browser)
home.netscape.com/browsers/

Microsoft Internet Explorer (browser)
www.microsoft.com/windows/ie/
www.microsoft.com/mac/ie/

Lynx (text-only browser)
lynx.browser.org

File transfer (FTP) programs

Telnet

Multimedia tools

Because this is a book for beginners, we won't be focusing on advanced multimedia elements; however, it is still useful to be aware of the software that is available to you should you choose to follow that specialty:

Macromedia Flash. This is the hands-down favorite for adding animation, sound, and interactive effects to web pages due to the small file size of Flash movies.

Macromedia Director. Although originally created for CD-ROM and kiosk presentations, Director can also be used to generate movies and interactive elements (called "Shockwave" files) for web delivery.

Adobe LiveMotion. Adobe's new multimedia package that can be used to create Flash files. It is well integrated with other Adobe products.

Internet tools

Because you will be dealing with the Internet, you need to have some tools specifically for viewing and moving files over the network:

A variety of browsers. Because browsers render pages differently, you'll want to test your pages on as many browsers as possible (Netscape Navigator and Microsoft Internet Explorer, at minimum), as well as a text-only browser such as Lynx.

A file-transfer program (FTP). This enables you to transfer (upload) your files to the computer that will serve your pages to the Web. There are many utilities that do file transfer exclusively, including Fetch (for the Mac), Interarchy (Mac), and WS_FTP (Windows). File-transfer functions are built into some web page authoring tools such as Macromedia Dreamweaver and Adobe GoLive. See Chapter 3, Getting Your Files on the Web, for more information on file uploading.

Telnet. If you are advanced and know your way around the Unix operating system, you may find a telnet program helpful for manipulating files on the server. If not, you can probably get along without it.

The Moral of the Story

Well, it's not really a moral, but the lesson of this chapter should be "you don't have to learn everything!" And even if you want to learn everything eventually, you don't need to learn it all at once. So relax, don't worry...

As you'll soon see, it's easy to get started designing web pages—you will be able to create simple pages by the time you're done reading this book. From there, you can continue adding to your bag of tricks and find your special niche in web design.

Chapter 2

How the Web Works

I got started in web design in early 1993—pretty close to the start of the Web itself. In web time, that makes me an old-timer, but it's not so long ago that I can't remember the first day I looked at a web page. Frankly, I was a bit confused. It was difficult to tell where the information was coming from and how it all worked.

This chapter sorts out the pieces and introduces some basic terminology you'll encounter. If you've already spent time perusing the Web, some of this information will be a review. If you're starting from scratch, it is important to have all the parts in perspective. We'll start with the big picture and work down to specifics.

IN THIS CHAPTER

An easy explanation of the Web, as it relates to the Internet

The role of the server

Introduction to URLs and their components

The anatomy of a web page

The function of a browser

The Internet Versus the Web

No, it's not a battle to the death, just an opportunity to point out the distinction between these two words that are increasingly being used interchangeably.

The Internet is a network of connected computers. No company owns the Internet (i.e., it is not equivalent to America Online); it is a cooperative effort governed by a system of standards and rules. The point of connecting these computers together, of course, is to share information. There are many ways information can be passed between computers, including email and file transfer (FTP), as well as outdated modes such as WAIS and gopher. A mode of communication is known as a protocol, and it requires special programs that know how to handle that flavor of information.

The World Wide Web (known affectionately as "the Web") is just one of the ways information can be shared; it is a subset of the information on the Internet, and it has its own protocol.

There are several aspects that make the Web unique among other protocols. First, and probably most significantly, you can easily link one document to another—the documents and their links form a huge "web" of connected information.

A Brief History of the Web

The Web was born in a particle physics laboratory (CERN) in Geneva, Switzerland in 1989. There, a computer specialist named Tim Berners-Lee first proposed a system of information management that used a "hypertext" process to link related documents over a network. He and his partner, Robert Cailliau, created a prototype and released it for review. For the first several years, web pages were text-only. It's difficult to believe that in 1992 (not long ago), the world had only 50 web servers, total!

The real boost to the Web's popularity came in 1992 when the first graphical browser (NCSA Mosaic) was introduced. This allowed the Web to break out of the realm of scientific research into mass media. The development of the Web is overseen by the World Wide Web Consortium (W3C), a volunteer organization at the Massachusetts Institute of Technology (MIT).

If you want to dig deeper into the Web's history, check out these sites:

A Short History of the Web
 www.inria.fr/Actualites/ Cailliau-fra.html

Web Developers' Virtual Library
 WDVL.com/Internet/History

W3C's History Archives
 www.w3c.org/History.html

The formal name for linked text is hypertext and the technical term for the way the Web transfers information is the Hypertext Transfer Protocol, or HTTP for short. If you've spent any time using the Web, that acronym should look familiar since it is the first four letters of all web site addresses. We'll look more closely at web addresses later in this chapter.

The popularity of the Web stems from the fact that it is a visual medium, combining text and graphics in a page-like layout. In addition, it doesn't require users to know any special commands or complex software; it's mostly point-and-click.

Serving Up Your Information

Let's talk more about the computers that make up the Internet. Because they "serve up" documents upon request, these computers are known as servers. More accurately, the server is the software program that allows the computer to communicate with other computers; however, it is common to use the word "server" to refer to the computer, as well. The role of server software is to wait for a request for information, then retrieve and send that information back as soon as possible.

There's nothing special about the computers themselves... picture anything from a high-powered Unix machine to a humble personal computer. It's the server software that makes it all happen. In order for a computer to be part of the Web, it must be running special web server software that allows it to "speak" the Hypertext Transfer Protocol. Web servers are also called "HTTP servers."

Each server is assigned a unique number (its IP address) and a corresponding name (its domain or hostname), such as *oreilly.com*. The number and name are used to identify that particular server on the Internet, so you can connect to the right information. On the Web, there is a convention that machines running web servers have a name starting with "www" (such as *www.oreilly.com*), but this is by no means a hard and fast rule.

Web Page Addresses (URLs)

With all those web pages on all those servers, how would you ever find the one you're looking for? Fortunately, each document has its own special address called a URL (Uniform Resource Locator). The Web is so popular now, it's nearly impossible to get through a day without seeing a URL (pronounced "U-R-L," not "erl") plastered on the side of a bus, shouting from a billboard, or broadcast on a television commercial.

URLs may look like crazy strings of characters separated by dots (periods) and slashes, but each part has a specific purpose.

The Parts of a URL

A complete URL is generally made up of four components, as shown in Figure 2-1. Let's examine each one.

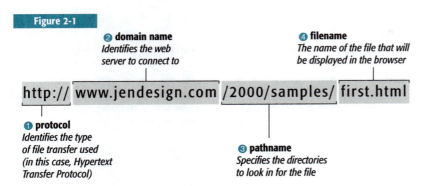

Figure 2-1

❷ domain name
Identifies the web server to connect to

❹ filename
The name of the file that will be displayed in the browser

http:// www.jendesign.com /2000/samples/ first.html

❶ protocol
Identifies the type of file transfer used (in this case, Hypertext Transfer Protocol)

❸ pathname
Specifies the directories to look in for the file

❶ `http://`

The first thing the URL does is define the protocol that will be used for that particular transaction. As we discussed earlier, the letters HTTP let the server know to use Hypertext Transfer Protocol, or get into "web-mode."

❷ `www.jendesign.com`

The next portion of the URL indicates the server to connect to. In most cases, the URL identifies a server by its domain name, but it could also call the server by its number (it's just easier for humans to ask for it by name). In this URL, I am asking to see a file on the "jendesign" server. The "www" is just a convention for indicating that this is a web server.

❸ `/2000/samples/`

If you see a series of words separated by slashes, that indicates a path through directory levels to a specific file. Because the Internet was originally comprised of computers running the Unix operating system, our current way of doing things still follows many Unix rules and conventions.

❹ `first.html`

The last part of the URL is the name of the file itself. It must end in *.htm* or *.html* in order to be recognized as a web page document.

Our example URL is saying it would like to use the HTTP protocol to connect to a web server on the Internet called *jendesign.com* and request the document *first.html* (located in the *samples* directory, which is in the *2000* directory).

Intranets and Extranets

When you think of a web site, you generally assume that it is accessible to anyone surfing the Web. However, many companies take advantage of the awesome information sharing and gathering power of web sites to exchange information just within their own business. These special web-based networks are called intranets. They are created and function like ordinary web sites, only they are on computers with special security devices (called firewalls) that prevent the outside world from seeing them. Intranets have lots of uses, such as sharing human resource information or providing access to inventory databases.

An extranet is like an intranet, only it allows access to selected users outside of the company. For instance, a manufacturing company may provide its customers with a password that allows them to check the status of their orders in the company's orders database. Of course, the passwords determine which slice of the company's information that user is allowed to see. This type of network sharing is changing the way many companies do business.

How the Web Works

> ## Servers and Clients
>
> As we discuss in this chapter, server software sends information upon request. Sometimes the word "server" is used to refer to the computer running that software.
>
> The other half of this equation is the software that makes the request. This software is called a "client."
>
> On the Web, the browser is the client software that makes requests for documents. The web server returns the documents for the browser to display.
>
> Often in web design, you'll hear reference to "client-side" or "server-side" applications. These terms are used to indicate which machine is doing the processing. Client-side applications run on the user's machine, while server-side applications and functions use the processing power of the server computer.

URL Shortcuts

Obviously, not every URL you see is so convoluted. Often, you see URLs that are short and sweet, like *www.oreilly.com*. Here's how that works.

http://

First, since all web pages use the Hypertext Transfer Protocol, "http://" is usually just omitted because it is implied. In addition, browsers are programmed to add that part automatically if it is not typed in explicitly. It's always in there, you just don't always need to deal with it.

Index files

Another implied part of a URL is any reference to a document called *index.html*. Most servers have a built-in default that causes them to search for a file called *index.html* if no filename is specified in the URL.* So, if I type in *www.oreilly.com*, the browser will retrieve the document *http://www.oreilly.com/index.html*. By naming the top-level document in your directory *index.html*, you can keep your URL simple (Figure 2-2).

If you don't want people snooping around your files, be sure there is an index file in every directory.

The index file is also useful for security. If a directory doesn't contain a file called *index.html*, and the server is set up to look for one, when someone types in a URL without a specific filename, the browser will display a list of all the files in that directory. If you don't want people snooping around your files, be sure there is an index file in every directory (Figure 2-3).

---

* The default file might have a different name, such as *default.html*. It depends on how the server software is configured, so be sure to ask your server administrator for the proper default filename.

Figure 2-2

Most browsers know to insert the "http://" if it is not typed in explicitly; some will also add a "www." and ".com" if a single word is requested.

Short and sweet URLs have implied components that you don't need to type in.

http:// www.oreilly.com /index.html

When no filename is provided the server will search for a default file, usually called "index.html".

Figure 2-3

Address: ▼ **http://www.littlechair.com/housepics/**

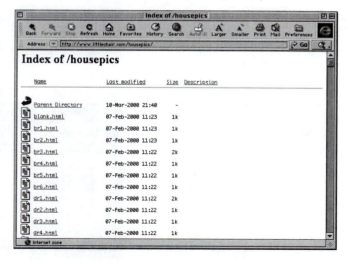

index.html

Typing in a URL without a specific filename prompts the server to look for the default page, usually named "index.html".

If the server doesn't find a file named "index.html", it returns the contents of the whole directory.

If you don't want the contents of your server visible to the whole world, be sure there is an index file in every directory.

Index of /housepics

Name	Last modified	Size	Description
Parent Directory	10-Mar-2000 21:40	-	
blank.html	07-Feb-2000 11:23	1k	
br1.html	07-Feb-2000 11:23	1k	
br2.html	07-Feb-2000 11:23	1k	
br3.html	07-Feb-2000 11:22	2k	
br4.html	07-Feb-2000 11:22	1k	
br5.html	07-Feb-2000 11:22	1k	
br6.html	07-Feb-2000 11:22	1k	
dr1.html	07-Feb-2000 11:22	2k	
dr2.html	07-Feb-2000 11:22	1k	
dr3.html	07-Feb-2000 11:22	1k	
dr4.html	07-Feb-2000 11:22	1k	

The Anatomy of a Web Page

Finally, we get to the real meat of the Web—web page documents! You know what they look like when you view them on your computer, but what's happening "under the hood"? Let's take a quick look at the stuff web pages are made of.

In Figure 2-4, you see a basic web page as it appears in a browser. Although you are able to view it as one coherent page, it is actually made up of three separate files: an HTML document (*simple.html*) and two graphics (*flower.gif* and *simpleheader.gif*). The HTML document is running the show.

Figure 2-4

```
<HTML>
<HEAD>
<TITLE>A Story</TITLE>
</HEAD>

<BODY>
<P><IMG SRC="flower.gif"><IMG SRC="simpleheader.gif"> <IMG SRC="flower.gif">
<H1>A Story</H1>
<P>Once there was a <EM>very</EM> simple web page. This page looked at
all the really cool web pages and felt a little inferior. But then the
little web page remembered, "HEY! I'm a web page all the same, and isn't
that cool enough?"</P>
<HR>
<P><B>The End</B>
</BODY>

</HTML>
```

simple.html

The simple web page displayed in this example is made up of three separate files: an HTML text document and two graphics.

flower.gif

simpleheader.gif

The browser brings these separate elements together in the window. Tags in the HTML file give the browser instructions for how the page is to be displayed.

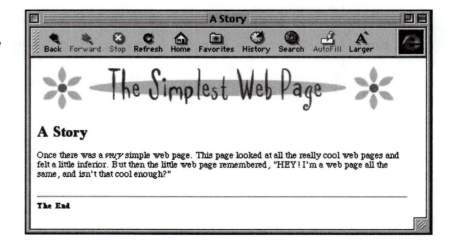

HTML Documents

You may be as surprised as I was to learn that the graphically rich and interactive pages we see on the Web are generated by simple, text-only documents. That's right: plain old ASCII text (meaning it has just letters, numbers, and a few symbol characters).

Take a look at *simple.html*, the text document that makes up our sample web page. You can see it contains the text content of the page; the "magic" lies in the special tags (indicated with angle brackets, ‹ and ›). They explain how the text is to be displayed, where the graphics should go, and where links occur. This system of tagging is called the HyperText Markup Language, or HTML for short, and the tags are commonly known as HTML tags.

But Where Are the Pictures?

Obviously, there are no pictures in the HTML file itself, so how do they get there when you view the final page?

You can see in Figure 2-4 that each image is a separate graphic file. The graphics are placed in the flow of the text with an image placement tag (‹IMG›) that tells the browser where to find the graphic (its URL). When the browser sees the ‹IMG› tag, it goes out and gets the graphic from the server and displays it seamlessly on the web page. So it's the browser that brings all the pieces together.

More About Tags

You'll be learning about HTML in detail in Part II: Learning HTML, so I don't want to bog you down with too much detail right now, but there are a few things I'd like to point out. Read through the HTML document and compare it to the browser results in Figure 2-4. It's easy to see how the page elements and tags relate.

First, you'll notice that anything within brackets does not display in the final page. Tags simply provide the browser with instructions for how the text or element is to be rendered on the page. Usually, the tag uses an abbreviation of the instruction, such as "H1" for "Heading Level 1," or "EM" for "Emphasized Text."

Second, you'll see that most HTML tags appear in pairs (sometimes called containers), the first one turning that attribute "on" and the second one (containing a slash) turning it "off." In our HTML document, ‹H1› indicates that the following text should be a Heading Level 1; ‹/H1› ends the heading and switches back to normal text.

There are some tags that don't use a closing tag. These are usually called "standalone" tags, and they are used for placing an element or instruction on a page. In our sample, the ‹HR› means "draw a horizontal rule (line) here."

TIP

View Source

You can see the HTML file for any web page by choosing View → Source or View → Page Source in your browser's menu. It is a good way to peek at the tagging that is responsible for an effect you like. Your browser will open the source document in a separate window.

Keep in mind that while learning from others' work is fine, the all-out stealing of other people's code is poor form. If you want to use code as you see it, ask permission and always give credit to those who did the work.

How the Web Works

The HTML Concept

It's significant to note that in "pure" HTML, tags merely specify the type of information that follows, not instructions for how the information should look. It's just like the style categories you might create in a word processing program or desktop publishing application.

So, when tagging a document properly, you indicate that a particular headline is a Heading Level 1 (<H1>), but it's the browser (controlled by the end user) that determines what an H1 looks like. Most browsers render first-level headings in the largest bold font available.

Fortunately, methods have been introduced to give the designer some control over how text is formatted, but the original intent of HTML was to keep style information separate from the content and structure of the document.

Browsers

As you probably know, a browser is a piece of software that displays web pages. It is the tool you use to view the Web, a little like a television set is the tool you use to view television programs.

The browser reads through the HTML file and renders the text and tags as it encounters them. When I first began writing HTML, it helped me to think of the tags and text as "beads on a string" that the browser deals with one by one, in sequence. Understanding the browser's method can be helpful when troubleshooting a misbehaving HTML document.

A browser is really a one-trick pony: it is programmed to request web pages and display their contents. You can't use the browser to edit the web file (you have to open the original file in an editor to do that)—you can only view it. Some "browsers" are bundles of programs that include a browser, email functionality, file transfer capabilities, even an HTML editor. Their capabilities are enhanced by the use of helper applications and plug-ins that help the browser present media other than HTML documents, including audio, video, and interactive presentations.

By far, the most popular browsers are Netscape Navigator and Microsoft Internet Explorer. But there are hundreds of smaller, lesser-known browsers out there.

One browser in particular you should know about is Lynx, a browser that displays only text and no graphics (Figure 2-5). Because it works on simple terminals, it is often used in academic and scientific networks. Sight-impaired users may have web pages spoken to them by a device that reads from Lynx or another text-only browser. Web designers often use Lynx to test their pages for functionality under the most rudimentary viewing conditions.

TIP

Because the browser is fundamental to how web pages appear to the end user, designers need to be especially aware of some of the complex issues surrounding browser software. We'll talk about some of those in Chapter 4, Why Web Design Isn't Like Print Design.

Figure 2-5

```
                                      MacLynx
                                                                    A Story

   [INLINE] [INLINE] [INLINE]

                                   A Story

   Once there was a very simple web page. This page looked at all the
   really cool web pages and felt a little inferior. But then the little
   web page remembered, "HEY! I'm a web page all the same, and isn't that
   cool enough?"
                                   _____

   The End




   Commands: Use arrow keys to move, '?' for help, 'q' to quit, '<-' to go back.
     Arrow keys: Up and Down to move. Right to follow a link; Left to go back.
    H)elp O)ptions P)rint G)o M)ain screen Q)uit /=search [delete]=history list
```

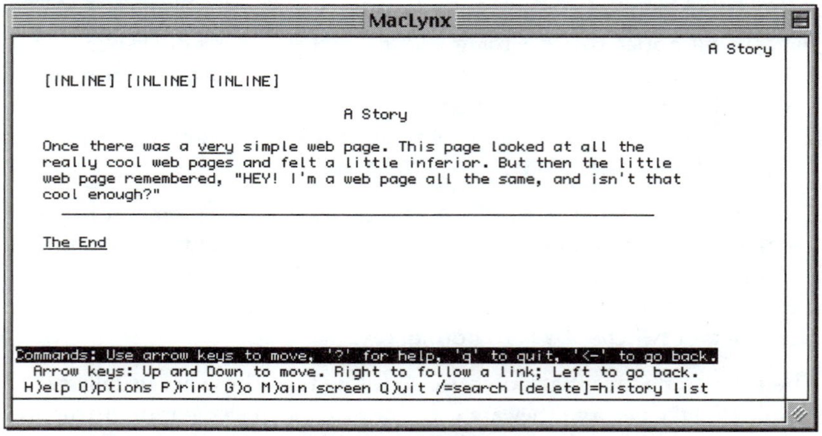

This is the way our simple web page looks when viewed in Lynx, a text-only browser.

Putting It All Together

To wrap up our introduction to how the Web works, let's trace the stream of events that occur with every web page that appears on your screen (Figure 2-6).

Figure 2-6

❶ You request a web page by either typing its URL (address) directly into the browser or by clicking on linked text. The URL contains all the information needed to target a specific document on the vast network of computers known as the Internet.

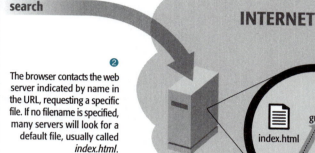

search

INTERNET

❷ The browser contacts the web server indicated by name in the URL, requesting a specific file. If no filename is specified, many servers will look for a default file, usually called *index.html*.

❸ The web server searches for the file and either returns it to the browser or returns an error saying that it can't be accessed. Assuming the file is found and returned successfully, the browser displays the document in its window according to the formatting specified in the document's HTML tags.

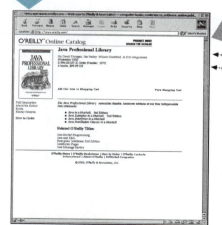

❹ If the page contains graphics (indicated by the `<IMG>` tag), the browser contacts the server again for each graphic. Each graphic is sent individually and is assembled into the final page by the browser.

And *voila*! The page is displayed for your viewing pleasure. All of this usually happens in an instant. If you have a slow connection to the Internet, you know that larger graphic files tend to lag behind the rest of the page.

Chapter 3

Getting Your Pages on the Web

Because browsers can view documents locally (right from your hard drive), you do not need an Internet connection to design web pages. However, eventually, you'll want to get them out there for the world to see. That is the point, right?

Putting a page on the Web is easy... just transfer your files to your web server and *ta da*—you're on the Web! What's that? You don't have a web server? This chapter will tell you where to look for one (you might even have server space and not know it).

But first, I want to show you how easy it is to put a page online. If you're one of those instant-gratification types (and have access to a web server), you can follow along and publish your first web page before the next chapter.

Putting Files Online (FTP)

Going online is a matter of transferring your web documents from your desktop computer to your web server computer. If you are in an office or at a school that has a web server as part of its network, you may be able to send the files directly over the network, as you would with any other file transfer.

More likely, your server will be out on the Internet. Files are transferred between computers on the Internet via FTP (File Transfer Protocol). Because FTP is a special Internet protocol, you'll need to use software made for the job.

In addition, you'll need to know these things to FTP files:

The name of your web server (host). For example, *www.jenware.com*.

Your login name or user ID. You'll get a login name from the server administrator when you set up your server account (or if you're a freelancer, you'll need access to your client's login).

Your password. This will also be provided by the server administrator or client.

The directory where your web pages reside. Your server administrator should also tell you which directory to use for your web pages (usually, it's *www* or *html*). Your server might be set up to send you to the correct directory when you log in, in which case, if you leave the directory blank, you will automatically be forwarded to the proper directory. Again, get directions from the administrator.

FTP Software

Before you can upload your files, you'll need to have FTP (file transfer) software and certain information about your web server.

The cool thing is that FTP functionality is now built into the better WYSIWYG web-authoring tools, such as Macromedia Dreamweaver, Adobe GoLive, and Microsoft FrontPage (just to name a few). This is a great feature, because you can build your pages and upload them all in one program.

If you haven't yet invested in one of these tools, there are a number of FTP-dedicated programs with simple interfaces that make file transfer as easy as moving files around on your own computer. For the Mac, both Fetch and Interarchie allow "drag and drop" transfers. On the PC, WS_FTP and AceFTP are quite popular. You can down these programs at CNET's *www.download.com*.

A Real, "Live" Web Page: Step-by-Step

Finally! Let's go through the process of making a page and putting it on the Web. In this scenario, I had an idea for a cooking resources web site, so I registered my own domain name, *jenskitchen.com*[*] (we'll discuss registering domain names later in this chapter). Now I want to put a page online to let folks know when the site will launch and the content will be available.

---

[*] This is a fictitious domain used for demonstration purposes only. It bears no relation to any site that may appear one day at that location.

Step 1: Create the web page

I've used an HTML editor to type out a simple HTML document, and saved it with the name *index.html* in a directory on my desktop called *mysite* (Figure 3-1). Before I put it on the server where everyone can see it, I check the page in a browser by opening the file that I just saved on my hard drive. This is called viewing the file "locally"—on your own machine. Since it looks fine, I'm ready to upload!

Figure 3-1

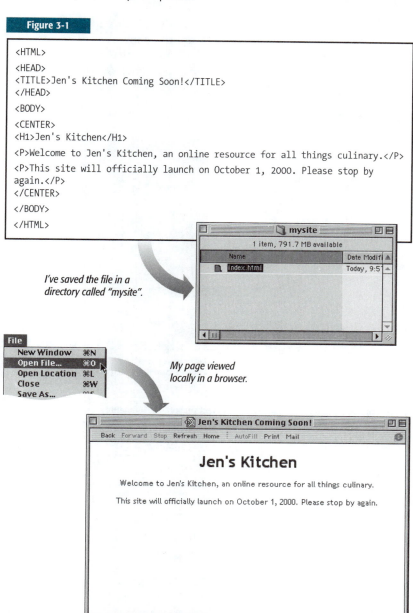

```
<HTML>
<HEAD>
<TITLE>Jen's Kitchen Coming Soon!</TITLE>
</HEAD>
<BODY>
<CENTER>
<H1>Jen's Kitchen</H1>
<P>Welcome to Jen's Kitchen, an online resource for all things culinary.</P>
<P>This site will officially launch on October 1, 2000. Please stop by again.</P>
</CENTER>
</BODY>
</HTML>
```

The HTML document I created in an HTML editor.

I've saved the file in a directory called "mysite".

My page viewed locally in a browser.

Step 2: Connect to the server with an FTP program

Since I work on a Mac I like to use Fetch for transferring files, but other FTP programs work similarly, so this demo should be useful for everyone.

The first thing I do, of course, is make sure that I'm connected to the Internet. I like my cable modem because it is always on, but you may need to dial in over a modem. Once I'm online, I can launch Fetch and connect to the server.

When I select "New Connection" (Figure 3-2), Fetch pops up a window that asks me the name of the server I want to connect to (in my case, it's *jenskitchen.com*) ❶. For security reasons, it asks for my username and password (I got these when I set up the server account) ❷. The last thing it asks for is the directory ❸. My server administrator told me to use *www*.

Figure 3-2

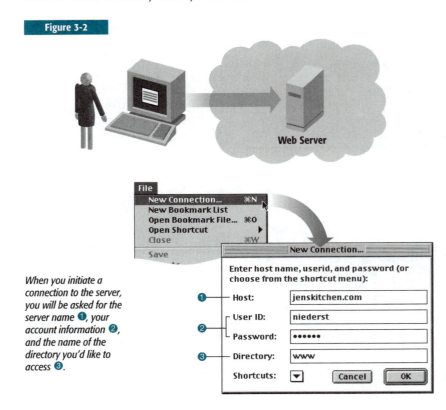

When you initiate a connection to the server, you will be asked for the server name ❶, your account information ❷, and the name of the directory you'd like to access ❸.

Step 3: Upload the file

Once I'm connected, Fetch gives me a window that shows the directory structure on the server (Figure 3-3). Since I want to "put" a file onto the server, I click the "Put File" button (other FTP programs may call this function "send" or "upload") ❶.

Clicking the "Put File" button gives me a window where I can browse through the directories on my desktop. I just select my *index.html* file and click "Open" to continue ❷.

The final bit of information you need to provide is the format of the file you are uploading ❸. While Fetch provides a number of options, the most useful ones are "Text," which is used for HTML documents, and "Raw Data," which is used when you are uploading images or other media. These options are also called "ASCII" and "Binary," respectively, by other FTP programs.

Once I select "Text" and hit OK, my file starts whizzing over the lines and onto the server. It'll take a moment to upload, but soon, you'll see the file pop up in the server directory in the main Fetch window ❹.

Click "Put File" when you want to upload files from your computer to the server. Click "Get File" when you want to download files from the server to your computer.

Getting Your Pages on the Web

Figure 3-3

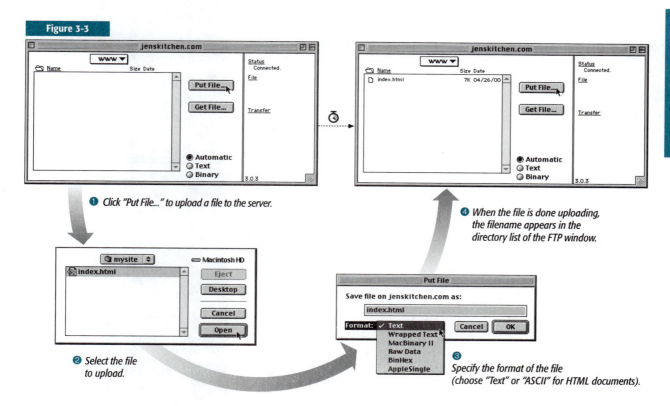

❶ Click "Put File..." to upload a file to the server.

❷ Select the file to upload.

❸ Specify the format of the file (choose "Text" or "ASCII" for HTML documents).

❹ When the file is done uploading, the filename appears in the directory list of the FTP window.

Step 4: Check the page

Cool! Now my page is officially on the Web. Just to be sure, I can check it with a browser (Figure 3-4). I open my favorite browser and enter the URL *http://www.jenskitchen.com/index.html*, and there it is.

Figure 3-4

Now the page is on the Web. We can view it by entering its URL in the browser.

Uploading from a Web Authoring Tool

Many web authoring tools come with FTP programs built right in, and using them is simple. In this example, I'm using Macromedia Dreamweaver on a Mac, but other tools work similarly.

Step 1: Create a new document

I've used Dreamweaver to create my *index.html* file and I've saved it in the *mysite* directory (Figure 3-5). You may want to open the file locally in a browser to make sure it works, as we did in the previous example.

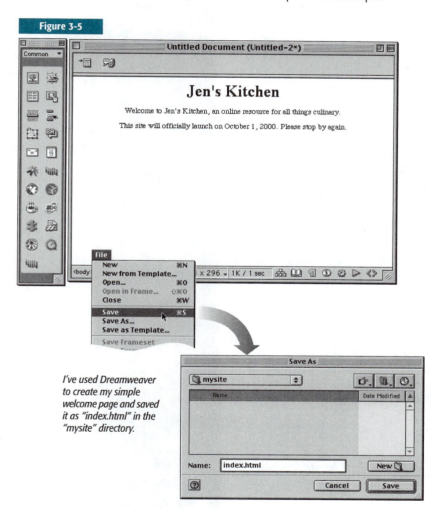

Figure 3-5

I've used Dreamweaver to create my simple welcome page and saved it as "index.html" in the "mysite" directory.

Step 2: Set up a new "site"

Dreamweaver uses the word "site" to refer to your project. Before you can upload, you need to define a new site and give it a name (Figure 3-6). The site manager (accessed through the Site window) keeps track of the documents on your hard drive and the server and allows you to transfer files between them.

Use the dialog box to provide information about each of the site categories listed on the left. The "Web Server Info" category lets you specify the host, username, password, and directory information that will be used for FTP transfers. In the "Local Info" category, point to the directory on your hard drive that contains the file (*mysite*).

Figure 3-6

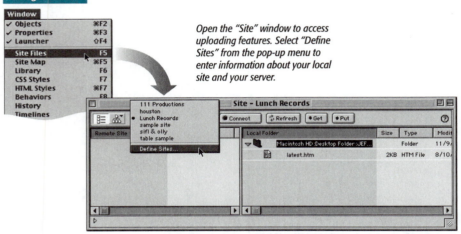

Open the "Site" window to access uploading features. Select "Define Sites" from the pop-up menu to enter information about your local site and your server.

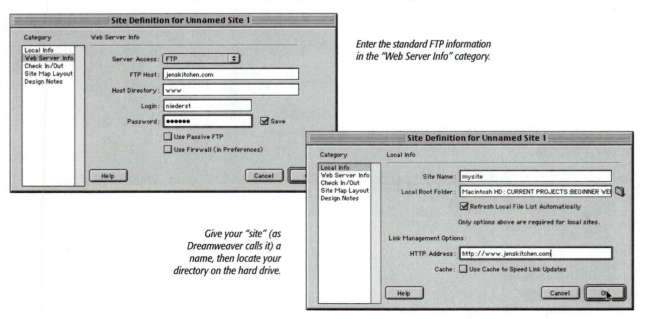

Enter the standard FTP information in the "Web Server Info" category.

Give your "site" (as Dreamweaver calls it) a name, then locate your directory on the hard drive.

Step 3: Upload the file

Making sure that you're connected to the Internet (whether via broadband or modem connection), you can now access your server by clicking the "Connect" button on the Site window (Figure 3-7). The server directory structure is visible in the left panel, and the local directory structure is in the right panel. Once the connection is established, highlight the directory or file to be transferred and hit the "Put" button. And away it goes! You'll see it appear in the left panel once it has arrived.

Figure 3-7

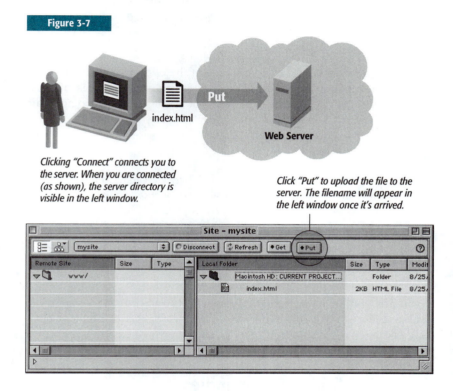

index.html

Put

Web Server

Clicking "Connect" connects you to the server. When you are connected (as shown), the server directory is visible in the left window.

Click "Put" to upload the file to the server. The filename will appear in the left window once it's arrived.

Step 4: Check the page

With the file on the server, you (and everyone else on the Internet) can view the page in a browser (you can look back at Figure 3-4 to see how this would look, since it's the same file).

Getting Your Pages on the Web

Organizing and Uploading a Whole Site

These examples show the creation and uploading of one web document, but chances are your site will consist of more than one page. If your site contains more than a dozen or so documents and graphics files, you should organize your files into directories and/or subdirectories. This requires some work and careful planning, but it makes site management much easier in the long run.

One common convention is to keep all of the graphics in a directory called *graphics* or *images*. In most cases, the overall directory structure is based on the structure of the site itself (for instance, if you have a "News" category on your site, there would be a corresponding *news* directory for those files). Site structure is discussed in more detail in Chapter 18, Building Usable Web Sites.

The good news is that you can upload an entire site in one go! When you select a directory to be FTP'd (whether in an authoring tool or with an FTP program), it will upload *everything* within that directory—leaving the subdirectory structure intact. Follow the instructions shown here, only select the directory name instead of a single filename for upload.

It is a good idea to set up your site directory structure as you want it on your local hard drive first, then upload everything to the final server once it is ready.

Finding Server Space

One of the first tasks in launching a new web site is finding a host (server space) for your files.

By now you know that in order for your pages to be on the Web, they must reside on a web server. Chances are, the machine you are working on is not set up with HTTP server software, so you'll need to get access to a computer that is equipped for the job. Looking for space on a web server is also called finding a host for your site.

Fortunately, there are many hosting options, ranging in price from free to many thousands of dollars a year. The one you choose should match your publishing goals. Will your site be business or personal? Will it get a few hits a month or thousands? How much can you (or your client) afford to pay for hosting services?

In this section, I'll introduce you to some of the options available for getting your web pages online. This should give you a general idea of what type of service you need. However, you should still count on doing a fair amount of research to find the one that's right for you.

Inherit a Server

If you are working as a web designer in an office, especially at a web design company, it is likely that there will be a server connected to your company's network. If this is the case, you can just copy your files to the specified server machine.

If you are a student, you may be given some space to publish personal pages as part of your school account. Ask the department that gives you your email account how to take advantage of web space.

If you are working as a freelancer, your clients will probably assume the responsibility of setting up server space for their sites. But smaller clients may ask for your assistance in finding space, in which case this chapter is for you.

Online Publishing Communities

If you just want to publish a personal site and don't want to sink any money into it, you might try picking up some free web space from an online publishing community such as Yahoo! GeoCities (*geocities.yahoo.com*) or Tripod (*www.tripod.lycos.com*). These services (and others like them) provide free server space in exchange for the opportunity to place *their* advertising on *your* content. The ads are annoying (especially if you go for the pop-up window option), but it might be an acceptable sacrifice if you're on a budget.

Advantages:	*Disadvantages:*
It's free!	You're stuck with annoying ad banners or pop-up windows.
Good for personal and hobbyist web pages. Also a good option for teens with limited budgets.	Not appropriate for business sites.

Online Services and ISPs

If you have an account with an online service such as America Online (*www.aol.com*) or CompuServe (*www.compuserve.com*), you probably already have some web server space just waiting to be filled. The online services usually provide tools and assistance with making web pages and getting them online. (Of course, after reading this book, you won't need 'em, right?!)

Likewise, ISPs (Internet service providers) such as Earthlink, MSN, and @Home provide a decent amount of web server space (5 or 6MB) for their members.

Advantages:	*Disadvantages:*
A low-cost alternative if you already have the service, or if you are shopping for both a hosting service and Internet access—usually just $15–25 per month.	Not desirable for business sites because of the limited space and the ISP-based domain name in the URL (for example, *www.earthlink.com/ members/~niederst*)
Good for small sites, such as personal and hobbyist web pages.	Service may be slow because you are sharing servers with hoards of other members.

Professional Hosting Services

If you are working on a serious business site, or if you are just serious about your personal web presence, you will probably want to rent server space from a professional hosting service. Hosting services focus their energies and resources on providing server space, dependable connections to those servers, and related services. Unlike ISPs, they do not offer Internet access.

Hosting companies usually offer a range of server packages, from just a few megabytes (MB) of space and one email address to full-powered e-commerce solutions with lots of bells and whistles. Of course, the more server space and more features, the higher your monthly bill will be, so shop wisely.

Advantages:	*Disadvantages:*
Scalable packages offer solutions for every size web site. With some research, you can find a host that matches your requirements and budget.	Finding the right one requires research (see the Shopping for Hosting Services sidebar).
You get your own domain name (for example, *www.littlechair.com*). We'll talk about domain names later.	Robust server solutions can get expensive, and you need to watch for hidden charges.

Shopping for Hosting Services

When you set out to find a host for your web site, you should begin by assessing your needs. Following are some of the first questions you should ask yourself or your client:

Is it a business or personal site? Some hosting services provide space for personal sites only; others charge higher rates for business sites than for personal sites. Make sure you are signing up for the appropriate hosting package for your site, and don't try to sneak a commercial site onto a personal account.

How much space do you need? Most small sites will be fine with 5MB of server space. You may want to invest in more if your site has hundreds of pages, a large number of graphics, or a significant number of audio and video files (which take up more space).

How much traffic will you get? Be sure to pay attention to the amount of data transfer you're allowed per month. This is a function of the size of your files and the amount of traffic you'll get (i.e., the number of downloads to browsers). Most hosting services offer 5–10 gigabytes (GB) of throughput a month (which is perfectly fine for low- or moderate-traffic sites), but after that, they start charging a few cents a megabyte. If you are serving media files like audio or video, this can really add up. I once ran a popular site with a number of movies that turned out to have over 30GB of data transferred a month! Fortunately, I had a service with unlimited data transfer (there are some out there), but other hosting companies could have racked up an extra $300 per month in fees.

How many email accounts do you need? Consider how many people will want email at that domain when you're shopping for the right server package. If you need many email accounts, you may need to go with a more robust and higher-priced package.

Do you need extra functionality? Many hosting services offer special web site features—some come as part of their standard service and others cost extra money. They range from libraries of spiffy scripts (for email forms or guestbooks), all the way up to complete, secure e-commerce solutions. When shopping for space, consider whether you need extra features, such as shopping carts, secure servers (for credit card transactions), a RealMedia server (for streaming audio and video), mailing lists, and so on.

Once you've identified your needs, it's time to do some hunting. First, ask your friends and colleagues if they have hosting services that they can recommend. There's nothing like firsthand experience from someone you trust. After that, the Web is the best place to do research. The following sites provide reviews and comparisons of various hosting services; they can be good starting points for your server shopping spree:

HostSearch
www.hostsearch.com

CNET Web Services
webhostlist.internetlist.com

HostIndex
www.hostindex.com

TopHosts.com
www.tophosts.com

www."YOU".com!

Your home page address is your identity on the Web. If you are posting a just-for-fun page and want to save money, an ISP URL (such as *www.earthlink.com/members/~niederst*) might be fine. More likely, you'll want your own domain name that better represents your business or content. For a small yearly fee, anyone can register a domain name.

What's in a Name?

A domain name is a human-readable name associated with a numeric IP address (the "IP" stands for Internet Protocol) on the Internet. While computers know that my site is on a server space numbered 206.151.75.9, you and I can just call it "littlechair.com." The IP address is important, though, because you'll need one (well, two, actually) to register your domain name.

Is It Available?

You might have already heard that the simple domain names in the coveted *.com* top-level domain are heavily picked over. Before you get too attached to a specific name, you'd better do a search to see if it is still available. The "Search for a domain name" box on the home page of Network Solutions, Inc. (*www.networksolutions.com*) is a reliable source.

Registering a Domain

Over the past year or so, registering a domain name has become a fairly painless, one-stop transaction. Most hosting companies will register a domain for you as part of the process of setting up a server account. But be sure to ask specifically! Some still require you to register your domain on your own.

If you do need to register a domain on your own, you have a number of options.

If you are registering a domain name that ends in *.com*, *.net*, or *.org*, you can go directly to Network Solutions (*www.networksolutions.com*) and register online. They will ask you for the following:

- An administrative contact for the account (name and address)
- A billing contact for the account (name and address)
- A technical contact for the account (generally the name and address of your hosting service)
- Two IP addresses for the server on which the domain will be hosted

---

Dot What?

The vast majority of web sites that you hear about end with *.com*, but there are other suffixes available for different purposes. These suffixes, used for indicating the type of site, are called top-level domains. Following are the most common top-level domains (also called TLDs by those not saturated with acronyms) in the United States and their uses:

.com	commercial/business
.org	nonprofit organization
.edu	educational institutions
.net	network organizations
.mil	military
.gov	government agencies

In late 2000, the governing body for top-level domains announced a list of potential new suffixes, including *.biz*, *.coop*, and *.pro*, so you'll probably start seeing some new names out on the Web.

As of this writing, it costs $35.00 per year to register a domain name with Network Solutions, and you can register for one to ten years.

If you don't have IP addresses, Network Solutions will offer to "park" the site for you for an additional fee. Parking a site means that you have reserved the domain name, but you can't actually *do* anything with it until you get a real hosting package. Basically, you're paying for the privilege of borrowing some IP addresses.

While Network Solutions used to be the only game in town, there are now several competing companies, such as Register.com and Domainname.com (and others like them sprouting up). In addition to *.com* domains, these services tend to register many more top-level domains, including domains in other countries. And in the spirit of competition, these services will park a domain name for you as well as provide basic hosting packages. Each has its own pricing structure, so check the going rates on their sites.

There are a few scams out there, so shop wisely. In addition to the $35 per year registration fee, do not spend more than $35 to $50 per year to park a site.

Chapter 4

Why Web Design Isn't Like Print Design

Like many people, I designed for print for years before I started designing for the Web. My transition was full of interesting twists and turns, and a few brick walls! The Web is a unique medium, and in my opinion... kinda weird. By its nature, it forces designers to give up control over the very things they are traditionally responsible for controlling. Many elements, such as colors, fonts, and page layout, are determined by the user or that user's browser software.

There is no guarantee that people will see your pages the same way you design them on your screen. The experience can be a shock until you get used to it. Then it can be downright frustrating!

Designing for the Unknown

Much of web design is "designing for the unknown": unknown users, unknown browsers, unknown platforms, unknown monitor sizes, and so on. In this chapter, I'll discuss the way these unknowns impact your role as designer.

Becoming a good web designer requires a solid understanding of the web environment in order to anticipate and plan for these shifting variables. Eventually, you'll develop a feel for it.

Unknown Browsers

You may be familiar with the two biggies in the browser arena, Netscape Navigator and Microsoft Internet Explorer, but did you know that there are actually hundreds of browsers in use today? In fact, there are dozens of versions of Navigator alone once you count all the past releases, partial releases, and the various platform versions of each.

IN THIS CHAPTER

The unknown factors that affect the web design process

Tips on surviving the frustration of "designing for the unknown"

What it means to design democratically

The importance of knowing your audience

Ten reasons why, in spite of it all, I still think web design is cool

What you'll quickly learn is that these browsers can display the same page differently (see Figure 4-1). This is due in part to built-in defaults for rendering fonts and form elements. Some browsers, such as Lynx, do not display graphics at all. Each browser has its own slight variation on how to interpret standard HTML tags in terms of fonts and sizes. Both Netscape and Microsoft have even created sets of HTML tags that work only with their respective browsers; if you use these tags, users with the competing browser won't see your content the way you intended.

Figure 4-1

| Internet Explorer 4.5 | Navigator 2 | Lynx |

The same web page may look different on different browsers. Dealing with browser variations is the trickiest part of web design.

The area where browser difference has the most impact is in the support of new web development technologies such as Cascading Style Sheets (a method for advanced control of text and page formatting) and DHTML (a method for adding interactivity and motion to web pages). Although it's tempting to use these new features, it's currently difficult to get them to work the same on both Navigator and Internet Explorer. In addition, there are enough out-of-date browsers still being used that it is guaranteed your special effects will be missed by a significant percentage of your audience.

The site in Figure 4-2 (names have been blurred to protect the innocent) uses a Java applet for its navigation bar at left. The applet makes the buttons appear to press down and makes a little "click-click" sound as you pass the mouse over them. But look what happens when users don't have Java activated on their browsers—no navigation at all! This is the danger of relying on a technology trick for crucial page elements.

Pressure from web developers has led to efforts from the big two browser companies to get this situation under control (see the Working Toward a Standard sidebar); however, the fact that your pages will be at the mercy of a myriad of browser interpretations is unlikely to change any time soon.

AT A GLANCE

When you design web pages, there are many unknown factors that affect how your page will look and function, including:

- Browser usage
- Platform
- User preference
- Window size
- Connection speed
- Computer speed
- Color support
- Font support

Figure 4-2

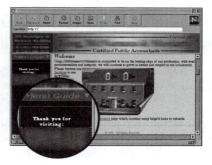

Internet Explorer 4.5 (Java enabled)   **Navigator 2** (no Java)

This web site uses a Java applet for its basic navigation. The applet changes the appearance of the buttons and adds a little clickety sound when the pointer passes over the button graphics. Unfortunately, for users with browsers that aren't Java-enabled, the applet doesn't appear at all and the page is a dead end.

Unknown Platforms

Another variable that affects how users see your pages is the platform, or operating system, of their computers. Although most web users have personal computers running some version of the Windows operating system, a significant portion view the Web from Macintoshes and Unix terminals. Each operating system has its own characteristics and quirks that affect how your page will look and perform.

For instance, Windows machines and Macs have different ways of displaying type, leading to the same size type appearing much larger on Windows than Mac. If you set the type on your web page to be small on your Windows machine, it may be completely illegible for Mac users.

Form elements such as scrolling lists and pull-down menus take on the general appearance of the operating system, and therefore appear quite differently (and at different sizes) depending on what type of machine you are viewing them on.

The viewers' platforms also have an effect on the way they see colors. See the section Unknown Colors later in this chapter.

In addition, there is usually a discrepancy between the functionality of browsers across different platforms. In general, browser and plug-in releases for the Macintosh lag behind the Windows versions. And although Unix was the platform upon which the Web was built, it is often ignored by software developers eager to hit the dominant Windows market.

Working Toward a Standard

Since the beginning, the World Wide Web Consortium (W3C), the organization that monitors and guides the development of the Web, has set the standards for how the Web should work. This includes minutely detailed specifications for HTML and how browsers should interpret them.

Not surprisingly, since the beginning the browser companies have been trying to stay one step ahead by introducing their own "improvements" to the standards. The result has been browser incompatibility, especially in emerging technologies such as style sheets and DHTML. Trying to get web features to work for all browsers is the single biggest frustration for web developers.

Fortunately, the web development community has made enough noise that the browser companies seem be listening. Both Netscape and Microsoft have vowed to be standards-compliant (as demonstrated by the efforts they put into Navigator 6 and Internet Explorer 5), which will hopefully mean more predictability for how web pages look and perform. Of course, this is all wishful thinking and it will take a few years before you can safely assume that users have ditched their old Version 3 and 4 browsers—but it's a start.

Figure 4-3

My browser preferences

A user's browser preferences

A document viewed on the same browser version can look very different as a result of the user's browser settings.

Unknown User Preferences

At the heart of the original web concept lies the belief that the end user should have ultimate control over the presentation of information. For that reason, browsers are built with the opportunity for users to set the default appearance of the pages they view. The user's settings will override yours, and there's not much you can do about it. Figure 4-3 shows how the same page might look for different users.

Now that web page design has become more exciting, I think users are less likely to alter the color settings in their browsers than they were when most web pages were comprised of black text on gray backgrounds. However, they can still tinker with the default font settings. I've seen CAD designers with super-high monitor resolution set their default type at 24 points to make it easily readable from a comfortable distance. I've looked over the shoulder of a kid who set his browser to render all text in a graffiti font, just because he could. You simply don't know how your page will look on the other end.

Users might also opt to turn the graphics off completely! You'd be surprised at the percentage of people who do this in order to alleviate the wait for bandwidth-hogging graphics over slow modem connections. Make sure your pages are at least functional with the graphics turned off. The web page in Figure 4-4 becomes unusable with the graphics turned off because the navigation elements lose their labels.

Figure 4-4

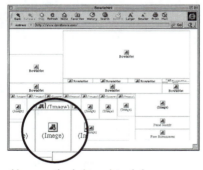

This web site looks great with all the graphics on, as the designers intended it to be seen.

But if someone decides to turn graphics off (because of a slow modem connection) or views it on a text-only browser, none of the links are labeled and the page is a dead end.

This could have been avoided if the designer had used alternative text labels in the image tags. This is discussed in Chapter 8, Adding GraphicsElements.

Unknown Window Size

When you design a printed piece, you know that your page is a certain size, so you design elements to fit that space. Another tricky thing about the Web is that you really have no idea how big your "page" will be. The available space is determined by the size of the browser window when the page is opened.

Web pages are more fluid than print; they reflow to fill the available space. Although you may prefer the way your page looks when the window is just larger than the headline graphic, the fact is users can set the window as wide or narrow as they please. This is one of the most vexing aspects of web design. Figure 4-5 shows how the elements on the page re-wrap to fill the available space when a browser window is resized. Notice how the text fills the width of the large window. Notice also how the flower graphic gets pushed to the next line when the window is really small.

The tricky thing about the Web is that you really have no idea how big your "page" will be.

Figure 4-5

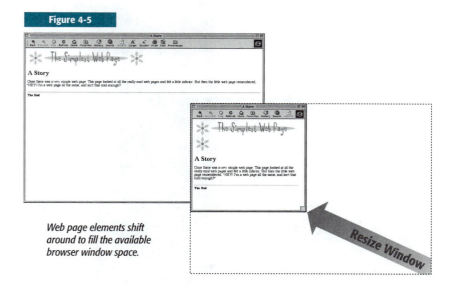

Web page elements shift around to fill the available browser window space.

Because browser windows can only be opened as large as the monitors displaying them, standard monitor resolution (the total number of pixels available on the screen) is useful in anticipating the likely dimensions of your page. This is particularly true on Windows machines, since the browser window is typically optimized to fill the monitor.

For instance, one of the lowest standard monitor resolutions still in use today is 640 × 480 pixels. After you allow for the space that the browser and all its rows of buttons and scrolls take up, that leaves a space as small as 623 × 278 pixels for your page. That's not very much space, but if you are designing a site for students or people who are likely to be using slightly older machines, you should keep this dimension in mind.

Figure 4-6

800 × 600

640 × 480

This page uses a table to fix the width of the page to 800 pixels wide. Notice how the navigation system falls out of view on the smaller monitor size. This is the risk of designing rigid page layouts. (In Adobe's case, a larger page size makes sense for their audience.)

Other common pixel dimensions are 800 × 600, 1024 × 768, and 1280 × 1024 (although they go even higher). At the highest resolutions, it's difficult to predict the browser window size because users are likely to resize the window smaller, or open several pages at once.

How do you cope with the unknown-window-size dilemma? One approach is to use a table to fix the dimensions of your content to a specific pixel width. That way, when the window is resized smaller, the elements do not shift, and users have a better chance of viewing the page as you intended.

Sounds great, right? Unfortunately, this solution has its drawbacks. When the window is resized smaller than the contents of the page, the content outside the browser window is simply no longer visible without horizontal scrolling. Users with smaller monitors may not even know it's there!

Figure 4-6 shows the Adobe web site, which has been designed to fit an 800 × 600 pixel browser window. Notice, however, that when the page is viewed on a smaller monitor (640 × 480), there's no way of knowing that there is a whole navigation system off the screen unless you happen to scroll to the right. This is one of the problems of fixing web pages to a particular width, especially if the width is larger than the lowest common denominator. In this case, it is Adobe's site, and since they can safely

Designing "Above the Fold"

Newspaper editors know the importance of putting the most important information "above the fold," that is, visible when the paper is folded and on the rack. This principle applies to web design as well.

Web designers have adopted the term "above the fold" to refer to the first screenful of a web page. It's what users will see without scrolling, and it bears the burden of holding their attention and enticing them to click in further. Some elements you should consider placing above the fold include:

- The name of the site and your logo (if you have one)
- Your primary message
- Some indication of what your site is about (e.g., shopping, directory, magazine, etc.)
- Navigation to key parts of the site
- Any other crucial information, such as a toll-free number
- An advertising banner (your advertisers may require it)

But how much is a "screenful"? Unfortunately, this varies by browser window size. Your available space could be as small as 623 × 278 pixels in a browser or a piddly 544 × 378 pixels on WebTV.

In general, the level of confidence in what will be seen on the first "page" is highest in the top-left corner of the browser window and then diminishes to the right and down from there. When the browser window is made very small, the bottom and the right edge are the most likely to be cut off. One strategy for page layout is to put your most important elements and messages in that top-left corner and work out from there through hierarchies of importance.

assume that their target audience (designers) will have larger monitors, their design decision to use a larger page grid is not off the mark. In fact, it serves their audience better.

You might choose to tell your users how you'd like them to size their screens. Every now and then (although not as often as in the early days of web design), you'll run into a friendly note at the top of a web page that says, "For optimal viewing of this site, please size your browser this wide," followed by a graphical bar of a certain width. The best you can do is hope that users will play along.

Another way to deal with unknown window size is to just accept it as the nature of the medium. It is possible to design for flexibility—good web pages are functional and not seriously compromised by a certain amount of shape-shifting. Learning to let go of some control is part of becoming a seasoned web designer.

Unknown Connection Speed

Remember that a web page is published over a network, and it will need to go zipping through the lines as little bundles of data before it reaches the end user. In most cases, the speed of that connection is a mystery. On the high end, folks with T1 connections, cable modems, ISDN, and other high-speed Internet access may be viewing your pages at a rate of up to 500K per second! On the other end of the scale are people who are dialing in with modems whose speed can range from 56Kbps down to 14.4Kbps (or even slower). For them, data transfer rates of only 1K per second are pretty common.

Keep your files as small as possible!

There are many factors that affect download times, including the speed of the server, the amount of traffic it is receiving when the web page is requested, and the general congestion of the lines.

It should be fairly intuitive that larger amounts of data will require more time to arrive. When you are counting on maintaining the interest of your readers, every millisecond counts. For this reason, it is wise to follow the golden rule of web design: *keep your files as small as possible!*

The worst culprits for hogging bandwidth are graphics files, so it is especially important that you spend time optimizing them for the Web. I discuss some strategies for doing this in Chapter 14, Creating GIFs, and Chapter 15, Creating JPEGs. HTML files, although generally just a few kilobytes (K) in size, can be optimized as well by removing redundant tags and extra spaces.

Unless you are designing specifically for high-bandwidth applications, assume the worst when it comes to connection speeds. Since you know a web page is designed to travel, do your best to see that it travels light.

Unknown Computer Speed

Another factor that affects the rate of page display is the speed of the user's computer. Assembling a web page in a browser requires a certain amount of computer processing power. The fancier you get with page formatting (for instance, using complex tables within tables), the longer it will take the browser to display the page on a slow machine. If you anticipate that your target audience may be working with outdated computers (such as in a home, library, or school setting), keeping your pages simple and straighforward will improve their experience.

Unknown Colors

I'll never forget my first lesson in web color. I had designed a headline graphic that used a rich forest green as a background. I proudly put the page up on the server, and when I went in to my boss's office to show him my work, the graphic came up on his screen with a background of rich *pitch black*! It was then that I learned that not everyone (including my boss) was seeing my colors the way I intended them.

When you are publishing materials that will be viewed on computer monitors, you need to deal with the varying ways computers handle color. The differences fall under two main categories: the number of colors and the brightness of colors.

Number of colors

Monitors differ in the number of colors they are able to display. They typically display 24-bit (approximately 17 million colors), 16-bit (approximately 65,000 colors), or 8-bit color (256 colors).

A full-color photograph may contain many thousands of shades of blended colors to produce a smooth image... not a problem for 24- or 16-bit monitors. But what happens to all those colors on an 8-bit monitor with only 256 available colors?

On 8-bit monitors, the image will be approximated out of the set of colors (called a palette) that the browser has on hand. Some colors from that full-color photo will shift to the nearest palette color. Others will be approximated by dithering (using a speckled pattern of two palette colors to create a color not in the palette, as in Figure 4-7, gallery). Be aware that colors may behave differently depending on the monitor used to view them.

Brightness

That rich forest green I described in my example above was a victim of varying gamma settings. Gamma refers to the overall brightness of a computer monitor's display, and its default setting varies from platform to platform. Images created on a Macintosh will generally look much darker

---

Figure 4-7 **G**

The image below shows a graphic as it might appear on a monitor that displays millions or thousands of colors (24-bit or 16-bit monitors). These monitors can smoothly display an enormous range of colors.

8-bit monitors, on the other hand, can display only 256 colors at a time. Within the browser, there are only 216 available colors to choose from.

The image above shows what happens to the same graphic when viewed on an 8-bit monitor. The close-up shows how the real color is approximated by mixing colors from the available palette of colors. This effect is called dithering.

when viewed on a Windows machine or Unix terminal (which is what happened to me). Images created under Windows will look washed out on a Mac. Figure 4-8, gallery, shows the same page viewed at different gamma settings.

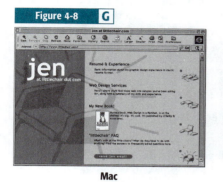
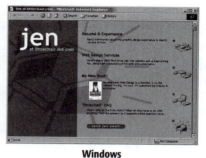

Figure 4-8 **G**

Mac   Windows

Gamma refers to the overall brightness of monitors. Windows machines tend to be darker (the result of higher gamma settings) than Macs.

Since the majority of the web audience today uses Windows machines, this shift is especially significant for designers using Macs. Try setting the gamma of your monitor darker to approximate the Windows viewing conditions, and as always, be sure to test your pages to make sure your color details aren't fading to black. There are also new web graphics tools that will give gamma previews and make brightness adjustments automatically.

Unknown Fonts

Another aspect of web design that you may find shocking is that you have virtually no control over the fonts used to display your content. The way text appears is a result of browser settings, platform, and user preferences.

You may find it shocking that you have virtually no control over the fonts used to display your content.

Even though there are methods for specifying a font face (the `<FONT>` tag and style sheets), the font will only display if it is already installed on the end user's machine. It's more like "suggesting" a font than specifying it. There's no guarantee your chosen font will be available. If it is not found, the default font will be used instead.

About the only thing you can be sure of is that you have two fonts to work with: a proportional font (such as Times or Helvetica) that is used for the majority of body copy and headlines on a page, and a monospaced font (such as Courier) that is used for code or text tagged with the "preformatted" tag `<PRE>`.

There are technologies for embedding fonts into a file, but due to the large file sizes and a cumbersome creation process, they have not been widely supported by the web community. This lack of control over fonts is something you have to get used to. Make your font suggestions, and let it go.

Surviving the Unknown

I can still remember my reaction to learning about this "unknown" stuff (it wasn't that long ago, after all)—it was somewhere between confusion and despair. If I couldn't control the size of the page, or the colors, or the type, what were they asking me to "design"... why did they need a designer at all? The answer is that the Web is a visual medium, and designers are needed for all the same reasons they've been needed in the past, including:

- Organizing information for the most effective communication
- Guiding readers' eyes through the page
- Creating an exciting visual experience that is in keeping with the goals and messages of the site

*My number one bit of advice for conquering the medium is to **let go!***

As a word of consolation, I can tell you that you will develop a feel for designing around the unknowns on the Web. If you've worked as a print designer, you know how you develop a feel for how an ink color will work on a particular paper. It takes practice. But after you've done a certain amount of testing, you'll know the types of things that are likely to go wrong, and you can avoid them. It just takes time to develop those chops.

My number one bit of advice for conquering the medium is to *let go*! Elements are going to shift and pages will look different to different people. Accept it as part of the medium and move on. You'll go batty trying to control every little thing, and then you'll stop having fun. Sometimes, you just have to go with the flow.

Designing Democratically

When you design for the Web, bear in mind that not everyone is equipped with the latest browser on a souped-up computer system with a lightning-fast connection. Although it's good to take advantage of the latest features in web publishing, you also have to design with the lowest common denominator in mind. In the web biz, this is also referred to as designing web pages that "degrade gracefully."

For instance, many of your users will not see your graphics because they have chosen to turn them off, or because they are using a text-only browser such as Lynx. Furthermore, some sight-impaired users will have your web pages read to them by a speech device attached to such a text-only browser. For this reason, you should design so that your pages are at least *functional* (although not beautiful) with the graphics turned off. Avoid putting important text, such as headlines and contact information, in graphics. When you do use a graphic, be sure to provide alternative text for the image (alternative text is discussed in Chapter 8.)

You should also avoid relying on effects that use cutting-edge technologies for your main message. For example, if the whole point of your web site is to distribute an "800" number, do not put that number in a Java applet that makes it scroll across the screen. A significant percentage of users who do not have Java activated on their browsers will miss it altogether. The safest way to present your most important information is in plain old HTML text; that way, everyone is sure to see it. It's okay to play with more adventurous web techniques, but use them as "icing."

I'll repeat this because it is the most important guideline for web design—keep your files as small as possible. Assume the worst when it comes to connection speed and everyone will benefit.

Take time to test your designs under less-than-optimum conditions before you put them online. Is it just a little less attractive (disappointing, but not critical) or is it totally unusable (back to the drawing board, as they say)?

Know Your Audience

We've established that there are a lot of unknown factors to consider when designing a web page. But there is something that you do know when you begin the design process: your target audience. In professional web development companies, researching the characteristics and needs of the target audience is one of the most important parts of the design process.

Having a good understanding of your audience can help you make better design decisions.

A good understanding of your audience can help you make better design decisions. Let's take a look at a few examples:

Scenario 1: A site that sells educational toys. If your site is aimed at a consumer audience, you should assume that a significant portion of your audience will be using your site from home computers. They may not keep up with the very latest browser versions, or they may be using an AOL browser or WebTV, so don't rely too heavily on cutting-edge web technologies. They are probably also connecting to the Internet through modem connections, so keep your files extra small to prevent long download times. You might want to use the smaller monitor size as a guideline for page layout. When your bread and butter depends on sales from ordinary consumers, it's best to play it safe with your page design. You can't afford to alienate anyone.

Scenario 2: A site with resources for professional graphic designers. Because graphic designers tend to have larger computer monitors, this is a case where you might safely design for an 800 × 600 pixel screen size. In addition, if they are accessing your pages from work, they are likely to have a connection to the Internet that is faster than the standard modem connection, so you can be a little more lax with the number of graphics you put on the screen (plus, a good-looking site will be part of the draw for your audience).

Scenario 3: A site used to share company information for in-house use only (also known as an "intranet"). This is the ideal situation for a web designer because many of the "unknowns" become easily known. Often, a company's system administrator will install the same browser on all machines and keep them up-to-date. Or you might know that everyone will be working on Windows machines with standard 800 × 600 monitors. Bandwidth becomes less of an issue when documents are served internally, as well. You should be able to take advantage of some features that would be risky in the standard web environment.

Why Web Design Is Cool

I feel like I've done a lot of complaining in this chapter about the frustrations of web design. Sure, it's different, but it's also exciting. I'd like to end on a positive note with my personal top-ten list of why I like being a web designer:

10. *It's paperless!* After years of being a print designer, there was something kind of spooky and cool about designing something that never hits paper.

9. *The limitations become a challenge.* If you're a problem-solving kind of designer like I am, you'll enjoy getting the most out of the medium.

8. *It taught me interface design.* You might find that you enjoy designing how a page works, as well as how it looks.

7. *It taught me multimedia design.* It has been interesting adding the dimension of time to my otherwise two-dimensional designs.

6. *Anyone can publish.* The real glory of the Web is that any individual can reach a worldwide audience.

5. *Instant gratification.* In print design, there's always a lag time while you wait to see how the piece prints. In web design, the results are immediate.

4. *It's easy to fix mistakes.* Because nothing's set in stone (or even paper), you can makes changes easily.

3. *I love being a geek.* Learning about new technology is a natural part of the job. I'm also proud to know basic Unix commands.

2. *There's lots of work out there.* Now that every company in the world is demanding a web presence, web designers are in hot demand.

...and the number one reason why web design is cool:

1. *My friends and family are impressed!* The Web is so new that it's still very hip to be a part of it.

Chapter 5

The Web Design Process

Web sites come in all shapes and sizes—from a single page about a favorite furry friend, to mega-sites conducting business for worldwide corporations such as American Express or FedEx. Regardless of the scale, the process for developing a site involves the same basic steps:

1. Conceptualize and research

2. Create and organize content

3. Develop the "look and feel"

4. Produce graphics and HTML documents

5. Create a prototype

6. Test, test, test!

7. Upload and test again

Of course, depending on the nature and scale of the site, these steps will vary in proportion, sequence, and number of people required, but in essence, they are a necessary journey for the creation of a site. This chapter examines each step of the web design process.

IN THIS CHAPTER

The standard steps in the web design process:

- Conceptualization and research
- Content organization and creation
- Art direction
- HTML production
- Prototype building
- Testing
- Uploading and final testing

1. Conceptualize and Research

Every web site begins with an idea. It's the result of some*one* wanting to get some*thing* online, be it for personal or commercial ends. This early phase is exciting! You start with the core idea ("photo album for my family," "shopping site for skateboarding gear," "online banking," etc.) then brainstorm on how it's going to manifest itself as a web page. This is a time for lists and sketches, whiteboards and notebooks. What's going to make it exciting? What's going to be on the first page?

Don't bother launching an HTML editor until you have your ideas and strategy together. This involves asking your client (or yourself) a number of questions regarding resources, goals, and most importantly, audience.

Some Questions Before You Begin

The following are just a few of the questions you should ask your clients during the research phase of design.

Strategy

- Why are you creating this web site? What do you expect to accomplish?
- What are you offering your audience?
- What do you want users to do on your web site? After they've left?

General Site Description

- What kind of site is it? (Purely promotional? Info-gathering? A publication? A point of sale?)
- What features will it have?
- What are your most important messages?
- Who are your competitors?

Target Audience

- Who is your primary audience?
- How Internet-savvy are they? How technically savvy?
- Can you make assumptions about an average user's connection speed? Platform? Browser use?
- How often do you expect them to visit your site? How long will they stay in an average visit?

Content

- Who is responsible for generating original content?
- How will content be submitted (process and format)?

Resources

- What resources have you dedicated to the site (budget, staff, time)?
- How often will the information be updated (daily, weekly, monthly)?
- Will updates require completely new page designs with graphics?
- Can maintenance be handled by your staff?
- Do you have a server for your site?
- Have you registered a domain name for your site?

Graphic Look and Feel

- Are you envisioning a certain look and feel for the site?
- Do you have existing standards, such as logos and colors, that must be incorporated?
- Is the site part of a larger site or group of sites with design standards that need to be matched?
- What are some other web sites you like? What do you like about them?

The Some Questions Before You Begin sidebar provides just a sampling of the sorts of questions you might ask before you start a project.

Many large web development and design firms spend more time on researching and identifying clients' needs than on any other stage of production. For large sites, this step may include case studies, interviews, and extensive market research. There are even firms dedicated to developing web strategies for emerging and established companies.

You may not need to put that sort of effort (or money) into preparing to publish, but it is still wise to be clear about your expectations and resources early on in the process, particularly when attempting to work within a budget.

Many web development and design firms spend more time on researching and identifying clients' needs than on any other stage of production.

2. Create and Organize Content

The most important part of a web site is its content. Despite the buzz about technologies and tools, content is still king on the Internet. There's got to be something of value, whether it's something to read or something to do, to draw visitors and keep them coming back. (Or as my editor says, "There's got to be a *there* there.") Even if you are working as a freelance designer putting your client's ideas online, it doesn't hurt to be sensitive to the need for good content.

Content Creation

When designing for a client, you need to immediately establish who will be responsible for generating the content that goes on the site. Some clients will arrive full of ideas but empty-handed, assuming that you will create the site, including all the content in it. Ideally, the client will be responsible for generating their own content and have allocated the appropriate resources to do so. Solid copy writing is an important, yet often overlooked component of a successful site.

The most important part of a web site is its content.

Information Design

Once you've got content—or at least a very clear idea of what content you will have—the next step is to organize the content so it will be easily and intuitively accessible to your audience. For large sites, the information design may be handled by a specialist in information architecture. It might also be decided by a team made up of designers and the client. Even personal sites require attention to the division and organization of information.

Again, this is a time for lists and sketchbooks! Get everything that you want in the site out there on the table. Organize it by importance, timeliness, category, and so on. Decide what goes on the home page and what gets divided into sections.

Viva la Pen and Paper!

There's still no beating pen and paper when it comes to firing up and documenting the creative process. Before you delve into the HTML and GIFs, what better way to hash out your ideas than in your handy notepad, on a napkin or whiteboard, or whatever surface is available (but remember, graffiti is a crime)? It's about creativity!

Make lists. Draw diagrams. Figure out that home page. Do it fast and loose, or include every minute detail and copy it faithfully online. It all comes down to your personal style.

The result of the information design phase is usually a diagram that reveals the overall "shape" of the site. Pages in diagrams are usually represented by rectangles; arrows indicate links between pages or sections of the site. The diagram gives designers a sense of the scale of the site and how sections are related, and aids in the navigation design.

Figure 5-1 shows the site diagram for my simple *www.littlechair.com* site. It is quite small compared to the diagrams for big e-commerce sites. I once saw a site diagram for a high-profile commercial site that, despite using postage-stamp-sized boxes to represent pages, filled the length and height of the hallway!

The effectiveness of a site's organization can make or break it. Don't underestimate the importance of this step. For a more thorough introduction to information and interface design, see Chapter 18, Building Usable Web Sites.

Figure 5-1

This is a diagram of my simple site, www.littlechair.com, as it existed in the spring of 2000. The boxes indicate pages and the arrows indicate links. The site diagrams for commercial websites are usually much more complicated, and even at this scale the printouts can be large enough to fill a wall.

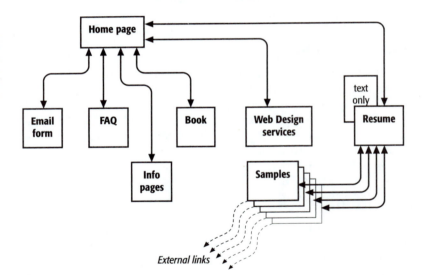

3. Develop the "Look and Feel"

The "look and feel" of a site refers to its graphic design and overall visual appearance, including its color scheme, typography, and image style (for example, photographic versus illustrative). As in the print world, this phase of design is often referred to as "art direction."

Sketch It

This is another chance to get out pads of paper and markers! Or perhaps you prefer to work out ideas right in Photoshop. Either way, it's your chance to be creative and try things. The end result is one or more sketches (sometimes called a "look and feel study") that show off your proposed visual style for the site.

A sketch is usually just a flat graphic file in the approximate dimensions of the browser window (usually 600 × 400 pixels or 800 × 500 pixels). When it is necessary to show interactivity (such as a "rollover" button effect), some designers use a layer in Photoshop that can be switched on and off to simulate the effect.

In some cases, it may be necessary to create a prototype home page in HTML to show off interactive and animated features, particularly if you have a client with no imagination (but a big budget to cover development costs). Keep in mind that the art direction phase is for exploring how the site will look, so flat graphic sketches are usually adequate.

The Art Direction Process

In most professional web development jobs, the client receives two or three sketches showing their home page in various visual styles. In some cases, a second- or third-level design might be included if it is important to show how the design plays out through several levels. Figure 5-2 shows a set of look and feel studies I created for a women's site several years ago.

The designer is usually provided with a basic list of elements and a manuscript for what should be included in the sketches, but don't be too surprised if you are asked to make stuff up on occasion.

Ideally, the client will choose one sketch, but with a list of changes, requiring another round of design until the final design is agreed upon. In my experience, clients usually see elements they like in each style and ask for some sort of hybrid. In this aspect, web designers face the same frustrations as traditional graphic designers.

Figure 5-2

As part of the art direction phase, I created three sketches for this women's site, demonstrating how the same material might look in three different visual styles.

BUSINESS TIP

Get It in Writing

Design comes down to a matter of taste, and clients don't always know what they want. When writing your contract for the job, it is a good idea to specify the number of initial sketches and the number of revisions that will be included for the project price. That way, you have the opportunity to ask for extra compensation should the art direction phase get out of control.

The Web Design Process

4. Produce Graphics and HTML Documents

Once the design is approved and the content is ready to go, the site enters the production phase. For small sites, the production may be done by one person. It is more common in commercial web design to have a team of people working on specialized tasks.

The art department uses their graphics tools to create all the graphics needed for the site. The content will be formatted into HTML documents by HTML whizzes who may write the code by hand or use a full-featured WYSIWYG program (such as Dreamweaver). There may also be multimedia elements produced and scripts and programs written. In short, all the elements of the site must be created.

5. Create a Prototype

At some point, all the pieces are brought together into a working site. This is not necessarily a distinct step; it is more likely to be an ongoing process as the HTML files and graphics are being produced (particularly if they are produced by the same person).

Once the pages are viewed in a browser, it is necessary to make a round of tweaks to both the HTML documents and the graphics until everything fits smoothly in place. As a solo web designer, I make a lot of rounds between my graphics program, HTML editor, and browser until the page works as I intended.

As in software design, the first prototype is often called the "alpha" release. It might only be made available to people within the web team for review and revisions before it is released to the client. The second release is called the "beta" and is generally the version that is sent to the client for approval. At this point, there is still plenty to do before the site is ready to go live on the Web.

6. Test, Test, Test!

Just because a page is working well on your machine doesn't mean it will look that way to everyone. As we discussed in Chapter 4, Why Web Design Isn't Like Print Design, your page will be viewed by seemingly infinite combinations of browsers, platforms, window sizes, and user settings.

For this reason, I strongly recommend (and many clients require) that you test your pages under as many conditions as possible. Professional web design firms build time and resources into the production schedule for rigorous testing. This phase is often called "QA" (short for "quality assurance"). They check that the site is in working order, that all the links work, and that the site performs appropriately on a wide variety of browsers and platforms. These firms have banks of various computer configurations, running numerous browser versions on various monitor setups.

Even if you're working on your own and can't afford to turn a room of your house into a testing lab, try viewing your web pages in a number of the following situations:

I strongly recommend (and many clients require) that you test your pages under as many conditions as possible.

- On another browser. If you developed your pages using Microsoft Internet Explorer, open them in Netscape Navigator. Hang onto old versions of browsers so you can open the pages in a less-technically advanced browser as well.

- On a different kind of computer than the one on which you developed the pages. You may need to visit a friend and use her computer. If you worked on a Windows machine, you may be surprised to see how your pages look on a Mac, and vice versa.

- With the graphics turned off, and with a text-only browser, such as Lynx. Is your page still functional?

- With the browser window set to different widths and lengths (be sure to check the extremes).

- With your monitor set to 8-bit color, grayscale, and black and white. Are your graphics still clear?

- Over a slow modem connection, particularly if you have fast Internet access where you are working.

You may need to make some adjustments to make the page (at the very least) acceptable even in the worst of conditions.

Another type of testing that is important to perform is user testing. This process involves sitting ordinary people down with your site and seeing how easily they are able to find information and complete tasks. User testing is generally conducted as early in the production process as possible so changes can be made to the final site.

7. Upload and Test Again

Once you have all the kinks worked out of the site, it's time to upload to the final server and make it available to the world. It's a good idea to do one final round of testing to make sure everything was transferred successfully and the pages function properly under the configuration of the final server. Check that the graphics still appear and the links are still working (link management is a big part of quality assurance).

This may seem like extra work, but if the reputation of your business (or your client's business) is riding on the success of the web site, attention to detail is essential.

Part II

Learning HTML

As we've already discussed, HTML is the stuff web pages are made of. In this section of the book, we finally dig into the details. I believe that it is important to learn HTML the old-fashioned way—writing it by hand (I explain why in Chapter 6, Creating a Simple Page). Don't worry, it's easy to get started.

However, I recognize that you most likely will use a web-authoring tool to create your pages (I do). For that reason, I have included "Tool Tips" in each chapter that show how to access the tags we discuss in three popular authoring programs: Macromedia Dreamweaver 3, Adobe GoLive 4, and Microsoft FrontPage 2000. There are plenty of other web tools out there, so if you've found one that works for you, feel free to stick with it. Understanding the tags and how HTML works will make using your tools even easier.

The chapters in Part II cover the major HTML topics in detail.

Chapter 6

Creating a Simple Page (HTML Overview)

In Part I: Getting Started, I provided a general overview of the web design environment. Now that we've covered the big concepts, it's time to roll up our sleeves and get started on the specifics of creating a real web page. It will be a simple page, but even the most complicated pages are based on the principles described in the following example.

In this chapter, I create a simple web page step by step. The important lessons here are:

- How HTML tagging works

- How an HTML document is structured

- How browsers display tagged documents

Don't worry about learning specific text-formatting tags at this point. All the tags will be discussed in detail in the following chapters. For now, just pay attention to the process and the overall structure of the document. Once you understand the basics, adding tags to your bag of tricks is simple.

HTML the Hard Way

With all the wonderful web-authoring tools out there today, chances are you will be using one to create your pages. In fact, I recommend it; the time and sanity savings are too good to pass up.

You may be asking, "If the tools are so great, do I need to learn HTML at all?" The answer is, you do. You may not need to have every tag memorized, but some familiarity is crucial for everyone who wants to make web pages. If you go looking for a job as a "web designer," it will probably be assumed that you know your way around an HTML document.

I stand by my method of teaching HTML the old-fashioned way—*by hand*! There's no way to truly understand how HTML works other than typing it out, one tag at a time, then opening your page in a browser. It doesn't take long to develop a feel for tagging documents properly.

Understanding HTML will make using your authoring tools easier and more efficient. In addition, you will be glad to be able to look at an HTML source file and understand what you're seeing. Say you see a really cool web page trick. You can always view the source to see how it's done, but if the source looks like a bunch of gibberish to you, it won't do much good.

Once you know the basics, you can continue your learning by reading *Web Design in a Nutshell* (O'Reilly, 1999) or *HTML & XHTML: The Definitive Guide, Fourth Edition* by Chuck Musciano and Bill Kennedy (O'Reilly, 2000).

Introducing... the HTML Tag

If you've read through Part I of this book, you know web pages are formatted using HTML tags. The characters within the tag are usually an abbreviation of a formatting instruction or an element to add to the page (Figure 6-1).

Figure 6-1

Container Tag Structure:

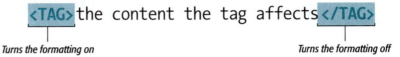

Turns the formatting on   Turns the formatting off

Standalone Tag Structure:

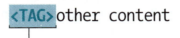

Places an element on the page (doesn't affect content display)

Most HTML tags are container tags. They consist of two tags (a beginning and an end tag) that are wrapped around a range of text. The tag instruction applies to all the content contained within the tags. Think of them as an "on" switch and "off" switch. The end tag looks the same as the start tag, only it begins with a slash (/).

A few tags are standalone tags: you just drop them into place where you want an element to appear. They do not have a closing tag.

We'll be using both types of tags in the following web page demo.

Assembling a Web Page

We are ready to make a web page. This demonstration has four steps:

Step 1: Setting up the HTML document. You'll learn about the tags used to give an HTML document its structure.

Step 2: Formatting text. We'll use container tags to format the text on the page.

Step 3: Adding graphical elements. We'll use standalone tags to add pictures and rules to the page. We'll also look at how tag attributes work.

Step 4: Adding a hypertext link. Since the Web is about linking, a web page demo would be incomplete without an introduction to linking.

I'll be typing the HTML by hand using an HTML editor called BBEdit (on a Mac). You could also use Allaire HomeSite if you're on a PC. Word processing programs such as Microsoft Word are not appropriate because they add hidden information to the code, and what we're after is pure text characters (ASCII).

I'll be checking my work in a browser frequently throughout this demonstration—probably more than you would in real life—but since this is a first introduction to HTML, I find it helpful to show the cause and effect of each change.

The end result will be the home page for a site called "Jen's Kitchen" (Figure 6-2) that links to a number of my favorite recipes.

Free Software Samples

You can try out these HTML editors for free!

For BBEdit, go to the Bare Bones Software site at *www.barebones.com/free/free.html* and download a free demo.

For Allaire HomeSite, start on the product page at *www.allaire.com/products/homesite/index.cfm* and choose "Download HomeSite 4.5." You'll need to fill out customer information, but when that's through, there is a free evaluation version of HomeSite available on the list of downloads.

Figure 6-2

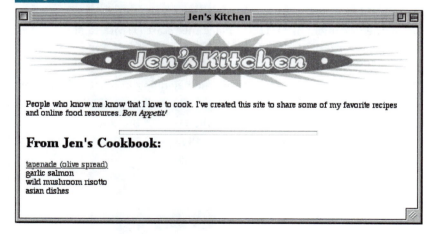

In this chapter, we'll assemble this web page step-by-step. It's not very fancy, but we have to start somewhere.

To Capitalize or Not to Capitalize

Throughout this book, I have written my tags in all capital letters, but they could also be lowercase. In other words, tags are not "case-sensitive." The choice is yours, but here are some things you might take into consideration:

On the one hand, using all capital letters makes the tags stand out against a sea of code. This is helpful when you are writing your HTML code from scratch.

On the other hand, as HTML evolves, related tagging systems (such as XML and XHTML) require lowercase tags only. If you are learning HTML for the first time and you anticipate becoming a web professional, you might want to get in the habit of writing all lowercase tags from the start.

Step 1: Setting Up the HTML Document

There are two things that make an ordinary text file a browser-readable web document. The document must have a name that ends in *.htm* or *.html* in order to be recognized by the browser, and it must contain the basic HTML tags that define the structure of the web document.

Basic structure

Begin a new web document by giving it a skeleton.

There are really only two parts to an HTML document: the head (also called the header) and the body. The head contains information about the document (its title, for instance); the body contains the actual content of the document. The structure of the document is identified by using the <HTML>, <HEAD>, and <BODY> container tags (Figure 6-3).

Figure 6-3

A document with no content would look like this.

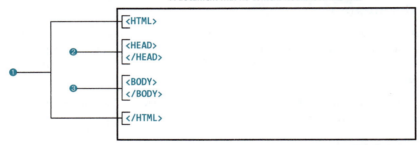

① First, tell the browser that the text is in HTML format by labeling the entire document as "HTML." Place the "start HTML" tag (<HTML>) at the very beginning of the text and the "end HTML" tag (</HTML>) at the end.

② The <HEAD>...</HEAD> tags define the beginning and end of the head section of the document. Right now, that section is empty.

③ The <BODY>...</BODY> tags define the body of the document. This is where we'll put the contents of the page; that is, everything we want to display in the browser window.

Giving the page a title

Another essential part of the document is its title. This is the name you give to the page; it is shown in the top bar of the browser window. If you don't give the document a title, the filename will be used instead. The title, indicated by the `<TITLE>` container tag, is placed within the head of the document (Figure 6-4).

The Importance of the Title

The title is one of the most important pieces of information you provide about your web page. In addition to appearing at the top of the browser when the page is open, it will be listed in the Bookmarks (or Favorites) menu when someone bookmarks your page. The title is also the first thing search engines look at when indexing your page. Make sure it is descriptive and useful. How many bookmarks would you want named "Welcome!"?

Figure 6-4

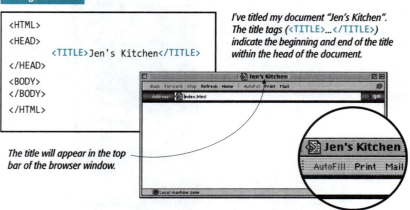

```
<HTML>
<HEAD>
        <TITLE>Jen's Kitchen</TITLE>
</HEAD>
<BODY>
</BODY>
</HTML>
```

I've titled my document "Jen's Kitchen". The title tags (`<TITLE>`…`</TITLE>`) indicate the beginning and end of the title within the head of the document.

The title will appear in the top bar of the browser window.

Adding content

So far, so good, but if we want something to appear in the browser window, we need to put some content in the body of the document. I've typed up a simple introduction and list (Figure 6-5).

Figure 6-5

```
<HTML>
<HEAD>
        <TITLE>Jen's Kitchen</TITLE>
</HEAD>
<BODY>
Jen's Kitchen

People who know me know that I love to cook. I've created
this site to share some of my favorite recipes and online food
resources. Bon Appetit!

From Jen's Cookbook:

    tapenade (olive spread)
    garlic salmon
    wild mushroom risotto
    asian dishes

</BODY>
</HTML>
```

I've added text to the body of the document.

TOOL TIP

Document Creation

When you use a web-authoring tool such as Macromedia Dreamweaver or Adobe GoLive, the structural tags are added automatically when you create a new document. The tools usually add some extra document information to the header as well (such as `<META>` tags that say what software was used to create the file). In most tools, the title is specified on the page that has settings for the whole document.

DREAMWEAVER 3

The document title is entered in the Page Properties dialog box.

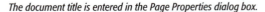

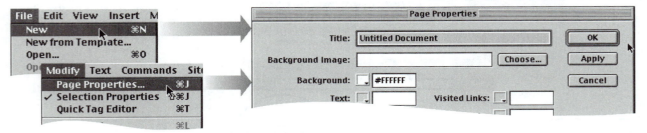
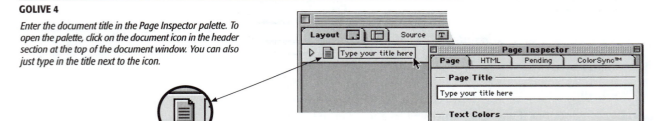

GOLIVE 4

Enter the document title in the Page Inspector palette. To open the palette, click on the document icon in the header section at the top of the document window. You can also just type in the title next to the icon.

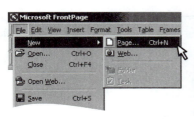

Document icon

FRONTPAGE 2000

Open a new page and default title will be highlighted in code. Type your title between `<TITLE>` and `</TITLE>` to replace.

Saving and viewing the page

We've got a document with the proper HTML structure and some content, but in order to view it in the browser, we need to save the file and give it a name (Figure 6-6). The filename needs to end in *.htm* or *.html* in order to be recognized by the browser as a web document. See the sidebar Naming Conventions for more tips on naming files. I've named my file *index.html*.

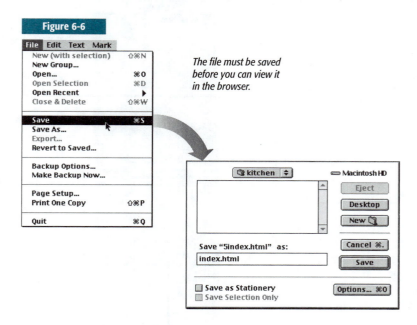

Figure 6-6

The file must be saved before you can view it in the browser.

Now we can view *index.html* in a browser. Opening a file from your computer's hard drive is called opening a file "locally." You don't need an Internet connection to check your work on a browser. Just launch your browser and choose "Open Page" or "Open Local" (or similar wording) from the File menu and locate your file in the dialog boxes (Figure 6-7, following page).

Naming Conventions

Follow these rules and conventions when naming your files:

* Use proper suffixes for your files. HTML files must end with *.html* or *.htm*. Web graphics must be labeled according to their file format: *.gif* or *.jpg* (*.jpeg* is also acceptable).

* Never use character spaces within filenames. It is common to use an underline character to visually separate words within filenames, such as *lynch_bio.html*.

* Avoid special characters such as ?, %, #, /, :, ;, ·, etc. Limit filenames to letters, numbers, underscores, hyphens, and periods.

* Filenames are case-sensitive in HTML. Consistently using all lowercase letters in filenames, while not necessary, makes your filenames easier to manage.

* Keep filenames short.

* If you really must give the file a long, multiword name, you can separate words with capital letters, such as *ALongDocumentTitle.htm*, or with underscores, such as *a_long_document_title.htm*, to improve readability.

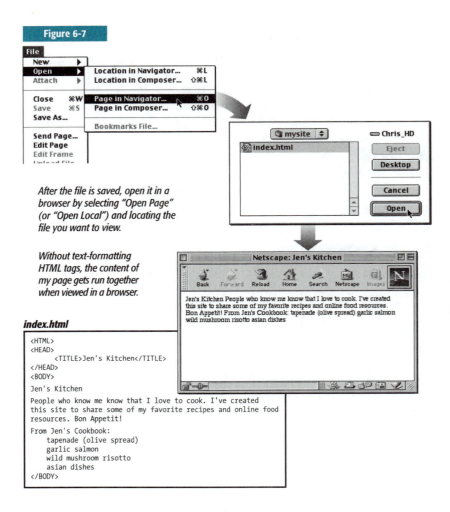

Figure 6-7

After the file is saved, open it in a browser by selecting "Open Page" (or "Open Local") and locating the file you want to view.

Without text-formatting HTML tags, the content of my page gets run together when viewed in a browser.

index.html

```
<HTML>
<HEAD>
        <TITLE>Jen's Kitchen</TITLE>
</HEAD>
<BODY>
Jen's Kitchen
People who know me know that I love to cook. I've created
this site to share some of my favorite recipes and online food
resources. Bon Appetit!
From Jen's Cookbook:
    tapenade (olive spread)
    garlic salmon
    wild mushroom risotto
    asian dishes
</BODY>
```

The only way a browser will make a new paragraph or add a space is if it sees a tag in the file that specifically tells it to do so. Otherwise, it will just ignore returns, tabs, and consecutive spaces.

Whoa! The text is all run together—not what I had in mind! My page title is up in the top bar of the browser, so that's a start. But let's look at what else happened. Notice how the browser ignored all of my line breaks. It also ignored the extra spaces I had added to indent the recipe names.

A browser will make a new paragraph or add a space only if it sees a tag in the file that specifically tells it to do so. Otherwise, it just ignores returns, tabs, and consecutive spaces in the text file.

This feature comes in handy, in a way, since you can enter as many returns and indents in your HTML document as you like. This makes it more readable while it's in the editor and won't affect your final product. The sidebar What Browsers Ignore provides some useful insights on how browsers interpret HTML code.

What Browsers Ignore

Some information in an HTML document will be ignored when it is viewed in a browser, including:

Line breaks (carriage returns). Line breaks are ignored. Text and elements will wrap continuously until a paragraph (`<P>`) or line break (`<BR>`) tag is encountered in the flow of the document text.

Tabs and multiple spaces. When a browser encounters a tab or more than one consecutive blank character space, it will display a single space. So if the document contains:

```
long,                long            ago
```

the browser will display:

```
long, long ago
```

Extra spaces can be added by using the "nonbreaking space" character string (` `) for each desired character space. (See the section Some Special Characters at the end of Chapter 7, Formatting Text.)

Multiple <P> tags. When a browser sees a `<P>` (paragraph) tag, it will add a line space; however, a series of `<P>` tags (or paragraph containers, `<P>...</P>`) with no intervening text is interpreted as redundant and will display as though it were only a single `<P>` tag. Most browsers will display multiple `<BR>` tags as multiple line breaks.

Unrecognized tags. A browser simply ignores any tag it doesn't understand or that was incorrectly specified. Depending on the tag and the browser, this can have varied results. Either the browser displays nothing at all, or it may display the contents of the tag as though it were normal text.

Text in comments. Browsers will not display text between the special `<!--` and `-->` elements used to denote a comment. Here is a sample comment:

```
<!-- This is a comment -->
<!-- This is a
multiple-line comment
that ends here. -->
```

There must be a space after the initial `<!--` and preceding the final `-->`, but you can put nearly anything inside the comment otherwise.

Step 2: Formatting Text

Let's quickly put some text-formatting tags in there to whip that text into shape (Figure 6-8, following page). At this point, don't worry too much about the specific tags—I just want you to get acquainted with the tagging process. We'll be discussing text-formatting tags in detail in Chapter 7.

At this point, don't worry too much about the specific tags— I just want you to get acquainted with the tagging process.

A Brief History of HTML

Before HTML there was SGML (Standard Generalized Markup Language), which established the system of describing documents in terms of their *structure*, independent of appearance. SGML tags work the same way as the HTML tags we've seen, but there can be far more of them, enabling a more sophisticated description of document elements.

Publishers began storing SGML versions of their documents so that they could be translated into a variety of end uses. For example, text that is tagged as a heading may be formatted one way if the end product is a printed book, but another way for a CD-ROM. The advantage is that a single source file can be used to create a variety of end products. The way it is interpreted and displayed (i.e., the way it *looks*) depends on the end use.

Because HTML is one application of an SGML tagging system, this principle of keeping style information (instructions for how elements look) separate from the structure of the document remains inherent to the HTML purpose. Over the past few years, this ideal has been muddied somewhat by the creation of HTML tags that contain explicit style instructions, such as the `<FONT>` tag, which gives designers control over the font, size, and color of text it contains, and the use of table tags for page layout.

A new system called Cascading Style Sheets has been introduced that promises to keep style information out of the content by storing all style instructions in a separate document (or separate section of the source document).

(continued on next page...)

Figure 6-8

I've added text-formatting tags to the HTML file to create headings (<H1>, <H2>), paragraphs (<P>), line breaks (<BR>), and italic text (<I>).

index.html

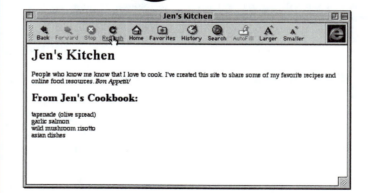

```
<HTML>
<HEAD>
            <TITLE>Jen's Kitchen</TITLE>
</HEAD>
<BODY>

❶  <H1>Jen's Kitchen</H1>

❷  <P>People who know me know that I love to cook. I've created
    this site to share some of my favorite recipes and online food
    resources. <I>Bon Appetit!</I></P>

❸  <H2>From Jen's Cookbook:</H2>
❹  <P>
        tapenade (olive spread)<BR>
        garlic salmon<BR>
        wild mushroom risotto<BR>
        asian dishes
</P>
</BODY>
```

Remember that you need to save your document in order for the changes to show up in the browser.

Because my page is already open in the browser, this time I can just hit "Refresh" (or "Reload") to see my new page.

Jen's Kitchen

People who know me know that I love to cook. I've created this site to share some of my favorite recipes and online food resources. *Bon Appetit!*

From Jen's Cookbook:

tapenade (olive spread)
garlic salmon
wild mushroom risotto
asian dishes

① `<H1>...</H1>`

I've placed start and end first-level heading tags around the headline of my page. The browser renders the text between `<H1>` tags in the largest bold text available. After the introduction, I've created a second-level heading (`<H2>`). You can see it is slightly smaller than the `<H1>` text. Notice also that these tags cause line breaks and extra space to be added above and below the headings.

② `<P>...</P>`

Paragraphs are indicated by wrapping the text in paragraph container tags (`<P>...</P>`). When you define a paragraph, the line automatically breaks and some space is added above and below.

It is possible to separate paragraphs by placing a single `<P>` tag between them. Browsers will render it the same as `<P>...</P>`. However, it is proper and preferable to use container tags, and furthermore, containers are required if you want to add formatting with style sheets. So you might as well start off on the right foot.

③ `<I>...</I>`

For emphasis, I've tagged the words "Bon Appetit!" with tags that start italic formatting (`<I>`), and then turn it off (`</I>`).

④ `<BR>`

To cause a line break without extra space (for instance, between recipe names), I added break tags (`<BR>`) at the points I want breaks to occur. The line break tag is an example of a standalone tag. It doesn't work on a range of text: it just inserts the break.

Again, I've saved my file and checked my progress in the browser window. This time, I was able to just hit the "Reload" or "Refresh" button since I already had the last version of the page in my browser window. Remember, your changes won't be visible on reload unless you save your file first.

Step 3: Adding Graphical Elements

By now, I'm sure you're getting the hang of container tags. Let's drop in some graphical elements to give the page more pizzazz. Again, don't worry too much about the specific tags at this point; they'll be covered in Chapter 8, Adding Graphic Elements.

I'll add a title graphic to the top of the page and a horizontal rule (a line) to break up the page (Figure 6-9, following page). These elements will give us a good opportunity to look at how standalone tags and attributes work.

A Brief History of HTML
(continued from previous page)

Style sheets are an advanced technique and therefore are not covered in depth in this book (see Chapter 20, How'd They Do That? for an introduction). Let's consider an example, though. Within the document, a heading will be labeled with a standard `<H1>` to indicate the type of information; elsewhere, in the style sheet, the designer specifies, "I'd like H1s to be 36 point, blue Helvetica type centered on the page." This pleases both the designers and the HTML purists. As Martha Stewart says, it's a "good thing."

Remember, your changes won't be visible on reload unless you save your file first.

Figure 6-9

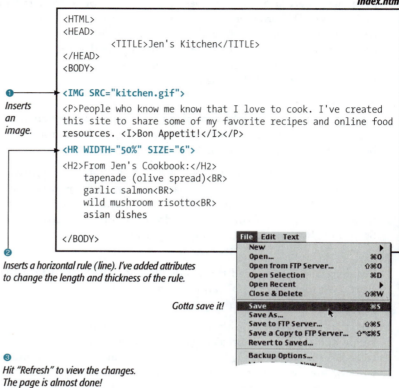

index.html

```
<HTML>
<HEAD>
        <TITLE>Jen's Kitchen</TITLE>
</HEAD>
<BODY>

<IMG SRC="kitchen.gif">

<P>People who know me know that I love to cook. I've created
this site to share some of my favorite recipes and online food
resources. <I>Bon Appetit!</I></P>

<HR WIDTH="50%" SIZE="6">

<H2>From Jen's Cookbook:</H2>
     tapenade (olive spread)<BR>
     garlic salmon<BR>
     wild mushroom risotto<BR>
     asian dishes

</BODY>
```

❶ *Inserts an image.*

❷ *Inserts a horizontal rule (line). I've added attributes
to change the length and thickness of the rule.*

Gotta save it!

❸ *Hit "Refresh" to view the changes.
The page is almost done!*

❶ I've replaced my text heading with a much spiffier graphic heading. The graphic is added to the page by placing an `<IMG>` tag where I want the graphic to appear. The image tag is a good example of a stand-alone tag—there is no closing or end tag, you just plop it into place.

❷ I've also added a horizontal rule (line) using the `<HR>` standalone tag. I've added some attributes within the tag to change the length (`WIDTH=`) and thickness (`SIZE=`) of the rule.

An `attribute` is a bit of information that is added to a tag to modify its action or behavior. Attributes are separated from their value settings by an equals sign (Figure 6-10). The sidebar About Attributes has more useful facts about this important feature of HTML.

Figure 6-10

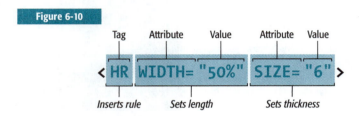

Tag | Attribute | Value | Attribute | Value

`< HR WIDTH= "50%" SIZE= "6" >`

Inserts rule | Sets length | Sets thickness

The `SRC=` part of the `<IMG>` tag is an example of a required attribute—without it, the browser wouldn't know which graphic to grab. The attributes in the `<HR>` tag are optional. Without the attributes, the default horizontal rule would be one pixel thick and the width of the browser window.

❸ I've saved and reloaded the page to check the progress so far. It's almost done! Just one more thing...

Step 4: Adding a Hypertext Link

What's a web page without links? Fairly pointless, if you ask me, so let's add one. Don't worry about learning everything about linking from this example. Linking is an important part of web design and I've dedicated a whole chapter to it (Chapter 9, Adding Links). For now, I just want to give you a flavor of how it's done.

In the end, I'd like each of my recipe names to link to their respective recipe pages, so I'll start with the first one in this example (Figure 6-11, following page).

About Attributes

The real power and flexibility of HTML lies in the attributes—small instructions added within a tag to modify its behavior or appearance. The formula for using attributes is as follows:

```
<TAG ATTRIBUTE="value">
affected text</TAG>
```

Here are some important things to know about attributes:

- Attributes go only in the opening container tag. The closing tag includes just the tag name, even if the opening tag is loaded with attributes.

- Most (but not all) attributes take values, which follow an equals sign (`=`) after the attribute's name. The value might be a number, a word, a string of text, a URL, or a measurement.

- You can add several attributes within a single tag.

- It is good practice to put quotation marks around values; however, they may be omitted if the value is a single word or number.

- Some attributes are required; for example, the `SRC` attribute within the `<IMG>` tag.

Figure 6-11

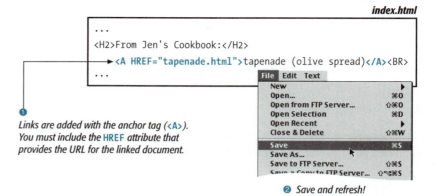

index.html

```
...
<H2>From Jen's Cookbook:</H2>
<A HREF="tapenade.html">tapenade (olive spread)</A><BR>
...
```

① *Links are added with the anchor tag (<A>). You must include the HREF attribute that provides the URL for the linked document.*

② *Save and refresh!*

And there we have it: a simple web page, complete with a graphic and a link. Not very fancy, but a web page nonetheless!

① Links are added with a container tag called an anchor (<A>...</A>). Like other container tags, anchor tags are placed around the text that you want to link. But you have to specify what page you want to link to, right? That's where the HREF= attribute comes in. It is a required attribute that gives the browser the URL of the target page. In my example, I've used a relative URL (a URL that points to a document on the same server) to create a link to the tapenade recipe page (*tapenade.html*).

② When I save my file and reload it in the browser, the anchor text will appear as blue, underlined, clickable text.

The page is done! At this point, I could upload it to the server. See Chapter 3, Getting Your Pages on the Web, for step-by-step instructions on uploading.

I know, I know... you're thinking, "That page is really boring." That's okay, I'm thinking the same thing. But it is a real web page nonetheless and we picked up some key concepts on the way. In future chapters, we'll add to your bag of tricks so you can make pages that are a bit more exciting.

When Good Pages Go Bad

The previous demonstration went very smoothly, but it's easy for small things to go wrong when typing out HTML code. Unfortunately, one missed character can break a whole page. I'm going to break my page on purpose so we can see what happens.

What if I had forgotten to type the slash (/) in the closing header tag (</H1>)? Just one character out of place (Figure 6-12). As you can see, the entire document displays in big bold heading text! That's because without that slash, there's nothing telling the browser to turn "off" the heading formatting, so it just keeps going.

Figure 6-12

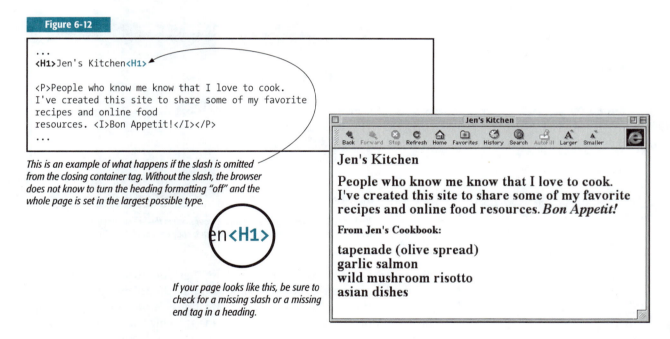

```
...
<H1>Jen's Kitchen<H1>

<P>People who know me know that I love to cook.
I've created this site to share some of my favorite
recipes and online food
resources. <I>Bon Appetit!</I></P>
...
```

This is an example of what happens if the slash is omitted from the closing container tag. Without the slash, the browser does not know to turn the heading formatting "off" and the whole page is set in the largest possible type.

If your page looks like this, be sure to check for a missing slash or a missing end tag in a heading.

Jen's Kitchen

Jen's Kitchen

People who know me know that I love to cook. I've created this site to share some of my favorite recipes and online food resources. *Bon Appetit!*

From Jen's Cookbook:

tapenade (olive spread)
garlic salmon
wild mushroom risotto
asian dishes

Having Problems?

The following are some typical problems that crop up when creating web pages and viewing them in a browser:

Q: I've changed my document, but when I reload the page in my browser, it looks exactly the same.

A: It could be you didn't save your HTML document before reloading. It's an important step.

Q: All the text on my page is HUGE!

A: Did you start a heading tag and forget to close it? Make sure each tag you've used has its end tag. Also, make sure that end tag has a slash (/)!

Q: Half my page disappeared!

A: This could happen if you are missing a closing bracket (>) or a quotation mark within a tag. This is a common error when writing HTML code by hand.

Q: I put in a graphic using the <IMG> tag, but all that shows up is a broken-graphic icon.

A: The broken graphic could mean a couple of things. First, it might mean that the browser is not finding the graphic. Make sure that the URL to the graphic is correct. (We'll discuss URLs further in Chapter 8, Adding Links.) Make sure that the graphic is actually in the directory you've specified. If the graphic is there, make sure it is in one of the formats that web browsers can display (GIF or JPEG) and that it is named with the proper suffix (*.gif* and *.jpeg* or *.jpg*, respectively).

I've fixed the slash, but this time, let's see what would have happened if I had accidentally omitted a bracket from the end of the first `<H2>` tag (Figure 6-13).

Figure 6-13

```
...
<H2From Jen's Cookbook:</H2>
<P>
    tapenade (olive spread)<BR>
    garlic salmon<BR>
    wild mushroom risotto<BR>
    asian dishes
</P>
...
```

In this example, I've accidently left out a bracket. Notice how "From Jen's Cookbook" disappears in the browser. Without that bracket, it's reading all the following characters as some elaborate tag it's never seen before.

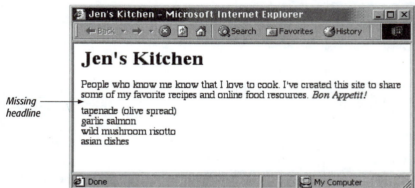

If you find text vanishing when you view your page in the browser, check for a missing bracket or missing quotation mark. They are usually to blame.

See how a whole chunk of text is missing? That's because without the closing tag bracket, the browser assumes that all the following text—all the way up to the next closing bracket (>) it finds—is part of that `<H2>` tag. Browsers don't display any text within a tag, so my heading disappeared. The browser just ignored the foreign-looking tag and moved on to the next element.

Making mistakes in your first HTML pages and fixing them is a great way to learn. If you write your first pages perfectly, I'd recommend fiddling with the code as I have here to see how the browser reacts to various changes. This can be extremely useful in troubleshooting pages later. I've listed some common problems in the sidebar, Having Problems? Note that these problems are not specific to beginners! Little stuff like this goes wrong all the time, even for the pros.

HTML Review—Structural Tags

In this chapter, we covered some important tags for establishing the structure of the document. The remaining tags introduced in the demonstration will be treated in more depth in the following chapters.

Tag	Function
<HTML>	Identifies the whole document as HTML
<HEAD>	Identifies the head of the document
<BODY>	Identifies the body of the document
<TITLE>	Gives the page a title

Chapter 7

Formatting Text

By this point, you should have an understanding of how HTML markup works. Are you ready for the nitty-gritty? In the following several chapters, we'll examine HTML one tag at a time, beginning with the tags that affect the appearance of text in a browser. But first, I want to reiterate a point we touched on in Chapter 4, Why Web Design Isn't Like Print Design.

"Typesetting" on the Web

Marking up text for the Web is not the same as specifying type for print. For one thing, there is no way of knowing exactly how your text is going to look. Scary, but true!

Take a look at your browser's preferences and you will find that you (and every other surfer out there) are able to specify the fonts and sizes that you prefer for online viewing. To access the font controls in Internet Explorer, choose Edit → Preferences, then select Language/Fonts under the Web Browser category. In Navigator, choose Edit → Preferences and select Fonts from the Appearance category. This is where users can choose any font for the browser default.

Although there are ways to override the browser default by specifying a font in the HTML document, it won't show up unless that exact font is already installed on the user's machine. Even then, you don't know how wide the window will be, so there is no guarantee that the lines will break the way they do on your machine. There is a lot that is out of your control.

Figure 7-1

Proportional fonts (variable width) allot different amounts of space for each character, based on its design.

In a constant-width (monospace) font, all characters are allotted the same width on the line.

Two Fonts

What you do have are two fonts to work with on the page: a proportional font and a fixed-width font (Figure 7-1). You can see their settings in your browser's font preferences.

The majority of your page—body text, headings, lists, blockquotes, etc.—will appear in the proportional font. A proportional font (called "Variable Width Font" in Netscape Navigator) is one that allots different amounts of space to each character; for example, a capital "W" takes up more space on the line than a lowercase "i." The default proportional font for the majority of web browsers is Times or Helvetica; as a very general guideline, you can assume body text will display in one of these two fonts at 10 or 12 points.*

The other available font is a fixed-width font, which is used for special types of information. A fixed-width font (also known as a "constant width" or "monospace" font) allots the same amount of horizontal space to all the characters; the capital "W" takes up no more space than the lowercase "i." Browsers use the fixed-width font for a few specific tags, usually related to the display of code, such as <PRE> or <TT> (we'll discuss these later in this chapter). You can usually assume these elements will display in some variation of Courier.

Text in Graphics

The only way you can have absolute control over the display of your type is to make it part of a graphic. It is common to see headlines, subheads, callouts, even whole web pages, put into big graphics rather than HTML text.

While the temptation of total control is strong, there are some very compelling reasons why you should resist sinking text into GIF files. First, graphics take much longer to download than text, and on the Web, download speed is everything. Second, any information in a graphic cannot be indexed or searched; in essence, it is removed from your document. And last, this content will be lost on non-graphical browsers or to users with graphics turned off. While using "alternative" text in the graphic tag may help, it is limited and not always reliable.

That said, let's look at some text tags.

---

* Internet Explorer 5.5 and Navigator 6.0 have started defining type sizes in pixels since point sizes are interpreted differently on Windows and Macs. The default size is 16 pixels, which will probably feel quite large to Mac users accustomed to smaller type.

Building Blocks: Headings and Paragraphs

In this section we'll look at the tags that format text on the paragraph level. These tags are also known as block elements, and they are the distinct units of text that make up the web page. Headings, paragraphs, quotations, and preformatted text are all block elements.

When a browser sees a block element tag, it will automatically insert a line break and add a little space above and below the text element. This is the characteristic that all block elements have in common. You cannot start paragraph text on the same line as a heading; it will always start as a new "block" of text. Following are examples of each block element.

Browsers automatically add space above and below block elements.

Headings

`<H#>...</H#>`
Heading level-#
(where "#" can equal 1 through 6)

In the last chapter, we used the `<H1>` tag to indicate a heading for our page. There are actually six levels of headings, `<H1>` through `<H6>` (Figure 7-2).

Headings are displayed in bold text. The first-level heading (`<H1>`) is displayed at the largest heading size, and the consecutive levels get smaller and smaller. In fact, fifth- and sixth-level headings tend to display the heading even smaller than regular text, and can be difficult to read. As a general rule, `<H3>` is as low as you'd want to go.

Since headings are used to provide logical structure to an HTML document, it is proper usage to start with the `<H1>` heading and work down in numerical order. But if you don't like how big and clunky the `<H1>` looks, you could start with an `<H2>` or `<H3>` instead. While the browser won't prevent you from doing this, there are certainly better ways to achieve the look you want (see the `<FONT>` tag later in this chapter).

Figure 7-2

Headings
There are six HTML heading levels.
`<H1>` *is the largest and each consecutive level gets smaller.*

```
<H1>First Level Heading</H1>
<H2>Second Level Heading</H2>
<H3>Third Level Heading</H3>
<H4>Fourth Level Heading</H4>
<H5>Fifth Level Heading</H5>
<H6>Sixth Level Heading</H6>
<P>Here's a little default body text for comparison.</P>
```

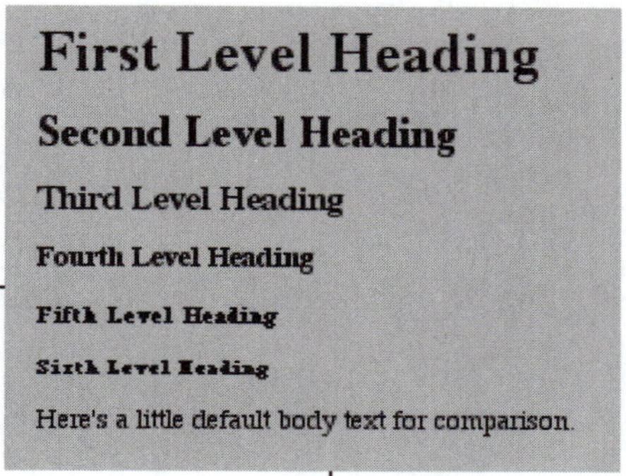

First Level Heading

Second Level Heading

Third Level Heading

Fourth Level Heading

Fifth Level Heading

Sixth Level Heading

Here's a little default body text for comparison.

Paragraphs

`<P>...</P>`
Body text paragraph

One of the simplest things you can do to HTML text is to break it into paragraphs. Paragraphs display in the browser's default proportional font with extra space above and below (Figure 7-3).

Figure 7-3

```
<P>Rinse fillets & pat dry. Add to marinade for 20 minutes. Drain and
discard ginger.</P>
<P>Heat oil in wok. Add seasonings & stir fry for 10 seconds. Add Fish
Sauce; heat 2 minutes, stirring constantly. Pour over fillets in baking
dish.</P>
```

Rinse fillets & pat dry. Add to marinade for 20 minutes. Drain and discard ginger.

Heat oil in wok. Add seasonings & stir fry for 10 seconds. Add Fish Sauce; heat 2 minutes, stirring constantly. Pour over fillets in baking dish.

Paragraphs display in the default font with space above and below.

Although most browsers will also recognize a single `<P>` placed between blocks of text as a paragraph break, many new technologies, such as JavaScript and style sheets, require both opening and closing tags. If you are learning HTML for the first time, you might as well learn it the proper way.

Browsers will not recognize a string of `<P></P>` tags or more than one consecutive `<P>` tag, so you can't use empty paragraphs to add extra space between elements, the way you can in a word processing program (Figure 7-4).

Figure 7-4

```
<P>Rinse fillets & pat dry. Add to marinade for 20 minutes. Drain and
discard ginger.</P>
<P></P>
<P></P>
<P></P>
<P></P>
<P>Heat oil in wok. Add seasonings & stir fry for 10 seconds. Add Fish
Sauce; heat 2 minutes, stirring constantly. Pour over fillets in baking
dish.</P>
```

Rinse fillets & pat dry. Add to marinade for 20 minutes. Drain and discard ginger.

Heat oil in wok. Add seasonings & stir fry for 10 seconds. Add Fish Sauce; heat 2 minutes, stirring constantly. Pour over fillets in baking dish.

Multiple paragraphs are ignored by the browser.

`<BR>`
Line break

While not a block element, I find it useful to introduce the break tag in relation to paragraphs. If you want to break a line of text, but not add space above and below (as with the `<P>` tag), you can insert a `<BR>` tag within a paragraph or other block element (Figure 7-5). A stack of `<BR>` tags will display as blank lines by most browsers.

Figure 7-5

```
2 slices ginger<BR>
1 T. rice wine or sake<BR>
1 t. salt<BR>
2 T. peanut oil
```

Line breaks

The `<BR>` tag starts a new line in a block element, but it doesn't add any extra space.

2 slices ginger
1 T. rice wine or sake
1 t. salt
2 T. peanut oil

Long Quotations

`<BLOCKQUOTE>...</BLOCKQUOTE>`
Blockquote

If you have a long quotation, you might try formatting it as a block-quote for added emphasis on the page. Blockquotes are generally displayed with an indent on the left and right margins, with a little extra space added above and below (Figure 7-6). For this reason, they are frequently used as a fudge to create narrow columns of text. Be aware that some older browser versions will display blockquote material in all italics, making it difficult to read.

Preformatted Text

`<PRE>...</PRE>`
Preformatted text

Preformatted text is a unique animal in the HTML world. It is displayed in the browser's constant-width font (usually Courier) with extra space added above and below. But what makes it really special is that each line will be displayed exactly as it is typed in—including all carriage returns, multiple character spaces, and tabs (Figure 7-7). As we saw in Chapter 6, Creating a Simple Page, browsers normally ignore these things in all other cases.

Preformatted text was originally created for the display of code, where spacing, indents, and alignment are important, but you can use it to control spacing and alignment of any content (as long as you don't mind everything set in Courier).

Figure 7-6

```
<P>The true test that meat is fully cooked is its
internal temperature. Cooks Illustrated Magazine had
this to say about safe internal temperatures
for poultry:</P>

<BLOCKQUOTE>The final word on poultry safety is this:
As long as the temperature on an accurate instant-
read thermometer reaches 160 degrees when inserted
in several places, all unstuffed meat (including
turkey) should be bacteria free. Dark meat is
undercooked at this stage and tastes better at 170
or 175 degrees.</BLOCKQUOTE>
```

The true test that meat is fully cooked is its internal temperature. Cooks Illustrated Magazine had this to say about safe internal temperatures for poultry:

> The final word on poultry safety is this: As long as the temperature on an accurate instant-read thermometer reaches 160 degrees when inserted in several places, all unstuffed meat (including turkey) should be bacteria free. Dark meat is undercooked at this stage and tastes better at 170 or 175 degrees.

Blockquotes are indented on the left and right margins.

Figure 7-7

```
<PRE>
1/4 c. chicken stock

        1 T. soy sauce

1 T. rice wine or sake

        1/2 t. sugar
</PRE>
```

Preformatted text is unique in that the browser displays the text as it is typed, including carriage returns and extra spaces.

```
1/4 c. chicken stock

        1 T. soy sauce

1 T. rice wine or sake

        1/2 t. sugar
```

Formatting Text

Putting It Together—Block Elements

Let's see what we can do with a simple recipe using block elements and line breaks to format the text (Figure 7-8).

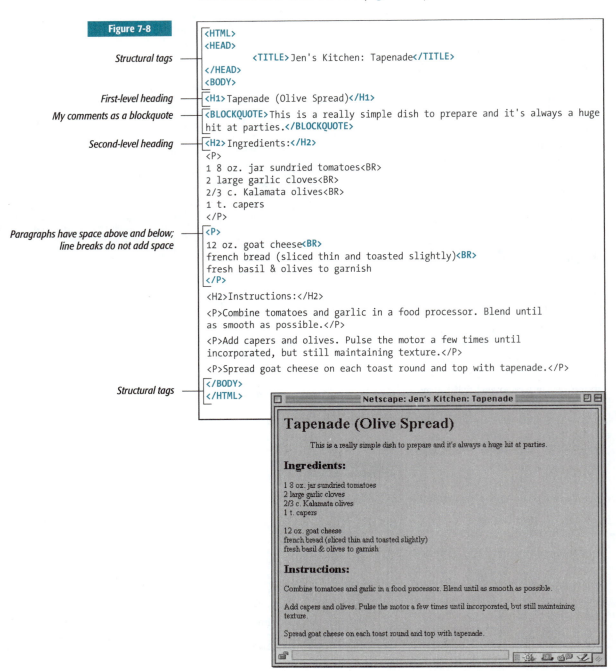

Figure 7-8

Structural tags →
```
<HTML>
<HEAD>
         <TITLE>Jen's Kitchen: Tapenade</TITLE>
</HEAD>
<BODY>
```

First-level heading → `<H1>Tapenade (Olive Spread)</H1>`

My comments as a blockquote → `<BLOCKQUOTE>This is a really simple dish to prepare and it's always a huge hit at parties.</BLOCKQUOTE>`

Second-level heading →
```
<H2>Ingredients:</H2>
<P>
1 8 oz. jar sundried tomatoes<BR>
2 large garlic cloves<BR>
2/3 c. Kalamata olives<BR>
1 t. capers
</P>
```

Paragraphs have space above and below; line breaks do not add space →
```
<P>
12 oz. goat cheese<BR>
french bread (sliced thin and toasted slightly)<BR>
fresh basil & olives to garnish
</P>

<H2>Instructions:</H2>

<P>Combine tomatoes and garlic in a food processor. Blend until
as smooth as possible.</P>

<P>Add capers and olives. Pulse the motor a few times until
incorporated, but still maintaining texture.</P>

<P>Spread goat cheese on each toast round and top with tapenade.</P>
```

Structural tags →
```
</BODY>
</HTML>
```

Netscape: Jen's Kitchen: Tapenade

Tapenade (Olive Spread)

This is a really simple dish to prepare and it's always a huge hit at parties.

Ingredients:

1 8 oz. jar sundried tomatoes
2 large garlic cloves
2/3 c. Kalamata olives
1 t. capers

12 oz. goat cheese
french bread (sliced thin and toasted slightly)
fresh basil & olives to garnish

Instructions:

Combine tomatoes and garlic in a food processor. Blend until as smooth as possible.

Add capers and olives. Pulse the motor a few times until incorporated, but still maintaining texture.

Spread goat cheese on each toast round and top with tapenade.

TOOL TIP

Paragraph Styles

Here's how you access paragraph controls in three of the more popular authoring programs.

DREAMWEAVER 3

❶ *With your text element highlighted, choose a paragraph style from the "Format" pull-down menu on the Properties palette.*

❷ *Blockquotes are set using the "Indent" button on the Properties palette.*

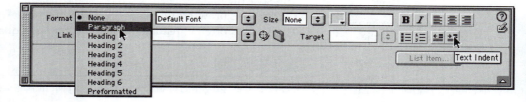

GOLIVE 4

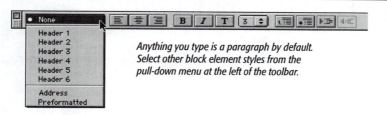

Anything you type is a paragraph by default. Select other block element styles from the pull-down menu at the left of the toolbar.

FRONTPAGE 2000

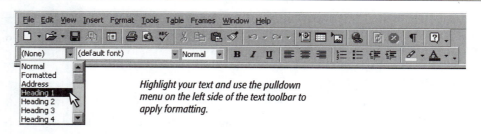

Highlight your text and use the pulldown menu on the left side of the text toolbar to apply formatting.

Formatting Text

Logical Versus Physical

The whole point of HTML is to define the logical structure of a document, not its appearance (see the sidebar A Brief History of HTML in Chapter 6). With this in mind, there are a few "logical" style tags built into the HTML specification. Logical styles describe the enclosed text's meaning or context. By contrast, "physical" style tags give the browser specific display instructions. To achieve a style effect such as italics, you have your choice of either a logical tag (e.g., <EM>) or a physical tag (e.g., <I>). Physical tags are by far more popular in practical use.

Inline Styles

Most text tags specify inline styles, meaning they are used right in the flow of text to affect the way the text looks. Unlike block element tags, using inline tags won't introduce line breaks or extra spaces.

<I>...</I>
Italic text

This style tag makes the enclosed text italic (Figure 7-9). Use italic text very sparingly, as browsers just slant the regular text font to achieve an "italic." The result is often unreadable, especially for large quantities of text.

Figure 7-9

```
<P>2 slices ginger <I>(smashed, then pinched in marinade)</I></P>

<P>2 slices ginger <EM>(smashed, then pinched in marinade)</EM></P>
```

2 slices ginger *(smashed, then pinched in marinade)*

2 slices ginger *(smashed, then pinched in marinade)*

Italic
Both <I> and <EM> (for emphasized) make text italic.

<EM>...</EM>
Emphasized text

This is the "logical" style equivalent (see the Logical Versus Physical sidebar) to the italic tag since most browsers display emphasized text in italics (Figure 7-9).

<B>...</B>
Bold text

TIP

Avoid using italics for more than just a few words of text; the result is often unreadable.

This style tag specifies that the enclosed text be rendered in bold type (Figure 7-10).

<STRONG>...</STRONG>
Strong text

This is the "logical" style equivalent to <B>, as most browsers render strong text in bold type (Figure 7-10).

Figure 7-10

```
<P>2 slices ginger <B>(smashed, then pinched in marinade)</B></P>

<P>2 slices ginger <STRONG>(smashed, then pinched in marinade)</STRONG></P>
```

2 slices ginger **(smashed, then pinched in marinade)**

2 slices ginger **(smashed, then pinched in marinade)**

Bold
Both <B> and <STRONG> tags make text bold.

`<TT>...</TT>`
Teletype (or typewriter text)

Text between these tags will be displayed in the browser's constant-width font (usually Courier) (Figure 7-11). Unlike preformatted text (`<PRE>`), teletype text can be used inline and extra character spaces or returns will be ignored by the browser (compare to Figure 7-7).

`<U>...</U>`
Underlined text

Enclosed text will be underlined when displayed. Be careful using this one, since your underlined text may be confused with a link (Figure 7-12).

`<STRIKE>...</STRIKE>`
Strikethrough text

You can use this tag to make text appear with a line through it, if that's the kind of thing you need to do (Figure 7-12).

`<SUB>...</SUB>`
Subscript

`<SUP>...</SUP>`
Superscript

These tags format enclosed text as subscript and superscript, respectively (Figure 7-12).

Figure 7-11

```
<TT>
1/4 c. chicken stock

          1 T. soy sauce

1 T. rice wine or sake

       1/2 t. sugar
</TT>
```

```
1/4 c. chicken stock 1 T. soy sauce 1 T. rice wine or sake 1/2 t.
sugar
```

Teletype
`<TT>` *displays text in a constant width font, but ignores line breaks and extra spaces, unlike* `<PRE>`.

Figure 7-12

```
<P>An example of <U>underlined</U> text and <STRIKE>strikethrough</STRIKE>
text.</P>
<P>You can make a superscript <SUP>word</SUP> and a subscript <SUB>word</SUB>.</P>
```

*Examples of **underlined, strikethrough, superscript,** and **subscript** text.*

An example of underlined text and strikethrough text.

You can make a superscript word and a subscript word.

Putting It Together—Style Tags

Now that we have a few more tricks up our sleeves, let's see what we can do to improve our recipe (Figure 7-13). Just adding simple touches like italic, bold, and constant-width type goes a long way toward differentiating content elements and making the recipe more readable at a glance.

Figure 7-13

I like my comments better in italics than as a blockquote.

Teletype sets the ingredient list apart from other text.

Special instructions appear in italics.

I've used bold to call attention to the main instructions.

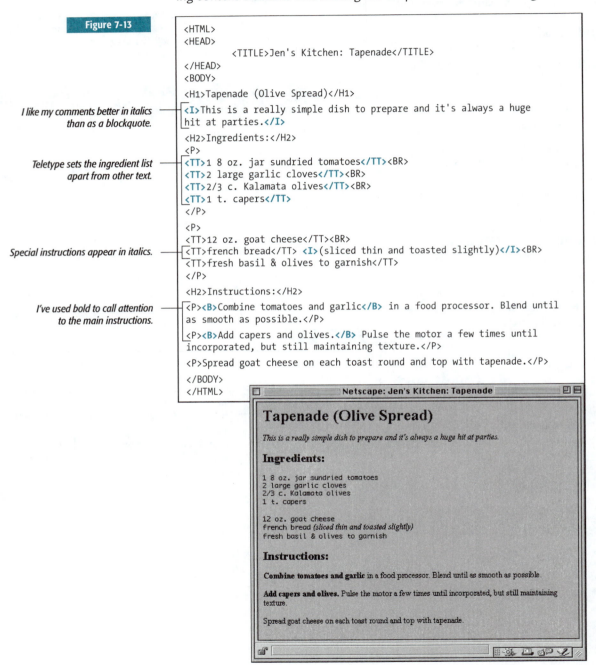

```
<HTML>
<HEAD>
          <TITLE>Jen's Kitchen: Tapenade</TITLE>
</HEAD>
<BODY>
<H1>Tapenade (Olive Spread)</H1>
<I>This is a really simple dish to prepare and it's always a huge
hit at parties.</I>
<H2>Ingredients:</H2>
<P>
<TT>1 8 oz. jar sundried tomatoes</TT><BR>
<TT>2 large garlic cloves</TT><BR>
<TT>2/3 c. Kalamata olives</TT><BR>
<TT>1 t. capers</TT>
</P>

<P>
<TT>12 oz. goat cheese</TT><BR>
<TT>french bread</TT> <I>(sliced thin and toasted slightly)</I><BR>
<TT>fresh basil & olives to garnish</TT>
</P>

<H2>Instructions:</H2>
<P><B>Combine tomatoes and garlic</B> in a food processor. Blend until
as smooth as possible.</P>

<P><B>Add capers and olives.</B> Pulse the motor a few times until
incorporated, but still maintaining texture.</P>

<P>Spread goat cheese on each toast round and top with tapenade.</P>

</BODY>
</HTML>
```

Netscape: Jen's Kitchen: Tapenade

Tapenade (Olive Spread)

This is a really simple dish to prepare and it's always a huge hit at parties.

Ingredients:

1 8 oz. jar sundried tomatoes
2 large garlic cloves
2/3 c. Kalamata olives
1 t. capers

12 oz. goat cheese
french bread *(sliced thin and toasted slightly)*
fresh basil & olives to garnish

Instructions:

Combine tomatoes and garlic in a food processor. Blend until as smooth as possible.

Add capers and olives. Pulse the motor a few times until incorporated, but still maintaining texture.

Spread goat cheese on each toast round and top with tapenade.

Text Size, Font, and Color

As we've seen so far, the formatting you can do with the basic set of HTML text tags is fairly limited. But there is a way to control the size, typeface, and color of text, and it's done with one little tag: the `<FONT>` tag. The `<FONT>` tag uses attributes (instructions added within the tag to expand its functionality) to control typeface, size, and color. Let's look at these one at a time.

Controlling Font Size

`<FONT SIZE=number>...</FONT>`
Font size

The `SIZE` attribute within the `<FONT>` tag controls the size of the enclosed text. Unfortunately, the `<FONT>` tag does not allow you to specify type by point or pixel size. In HTML, you can only specify the size of the text relative to the default font size.

Frankly speaking, the system HTML uses for sizing type is very strange. First, you need to know that the browser's default font size is given the value of "3." Some users have their default font size set quite small; others have it large enough to view from a distance. Whatever the size, the user's default text has the value of 3.

With that established, you can use the `SIZE` attribute to specify larger and smaller type in relation to the default value of 3. The value of the `SIZE` attribute can be either absolute or relative (Figure 7-14).

Absolute values are the numerals 1 through 7, with each size increment about 20% larger than the size before. Therefore, type set to `SIZE=4` would be approximately 20% larger than type set to `SIZE=3` (the default text size, whatever that might be). The largest size the browser will display using the `<FONT>` tag is 7; if you try to specify a higher value, it will just display at the same size as text set to 7.

Relative values are indicated with a plus or minus sign, added or subtracted from the default 3. So `SIZE=+1` displays exactly the same as `SIZE=4` (because 3+1=4). And because the browser won't display text with a size value higher than 7, the highest relative value that will work is +4 (3+4=7).

The Problem with `<FONT>`

While the `<FONT>` tag offers a way to make text look more interesting, it does have some downsides. First, it is not "good" HTML practice, in that it does nothing to structure the document logically and instead inserts display information right into the document (see the sidebar A Brief History of HTML in Chapter 6 for why this is undesirable). Furthermore, in practical terms, it is more cumbersome to make changes to the styles, because every individual `<FONT>` tag needs to be changed.

For these reasons, there has been a movement away from the `<FONT>` tag and toward Cascading Style Sheets (CSS). Style sheets enable you to do more sophisticated text formatting, and they store this information in a separate style sheet (not dispersed throughout the content). See Chapter 20, How'd They Do That?, for more information on Cascading Style Sheets.

Figure 7-14

	default						
Absolute Values	1	2	**3**	4	5	6	7
Relative Values	−2	−1	**−**	+1	+2	+3	+4
On a browser with its default font set to 10 points, these values might translate to approximately	6pt	8pt	10pt	12pt	14pt	18pt	27pt

Let's see the `<FONT>` tag in action. Because it is a container tag, just wrap the tag around the text you want to change, then use the SIZE attribute to specify how much larger or smaller than the default size you'd like it to be (Figure 7-15). Notice that the final size of the text depends on the default font size in the browser.

Figure 7-15

Notice that we still need `<P>` tags for paragraphs.

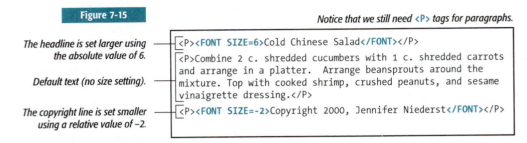

The headline is set larger using the absolute value of 6.

`<P><FONT SIZE=6>Cold Chinese Salad</FONT></P>`

Default text (no size setting).

`<P>Combine 2 c. shredded cucumbers with 1 c. shredded carrots and arrange in a platter.  Arrange beansprouts around the mixture. Top with cooked shrimp, crushed peanuts, and sesame vinaigrette dressing.</P>`

The copyright line is set smaller using a relative value of –2.

`<P><FONT SIZE=-2>Copyright 2000, Jennifer Niederst</FONT></P>`

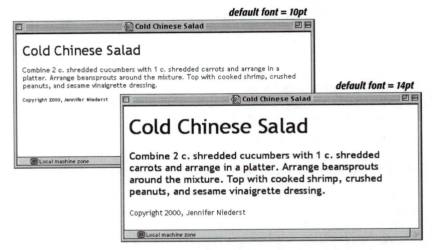

default font = 10pt

default font = 14pt

The resulting text size depends on the default browser font setting. See how text set to SIZE=6 is much larger when the default font is set larger.

TIP

As a rule of thumb, you should avoid changing the font size more than +1 or –1. Because type displays differently across platforms and for each user, you risk making your text too small to be legible or too large and clunky.

Changing the default text size

`<BASEFONT SIZE=`*number*`>`
Sets the base (default) size

You're not stuck with the default font set at 3. You can use the `<BASEFONT>` tag to set the default size of the text. When you use `<BASEFONT>`, any relative size specifications you make (with a plus or minus sign) in the document will be applied to the new base font size.

When placed in the `<HEAD>` of the document, the `<BASEFONT>` tag affects all the text in the document. So if you wanted the text in the whole document to be slightly larger than standard, set `<BASEFONT SIZE=4>` in the header, like this:

```
<HTML>
<HEAD>
<TITLE>Sample Document</TITLE>
<BASEFONT SIZE=4>
</HEAD>
<BODY>...
```

If you want to change the default text for a portion of the document, you can place the `<BASEFONT>` tag in the flow of text. All the text following the tag will be the new basefont size. And of course, any relative font size settings will be relative to that size (Figure 7-16).

(Figure 7-16)

> **TIP**
>
> Although you can change the default font size for a page, that doesn't mean you should. Keep in mind that users are likely to be viewing the text on their browsers at a size that is comfortable for them. You're not necessarily doing them a favor by changing it.

Formatting Text

Figure 7-16

The page starts with regular default text (SIZE=3).

The `<BASEFONT>` tag changes the default to 4.

Now text appears at SIZE=4, even with no `<FONT>` setting.

When I use a relative font size (+1), it is added to the new default size. The result is equivalent to a font setting of 5 (4+1).

```
<P>Put grated ginger in a fine strainer set over a bowl.
Press to extract the juice; discard the pulp. Stir sake,
soy sauce, vegetable oil, and mustard into the juice and
season with salt and pepper.</P>
<BASEFONT SIZE=4>
<P>Set salmon in a broiler pan. Marinate in sauce for
30 to 40 minutes.</P>
<P><FONT SIZE=+1>Broil approx. 6 minutes until just
cooked through. Serve with steamed rice and stir-fried
vegetables.</FONT></P>
```

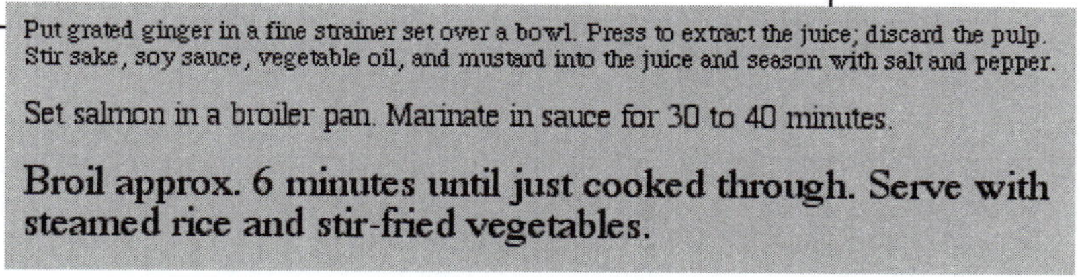

Put grated ginger in a fine strainer set over a bowl. Press to extract the juice; discard the pulp. Stir sake, soy sauce, vegetable oil, and mustard into the juice and season with salt and pepper.

Set salmon in a broiler pan. Marinate in sauce for 30 to 40 minutes.

Broil approx. 6 minutes until just cooked through. Serve with steamed rice and stir-fried vegetables.

Specifying a Typeface

Figure 7-17

❶ `<P>Saute mushrooms in butter. Add prosciutto when mushrooms are soft and have given up their juices.</P>`

❷ `<P><FONT FACE="trebuchet ms, arial, sans-serif">Saute mushrooms in butter. Add prosciutto when mushrooms are soft and have given up their juices.</FONT></P>`

❸ `<P><FONT FACE="ponyface">Saute mushrooms in butter. Add prosciutto when mushrooms are soft and have given up their juices.</FONT></P>`

❶ Saute mushrooms in butter. Add prosciutto when mushrooms are soft and have given up their juices.

❷ Saute mushrooms in butter. Add prosciutto when mushrooms are soft and have given up their juices.

❸ Saute mushrooms in butter. Add prosciutto when mushrooms are soft and have given up their juices.

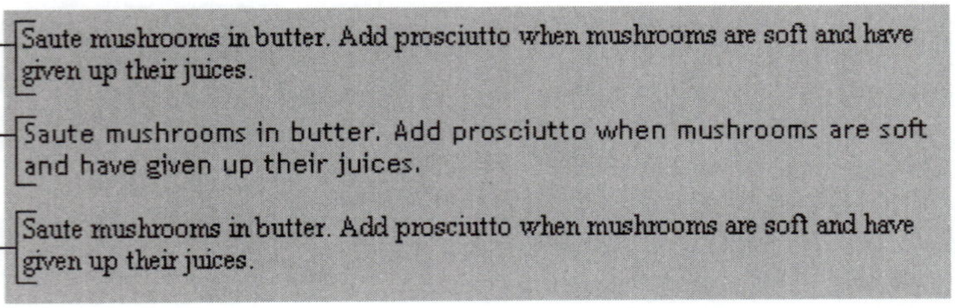

❶ *The default font as set in the browser (in this case, it's Times).*

❷ *I've used the `<FONT FACE= >` tag to set this line to Trebuchet MS. If the browser doesn't have Trebuchet on the user's machine, it can use Arial or any sans-serif font instead.*

❸ *When the browser doesn't find the specified font (in this case, my made up "ponyface" font), it will just display the text in the default font. Notice how line ❸ is identical to line ❶.*

Figure 7-18

The COLOR attribute is used to specify text color.

```
<P><FONT COLOR="gray">Fish in Black Bean Sauce</FONT></P>
<P><FONT COLOR="#808080">Fish in Black Bean Sauce</FONT></P>
```

Fish in Black Bean Sauce

Fish in Black Bean Sauce

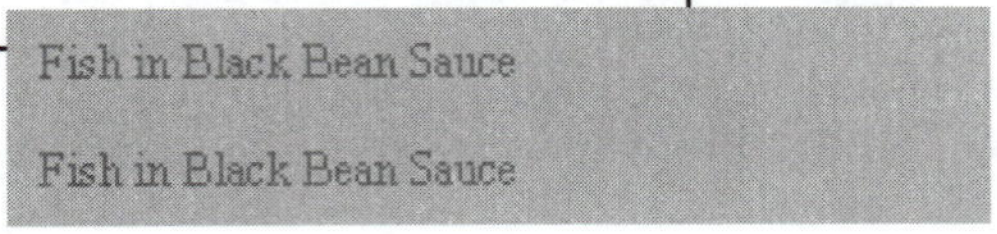

Colors can be specified by name or numeric value.

Specifying a Typeface

**`<FONT FACE="`*fontname*`">`
`...</FONT>`**
Specifies typeface

The FACE attribute is used to specify a typeface for the text. Remember that the selected typeface will be used only if it is found on the user's machine. You may provide a list of fonts (separated by commas and enclosed in quotation marks) and the browser will use the first font it finds in the string (Figure 7-17). You can also include a generic font family (serif, sans-serif, monospace, cursive, or fantasy) as the last choice in your list. That way, if the browser can't find any of your named fonts, it will try to substitute a font from your chosen style.

Specifying Type Color

**`<FONT COLOR="`*color*`">`
`...</FONT>`**
Specifies font color

You can change the color of type by using the COLOR attribute within the `<FONT>` tag. The value of this attribute can be one of 140 preset color names, or it can be the numeric value for any color you choose. These systems for specifying colors on the Web are explained in more detail in the aptly named Chapter 12, Color on the Web. The sample shows two ways to make the text color gray (Figure 7-18).

We've just seen the separate attributes of the `<FONT>` tag that control size, face, and color. But what if we want to make a headline large and Helvetica and blue? Do we have to use the `<FONT>` tag three times?

Not at all. You can put many attributes within a single opener tag. So you can control the size, font, and color of your text in one fell swoop, as shown here:

```
<FONT SIZE="+2" FACE="Helvetica" COLOR="teal">
```

Combining Styles

Now that you're getting the hang of container tags, it's time for a quiz. What do you think the following HTML code will look like when viewed in a browser?

```
<B><I><FONT COLOR="red" SIZE="6">CAUTION!!</FONT></I></B>
```

First of all, we can see it will display the word "CAUTION!!" And the `<FONT>` tag around that word means it will be large and red. But we've also got an italic tag (`<I>`) and a bold tag (`<B>`) wrapped around everything. I bet you've guessed by now that the word will display in large, red text that is also italic and bold. (Or you could just look at Figure 7-19.)

When nesting style tags, be sure that one set is completely enclosed within the other and the tags are not overlapping.

Figure 7-19

```
<B><I><FONT COLOR="red" SIZE=6>CAUTION!!</FONT></I></B> Melted sugar is
very hot!
```

Combine styles by nesting the style tags.

CAUTION!!   Melted sugar is very hot!

In HTML, you can apply several styles to the same piece of text by wrapping one set of style tags around another. This is known as nesting tags or elements.

The only rule is that one set of tags must be completely enclosed within the other—no overlapping. Take a look at this code example:

```
<B><FONT FACE="Verdana">Step-by-step</B></FONT>
```

It is incorrect because both the opening `<FONT>` tag and the closing `</FONT>` tag are not within the bold `<B>` tags. This may not display properly in a browser (although some browsers are more forgiving than others).

Putting It Together—The <FONT> Tag

Let's go back and have a little fun with my recipe page, using the <FONT> tag and its attributes to make the headline and section titles more interesting (Figure 7-20). Note that SIZE, FACE, and COLOR are attributes, not tags in themselves; they must go inside a <FONT> tag. I've also combined styles by nesting tags.

Figure 7-20

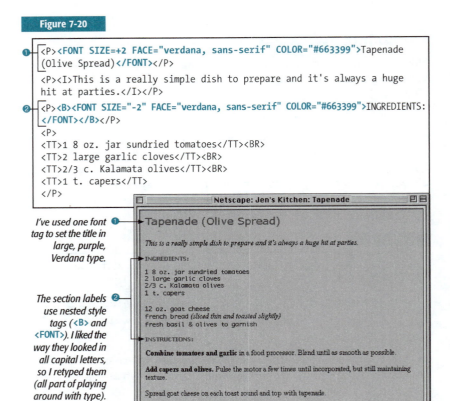

❶ ```
<P><FONT SIZE=+2 FACE="verdana, sans-serif" COLOR="#663399">Tapenade
(Olive Spread)</FONT></P>

<P><I>This is a really simple dish to prepare and it's always a huge
hit at parties.</I></P>
```
❷ ```
<P><B><FONT SIZE="-2" FACE="verdana, sans-serif" COLOR="#663399">INGREDIENTS:
</FONT></B></P>
<P>
<TT>1 8 oz. jar sundried tomatoes</TT><BR>
<TT>2 large garlic cloves</TT><BR>
<TT>2/3 c. Kalamata olives</TT><BR>
<TT>1 t. capers</TT>
</P>
```

❶ *I've used one font tag to set the title in large, purple, Verdana type.*

❷ *The section labels use nested style tags (<B> and <FONT>). I liked the way they looked in all capital letters, so I retyped them (all part of playing around with type).*

Netscape: Jen's Kitchen: Tapenade

Tapenade (Olive Spread)

This is a really simple dish to prepare and it's always a huge hit at parties.

INGREDIENTS:

1 8 oz. jar sundried tomatoes
2 large garlic cloves
2/3 c. Kalamata olives
1 t. capers

12 oz. goat cheese
french bread *(sliced thin and toasted slightly)*
fresh basil & olives to garnish

INSTRUCTIONS:

Combine tomatoes and garlic in a food processor. Blend until as smooth as possible.

Add capers and olives. Pulse the motor a few times until incorporated, but still maintaining texture.

Spread goat cheese on each toast round and top with tapenade.

Formatting Text

TOOL TIP

Text Styles

Here's how you access style controls in three of the more popular authoring programs.

DREAMWEAVER 3

❶ *The most common text style adjustments are available right on the Properties palette when text is highlighted.*

❷ *Additional styles are available under the Text → Style menu.*

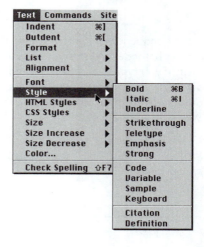

GOLIVE 4

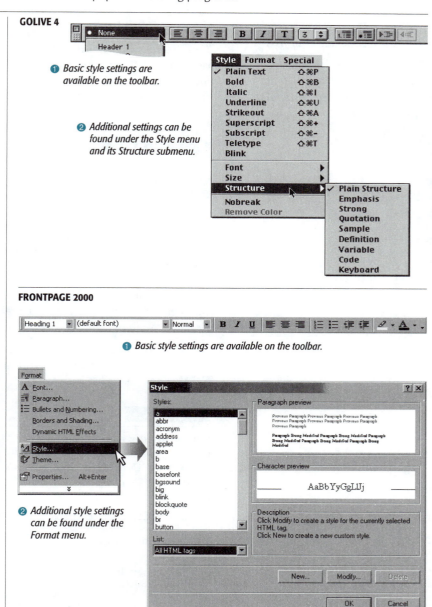

❶ *Basic style settings are available on the toolbar.*

❷ *Additional settings can be found under the Style menu and its Structure submenu.*

FRONTPAGE 2000

❶ *Basic style settings are available on the toolbar.*

❷ *Additional style settings can be found under the Format menu.*

Lists

Sometimes it is necessary to itemize information, instead of presenting it in paragraphs. For instance, you might want to list items with bullets. Or you might have detailed instructions that must appear in numerical order.

There are three kinds of lists you can define with HTML: ordered lists (numbered lists), unordered lists (bulleted lists), and definition lists (for terms and their definitions). Each list type has its own tag that you use to indicate the beginning and end of the list as a whole. You must also identify each item within that list. Let's look at how you create formatted lists in HTML.

There are three kinds of lists you can define with HTML: ordered (numbered) lists, unordered (bulleted) lists, and definition lists (for terms and their definitions).

Ordered Lists

`<OL>...</OL>`
Ordered list

`<LI>`
List item

An ordered (numbered) list is used when the sequence of items is important. Browsers automatically insert a number before each list item, so you do not need to type the number in yourself (if you type in a number, you'll see two numbers when the document displays). The advantage to using a numbered list is that the list will be renumbered automatically if you insert or delete an item (plus, you get a nicely indented left edge).

The `<OL>` container tag is used to identify the entire list as "ordered." Each item within the list is then indicated with an `<LI>` (list item) tag (Figure 7-21). The closing list item tag (`</LI>`) is optional.

Figure 7-21

```
<P><B>Instructions:</B></P>
<OL>
<LI>Rinse fillets & pat dry. Add to marinade for 20 minutes. Drain and
discard ginger.
<LI>Heat oil in wok. Add seasonings & stir fry for 10 seconds. Add Fish
Sauce;
heat 2 minutes, stirring constantly. Pour over fillets in baking dish.
<LI>Fill wok with water to bottom of steamer tray. Heat til boiling. Steam
fish for 10 minutes, covered, high heat until flakey.
</OL>
```

Instructions:

1. Rinse fillets & pat dry. Add to marinade for 20 minutes. Drain and discard ginger.
2. Heat oil in wok. Add seasonings & stir fry for 10 seconds. Add Fish Sauce; heat 2 minutes, stirring constantly. Pour over fillets in baking dish.
3. Fill wok with water to bottom of steamer tray. Heat til boiling. Steam fish for 10 minutes, covered, high heat until flakey.

__Ordered (numbered) lists__ are indicated by the `<OL>` tag. Each item in the list is preceded by a list item tag `<LI>`. The numbers are added automatically by the browser.

You can get fancy with ordered lists and change the style of numbering with the TYPE attribute. There are five possible values: 1 (numbers), A (uppercase letters), a (lowercase letters), I (uppercase roman numerals), and i (lowercase roman numerals). Regular numbers are the default. The other variations are shown in Figure 7-22.

Figure 7-22

You can change the numbering style with the TYPE attribute and its following values:

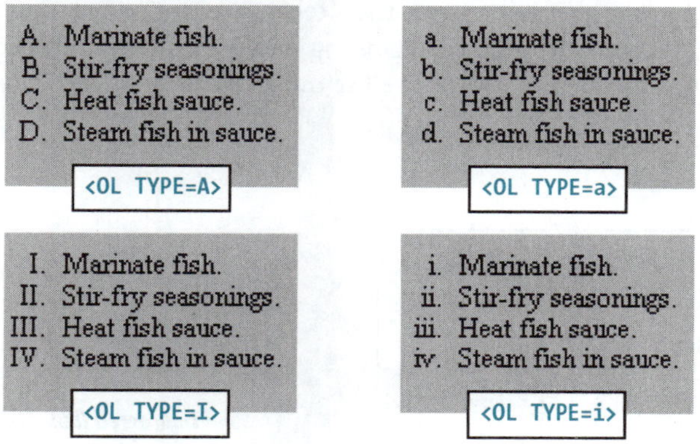

```
A. Marinate fish.
B. Stir-fry seasonings.
C. Heat fish sauce.
D. Steam fish in sauce.
```
<OL TYPE=A>

```
a. Marinate fish.
b. Stir-fry seasonings.
c. Heat fish sauce.
d. Steam fish in sauce.
```
<OL TYPE=a>

```
  I. Marinate fish.
 II. Stir-fry seasonings.
III. Heat fish sauce.
 IV. Steam fish in sauce.
```
<OL TYPE=I>

```
  i. Marinate fish.
 ii. Stir-fry seasonings.
iii. Heat fish sauce.
 iv. Steam fish in sauce.
```
<OL TYPE=i>

When you use an ordered list, the browser adds the numbers automatically, so you don't need to type them yourself. You can specify the type of numbering and the starting number.

Formatting Text

You can also start the list with a number (or letter value) other than "1" by using the START attribute as shown in Figure 7-23.

Figure 7-23

Use the START attribute to specify the first number in the list.

```
<B>Instructions:</B></P>
<OL START=17>
<LI>Marinate fish.
<LI>Stir-fry seasonings.
<LI>Heat fish sauce.
<LI>Steam fish in sauce.
</OL>
```

Instructions:

```
17. Marinate fish.
18. Stir-fry seasonings.
19. Heat fish sauce.
20. Steam fish in sauce.
```

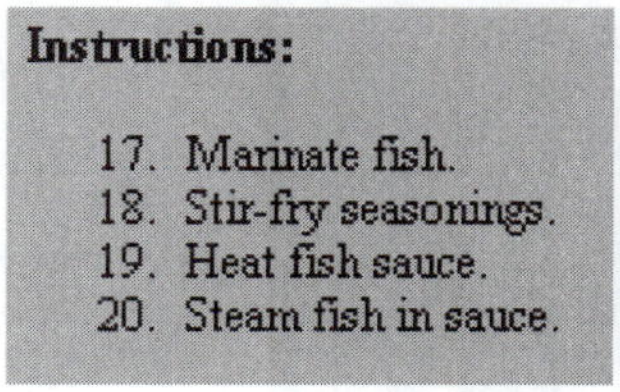

You can combine the START and TYPE attributes in one tag.

```
<B>Instructions:</B></P>
<OL TYPE=a START=10>
<LI>Marinate fish.
<LI>Stir-fry seasonings.
<LI>Heat fish sauce.
<LI>Steam fish in sauce.
</OL>
```

Instructions:

```
j. Marinate fish.
k. Stir-fry seasonings.
l. Heat fish sauce.
m. Steam fish in sauce.
```

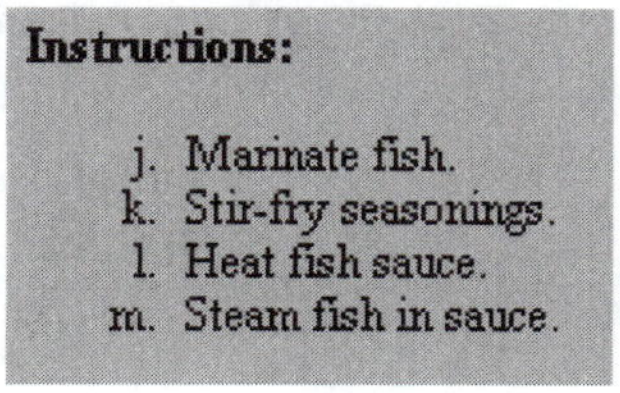

Unordered Lists

`<UL>...</UL>`
Unordered list

`<LI>`
List item

Unordered lists are displayed as bulleted lists. The bullets are added automatically by the browser and the items are set on an indent. The `<UL>...</UL>` tags indicate the beginning and end of the bulleted list. Like ordered lists, each item within the list must be marked with the `<LI>` (list item) tag (Figure 7-24).

The bullets in unordered lists are added automatically by the browser.

Figure 7-24

```
<P><B>From the pantry:</B></P>
<UL>
<LI>rice wine
<LI>soy sauce
<LI>garlic
<LI>chicken stock
</UL>
```

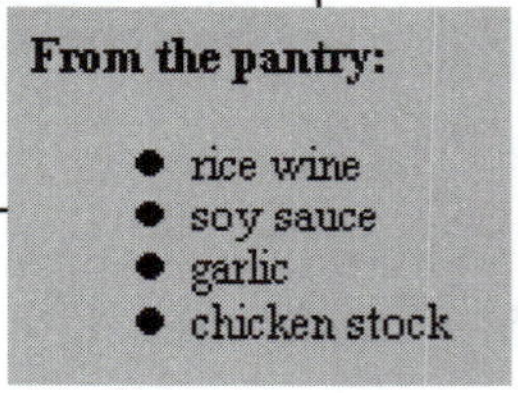

From the pantry:

- rice wine
- soy sauce
- garlic
- chicken stock

Unordered (bulleted) lists are indicated by the `<UL>` tag. Notice that the bullets are added automatically for each list item (`<LI>`).

If you aren't excited about black dot bullets, you can use circles or squares. The TYPE attribute in the `<UL>` tag gives you minimal control over the appearance of bullets. The values may be disc (the black dot default), circle, or square (Figure 7-25). If you want to use one of your own graphics as bullets, you'll need to use one of the tricks demonstrated in Chapter 17, Web Design Techniques.

Figure 7-25

Use the TYPE attribute to specify the bullet type.

From the pantry:

- rice wine
- soy sauce
- garlic
- chicken stock

`<UL TYPE=disc>`

From the pantry:

- rice wine
- soy sauce
- garlic
- chicken stock

`<UL TYPE=circle>`

From the pantry:

- rice wine
- soy sauce
- garlic
- chicken stock

`<UL TYPE=square>`

Definition Lists

<DL>...</DL>
Dictionary (or definition) list

<DT>
Dictionary term

<DD>
Dictionary definition

Dictionary lists are used for displaying lists of words with blocks of descriptive text. They are a bit different from the other two HTML lists in format. The <DL>...</DL> tags are used to mark the beginning and end of the list. Within the list, each word (term) is marked with the <DT> tag (the closing </DT> tag is usually omitted) and its definition is marked with a <DD>.

Terms are displayed against the left margin with no extra space above or below. The definition is displayed on an indent (Figure 7-26).

Nesting Lists

Any list can be nested within another list (Figure 7-27). For instance, you could add a bulleted list item under an item within a numbered list, or add a numbered list within a definition list, and so on. Lists can be nested several layers deep; however, since the left indent is cumulative, it doesn't take long for the text to end up pressed against the right margin.

Formatting Text

Figure 7-26

```
<DL>
<DT>rice vinegar
<DD>Rice vinegar is made from fermented rice and has
a light, clean flavor that goes well with ginger.
<DT>soy sauce
<DD>This sauce based on fermented soy beans is probably
the best-known Asian seasoning.
<DT>fermented black beans
<DD>A staple of Chinese cuisine, these beans are
preserved in salt. The salt must be rinsed off before
the beans are used.
</DL>
```

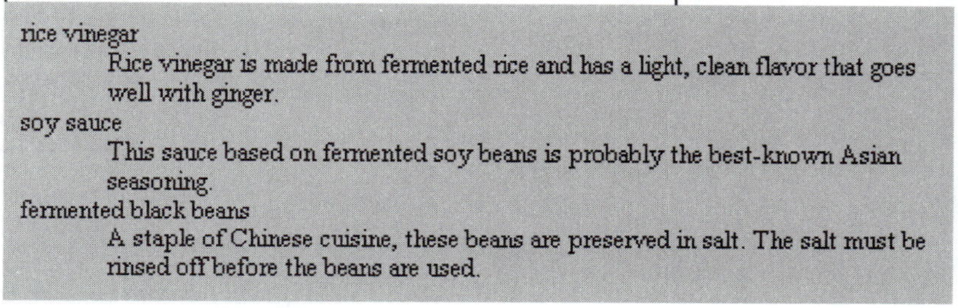

Definition lists are marked with <DL> tags. Each term is preceded by a <DT>; each definition gets a <DD>.

rice vinegar
Rice vinegar is made from fermented rice and has a light, clean flavor that goes well with ginger.
soy sauce
This sauce based on fermented soy beans is probably the best-known Asian seasoning.
fermented black beans
A staple of Chinese cuisine, these beans are preserved in salt. The salt must be rinsed off before the beans are used.

Figure 7-27

```
<OL>
<LI>Mix Marinade
        <UL>
        <LI>2 slices ginger <EM>(smashed, then pinched
in marinade)</EM>
        <LI>1 T. rice wine or sake
        <LI>1 t. salt
        <LI>2 T. peanut oil
        </UL>
<LI>Stir-fry seasonings
<LI>Add fish sauce
</OL>
```

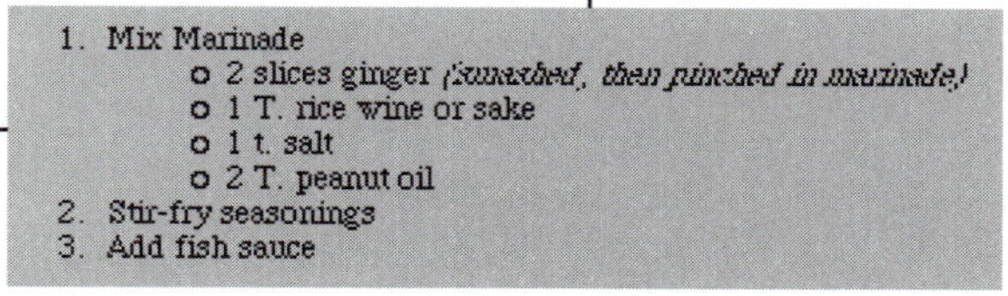

This example nests an unordered list within an ordered (numbered) list.

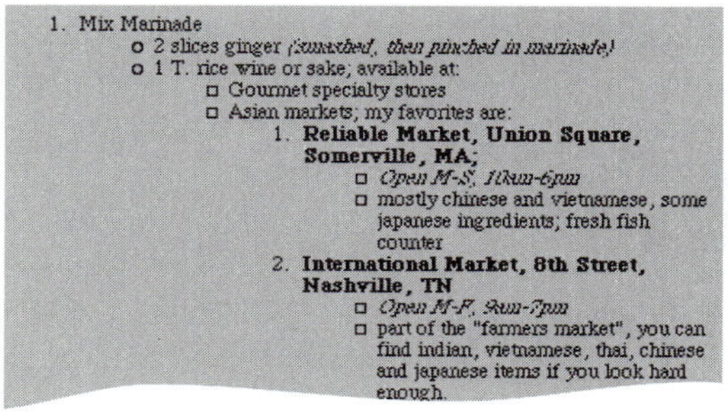

1. Mix Marinade
   o 2 slices ginger *(smashed, then pinched in marinade)*
   o 1 T. rice wine or sake
   o 1 t. salt
   o 2 T. peanut oil
2. Stir-fry seasonings
3. Add fish sauce

If you use too many nested lists, your content will end up shoved against the right margin.

Putting It Together–Lists

Because a recipe has step-by-step instructions, it provides a good opportunity to use a list. The raw text for my recipe instructions appears below
(Figure 7-28). What HTML tags would you add to get them to look as they
do in the sample output? (The answer follows.)

Figure 7-28

*What list tags
would you add to
these instructions
to make them
match the sample?*

```
<P><B><FONT SIZE="-2" FACE="verdana, sans-serif"
COLOR="#663399">INSTRUCTIONS:</FONT></B></P>

<B>Combine tomatoes and garlic</B> in a food processor.
Blend until as smooth as possible.

<B>Add capers and olives.</B> Pulse the motor a few times
until incorporated, but still maintaining texture.

Spread goat cheese on each toast round and top with tapenade.
```

INSTRUCTIONS:

  I. **Combine tomatoes and garlic** in a food processor. Blend until as smooth
      as possible.
 II. **Add capers and olives.** Pulse the motor a few times until incorporated,
      but still maintaining texture.
III. Spread goat cheese on each toast round and top with tapenade.

Answer:

```
<P><B><FONT SIZE="-2" FACE="verdana, sans-serif"
COLOR="#663399">INSTRUCTIONS:</FONT></B></P>
<OL TYPE=I>
<LI><B>Combine tomatoes and garlic</B> in a food processor.
Blend until as smooth as possible.
<LI><B>Add capers and olives.</B> Pulse the motor a few times
until incorporated, but sill maintaining texture.
<LI>Spread goat cheese on each toast round and top with tapenade.
</OL>
```

TOOL TIP

Formatting Lists

Here's how you access list controls in three of the more popular authoring programs.

DREAMWEAVER 3

❶ *With the entire list selected, choose the appropriate list style from the Text → List menu.*

❷ *With a specific list item selected, open the List Properties dialog box from the Text → List menu. Here you can fine-tune the list item.*

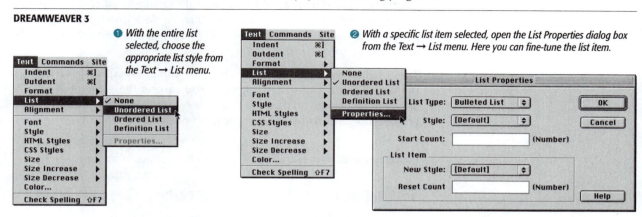

GOLIVE 4

❶ *All list settings are available from the Format → List menu.*

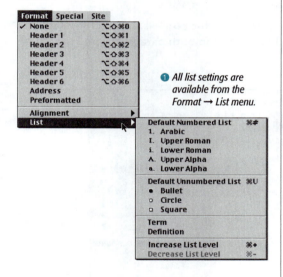

❷ *For quick numbered or bulleted lists, use the buttons on the Toolbar.*

FRONTPAGE 2000

❶ *Insert the cursor where you'd like to start a numbered list. Then select Format → Bullets and Numbering. Click the Numbers tab and select the style.*

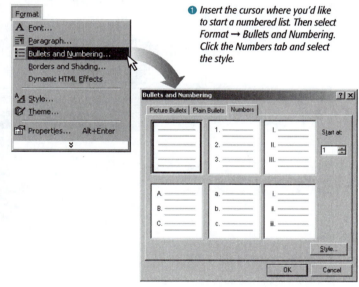

❷ *A quick method is to type and select items to be included in a list. Then click the Numbering icon on the toolbar. The items will automatically format to the default number list.*

Formatting Text

Aligning Text

Unfortunately, HTML alone provides few tools for adjusting text alignment.

HTML gives designers precious little control over text alignment. For the most part, you get your choice of text aligned on the left margin (left-justified), aligned on the right margin (right-justified), or centered. If you want your text left-justified, you don't have to do anything; it will be displayed that way automatically. But if that's not what you're after, let's look at ways to move your text around.

The `ALIGN` attribute can be used in heading and paragraph tags to change the text alignment of that paragraph. You can set the value of the `ALIGN` attribute to `left` (the default), `right`, or `center`. If you have multiple paragraphs you want to realign, you need to put the `ALIGN` attribute in every `<P>` tag.

Following are a few examples of the `ALIGN` attribute in action.

Setting Text on the Right Margin

`<P ALIGN=right>`
Right alignment

When you set the `ALIGN` value to `right`, the text will align on the right margin (Figure 7-29). Notice that it works in both paragraphs and headings.

Figure 7-29

```
<H2 ALIGN=right>Fish in Black Bean Sauce</H2>
<P ALIGN=right>The Chinese fermented black beans in this recipe give the
dish an unusual earthy aroma.</P>
<P ALIGN=right>It is a richly flavored dish that is also low in fat.</P>
```

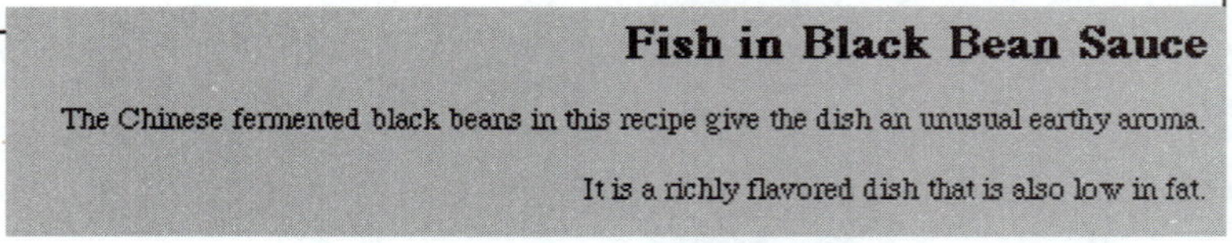

Fish in Black Bean Sauce

The Chinese fermented black beans in this recipe give the dish an unusual earthy aroma.

It is a richly flavored dish that is also low in fat.

To align text flush-right, use the `ALIGN=right` attribute.

Centering Text

<P ALIGN=center>
Center alignment

Set the value of the ALIGN attribute to center to center the paragraph or heading on a page. Remember, to center the whole page with this method, every element needs to have the ALIGN=center attribute in its opening tag (Figure 7-30).

Figure 7-30

```
<H2 ALIGN=center>Fish in Black Bean Sauce</H2>
<P ALIGN=center>The Chinese fermented black beans in this recipe give the
dish an unusual earthy aroma.</P>
<P ALIGN=center>It is a richly flavored dish that is also low in fat.</P>
```

Fish in Black Bean Sauce

The Chinese fermented black beans in this recipe give the dish an unusual earthy aroma.

It is a richly flavored dish that is also low in fat.

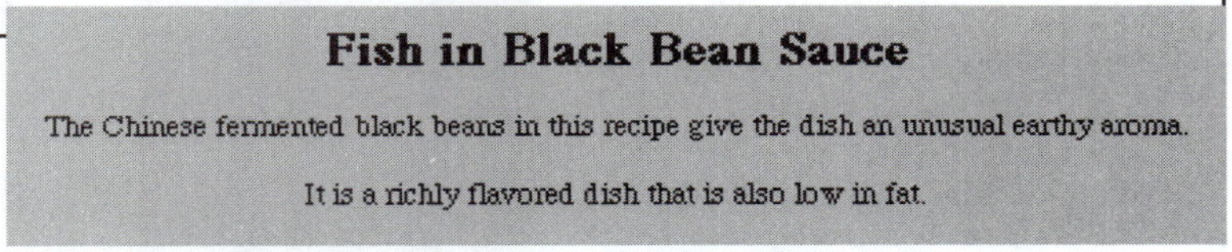

These headings and paragraphs are centered using the ALIGN=center attribute in each tag.

<CENTER>
Center alignment

Another way to center text is to use the <CENTER> container tag (Figure 7-31). This tag centers all of the text within it—you could center your whole page this way, if you like. Because it is so straightforward to use, the <CENTER> tag is by far the most popular way to center; however, it is not part of the official HTML specification. The proper way to center the whole page is to use a <DIV> (division) tag, as explained next.

Figure 7-31

```
<CENTER>
<H2>Fish in Black Bean Sauce</H2>
<P>The Chinese fermented black beans in this recipe give the
dish an unusual earthy aroma.</P>
<P>It is a richly flavored dish that is also low in fat.</P>
</CENTER>
```

Fish in Black Bean Sauce

The Chinese fermented black beans in this recipe give the dish an unusual earthy aroma.

It is a richly flavored dish that is also low in fat.

You can center many elements at once (or a whole page) using the <CENTER> tag.

The <DIV> Tag

The <DIV> container tag is used to indicate a division. A division is like a generic block element; it's not a formal structural element, but you can use it to apply style attributes (like alignment) across a whole chunk of a page. You can wrap <DIV>...</DIV> tags around a whole page or any part of it.

Used by itself, the <DIV> tag doesn't affect the way the text looks in the browser. However, you can use the ALIGN attribute with it to affect the alignment of the whole division (Figure 7-32). <DIV> is also extremely useful with Cascading Style Sheets because you can apply display instructions to everything it contains (see Chapter 20 for more about style sheets). You'll find that web authoring programs such as Macromedia Dreamweaver use the <DIV> tag liberally to format pages. It's a good tag to be familiar with, even if you're a beginner.

TIP

Although the ALIGN attribute will not work in lists and blockquotes, if for some reason you really need to realign these elements, you can put everything inside <DIV> tags and set the alignment there. It will override the inherent alignment of the tag.

Figure 7-32

```
<DIV ALIGN=center>
<H2>Fish in Black Bean Sauce</H2>
<P>The Chinese fermented black beans in this recipe give the
dish an unusual earthy aroma.</P>
<P>It is richly flavored dish that is also low in fat.</P>
</DIV>
```

Fish in Black Bean Sauce

The Chinese fermented black beans in this recipe give the dish an unusual earthy aroma.

It is a richly flavored dish that is also low in fat.

The preferred method for centering several elements is to identify a division (with the <DIV> tag), then center the division with ALIGN.

Indents

Unfortunately, there is no "indent" function in standard HTML, so designers must resort to the creative use (or misuse) of existing tags to get text to indent.

A few popular HTML cheats include (Figure 7-33):

- Using the `<BLOCKQUOTE>` tag to produce an indent on both the left and right margins.

- Using an unordered list (`<UL>...</UL>`) with no list items (`<LI>`) specified to display text as indented.

- Using a dictionary list (`<DL>...</DL>`) with only definitions (`<DD>`) and no terms to display text as indented.

It's generally not a good idea to write illegal HTML to achieve a visual effect. It can come back to bite you later.

Formatting Text

Figure 7-33

```
<BLOCKQUOTE>Heat oil in wok. Add seasonings & stir fry for 10
seconds. Add Fish Sauce; heat 2 minutes, stirring constantly.
Pour over fillets in baking dish.</BLOCKQUOTE>

<UL>Heat oil in wok. Add seasonings & stir fry for 10 seconds.
Add Fish Sauce; heat 2 minutes, stirring constantly. Pour over
fillets in baking dish.</UL>

<DL>
<DD>Heat oil in wok. Add seasonings & stir fry for 10 seconds.
Add Fish Sauce; heat 2 minutes, stirring constantly. Pour over
fillets in baking dish.
</DL>
```

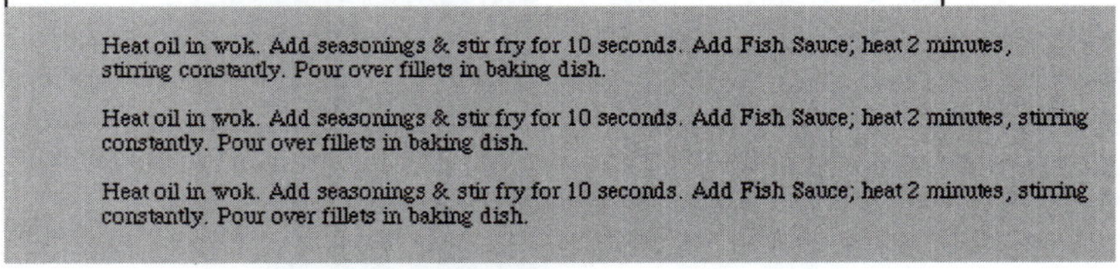

Heat oil in wok. Add seasonings & stir fry for 10 seconds. Add Fish Sauce; heat 2 minutes, stirring constantly. Pour over fillets in baking dish.

Heat oil in wok. Add seasonings & stir fry for 10 seconds. Add Fish Sauce; heat 2 minutes, stirring constantly. Pour over fillets in baking dish.

Heat oil in wok. Add seasonings & stir fry for 10 seconds. Add Fish Sauce; heat 2 minutes, stirring constantly. Pour over fillets in baking dish.

Three "cheats" for indenting HTML text.

Even with these workarounds, you only get an automatic indent of about a half-inch on the left or both margins. You can't indent just the first line, or specify the amount of indent. It's kind of a bummer. Style sheets offer some additional control, but unfortunately, browser support for indenting functions is inconsistent as of this writing.

If you want more sophisticated indenting and text alignment, you're better off using tables, as discussed in Chapter 10, Tables. Some designers use 1-pixel transparent graphics, which they size to push text out of the way. This technique is discussed in Chapter 17.

Preventing Line Breaks

Text or images between "no break" tags will stay on one line, regardless of the width of the browser window.

Say you want to keep a line of text all on one line, even if the window is resized. Well, there's a tag for that! It's the "no break" tag (`<NOBR>`). Text and graphics that appear within this tag will not be broken by the automatic wrapping function of the browser (Figure 7-34). If the string of elements is very long, it will continue off the browser page and users will have to scroll to the right to see it. This tag is useful for holding a row of individual graphics (such as a navigational toolbar) together, even when the window is resized very small.

Figure 7-34

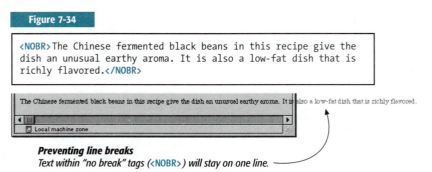

Preventing line breaks
Text within "no break" tags (`<NOBR>`) will stay on one line.

Preformatted Text

Preformatted text is unique in that it displays extra characters and carriage returns just as they are typed.

As we saw earlier in this chapter, the preformatted text tag (`<PRE>`) gives you character-by-character control over text alignment. Of course, you have to live with your text displayed in Courier. Since `<PRE>` text honors blank character spaces, it's possible to use this tag to align other elements precisely on the page (although you'd probably be better off using tables). Figure 7-35 shows preformatted text used for precise alignment.

Figure 7-35

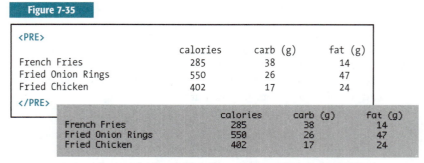

An example of precise text alignment using preformatted text (`<PRE>`).

Putting It Together—Aligning Text

In HTML, there is often more than one way to achieve a particular effect. Two of the code examples listed here will center the recipe title and comments as shown in Figure 7-36; the other two will not. Which two code examples will not work? What's wrong with them?

Figure 7-36

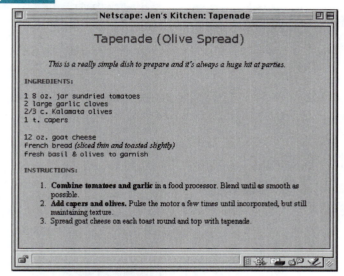

The recipe title and comments are now centered.

❶ `<P ALIGN=center><FONT SIZE=+2 FACE="verdana, sans-serif" COLOR="#663399">Tapenade (Olive Spread)</FONT></P>`
`<P ALIGN=center><I>This is a really simple dish to prepare and it's always a huge hit at parties.</I></P>`

❷ `<ALIGN=center>`
`<P><FONT SIZE=+2 FACE="verdana, sans-serif" COLOR="#663399">Tapenade (Olive Spread)</FONT></P>`
`<P><I>This is a really simple dish to prepare and it's always a huge hit at parties.</I></P>`
`</ALIGN>`

❸ `<DIV ALIGN=right>`
`<P><FONT SIZE=+2 FACE="verdana, sans-serif" COLOR="#663399">Tapenade (Olive Spread)</FONT></P>`
`<P><I>This is a really simple dish to prepare and it's always a huge hit at parties.</I></P>`
`</DIV>`

❹ `<CENTER>`
`<P><FONT SIZE=+2 FACE="verdana, sans-serif" COLOR="#663399">Tapenade (Olive Spread)</FONT></P>`
`<P><I>This is a really simple dish to prepare and it's always a huge hit at parties.</I></P>`
`</CENTER>`

Answers:

❶ Works. Each element is centered with the `ALIGN` attribute.

❷ Won't work. `ALIGN` is an attribute, not a tag.

❸ Won't work. The `<DIV>` tag is used correctly, but its value is set to right, not center.

❹ Works. The `<CENTER>` tag centers everything it contains.

Some Special Characters

Some common characters, such as ©, are not part of the standard set of ASCII characters (which contains only letters, numbers, and a few basic symbols). To get these characters on a web page, you have to call them by their character entity names in the HTML document. A character entity is a string of text that identifies a specific character. Characters can be defined by name or by their numeric values.

Figure 7-37

```
<P>Copyright &copy; 2000 Jennifer Niederst</P>

<P>Copyright &#169; 2000 Jennifer Niederst</P>
```

Copyright © 2000 Jennifer Niederst

Copyright © 2000 Jennifer Niederst

Most special characters can be called by name or by number. The browser displays the special character in place of the character entity string.

An example will make this clearer. I'd like to add a copyright symbol to my page. The typical Mac keyboard command, *Option-g*, which works in my word processing program, won't work on an HTML page. Instead, I use the character entity name © (or its numerical value ©) where I want the symbol to appear (Figure 7-37).

Figure 7-38

```
<P>The beginning     The End</P>
<P>The beginning   The End</P>
```

The beginning The End

The beginning   The End

Browsers ignore multiple character spaces in an HTML file, but you can add hard spaces using the "nonbreaking space" character entity.

Remember how extra character spaces in an HTML document are ignored by browsers? If you need to add a hard character space (or a string of them) to a page, you can insert them using the character entity for a "nonbreaking space,"   (Figure 7-38).

Table 7-1 lists some commonly used character entities. Of course, there are many more than are listed here. For a complete list, see Webmonkey's useful Special Characters Quick Reference at *hotwired.lycos.com/webmonkey/ reference/special_characters/*.

Table 7-1: Common Special Characters and Their Character Entities

Character	Description	Name	Number
	Character space (nonbreaking space)		
©	Copyright	&copy;	&#169;
®	Registered trademark	&reg;	&#174;
™	Trademark	*(none)*	&#153;
£	Pound	&pound;	&#163;
¥	Yen	&yen;	&#165;
"	Left curly quotes	*(none)*	&#147;
"	Right curly quotes	*(none)*	&#148;
<	Greater-than symbol; left bracket (useful for displaying tags on a web page)	*(none)*	&#155;
>	Less-than symbol; right bracket (useful for displaying tags on a web page)	*(none)*	&#139;

TOOL TIP

Character Entities

Here's how you add character entities in three of the more popular authoring programs.

Formatting Text

DREAMWEAVER 3

❷ *This accesses a palette of common characters that you can drag into place on your page. The complete list of character entities is also available.*

❶ *First, select Characters from the Objects palette pull-down menu.*

GOLIVE 4

❶ *Character entities are accessed via the Web Database (located under the Special menu). To use a character, simply select it and drag it into place in the document.*

❷ *While it is selected, you can get more information about it in the Inspector.*

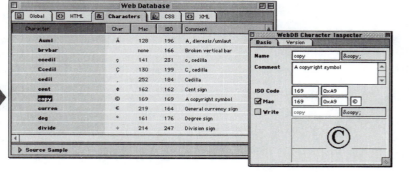

FRONTPAGE 2000

Place the insertion point where you want to insert a character. Go to Insert → Symbol. Select the character you want to insert, and click Insert.

HTML Review—Text Formatting Tags

The following is a summary of the tags we covered in this chapter:

Tag and Attributes	Function
`<B>`	Bold text
`<BLOCKQUOTE>`	Lengthy quotation
` `	Line break
`<CENTER>`	Centers elements on the page
`<DD>`	Definition item (in a definition list)
`<DIV>`	Division (used for applying styles)
`ALIGN=left|right|center`	Horizontal alignment
`<DL>`	Definition list
`<DT>`	Term item (in a definition list)
`<EM>`	Emphasized (italic) text
`<FONT>`	Uses attributes to specify size, font face, and color
`SIZE=1 to 7`	Text size
(or relative value)	
`FACE="name"`	Typeface for the enclosed text
`COLOR="number" or "name"`	Color of the enclosed text
`<H#>`	Heading level (from 1 to 6)
`ALIGN=left|right|center`	Horizontal alignment
`<I>`	Italic text
`<LI>`	List item (in an ordered or unordered list)
`<NOBR>`	"No break"; prevents line breaks in the enclosed text
`<OL>`	Ordered (numbered) list
`<P>`	Paragraph
`ALIGN=left|right|center`	Horizontal alignment
`<PRE>`	Preformatted text
`<STRIKE>`	Strikethrough text
`<STRONG>`	Strong (bold) text
`<SUB>`	Subscript
`<SUP>`	Superscript
`<TT>`	Teletype (or typewriter text)
`<U>`	Underlined text
`<UL>`	Unordered (bulleted) list

Chapter 8

Adding Graphic Elements

A web page with all text and no pictures isn't much fun! The Web's explosion into mass popularity is due in part to the fact that there are images right there on the page. Images are used in obvious and subtle ways. For instance, it may be apparent that photographs, icons, and buttons are graphics, but graphics can also be used as spacing devices or to create visual effects like rounded corners on boxes (these tricks are discussed in Chapter 17, Web Design Techniques).

In this chapter, we'll take a detailed look at the tags used for adding graphics to a page, both in the flow of text and as background images. We'll also look at that handy little page-divider, the horizontal rule.

Adding Inline Images

Most graphics on the Web are used as inline images, graphics that are part of the flow of the HTML content. These include all the illustrations, banner headlines, navigational toolbars, advertisements, etc., that you see on web pages. In other words, if it's not a background tiling image, it's an inline image. All inline images are placed in the HTML document using the `<IMG>` tag.

In order to be displayed in the browser, the graphics must be in the GIF or JPEG file format* (see Chapter 13, All About Web Graphics, if you are not familiar with these formats). Furthermore, the files need to be named with the proper suffixes—.gif and .jpg (or .jpeg), respectively—in order to be recognized by the browser. Simply being in the right format is not enough.

Let's take a look at the `<IMG>` tag and all its attributes that give you control over the graphic's placement and appearance.

---

* There is a third acceptable graphic format called PNG (pronounced "ping") that has some advantages over GIF, but it is less supported and less popular.

Pointing to Graphics

If the graphic you're placing on the page is in the same directory as the HTML file, you can just specify the filename of the graphic in the SRC attribute.

If it's in another directory, you'll need to provide the pathname to the graphic so the browser can find it. The pathname is a list of the directories and subdirectories the graphic is in, separated by slashes. It describes the location of the graphic relative to the current HTML file.

Pathnames in the <IMG> tag work the same as in link tags. They are discussed in more detail in Chapter 9, Adding Links.

The Image Tag

`<IMG SRC="`*`filename`*`"` or `"`*`URL`*`">`
Adds an image to the page

This is the basic tag that tells the browser "place a graphic here." There are a number of useful attributes that can be used to manipulate the image (we'll get to those next). Only one attribute, SRC (short for "source"), is required because it tells the browser which graphic to use. The value of the SRC attribute is the URL of the graphic. If the graphic file is in the same directory as the HTML file, you can just use its filename. The sidebar Pointing to Graphics gives more details about referring to graphics.

By default, graphics are displayed with their bottom edges lined up with the baseline of the surrounding text (Figure 8-1). Text will not automatically wrap around a graphic unless specified with the ALIGN attribute, described later in this chapter.

Figure 8-1

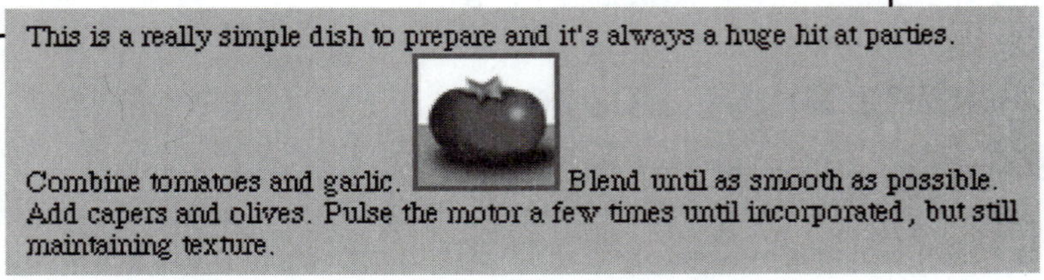

By default, the `<IMG>` *tag aligns the bottom edge of the graphic with the text baseline and holds the space around the graphic clear.*

TOOL TIPS

Adding Images

Here's how you add images to a web page in three of the more popular authoring programs.

DREAMWEAVER 3

❶ *Drag the image icon from the list of Common elements on the Objects palette into place on your document.*

❷ *A dialog box will open asking which graphic file to use.*

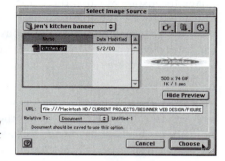

GOLIVE 4

To add an image, drag the image icon (question mark) from the Palette into place in the document window. You can also drag a file directly from your desktop onto the page.

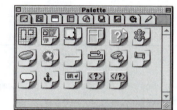

FRONTPAGE 2000

To add an image, click the Insert Image icon. A window will pop up, browse to the picture you want from your local file system and select the file.

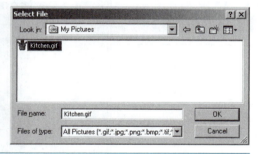

Adding Graphic Elements

Alternative Text

ALT="*text*"
Alternative text

The alternative text will
appear next to or within the
generic graphic icon if the
image doesn't display.

The ALT attribute allows you to provide a brief text description of your
image for instances when the graphic cannot be displayed in a browser.
The alternative text will appear next to or within the generic graphic icon
if the image is missing or if the user has graphics turned off in the browser
for faster downloading (and many people do). For non-graphical browsers,
such as Lynx, the alternative text will appear in brackets in place of the
graphic.

Too often, I see home pages with graphical button links to sections of the
site without alternative text. When the graphics are not available, these
home pages become dead ends (Figure 8-2). Taking the extra time to add
alternative text (especially to graphics that serve as navigational links) can
save the day.

Figure 8-2

```
<CENTER>
<H1>Welcome to Our Site</H1>
<P>Here you will find useful information about Our Products and Our Company.</P>
<P><IMG SRC="products.gif" ALT="PRODUCTS"></P>
<P><IMG SRC="history.gif" ALT="HISTORY"></P>
<P><IMG SRC="jobs.gif" ALT="JOBS"></P>
<P><IMG SRC="contact.gif" ALT="CONTACT US"></P>
</CENTER>
```

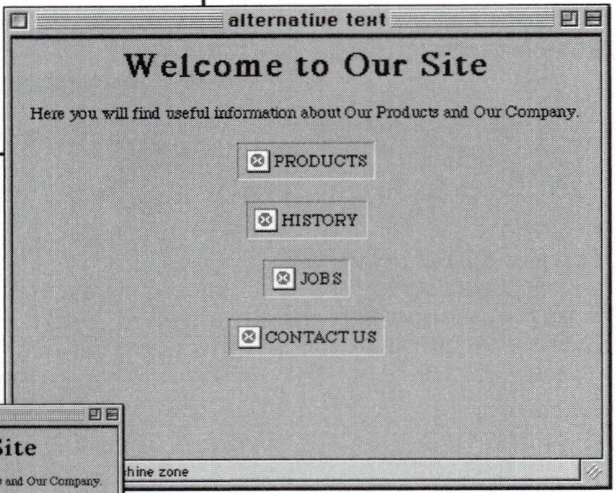

*Alternative text
appears when the
graphic doesn't.*

*This is what users see when the graphics
load properly.*

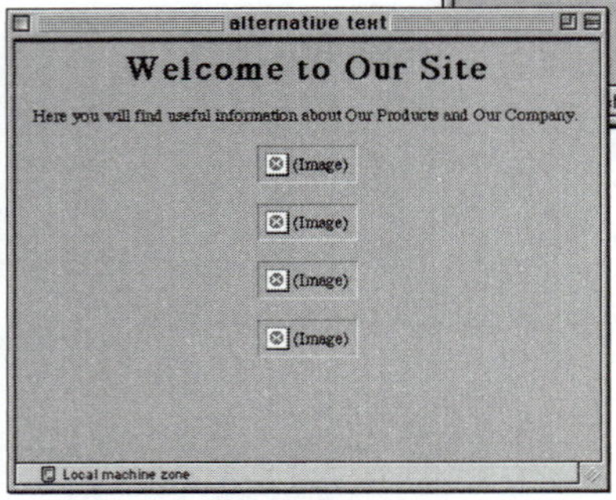

*Without alternative text, and with no
graphics visible, this page is a dead end.*

Image Size

WIDTH=*number*
Image width in pixels

HEIGHT=*number*
Image height in pixels

The WIDTH and HEIGHT attributes indicate the dimensions of the graphic in pixels. Sounds mundane, but these attributes are your best friends because they speed up the time it takes to display the final page.

When the browser knows the dimensions of the graphics, it can busy itself laying out the page while the graphics themselves are downloading. Without width and height values, the page is laid out immediately, and then reassembled each time a graphic arrives. Telling the browser how much space to hold for each graphic can make the final page appear seconds faster.

If you are using a web-authoring tool, the WIDTH and HEIGHT values will be added automatically when you place a graphic. You'll need to remember to type them in by hand if you are using a simple HTML editor.

It's important to note, however, that if your pixel values are different from the actual dimensions of your image, the browser will resize your image to match your specified values (Figure 8-3). Although it may be tempting to resize images in this manner, you should know that the image can get blurry and deformed. In fact, if your graphics ever look blurry when viewed in a browser, the first thing to check is that your width and height values match the dimensions of the image exactly.

WIDTH and HEIGHT attributes can speed up the display of your page.

TIP

If you have resized a graphic in an image-editing program, be sure to also update its dimensions in the HTML file.

Adding Graphic Elements

Figure 8-3

```
<IMG SRC="tomato.gif" WIDTH=72 HEIGHT=72>
```

Width and height values help the browser lay out the page more efficiently.

Be aware that if the measurements are not accurate, the browser will resize the image to match the specified width and height values.

```
<IMG SRC="tomato.gif" WIDTH=144 HEIGHT=36>
```

Image Borders

BORDER=*number*
Border thickness in pixels

TIP

Turn off borders on linked images by
adding BORDER=0, as in:

    <IMG SRC="picture.gif" BORDER=0>

When you use an image as a link, the browser automatically adds a colored border around the graphic to indicate that it's a link. (See Chapter 9
for how to link a graphic.) The color of the border will match the color of
linked text on the page (dark blue by default). You can control the thickness of the border using the BORDER attribute within the image tag.

In most cases, you'll probably want to turn the border off by setting the
value to zero pixels, but you can also make it extra thick by specifying a
higher pixel value (Figure 8-4).

Figure 8-4

Default behavior: BORDER=1 *(for linked graphics)*

    <A HREF="recipe.html"><IMG SRC="tomato.gif"></A>

*When an image is linked, the
browser adds a 1-pixel wide
border in the link color.*

Turn off border: BORDER=0

    <A HREF="recipe.html"><IMG SRC="tomato.gif" BORDER=0></A>

*You can turn this border off
by setting the BORDER
attribute to 0.*

Increase border: BORDER=*x*

    <IMG SRC="tomato.gif" BORDER=10>

*You can add a border to any
graphic. If it is linked it will
appear in the linked color. If
it is not linked, the border
appears in the text color.*

Positioning Graphics

The ALIGN attribute tells the browser how you want to align the graphic, horizontally or vertically, relative to the neighboring lines of text. The values top, middle, and bottom affect the vertical alignment of a graphic in relation to a neighboring single line of text (such as a label). The values left and right affect the horizontal alignment of the graphic (i.e., the margin the graphic is placed against). Let's look at how they work.

The ALIGN attribute is used to position graphics vertically and horizontally, depending on the values you specify.

Vertical alignment

ALIGN=top, middle, or bottom
Vertical alignment relative to neighboring text line

By setting the value of the ALIGN attribute to either top, middle, or bottom, you affect the positioning of the graphic in relation to the neighboring line of text. By default (that is, if you don't specify anything), the neighboring text line will align with the bottom of the image. This is the same as specifying ALIGN=bottom. If you want the text baseline to line up with the middle of the graphic, set the value to middle; top aligns the text with the top edge of the image (Figure 8-5).

Figure 8-5

```
<P><IMG SRC="tomato.gif" ALIGN=bottom>You say tomato! I say tomahto!</P>
```

ALIGN=bottom *is the default vertical alignment for all images.*

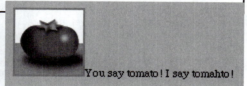

```
<P><IMG SRC="tomato.gif" ALIGN=middle>You say tomato! I say tomahto!</P>
```

ALIGN=middle *aligns the middle of the graphic with the neighboring text.*

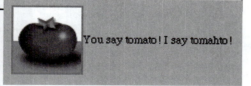

```
<P><IMG SRC="tomato.gif" ALIGN=top>You say tomato! I say tomahto!</P>
```

ALIGN=top *puts the text at the top edge of the graphic.*

Wrapping text around a graphic

ALIGN=left or right
Horizontal alignment with text wrap

To make text wrap around a graphic, set the ALIGN attribute to left or right.

The ALIGN attribute also adjusts the horizontal positioning of the graphic when you set the value to either left (against the left margin) or right (against the right margin).

This attribute is a favorite of mine because, in addition to specifying whether the graphic should appear against the left or right margin, it makes the following text wrap around the graphic (Figure 8-6). As we've seen in earlier examples, without horizontal alignment values, the space next to the graphic is held blank.

Figure 8-6

Aligning an image left or right makes the text wrap around the graphic.

```
<P>
<B>SAUCE:</B><BR>
Cut prosciutto into 1/2" chunks and fry with chopped onion in olive oil
over low heat, until fat is rendered and meat is crisp. Remove meat and
set aside.<BR>
<IMG SRC="tomato.gif" ALIGN=left> Drain the tomatoes, finely chop them and
add to the onion in the pan. Season with red pepper flakes and salt and
pepper. Simmer 20 minutes, stirring occasionally.<BR>
<B>TO SERVE:</B><BR>
Cook pasta according to directions on package. Drain well.<BR>
Transfer sauce to large skillet over medium-high heat. Add the pasta and
reserved meat and cook for 30 seconds. Remove the skillet from heat. Add
cheese.
</P>
```

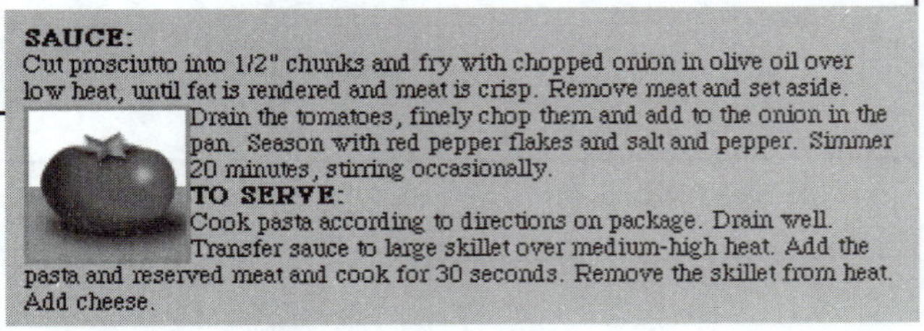

SAUCE:
Cut prosciutto into 1/2" chunks and fry with chopped onion in olive oil over low heat, until fat is rendered and meat is crisp. Remove meat and set aside. Drain the tomatoes, finely chop them and add to the onion in the pan. Season with red pepper flakes and salt and pepper. Simmer 20 minutes, stirring occasionally.
TO SERVE:
Cook pasta according to directions on package. Drain well.
Transfer sauce to large skillet over medium-high heat. Add the pasta and reserved meat and cook for 30 seconds. Remove the skillet from heat. Add cheese.

```
<IMG SRC="tomato.gif" ALIGN=right> Drain the tomatoes, finely chop them
and add to the onion in the pan. Season with red pepper flakes and salt
and pepper. Simmer 20 minutes, stirring occasionally.<BR>
```

SAUCE:
Cut prosciutto into 1/2" chunks and fry with chopped onion in olive oil over low heat, until fat is rendered and meat is crisp. Remove meat and set aside.
Drain the tomatoes, finely chop them and add to the onion in the pan. Season with red pepper flakes and salt and pepper. Simmer 20 minutes, stirring occasionally.
TO SERVE:
Cook pasta according to directions on package. Drain well.
Transfer sauce to large skillet over medium-high heat. Add the pasta and reserved meat and cook for 30 seconds. Remove the skillet from heat. Add cheese.

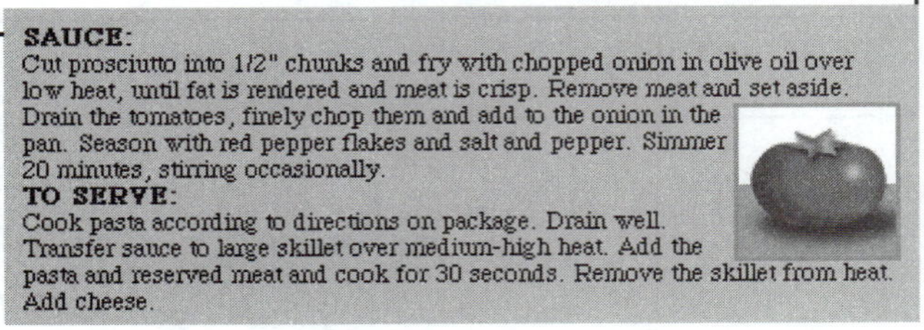

HSPACE=*number*
Horizontal space

VSPACE=*number*
Vertical space

The HSPACE and VSPACE attributes are used in conjunction with the ALIGN=left and ALIGN=right settings. Without them, the browser runs the wrapped text right up to the edge of the graphic. Chances are, you'll want to give your image a little breathing room. Use the HSPACE attribute to specify an amount of space (in pixels) to be held clear on the left and right of the image (Figure 8-7). Similarly, VSPACE holds a specified amount of space above and below. I find that 6 to 9 pixels usually does the trick.

Figure 8-7

```
<IMG SRC="tomato.gif" ALIGN=left HSPACE=12 VSPACE=12> Drain the tomatoes,
finely chop them and add to the onion in the pan. Season with red pepper
flakes and salt and pepper. Simmer 20 minutes, stirring occasionally.<BR>
```

SAUCE:
Cut prosciutto into 1/2" chunks and fry with chopped onion in olive oil over low heat, until fat is rendered and meat is crisp. Remove meat and set aside.

Drain the tomatoes, finely chop them and add to the onion in the pan. Season with red pepper flakes and salt and pepper. Simmer 20 minutes, stirring occasionally.

TO SERVE:
Cook pasta according to directions on package. Drain well.
Transfer sauce to large skillet over medium-high heat. Add the pasta and reserved meat and cook for 30 seconds. Remove the skillet from heat. Add cheese.

Using our same example, I've added HSPACE to the <IMG> tag to insert 12 pixels of space to the left and right of the graphic and VSPACE to add 12 pixels above and below.

Right Alignment, No Wrap

If you want to position a graphic on the right edge of the page without text wrap, put the image tag in a paragraph (<P>), then align the paragraph to the right, as shown below:

```
<P ALIGN=right><IMG SRC="tomato.gif"></P>
<P ALIGN=right>Drain the tomatoes, finely chop them and add to
the onion in the pan. Season with red pepper flakes and salt
and pepper. Simmer 20 minutes, stirring occasionally.</P>
```

Drain the tomatoes, finely chop them and add to the onion in the pan. Season with red pepper flakes and salt and pepper. Simmer 20 minutes, stirring occasionally.

Stopping the text wrap

<BR CLEAR=all>

Insert line break; start next line below the graphic

To turn the text wrap off, insert a <BR CLEAR=all> just before the line that you want to start under the graphic.

You may decide you don't want all the following text to wrap around a graphic; for instance, if you have a headline or some other text that you want to start against the margin.

The way you "turn off" the text wrap is by inserting a line break (<BR>) enhanced with the CLEAR attribute, which instructs it to start the next line below the image... when the margin is clear (Figure 8-8).

The CLEAR attribute actually has three possible values: left, right, and all. Use left only when you want to start the next line below a graphic that is against the left margin; use right when you want to start the next line below a graphic on the right margin. The all value starts the next line below graphics on either or both sides, so it'll do the job for most cases (I use it almost exclusively).

Figure 8-8

```
<IMG SRC="tomato.gif" HSPACE=12 VSPACE=12 ALIGN=left> Drain the
tomatoes, finely chop them and add to the onion in the pan. Season
with red pepper flakes and salt and pepper. Simmer 20 minutes,
stirring occasionally.<BR CLEAR=all>

<B>TO SERVE:</B><BR>
Cook pasta according to directions on package. Drain well.<BR>
```

SAUCE:
Cut prosciutto into 1/2" chunks and fry with chopped onion in olive oil over low heat, until fat is rendered and meat is crisp. Remove meat and set aside.

Drain the tomatoes, finely chop them and add to the onion in the pan. Season with red pepper flakes and salt and pepper. Simmer 20 minutes, stirring occasionally.

TO SERVE:
Cook pasta according to directions on package. Drain well. Transfer sauce to large skillet over medium-high heat. Add the pasta and reserved meat and cook for 30 seconds. Remove the skillet from heat. Add cheese.

The CLEAR=all attribute tells the browser to add a line break and position the next line when all margins are "clear" (in other words, when there are no graphics). Now my "To Serve" section starts below the graphic, where I want it.

Setting Image Attributes

Here's how you access image attribute controls in three of the more popular authoring programs.

DREAMWEAVER 3

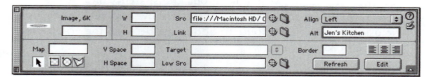

With the image selected (handles will be visible), all the settings for the image are available on the Properties palette.

GOLIVE 4

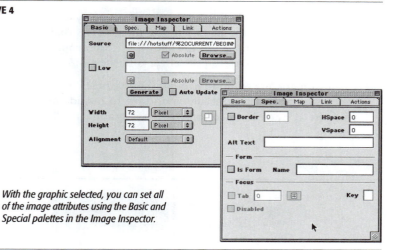

With the graphic selected, you can set all of the image attributes using the Basic and Special palettes in the Image Inspector.

FRONTPAGE 2000

Right click the graphic to bring up Picture Properties on the shortcut menu. Then click the Appearance tab to see the attributes for the graphic within the layout.

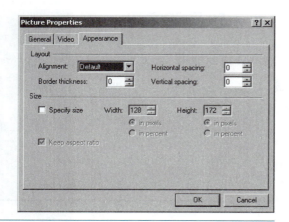

Adding Graphic Elements

Putting It Together—Placing Graphics

To show off the `<IMG>` tag in action, I've spruced up the home page of the cooking site I started in Chapter 6, Creating a Simple Page, with a few graphics (Figure 8-9). Let's look at what I've done:

❶ The banner graphic is transparent, allowing the background graphic to show through (we'll talk about transparency in Chapter 14, Creating GIFs). I added 8 pixels of space above and below the graphic using the VSPACE attribute to add space between the graphic and the top border of the browser.

One other thing to note: you can tell from the URL in the `<IMG>` tag that all my graphics for this page are stored in a directory called *graphics*. The pathname tells the browser where to look for each graphic on the current server.

❷ I got a little fancy and replaced the first letter of my introduction with a graphic to match the banner text. Capital letters that sink into the first few lines of text like this are known as "drop-caps" in the design biz. It is easy to accomplish the effect with the ALIGN=left attribute.

❸ I've also made my section headings into graphics. Any time you put text in a graphic, it especially important to include alternative text with the ALT attribute so folks without graphics will still get your message.

Figure 8-9

Figure 8-9 (cont.)

```
<HTML>
<HEAD>
        <TITLE>Jen's Kitchen</TITLE>
</HEAD>
<BODY>
<CENTER>
<IMG SRC="graphics/kitchen.gif" VSPACE=8>
</CENTER>

<BLOCKQUOTE>
<FONT FACE="Trebuchet MS, Arial, sans-serif">
<IMG SRC="graphics/W.gif" ALIGN=left WIDTH=40 HEIGHT=28 ALT="W">elcome to
my kitchen! People who know me know that I love to cook. I've created this
site to share some of my favorite recipes and online food resources. <I>Bon
Appetit!</I></FONT>
</BLOCKQUOTE>

<CENTER>
<P><IMG SRC="graphics/fromjensbook.gif" WIDTH=200 HEIGHT=28 ALT="From Jen's
Cookbook"><P>

<P><FONT FACE="Trebuchet MS, Arial, sans-serif">
tapenade (olive spread)<BR>
garlic salmon<BR>
wild mushroom risotto<BR>
asian dishes</FONT></P>

<P><IMG SRC="graphics/outthere.gif" WIDTH=217 HEIGHT=30
    ALT="Good Stuff 'Out There'"></P>

<P><FONT FACE="Trebuchet MS, Arial, sans-serif">
The Food Network Epicurious</FONT></P>
</CENTER>

</BODY>
</HTML>
```

❶ Banner graphic →

❷ Dropped capital letter → (a.k.a. "drop cap")

❸ Section titles in graphic →

❶ **kitchen.gif**

❷ **W.gif**

These checkerboard patterns indicate that these are transparent graphics (as viewed in Adobe Photoshop).

❸ **fromjensbook.gif**

❸ **outthere.gif**

Background Tiles

One easy way to jazz up a web page is to use a graphic as a tiling background image.

`<BODY BACKGROUND="`*`filename`*`"` or `"`*`URL`*`">`
Adds tiling background image

The key to a successful tiling background is subtlety—you need to be able to read text over it easily.

Tiled backgrounds are created using the BACKGROUND attribute within the `<BODY>` tag. We've used the `<BODY>` tag earlier as the structural tag that defines the visible part of the web document. It can also be used for certain settings that affect the whole page, such as background tiles and color settings. (Using the `<BODY>` tag to change color settings is discussed in Chapter 12, Color on the Web.)

In Figure 8-10, I've specified that the graphic *tile.gif* be used as a tiling background. The graphic pattern starts in the upper-left corner of the page and is repeated automatically.

The key to successful tiling backgrounds is *subtlety*. Nothing can ruin a web page faster than a tiled background that is too bold and busy, making the text virtually unreadable. So, please, tile with care.

Figure 8-10

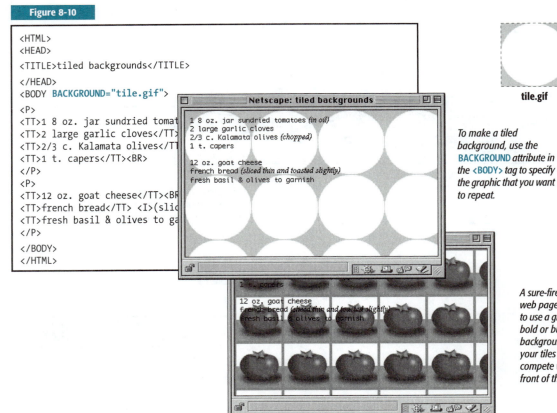

```
<HTML>
<HEAD>
<TITLE>tiled backgrounds</TITLE>
</HEAD>
<BODY BACKGROUND="tile.gif">

<P>
<TT>1 8 oz. jar sundried tomat
<TT>2 large garlic cloves</TT>
<TT>2/3 c. Kalamata olives</TT
<TT>1 t. capers</TT><BR>
</P>
<P>
<TT>12 oz. goat cheese</TT><BR
<TT>french bread</TT> <I>(slic
<TT>fresh basil & olives to ga
</P>

</BODY>
</HTML>
```

tile.gif

To make a tiled background, use the **BACKGROUND** *attribute in the* `<BODY>` *tag to specify the graphic that you want to repeat.*

A sure-fire way to make a web page unreadable is to use a graphic that is too bold or busy as a background tile. Design your tiles so they do not compete with the text in front of them.

Adding Tiling Backgrounds

Here's how you add tiled background graphics in three of the more popular authoring programs.

DREAMWEAVER 3

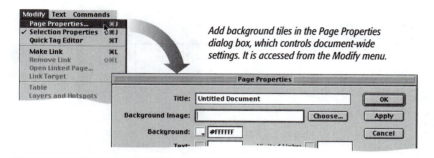

Add background tiles in the Page Properties dialog box, which controls document-wide settings. It is accessed from the Modify menu.

GOLIVE 4

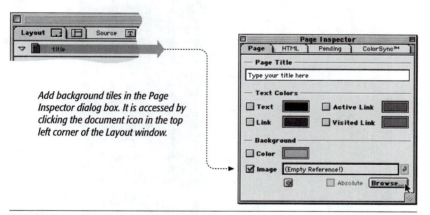

Add background tiles in the Page Inspector dialog box. It is accessed by clicking the document icon in the top left corner of the Layout window.

FRONTPAGE 2000

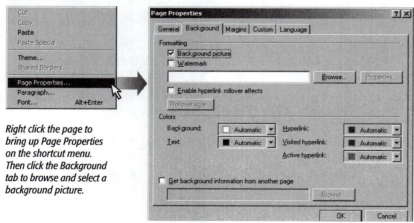

Right click the page to bring up Page Properties on the shortcut menu. Then click the Background tab to browse and select a background picture.

Solid Background Colors

The `<BODY>` tag is also used to make the background a solid color using the BGCOLOR attribute as shown in this example:

```
<BODY BGCOLOR="color name or
    number">
```

The system for specifying colors in HTML is discussed in detail in Chapter 12.

I often will use the BGCOLOR and BACKGROUND attributes at the same time. The BGCOLOR attribute loads a solid color that is the same as the dominant color of the background tile. That way, the tone for the page is set immediately while the background tile graphic is still downloading.

Adding Graphic Elements

Putting It Together—Background Tiles

I've actually designed the graphics for the Jen's Kitchen home page to be viewed against a dark background color. To give the page a little polish, I've added a tiling background image (Figure 8-11, gallery). Because the tile graphic is so tall, most users will only see the band of color at the top of the page. This technique is discussed in more detail in Chapter 17.

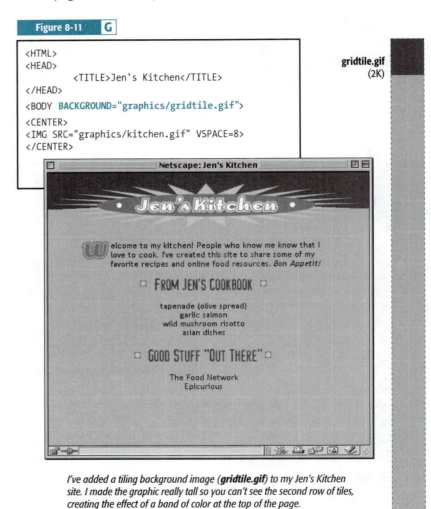

Figure 8-11   **G**

```
<HTML>
<HEAD>
          <TITLE>Jen's Kitchen</TITLE>
</HEAD>
<BODY BACKGROUND="graphics/gridtile.gif">
<CENTER>
<IMG SRC="graphics/kitchen.gif" VSPACE=8>
</CENTER>
```

gridtile.gif
(2K)

*I've added a tiling background image (**gridtile.gif**) to my Jen's Kitchen site. I made the graphic really tall so you can't see the second row of tiles, creating the effect of a band of color at the top of the page.*

Horizontal Rules

If you need to break up a long flow of text into more manageable chunks, you can use a horizontal rule. ("Rule" is another term for a line.)

<HR>
Horizontal rule

Horizontal rules are plopped on the page with the <HR> tag. When the browser sees the <HR> tag alone, it draws an "embossed" shaded line across the full available width of the page (Figure 8-12). Rules are block elements, so some space will be added above and below. This means you can't place a rule on the same line as text.

There are a number of attributes that allow you to create different effects with horizontal rules. Let's take a look.

SIZE=*number*
Rule thickness

This attribute specifies the thickness of the rule in pixels (Figure 8-13).

How Do I Make a Vertical Rule?

While adding a horizontal rule is easy with the <HR> tag, there is no similar tag for adding a vertical rule to a web page, unfortunately. However, there are a number of ways you can fake it using tables and graphics, as demonstrated in Chapter 17, Web Design Techniques.

Figure 8-12

```
<HR>
<B>SAUCE:</B><BR>
Cut prosciutto into 1/2" chunks and fry with chopped onion in olive oil
over low heat, until fat is rendered and meat is crisp. Remove meat and
set aside. Drain the tomatoes, finely chop them and add to the onion in
the pan. Season with red pepper flakes and salt and pepper. Simmer 20
minutes, stirring occasionally.<BR>

<HR>
<B>TO SERVE:</B><BR>
Cook pasta according to directions on package. Drain well.<BR>

Transfer sauce to large skillet over medium-high heat. Add the pasta and
reserved meat and cook for 30 seconds. Remove the skillet from heat. Add
cheese.
<HR>
```

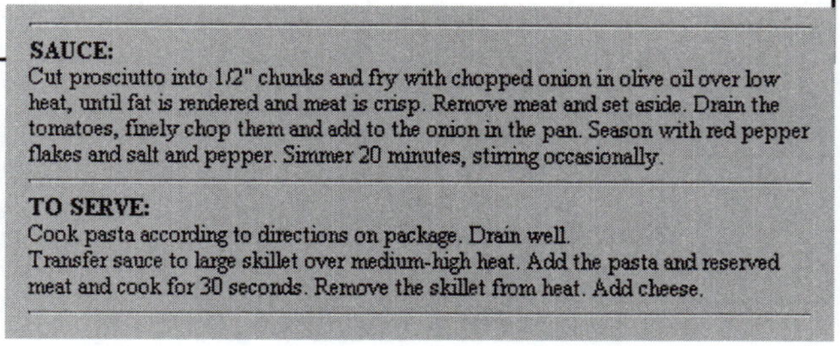

The default horizontal rule is a "beveled" line that fills the width of the browser window.

SAUCE:
Cut prosciutto into 1/2" chunks and fry with chopped onion in olive oil over low heat, until fat is rendered and meat is crisp. Remove meat and set aside. Drain the tomatoes, finely chop them and add to the onion in the pan. Season with red pepper flakes and salt and pepper. Simmer 20 minutes, stirring occasionally.

TO SERVE:
Cook pasta according to directions on package. Drain well.
Transfer sauce to large skillet over medium-high heat. Add the pasta and reserved meat and cook for 30 seconds. Remove the skillet from heat. Add cheese.

Figure 8-13

```
<P>12 pixels thick.</P>
<HR SIZE=12>
```

12 pixels thick.

The SIZE attribute affects the thickness of the rule.

Adding Graphic Elements

Figure 8-14

```
<P>100 pixels long:</P>
<HR WIDTH=100>
<P>
<P>50% of the width of the page:</P>
<HR WIDTH=50%>
```

Pixel value

Percent value

The WIDTH attribute affects the length of the rule.

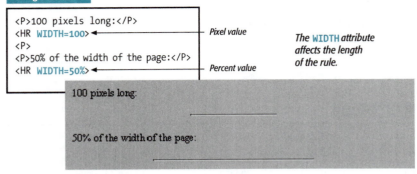

Figure 8-15

```
<P>100 pixel wide rule positioned on the right margin:</P>
<HR WIDTH=100 ALIGN=right>
```

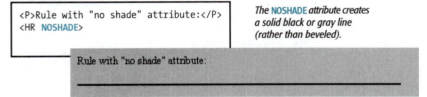

Use the ALIGN attribute to position the rule horizontally on the page.

Figure 8-16

```
<P>Rule with "no shade" attribute:</P>
<HR NOSHADE>
```

The NOSHADE attribute creates a solid black or gray line (rather than beveled).

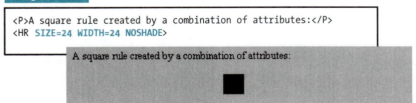

Figure 8-17

```
<P>A square rule created by a combination of attributes:</P>
<HR SIZE=24 WIDTH=24 NOSHADE>
```

A square rule created by a combination of attributes:

You can combine attributes to radically change the way a rule looks.

WIDTH=*number* or *%*
Rule width

WIDTH determines how long the rule should be (in other words, its width across the page). You can specify a pixel measurement, or a percentage of the available page width (Figure 8-14).

ALIGN=left, right, or center
Horizontal alignment

You can specify where you'd like the rule positioned across the page with this attribute (Figure 8-15). Rules are centered by default.

NOSHADE
Turns off shading

If you don't like the shaded bar effect, add this attribute to the <HR> tag to make the rule a solid line (Figure 8-16). This attribute is just an instruction; it doesn't take a value.

Remember that attributes can be used in combination in a single tag, so feel free to get creative. In the following example, the rule has been manipulated to form a small square centered on the page (Figure 8-17).

TOOL TIP

Adding Horizontal Rules

Here's how you add horizontal rules in three of the more popular authoring programs.

DREAMWEAVER 3

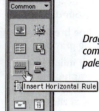

Drag the rule icon from the list of common elements on the Objects palette into place in your document.

GOLIVE 4

❶ *Drag the rule icon from the Palette window into place in your document.*

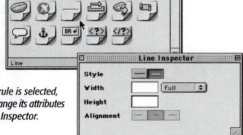

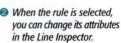

❷ *When the rule is selected, you can change its attributes in the Line Inspector.*

FRONTPAGE 2000

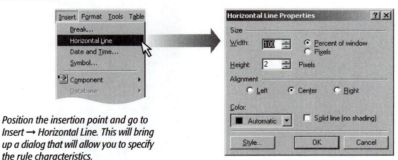

Position the insertion point and go to Insert → Horizontal Line. This will bring up a dialog that will allow you to specify the rule characteristics.

Adding Graphic Elements

HTML Review–Graphic Element Tags

The following is a summary of the tags we covered in this chapter.

Tag and Attributes	Function
`<BODY>`	Body of the document; can contain attributes that affect document appearance
`BACKGROUND="url"`	Tiling background graphic
`BGCOLOR="number"` or `"name"`	Background color
`<BR CLEAR=all>`	Inserts line break and starts next line below the graphic
`<IMG>`	Inserts an inline image
`SRC="url"`	The graphic file to use
`ALT="text"`	Alternative text
`WIDTH=number`	Width of the graphic
`HEIGHT=number`	Height of the graphic
`BORDER=number`	Thickness of border when graphic is linked
`ALIGN=left|right`	Horizontal alignment
`ALIGN=top|middle|bottom`	Vertical alignment
`HSPACE=number`	Space held to the left and right of a graphic
`VSPACE=number`	Space held above and below a graphic
`<HR>`	Inserts a horizontal rule (a line)
`SIZE=number`	Adjusts the thickness of the rule
`WIDTH=number`	Adjusts the length of the rule
`ALIGN=left|right|center`	Horizontal positioning
`NOSHADE`	Turns off 3-D bevel

Chapter 9

Adding Links

If you're creating a page for the Web, chances are you'll want it to point to other web pages, whether to another section of your own site or to someone else's. You can even link to another spot on the same page. Linking, after all, is what the Web is all about!

In this chapter, we'll look at the HTML that makes linking work: to other sites, to your own site, and within a page. In addition, we'll cover imagemaps, single images that contain a number of links.

If you've used the Web at all, you should be familiar with the highlighted text and graphics that indicate "click here." There is one tag that makes linking possible, the anchor tag (<A>). The anchor tag is a container tag; it has start and end tags that you wrap around a span of text.

To use it, just wrap the tag around the text you want linked, like this:

```
<A HREF="http://www.oreilly.com">Go to O'Reilly.com</A>
```

To make a graphic a link, simply place the anchor tag around the entire image tag, as shown here:

```
<A HREF="http://www.oreilly.com"><IMG SRC="ora.gif"></A>
```

IN THIS CHAPTER

Making links to external pages

Making relative links to documents on your own server

Linking within a page

Creating imagemaps

Adding "mailto" links

Anchor Tag Syntax

The simplified structure (or syntax) for the anchor tag is:

```
<A HREF=url>linked text or image</A>
```

Changing Link Colors

Tired of your links always being that default bright blue? Well, you can change them! Special attributes in the `<BODY>` tag assign colors for links for the whole document. In addition to ordinary links, you can specify the color of links that have already been clicked ("visited links") and the color that links appear while they are being clicked ("active links"):

`LINK="color name or number"`
Sets the link color (blue by default)

`VLINK="color name or number"`
Sets the color of visited links (purple by default)

`ALINK="color name or number"`
Sets the color of active links

Of course, you can use all of these attributes in a single `<BODY>` tag as follows:

```
<BODY LINK="aqua"
VLINK="teal" ALINK="red">
```

The system for specifying colors in HTML is covered in detail in Chapter 12, Color on the Web.

One word of caution, however: if you do choose to change your link colors, it is recommended that you keep them consistent throughout your site so as not to confuse your users. For a more thorough discussion, see the section Color Coding in Chapter 18, Building Usuable Web Sites.

When viewed in a browser, the marked text is blue and underlined (by default) and the linked graphic appears with a blue outline (unless you turn it off; see Chapter 8, Adding Graphic Elements). When a user clicks on the linked text or graphic, the page you specify in the anchor tag will load in the browser window. The code listed previously would look like Figure 9-1.

Figure 9-1

When a user clicks on the linked text or graphic, the page you specify in the anchor tag will load in the browser window.

The Anchor Tag Dissected

The anchor tag is an ordinary container tag with one attribute, so you should already have a good idea of how it works. Let's look at the parts of the tag.

`<A>...</A>`
Anchor tag

The anchor tag is a container tag that is placed around whatever text or graphic you'd like linked. Whatever is within the anchor tag will display as a link in the browser. By default, links appear as blue underlined text or as blue outlined graphics in most browsers.

`HREF=url`
The location of the linked file

You'll need to tell the browser which document to link to, right? HREF is the attribute that provides the URL of the page (its address) to the browser. It's unclear what "HREF" actually stands for (maybe hypertext reference). Most of the time you'll be pointing to other web pages; however, you can also point to other web resources, such as images and audio or video files.

The URL can be either absolute (with the protocol and complete path-name) or relative to the document currently displayed in the window. Absolute URLs are used when you are pointing to a document out on the Web. If you are pointing to another document on your own site (i.e., on your own server), you can use a relative URL and omit the *http://* proto-col. Both absolute and relative URLs are discussed in this chapter.

Since there's not much to slapping an anchor tag around some text, the real art of linking comes in getting the URL correct.

Linking to Pages on the Web

Many times, you'll want to create a link to a page that you've found on the Web. This is known as an "external" link because it is going to a page out-side of your own server or site.

To make an external link, you need to provide the complete URL (also called an absolute URL), beginning with the *http://* part (the protocol). This tells the browser, "Go out on the Web and get the following docu-ment." For more information on the parts of a URL, go back to our URL dissection example in Chapter 2, How the Web Works.

Use the complete URL (including "http://") when linking to pages on the Web.

I've added some external links to popular cooking sites to the bottom of my cooking home page (Figure 9-2).

Figure 9-2

To make a link, wrap the anchor tag `<A>` *around the text or graphic you want to link. The* `HREF` *attribute tells the browser which file to link to.*

When linking to a page out on the Web, use the absolute URL (including the HTTP protocol) in the anchor tag.

```
<P><IMG SRC="graphics/outthere.gif"></P>
<P><FONT FACE="Trebuchet MS, Arial, sans-serif">

<A HREF="http://www.foodtv.com">The Food Network</A><BR>

<A HREF="http://www.epicurious.com">Epicurious</A></BR>
```

In the browser, the links appear as blue underlined text.

GOOD STUFF "OUT THERE"

The Food Network
Epicurious

Adding Links

Sometimes, when the page you're linking to has a long URL pathname, the link can end up looking pretty confusing (Figure 9-3). Just keep in mind that the structure is still a simple container tag with one attribute. Don't let the pathname intimidate you.

TIP

If you are linking to a page with a long URL, it is useful to copy the URL from the location toolbar in your browser and paste it into your HTML document. That way, you avoid mistyping a single character and breaking the whole link.

Figure 9-3

An example of a long URL. Although it may make the anchor tag look confusing, the structure is the same.

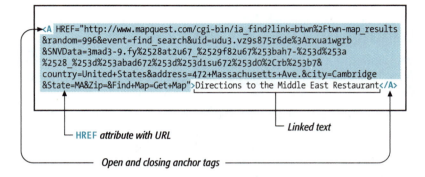

```
<A HREF="http://www.mapquest.com/cgi-bin/ia_find?link=btwn%2Ftwn-map_results
&random=996&event=find_search&uid=udu3.vz9s875r6de%3Arxua1wgrb
&SNVData=3mad3-9.fy%2528at2u67_%2529f82u67%253bah7-%253d%253a
%2528_%253d%253abad672%253d%253d1su672%253d0%2Crb%253b7&
country=United+States&address=472+Massachusetts+Ave.&city=Cambridge
&State=MA&Zip=&Find+Map=Get+Map">Directions to the Middle East Restaurant</A>
```

        HREF *attribute with URL*   *Linked text*

                    Open and closing anchor tags

Linking Within Your Own Site

The <IMG> Tag and Relative URLs

The SRC attribute in the <IMG> tag works the same as the HREF attribute in anchors when it comes to specifying URLs. Since you'll most likely be using graphics files from your own server, the SRC attributes within your image tags will be set to relative URLs. All of the rules and guidelines for writing pathnames described here apply to pointing to graphic files as well.

A large portion of the linking you'll do will be between pages of your own site: from the home page to section pages, from section pages to content pages, and so on. In these cases, you can provide a relative URL—one that calls for a page on your own server, relative to the page that is currently displayed in the browser.

For relative links, you can omit the *http://*. Without it, the browser starts looking on the current server for the linked document. But you have to tell the browser which directory the document is in by providing the pathname. A pathname is the notation used to point to a particular file or directory. It follows the Unix convention of separating directory and filenames with forward slashes / .

Starting with the current document, you need to describe the path to the target document. This is where relative URLs get a little bit tricky. We'll go through a few examples to show you how they work.

Linking Within a Directory

The simplest relative link is to another file within the same directory. (Macintosh users, you are probably accustomed to thinking in terms of "folders," but for purposes of the Web, you'll need to shift your thinking slightly to the directory model.)

When you are linking to a file in the same directory, you only need to provide the name of the file (its filename). Without any path information, the browser will assume that the file is in the same directory as the current document.

In my example, I want to make a link from my home page (*index.html*) to a general information page (*information.html*). Currently, both files are in the same directory, called *jenskitchen*. So from my home page, I can make a link to the information page by simply providing its filename in the URL (Figure 9-4):

```
<A HREF="information.html">About this Site</A>
```

A link to just the filename indicates the file is in the current directory.

Figure 9-4

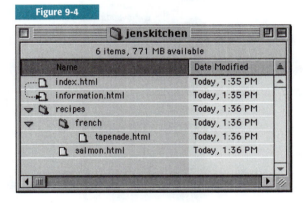

*The desktop view and the illustration show that **index.html** and **information.html** are in the same directory.*

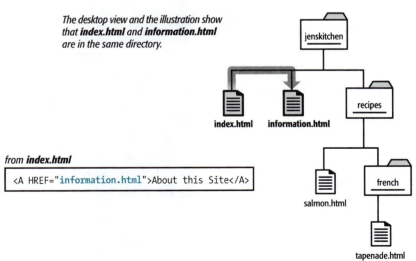

from ***index.html***

```
<A HREF="information.html">About this Site</A>
```

Adding Links

Linking to a Lower Directory

But what if the files aren't in the same directory? You have to give the browser directions by including the pathname in the URL. Let's see how this works.

Getting back to our example, my recipe files are stored in a subdirectory called *recipes*. I want to make a link from *index.html* to a file in that directory called *salmon.html*. I first must tell the browser to look in the subdirectory called *recipes*, and then look for the file *salmon.html* (Figure 9-5):

```
<A HREF="recipes/salmon.html">garlic salmon</A>
```

When linking to a file in a lower directory, the pathname must contain the names of the subdirectories you go through to get to the file.

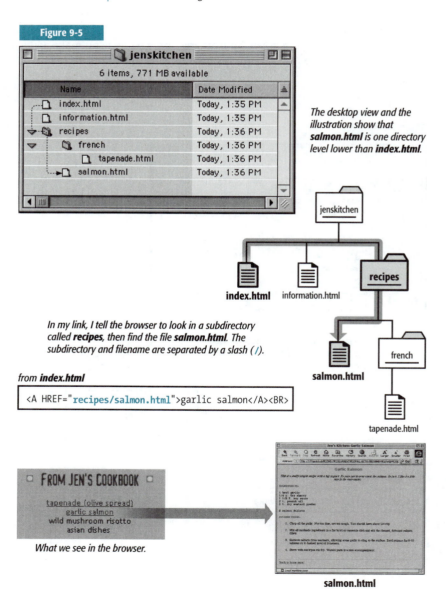

Figure 9-5

*The desktop view and the illustration show that **salmon.html** is one directory level lower than **index.html**.*

*In my link, I tell the browser to look in a subdirectory called **recipes**, then find the file **salmon.html**. The subdirectory and filename are separated by a slash (/).*

from **index.html**

```
<A HREF="recipes/salmon.html">garlic salmon</A><BR>
```

What we see in the browser.

salmon.html

Now let's link down one more directory level to the file called *tapenade.html*, which is located in the *french* subdirectory. All we need to do is provide the directions through two subdirectories, *recipes* and *french*, to our file (Figure 9-6):

```
<A HREF="recipes/french/tapenade.html">tapenade (olive spread)</A>
```

The resulting anchor tag is telling the browser, "Look in the current directory for a directory called *recipes*. There you'll find another directory called *french*, and in there is the file I'd like to link to, *tapenade.html*."

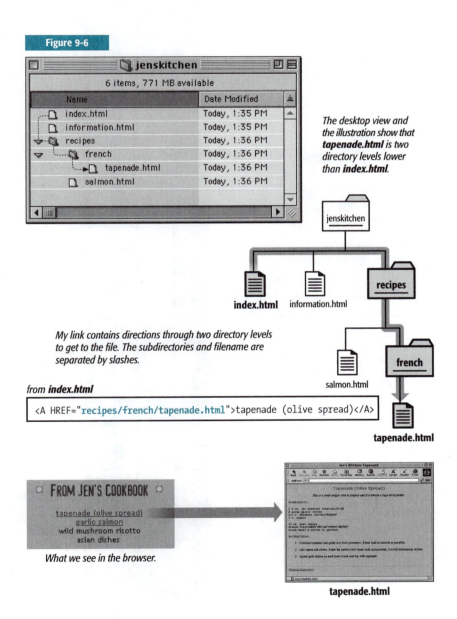

Figure 9-6

The desktop view and the illustration show that **tapenade.html** *is two directory levels lower than* **index.html**.

My link contains directions through two directory levels to get to the file. The subdirectories and filename are separated by slashes.

from **index.html**

```
<A HREF="recipes/french/tapenade.html">tapenade (olive spread)</A>
```

What we see in the browser.

Linking to a Higher Directory

We've seen how to write a pathname to a file in a directory that is lower in the hierarchy than the current file. Now let's go in the other direction—from the recipe page back to the home page, which is on a higher level.

In Unix, there is a pathname convention just for this purpose, the "dot-dot-slash" (../). When you begin a pathname with a ../ it's the same as telling the browser "go up a level" and then follow the path to the specified file.

Each ../ at the beginning of the pathname tells the browser to go up one directory level to look for the file.

Let's start by making a link back to the home page (*index.html*) from *salmon.html*. In order to do that, we need to link to a file that's one directory level higher than the current document. In the pathname, we need to tell the browser to "go up one level" then look for a file called *index.html* (Figure 9-7):

```
<A HREF="../index.html">[back to home page]</A>
```

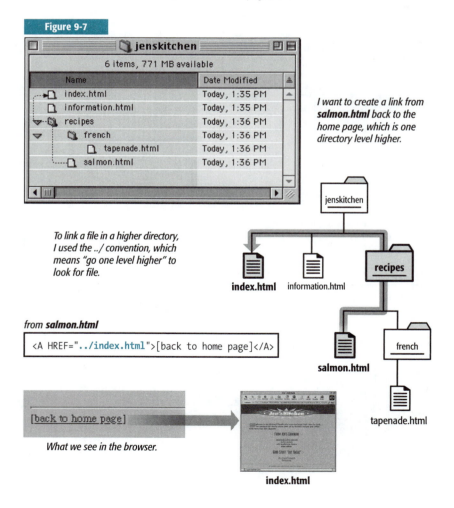

Figure 9-7

I want to create a link from **salmon.html** *back to the home page, which is one directory level higher.*

To link a file in a higher directory, I used the ../ convention, which means "go one level higher" to look for file.

from **salmon.html**

```
<A HREF="../index.html">[back to home page]</A>
```

What we see in the browser.

index.html

But how about linking back to the home page from *tapenade.html*? Can you guess how you'd back your way out of two directory levels? Simple, just use the dot-dot-slash twice (Figure 9-8)!

I confess to still sometimes silently chanting "go-up-a-level, go-up-a-level" for each ../ when trying to decipher a complicated relative URL. It helps me sort things out.

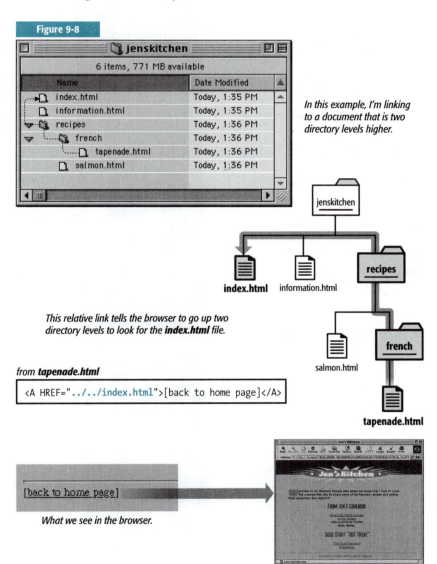

Figure 9-8

In this example, I'm linking to a document that is two directory levels higher.

*This relative link tells the browser to go up two directory levels to look for the **index.html** file.*

from **tapenade.html**

```
<A HREF="../../index.html">[back to home page]</A>
```

[back to home page]

What we see in the browser.

index.html

The Root Directory

The "root" directory refers to the top directory level of the server. If you keep files in the first directory level of your hard drive, you are keeping those files in your computer's root directory.

The root directory is indicated with a slash at the beginning of the pathname. When the browser sees a pathname that starts with a slash, it goes to the very top level of the server and begins working its way through directories and subdirectories from there. If you are getting confused with relative directories, you can always start from the top level and point to the file from there.

The pathname to the *tapenade.html* file in our sample, starting at the root directory, might look like this:

/jenskitchen/recipes/french/
tapenade.html

The first slash is the giveaway!

Adding Links

Most web-authoring tools will write the relative pathnames for you when you use the "browse" or drag-and-drop function for linking documents on your site.

Don't Worry!

The good news is that if you use a WYSIWYG authoring tool to create your site, the tool can take care of generating the relative URLs for you. Be sure to use one of the automated link tools (such as the Browse button, or a drag-and-drop function) to make links between pages of your site and to place graphics. The tool should handle the rest. Some, like Macromedia Dreamweaver and Adobe GoLive, have built-in site management functions that will adjust your relative URLs if you reorganize the directory structure.

But if you anticipate writing lots of HTML by hand, you'll need to know your way around relative pathnames and other Unix conventions. There is a summary of Unix server functions and operating commands in *Web Design in a Nutshell* (O'Reilly, 1999), and if you want to go even deeper, try *Unix in a Nutshell* by Arnold Robbins (O'Reilly, 1999).

Putting It Together–Making Links

If you want to try your hand at relative URLs, try this little pathname puzzler!

We're starting with a file called *index.html* which is located in the *three* directory on a server with this directory structure:

```
/one/two/three/four/five
```

We want to create a link to a file called *a.html*. The pathname to that file is going to depend on which directory the file is in. Your challenge is to write out the pathnames to *a.html*, when it is located in various directories on the server. Remember, you're starting in the *three* directory. I've started you out with the easy one!

	If a.html is in this directory	The pathname will be:
a.	*three*	HREF="a.html"
b.	*two*	HREF=
c.	*one*	HREF=
d.	*four*	HREF=
e	*five*	HREF=

[Answers: b: ../a.html c: ../../a.html d: four/a.html e. four/five/a.html]

TOOL TIPS

Adding Links

Here's how you add links to a page in three of the more popular authoring programs.

DREAMWEAVER 3

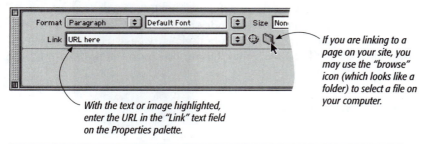

If you are linking to a page on your site, you may use the "browse" icon (which looks like a folder) to select a file on your computer.

With the text or image highlighted, enter the URL in the "Link" text field on the Properties palette.

GOLIVE 4

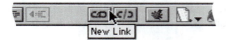

To add a link, click the "New Link" button on the toolbar while your text or image is selected. Then enter the URL in the Link palette of the Text Inspector. You can type in a complete URL or browse from files on the desktop. You can also use the "Point and Shoot" button to point to a file in the Site window.

FRONTPAGE 2000

Selected text can be linked from the toolbar, using Insert → Hyperlink. The URL can be typed or the file, if local, can be selected from the Finder.

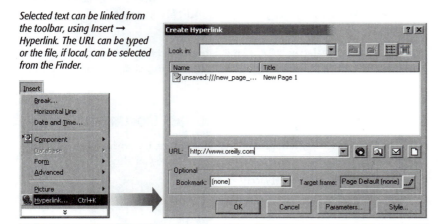

Adding Links

Linking Within a Page

Did you know you can link to a specific point in a web page? This is a useful trick for providing shortcuts to information at the bottom of a long scrolling page, or for getting back to the top of a page with just one click.

Linking to another spot on the same page works well for long scrolling pages, but the effect may be lost on a short web page.

Linking to a fragment within a page is a two-part process. First you need to give the fragment a name, and then you make a link to it. In my example, I'm creating an alphabetical index at the top of the page that links down to each alphabetical section of my glossary page (Figure 9-9). When users click on the letter "C", they'll jump down on the page to the first term starting with C.

Step 1: Naming a Fragment

`<A NAME="`*text*`">`
Named anchor

The anchor tag (`<A>`) with the NAME attribute is used to give a section of the page a name that can be referenced elsewhere. It's like putting a marker or a flag in the file so you can get back to it easily.

❶ I've added a named anchor at "CGI" (my first term starting with C), and I've given it the name "startC".

Step 2: Linking to a Fragment

`<A HREF="#`*text*`">`
Link to a fragment (a "named anchor")

Next, at the top of the page, I'll create a link down to the named anchor. The link is an ordinary link (using the HREF attribute), only it includes a hash (#) symbol before the name to indicate that we're linking to a fragment.

❷ I've linked the letter "C" in my alphabetical index to the fragment labeled "startC". And we're done! Now, if you click on the C, you are transported to the first C term.

Linking to a Fragment in Another Document

You can link to a fragment in another document by adding the fragment name to the end of the URL (absolute or relative) as shown here:

```
<A HREF="http://www.oreilly.com/niederst.html#fragment">
```

```
<A HREF="content/glossary.html#fragment">
```

Figure 9-9

❶ *Add the named anchor.*

```
<DT><A NAME="startC">CGI</A>
<DD>Common Gateway Interface; the mechanism for communication between the
web server and other programs (CGI scripts) running on the server.
<P>
<DT>character entities
<DD>Strings of characters used to specify characters not found in the
normal alphanumeric character set in HTML documents.
<P>
<DT>character set
<DD>An organization of characters (units of a written language system)
in which each character is assigned a specific number.
```

❷ *Create a link to the anchor.*

```
<HTML>
<HEAD>
        <TITLE>Named Anchor</TITLE>
</HEAD>
<BODY>

<PRE>A B <A HREF="#startC">C</A> D E F G H I J K L M N O P Q R S T U V W
X Y Z</PRE>
```

When you click on the link, it drops you down lower on the page to the position of the named anchor.

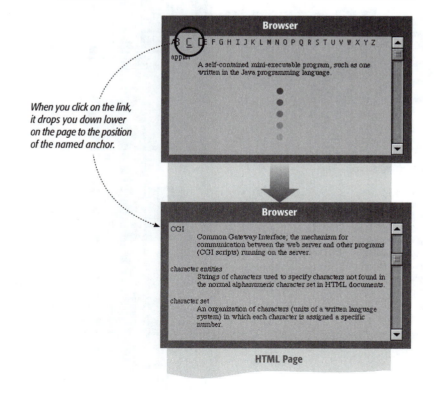

Adding Links

TOOL TIPS

Adding Named Anchors

Here's how you add named anchors to a page in three of the more popular authoring programs.

DREAMWEAVER 3

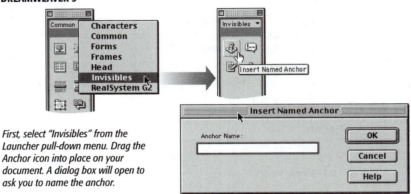

First, select "Invisibles" from the Launcher pull-down menu. Drag the Anchor icon into place on your document. A dialog box will open to ask you to name the anchor.

GOLIVE 4

Drag the Anchor object icon from the Palette into place in the document window. With the anchor selected, enter the name in the Anchor Inspector.

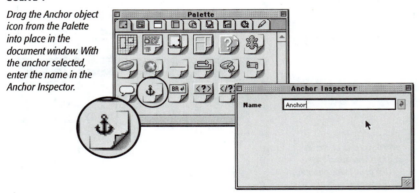

FRONTPAGE 2000

An "Anchor" (bookmark), can be added to the page with Insert → Bookmark. The dialog box will prompt you for a unique name.

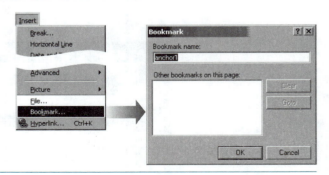

Several Links in One Graphic (Imagemaps)

In your web travels, I'm sure you've run across a single graphic that has multiple "hot spots," or links, within it. These graphics are called imagemaps.

Putting the links in one graphic has nothing to do with the graphic itself; it's just an ordinary graphic. Rather, the graphic serves as a frontend to the mechanisms that match a particular mouse-click to a URL.

The real work is done by a map that contains sets of pixel coordinates and their respective link information. When the user clicks somewhere within the image, the browser passes the pixel coordinates of the pointer to the map, which, in turn, generates the appropriate link.

We'll be focusing on client-side imagemaps in our example, which puts the map directly in the HTML file. The mouse-clicks and URLs are matched up by the browser on the user's machine (thus, client-side). See the sidebar The Other Imagemap for more information on server-side imagemaps.

Client-side imagemaps have three components:

- An ordinary graphic file (*.gif*, *.jpg* or *.jpeg*, or *.png*)

- The USEMAP attribute within that graphic's `<IMG>` tag, which identifies which map to use

- A map file (identified with the `<MAP>` tag) located within the HTML document

An imagemap is a single graphic file that contains a number of links, or hot spots.

The Other Imagemap

Before there were client-side imagemaps, all imagemaps were server-side. There are a few significant differences.

For server-side imagemaps, the map is a separate file (named with the *.map* suffix) that lives on the server. It relies on a special program (called a CGI script) to interpret the *.map* file and send the correct URL back to the browser. All of the processing for matching coordinates takes place on the server. The whole graphic gets linked to the *.map* file via a regular anchor tag, as shown here:

```
<A HREF="/cgi-bin/veggie.map"><IMG SRC="veggie.gif" ISMAP></A>
```

The other thing to note is that the `<IMG>` tag uses the simple ISMAP attribute to indicate it is an imagemap.

The advantage to server-side imagemaps is that they are universally supported (client-side imagemaps aren't supported in Netscape Navigator 1.0 and Internet Explorer 2.0), but they are trickier to use. Because they are so dependent on the configuration of the server, you need to coordinate with your server administrator if you plan on implementing them. They also add extra work for your server.

Creating the Map

Fortunately, there are tools that generate maps so you don't have to write out the map by hand. You can download shareware imagemap programs (see the sidebar Imagemap Tools). Also, you will find that nearly all web-authoring tools have imagemap generators built in. Regardless of the tool you use, the process for creating the map is essentially the same and follows these steps:

1. Place the graphic on the page (or open it in an imagemap program).

2. Define areas that will be "clickable" by using the appropriate shape tools: rectangle, circle, or polygon (for tracing irregular shapes).

3. While the shape is still highlighted, enter a URL for that area in the text entry field provided.

4. Continue adding shapes and their respective URLs for each clickable area in the image.

5. Select the type of imagemap you want to create (we're focusing on client-side in this example). If you choose server-side, you will also have to define a default URL, which is the page that will display if users click outside one of the defined areas.

6. Give the map a name and add the map to the HTML file. Web-authoring tools will insert the map automatically.

7. Save the HTML document and open it in your browser.

Figure 9-10 demonstrates how a map is created using Macromedia Dreamweaver 3.

Imagemap Tools

There are many imagemap-creation tools available as shareware and freeware for both Windows machines and Macs. You can do a search for "imagemap" at CNET's Download.com (*www.download.com*), or try one of these popular programs:

Windows

MapEdit by Tom Boutell, available at *www.boutell.com/mapedit/*.

Mac

MapMaker 1.1.2 by Frederic Eriksson, available at *www.kickinit.com/mapmaker/*.

Figure 9-10

I start with my graphic placed on the web page document. (If you are using an imagemap tool, simply open the graphic file.)

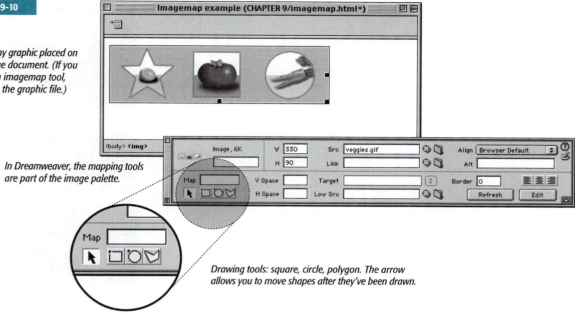

In Dreamweaver, the mapping tools are part of the image palette.

Drawing tools: square, circle, polygon. The arrow allows you to move shapes after they've been drawn.

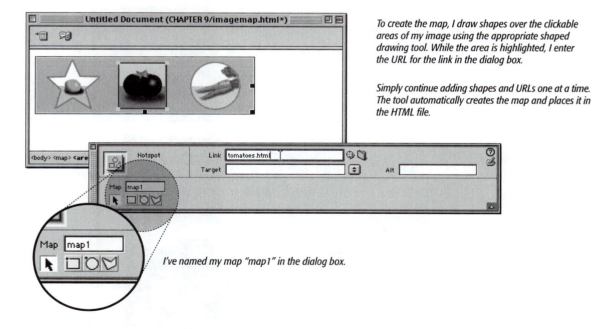

To create the map, I draw shapes over the clickable areas of my image using the appropriate shaped drawing tool. While the area is highlighted, I enter the URL for the link in the dialog box.

Simply continue adding shapes and URLs one at a time. The tool automatically creates the map and places it in the HTML file.

I've named my map "map1" in the dialog box.

Adding Links

Now let's look at the map file Dreamweaver generated (Figure 9-11):

❶ The <IMG> tag now sports the USEMAP attribute, which tells the browser which map to use. You could include several imagemapped graphics and their respective map files in a single HTML document.

❷ This marks the beginning of the map. The map is named map1, as I entered it in the dialog box. Within the <MAP> tag there are <AREA> tags for each hot spot in the image.

❸ Each <AREA> tag contains the shape identifier (SHAPE), pixel coordinates (COORDS), and the URL for the link (HREF). In this map there are three areas corresponding to the square, circle, and polygon that I drew over my image.

Figure 9-11

```
<html>
<head>
<title>Imagemap example</title>
</head>

<body bgcolor="#FFFFFF">
<img src="veggies.gif" width="330" height="90" border="0" usemap="#map1">

<map name="map1">
<area shape="rect" coords="125,8,199,82" href="tomatoes.html">
<area shape="circle" coords="271,46,37" href="carrots.html">
<area shape="poly"
coords="55,5,66,32,96,32,74,54,82,81,54,66,28,81,38,50,18,31,46,33"
href="peas.html">

</map>

</body>
</html>
```

In the browser, each spot will link to the file I've specified (Figure 9-12). The cursor will change when it passes over each hot spot to indicate that it is a link and the URL will appear in the status bar.

Figure 9-12

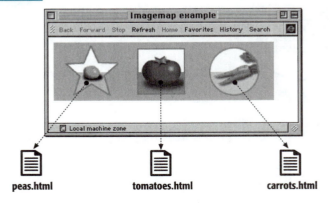

Mail Links

Here's a nifty little linking trick: the "mailto" link. By using the *mailto* protocol in a link, you can link to an email address. When you click on a "mailto" link, the browser opens a new mail message in a designated mail program. The browser has to be configured to launch a mail program, so the effect won't work for 100% of your audience, but it reaches enough people to be a worthwhile shortcut.

Figure 9-13 shows the structure of a "mailto" link and what happens when you click on it in a browser.

TIP

If you use the email address itself as the linked text, nobody will be left out if the "mailto" function does not work.

Figure 9-13

Use the standard anchor tag to create the link.

`<A HREF="mailto:aklecker@hotmail.com">Contact Al Klecker.</A>`

Set the URL value to `mailto` *followed by the email address.*

When you click on a mailto *link, many browsers will open a new outgoing message addressed to the specified email address. The browser needs to be configured with a helper email program for the* mailto *protocol.*

WARNING

Spam-bots

Be aware that by putting an email address on a page you will make it susceptible to receiving unsolicited junk email (known as spam). People who generate spam lists sometimes use automated search programs (called bots) to scour the Web for email addresses. So, if you don't want to risk getting spammed, keep your email address off your web page.

Adding Links

HTML Review—Link Tags

The following is a summary of the tags covered in this chapter.

Tag and Attributes	Function
`<A>`	Anchor tag
`HREF="url"`	Location of the target file
`NAME="text"`	Name for the location in the page
`<MAP>`	Map information for an imagemap
`NAME="text"`	Name for the map
`<AREA>`	Link information in an imagemap
`SHAPE=rect|circle|poly`	Shape of the linked area
`COORDS="numbers"`	Pixel coordinates for the linked area
`HREF="url"`	Target file for the link

Chapter 10

Tables

Tables are the web designer's best friend and worst enemy. While they offer much welcomed control over text alignment and page layout, the HTML code behind them is not especially intuitive and is prone to going haywire.

You'll be much better off relying on a web-authoring tool to create tables rather than writing them out by hand (although it's not *that* difficult, once you get used to it). Web tools, such as Macromedia Dreamweaver and Adobe GoLive, have built-in tricks that anticipate some common table problems, and they'll save you a lot of time. However, even with the tools, it's beneficial to understand how tables work, and to be familiar with table terminology.

In this chapter, I'll give you a thorough introduction to tables, how they're made, how to plan and design them, the specific tags that control them, and how they tend to go wrong.

How Tables Are Used

Although originally intended for the display of rows and columns of data, tables were quickly coopted to serve many purposes. In each of the examples below, the table border has been turned on to reveal the structure of the table and its cells. With the borders turned off, these pages would be seamless and clean. Some uses for tables include:

For data display. Ah, the beauty of the table used as it was originally intended—rows and columns full of data (Figure 10-1). Very tidy and useful.

For better text alignment. As we saw in Chapter 7, Text Formatting, HTML alone offers little control over how text is aligned (you can't even indent). Putting text in tables allows you to format indents and columns and add whitespace to a page (Figure 10-2).

For overall page structure. One common use of tables is to divide a page into major sections. In this example, the column on the left is for navigational items and the main column is for content (Figure 10-3).

For holding together a multipart (sliced) image. Tables can be used to hold together an image that has been divided up to accommodate animations, rollovers, etc. (Figure 10-4). The best way to create these tables is to use a web image program such as Macromedia Fireworks or Adobe ImageReady. With the tool, you just drag guides where you want the image to be sliced, and the tool divides up the image and writes all the code for the table.

Figure 10-1

Values That Make Up the Web Palette		
Decimal	**Hexadecimal**	**Percentage**
0	00	0%
51	33	20%
102	66	40%
153	99	60%
204	CC	80%
255	FF	100%

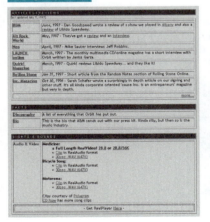

Figure 10-2

Figure 10-3

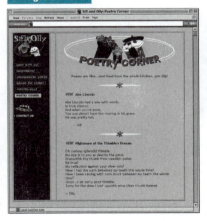

Figure 10-4

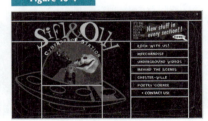

How Tables Work

Let's take a look at a simple table to see what it's made of. At their most basic, tables are made up of cells, arranged into rows and columns (Figure 10-5).

Tables are made up of cells, arranged into rows and columns

Figure 10-5

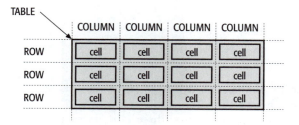

Tables are divided into rows and columns. Cells are the containers for content.

Simple enough, right? Let's look at how the table elements translate into HTML.

It's a Cell Thing

As shown in Figure 10-6, there are tags that identify the table (<TABLE>), rows (<TR>), and cells (<TD>, for "table data"). Cells are the heart of the table, since that's where the actual content goes. The other tags hold things together.

Figure 10-6

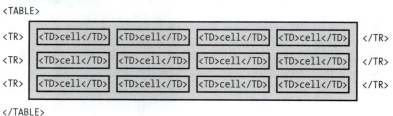

The <TABLE> tag identifies the beginning and end of the table.

Rows are created with <TR> (table row) tags.

Cells are created with table data (<TD>) tags placed within each row.

What we don't see are tags for columns. The number of columns in a table is determined by the number of table cells in each row. This is one of the things that make HTML tables tricky to deal with. Rows are easy—if you want the table to have three rows, just use three <TR> tags. Columns are different. For a table with four columns, you need to make sure that every row has four sets of <TD> tags; the columns are implied.

Tables

Following is the source code for another table as it might appear in an HTML document. Can you tell how many rows and columns it will have when it is displayed in a browser?

```
<TABLE>
<TR>
   <TD>Elliott Smith</TD>
   <TD>Supergrass</TD>
   <TD>Wheat</TD>
</TR>
<TR>
   <TD>Cat Power</TD>
   <TD>The Magnetic Fields</TD>
   <TD>Orbit</TD>
</TR>
</TABLE>
```

TIP

Be sure to close your table tags! Some browsers will not display the table at all if the end tag (`</TABLE>`) is missing.

If you guessed that it's a table with two rows and three columns, you're right! It's a stripped-down version of the table in Figure 10-22 later in the chapter. Two `<TR>` tags create two rows; three `<TD>`s in each row create three columns.

Remember all content for a table must go in cells; that is, within `<TD>` tags. You can put any HTML content in a cell: text, a graphic, even another table. `<TABLE>` tags are used to set the beginning and end of the table. The only thing that can go between `<TR>` tags is some number of `<TD>`s.

Spanning Cells

One fundamental feature of tables is cell spanning, the stretching of a cell to cover several rows or columns (Figure 10-7). Row spanning is when a cell is stretched downward to span across several rows. Column spanning is when a cell is stretched to the right to span over subsequent columns. They are controlled by the attributes ROWSPAN and COLSPAN, respectively.

The ability to span cells gives you more flexibility when designing tables; however, they can also make things a little more difficult to keep track of. The table we'll be working with in the next section (previewed in the sidebar The Finished Product) is an excellent example of column spans at work.

Figure 10-7

When a cell's "rowspan" is set to three, the cell extends down to span three rows.

When a cell's "colspan" is set to three, the cell extends to the right to span three columns.

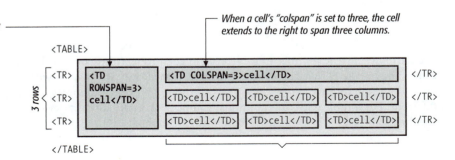

Table and Cell Controls

In addition to forming the overall structure of the table, the table and cell tags have attributes that you can use to adjust the formatting and appearance of the table.

At the table level (using the `<TABLE>` tag), you can specify the width and height of the whole table, the space between the cells (called cell spacing), the space within each cell (cell padding), the background color, and the border thickness for the table.

At the cell level (in the `<TD>` tag), there are attributes for controlling the width of the column, the height of the row, the background color of the cell, and the alignment of the elements within the cell.

We will discuss all of these attributes in detail later in this chapter. For now, I want to give you a flavor of the table design process.

The difficult part of writing code for tables is remembering which elements you control at the table level and which you control at the cell level.

Designing Tables

When it comes to creating tables, particularly complicated ones, I highly recommend WYSIWYG web-authoring tools over writing out the HTML by hand. (I'll show both ways in this demo.) With web-authoring software, you fill out the dialog boxes, and the tool keeps track of the code.

But even with a good tool, designing tables requires some planning and strategy. Of course, every designer has his or her own approach, but the process I'll outline covers some of the key issues you'll face. Again, don't worry about the specific tags; it's the process that's important.

We'll start with good old pencil and paper.

The Finished Product G

The table demonstration in this section walks you through the creation of the order form on the Sifl & Olly web site (designed by yours truly). You can see the final working page online at *www.sifl-n-olly.com/merch*, and a color version in this book's gallery.

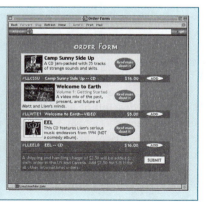

Tables

Step One: Sketch It!

One key in preventing being overwhelmed with an avalanche of <TR>s and <TD>s is to plan your table in advance. Even if you are using a web-authoring program, you'll need to know how many rows and columns your table has, and sometimes that's not evident, especially if there are overlapping spanned cells.

I start with a sketch of the page I want to make. I often use Photoshop to make a mock-up of a page; however, this time I'm using pencil and paper to sketch out my page quickly.

In this example, I'm designing an order form (the completed form is shown in the sidebar "The Finished Product" on the previous page). I've sketched out the basic structure of the page and the information I need to include with each entry (Figure 10-8).

Figure 10-8

A rough sketch of the merchandise interface that will be held together with a fairly complex table.

Step Two: Find the Grid

Next, I'll draw a grid over the sketch, making sure there is a line at each significant division of information. I find it easiest to start by drawing the lines between every row. Then I go back and drag my ruler across the page, drawing a vertical line at every point where there should be a column break in any of the rows.

This exercise reveals the total number of rows and columns in the table (Figure 10-9). It is also a good opportunity to assign pixel measurements to the columns and rows if you intend to restrict the size of the table. In this case, I want to control the column widths, but I'm allowing the heights of the rows to resize automatically.

Step Three: Plan the Spans

Once I have my master grid, I start knocking out cells with row and column spans until the grid resembles the structure of my sketch (Figure 10-10). This step could be done in a web-authoring tool as well, but I find it useful to draw shaded boxes on the sketch itself (either on paper or with guides and layers in Photoshop).

TIP

Table Getting Too Complicated?

If your table is looking totally out of control with tiny rows and columns and a bizillion spans, consider breaking some of the information out into smaller, more controllable tables. Those tables can be nested inside the cells of a larger, simpler table that provides the overall table structure.

Figure 10-9

I draw a grid over my sketch to figure out the total number of rows and columns. (Believe me. It's not always evident just by looking, especially if there are a lot of spanned cells.)

This is also a good time to plan the dimensions of the table and each row and column. In the example I'm going to let the table and row heights size automatically, but I want to constrain the widths.

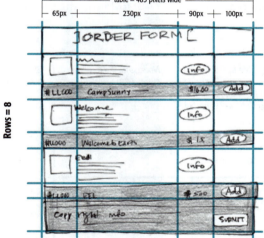

Figure 10-10

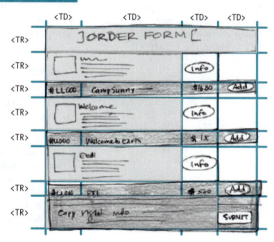

Blocking out the main areas of the table helps me plan the row spans and column spans (although there are no row spans in this example).

Tables

Use Comments to Label Your Document

The code for tables can get complicated, particularly for complex tables or tables nested within other tables.

This is a good opportunity to use comment tags to leave notes for yourself in the document. Anything you put between comment tags (`<!-- -->`) will not show in the browser and it will not have any effect on the rest of the HTML page.

For instance, if you have a table holding your navigation system together, you might insert the following comments to make it easier to find in the HTML source code:

```
<!-- Start nav. table -->
<TABLE>
...
</TABLE>
<!-- end nav. table -->
```

Step Four: Start Building

When all the planning is done, building the table should be a breeze. You can write out the HTML by hand (it wouldn't hurt to try a few to get a feel for it), or get some help from a web-authoring tool such as Macromedia Dreamweaver. Let's start by doing it the hard way.

Creating the structure in HTML

There are many ways to approach table construction in HTML, depending on the complexity of the table and your style of working. I'm going to build the table framework first (working from my grid layout). I usually design with the border turned on (`BORDER=1`) so I can see if the table is structured the way I want it. Once the table is working properly, I turn the border off and add all the content.

I find it useful to write in the row and cell tags right on my sketch. This helps me get the right number of `<TD>`s in each row and set the spans correctly. Using that marked-up sketch as a map, it's simple to write out the actual HTML file (Figure 10-11).

I've also inserted the column widths in one of the rows (one row is enough to set the widths for the whole table) and specified varying colors to set apart certain cells and rows. (Don't worry if the color values look strange—I will discuss colors in Chapter 12, Color on the Web.)

Figure 10-11

I am writing the HTML for my table by hand. I use my grid to fill in every `<TR>` and `<TD>`. The grid makes it easy to keep track of the final number of cells in each row after some cells have expanded.

Notice that the total of cells (`<TD>`s) and column spans (`COLSPAN`) equals 4 in every row.

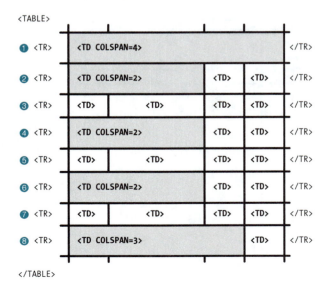

Figure 10-11 (cont.)

This is the HTML structure for the table in my sketch. You can compare the resulting tags with the sketch row-by-row. You will also notice that I've added tag attributes for column widths (WIDTH) and background colors (BGCOLOR).

```
<TABLE CELLPADDING=6 CELLSPACING=0 BGCOLOR="#0099CC" WIDTH="485">
❶  <TR>
        <TD COLSPAN=4 > </TD>
    </TR>
❷  <TR>
        <TD COLSPAN=2 BGCOLOR="#CCFFFF"> </TD>
        <TD BGCOLOR="#CCFFFF"> </TD>
        <TD> </TD>
    </TR>
❸  <TR BGCOLOR="#0066CC">
        <TD WIDTH=65> </TD>
        <TD WIDTH=230> </TD>
        <TD WIDTH=90> </TD>
        <TD WIDTH=100> </TD>
    </TR>
❹  <TR>
        <TD COLSPAN=2 BGCOLOR="#CCFFFF"> </TD>
        <TD BGCOLOR="#CCFFFF"> </TD>
        <TD> </TD>
    </TR>
❺  <TR BGCOLOR="#0066CC">
        <TD> </TD>
        <TD> </TD>
        <TD> </TD>
        <TD> </TD>
    </TR>
❻  <TR>
        <TD COLSPAN=2 BGCOLOR="#CCFFFF"> </TD>
        <TD BGCOLOR="#CCFFFF"> </TD>
        <TD> </TD>
    </TR>
❼  <TR BGCOLOR="#0066CC">
        <TD> </TD>
        <TD> </TD>
        <TD> </TD>
        <TD> </TD>
    </TR>
❽  <TR BGCOLOR="#0066CC">
        <TD COLSPAN=3 > </TD>
        <TD> </TD>
    </TR>
    </TABLE>
```

Put content in the cells

Now that the table structure is established, I can write in the content for each cell. Because the final file is quite lengthy, I'll show just a portion of it here, as well as a shot of the table as it's viewed in a browser (Figure 10-12). In reality, I had many trips to the browser to check my progress as I went along, making tweaks to the HTML code and viewing it again until I got something I liked.

Figure 10-12

```
<HTML>
<HEAD>
    <TITLE>Order Form</TITLE>
</HEAD>
<BODY BGCOLOR="#0099CC">

<CENTER>

<TABLE WIDTH=485 CELLPADDING=5 CELLSPACING=0 BGCOLOR="#0099CC">
<TR>
    <TD COLSPAN=4 ALIGN=center><IMG SRC="orderform.gif"></TD>
</TR>

<TR>
    <TD COLSPAN=2 BGCOLOR="#CCFFFF"><IMG SRC="camp.gif" ALIGN=left HSPACE=5>
<FONT SIZE=+1><B>Camp Sunny Side Up</B></FONT><BR>
A CD jam-packed with 35 tracks of strange sounds and skits.</TD>
    <TD BGCOLOR="#CCFFFF" VALIGN=middle><A HREF="cssu-cd.html"><IMG
SRC="readmore.gif" BORDER=0></A></TD>
    <TD> </TD>
</TR>

<TR BGCOLOR="#0066CC">
    <TD WIDTH=65><FONT COLOR="#CCFFFF"><B>#LLCSSU</B></FONT></TD>
    <TD WIDTH=230><FONT COLOR="#FFFFFF"><B>Camp Sunny Side Up --
CD</B></FONT></TD>
    <TD WIDTH=90 ALIGN=right><FONT COLOR="#FFFFFF"><B>$16.00</B><
    <TD WIDTH=100 ALIGN=center><IMG SRC="add.gif"></TD>
</TR>

<TR>
    <TD COLSPAN=2 BGCOLOR="#CCFFFF"><IMG SRC="welcome.gif" ALIG
HSPACE=5><FONT SIZE=+1><B>Welcome to Earth</B></FONT><BR>
<FONT COLOR="#0066CC">Volume 1: Getting Started</FONT><BR>
A video mix of the past, present, and future of Matt and Liam's
    <TD BGCOLOR="#CCFFFF"><A HREF="wte-vid.html"><IMG SRC="read
BORDER=0></A></TD>
    <TD> </TD>
</TR>

<TR BGCOLOR="#0066CC">
    ...OR="#CCFFFF"><B>#LLWTE1</B></FONT...
    ...FFF"><B>Welcome...
```

Here is an excerpt from the final HTML file, including all the content.

All the tags in this file (with the exception of color specifications) have been covered in the preceding chapters. Try reading through the source code and matching it with effects on the final page. This is a good skill to have if you ever need to troubleshoot a page.

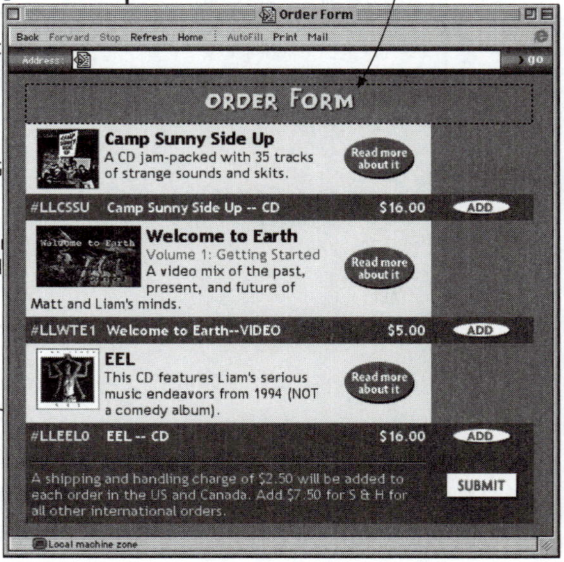

Same Thing, This Time Using Dreamweaver

Let's create the same table, starting with the map we made in Figure 10-8, using a WYSIWYG web-authoring tool. Although I'll be using Dreamweaver in this example, other tools also offer time and patience savings (of course, the features and interface will be slightly different).

Start with a new Dreamweaver document. I've already named and saved the document, and have entered some document-level settings such as the background color and title. Now, I'm ready to insert a new table into the page, either by choosing "Table" from the "Insert" menu or by dragging the table icon onto the page. This will launch a dialog box that asks for all the table-level settings (Figure 10-13).

Using a WYSIWYG web-authoring tool makes the table design process much faster and easier.

Figure 10-13

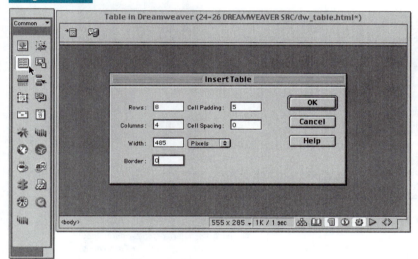

I used the Table button in the Objects window to insert a new table on my page. The dialog box allows me to enter table-level settings all in one step, including:

- *Number of rows and columns*
- *Cell padding and spacing*
- *Overall width of the table*
- *Border thickness*

Now I can start formatting all my cells, including setting the column widths in a row that will keep all its cells intact, knocking out cells with column spans, and assigning cell background colors, while using my sketch as a guide (Figure 10-14, following page).

Figure 10-14

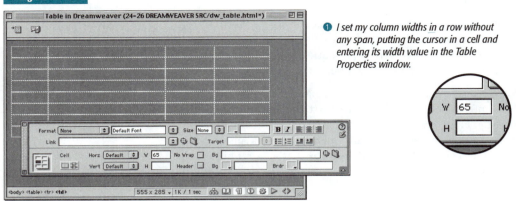

❶ I set my column widths in a row without any span, putting the cursor in a cell and entering its width value in the Table Properties window.

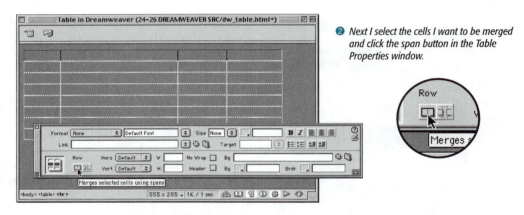

❷ Next I select the cells I want to be merged and click the span button in the Table Properties window.

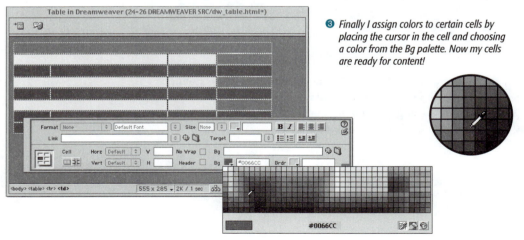

❸ Finally I assign colors to certain cells by placing the cursor in the cell and choosing a color from the Bg palette. Now my cells are ready for content!

Now that the table is formatted, I can add the content within each cell (Figure 10-15). I've used the Objects window to add graphics to my page. The Properties window makes formatting text and adding links fast and easy.

Figure 10-15

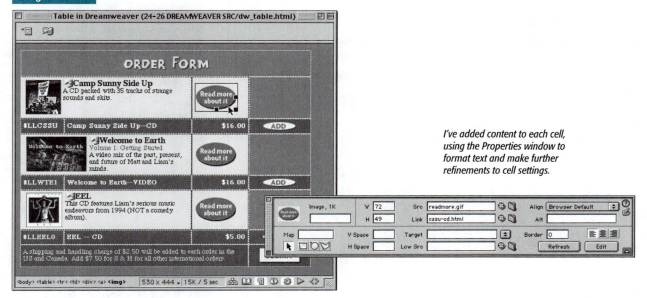

I've added content to each cell, using the Properties window to format text and make further refinements to cell settings.

And it's done! As you can see, it looks just the same in the browser window as the table I wrote by hand. However, take a look at the source code generated by Dreamweaver (Figure 10-16, following page). You'll see subtle differences in the way tools generate code to achieve the same visual effect. In HTML, there are often several solutions to a formatting task.

This section gives you an overview of the table design process. I find when you use the latest versions of the big-name web-authoring tools, table-making goes smoothly. However, even the most carefully crafted tables are prone to misbehaving, so it is important to understand how table tags work in HTML.

Tables

Figure 10-16

```
<html>
<head>
<title>Table in Dreamweaver</title>
<meta http-equiv="Content-Type" content="text/html; charset=iso-8859-1">
</head>

<body bgcolor="#0099CC">
<div align="center">
  <table width="485" border="0" cellspacing="0" cellpadding="5">
    <tr>
      <td colspan="4">
        <div align="center"><img src="orderform.gif" width="160" height="36"></div>
      </td>
    </tr>
    <tr>
      <td colspan="2" bgcolor="#CCFFFF">
        <p><img src="camp.gif" width="60" height="60" align="left"><b><font
size="+1">Camp
          Sunny Side Up</font></b><br>
          A CD packed with 35 tracks of strange sounds and skits.</p>
      </td>
      <td bgcolor="#CCFFFF">
        <div align="left"><a href="cssu-cd.html"><img src="readmore.gif"
width="72" height="49" border="0"></a></div>
      </td>
      <td> </td>
    </tr>
    <tr>
      <td width="65" bgcolor="#0066CC"><b><font
color="#FFFFFF">#LLCSSU</font></b></td>
      <td width="230" bgcolor="#0066CC"><b><font color="#FFFFFF"
Side
        Up--CD</font></b></td>
      <td width="90" bgcolor="#0066CC">
        <div align="right"><b><font color="#FFFFFF">$16.00</font>
      </td>
      <td width="100" bgcolor="#0066CC">
        <div align="center"><img src="add.gif" width="58" height=
      </td>
    </tr>
    <tr>
                      "2" bgcolor="#CCFFFF"><img src="
                              come
```

Here is the final HTML, as created in Dreamweaver. It is slightly different from the HTML I wrote by hand, but the results in the browser are identical.

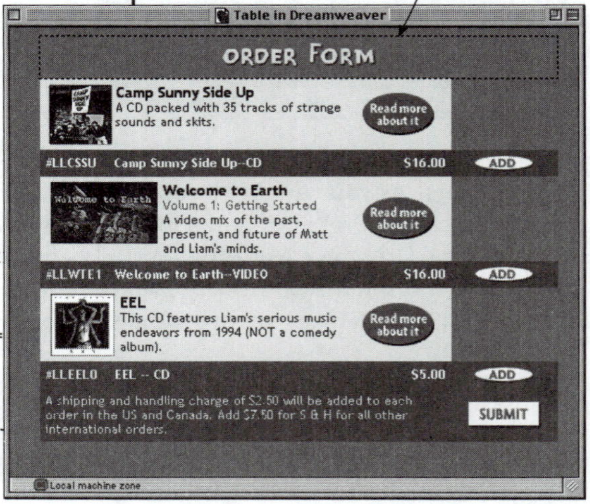

HTML for Tables

Now that we have a feel for how tables are put together, let's dive into the nitty-gritty of the tags and how they work. Even if you're using an authoring tool, knowing the terminology will help you use it more efficiently.

Like so many other web elements, the real control over table display lies in the attributes. Some settings apply to the whole table, while others affect individual cells.

Even if you're using a web-authoring tool, understanding the tags and the terminology will help you use the tool more efficiently.

Formatting the Whole Table

At the table level (that is, using attributes in the <TABLE> tag), you can control the following aspects of how the whole table is formatted:

- Thickness of the border around the table

- Dimensions of the table

- Amount of space within and between table cells

- Background color for the table

Let's look at each of these <TABLE> attributes.

<TABLE BORDER=*number*>
Border thickness

The BORDER attribute indicates the thickness (in pixels) of the border around the outside edge of the table (Figure 10-17). The most popular setting for this attribute is zero, which makes the table and cell borders invisible. Using the attribute BORDER alone, without a value, will result in the default 1-pixel border. If you omit the BORDER attribute most browsers will display the table without a border, but it's best to set the border to zero to be on the safe side.

Figure 10-17

```
<TABLE BORDER=0>
<TR>
<TD>Cell 1</TD><TD>Cell 2</TD>
</TR>
<TR>
<TD>Cell 3</TD><TD>Cell 4</TD>
</TR>
</TABLE>
```

To be sure the border is not visible, set the BORDER value to zero.

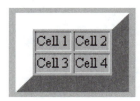

```
<TABLE BORDER=15>
<TR>
<TD>Cell 1</TD><TD>Cell 2</TD>
</TR>
<TR>
<TD>Cell 3</TD><TD>Cell 4</TD>
</TR>
</TABLE>
```

You can make the border as wide as you like. Notice that it only affects the outside edge of the table.

Tables

Figure 10-18

```
<TABLE WIDTH=200 HEIGHT=100 BORDER>
<TR>
<TD>Cell 1</TD><TD>Cell 2</TD>
</TR>
<TR>
<TD>Cell 3</TD><TD>Cell 4</TD>
</TR>
</TABLE>
```

The dimensions of a table can be specified in numbers of pixels …

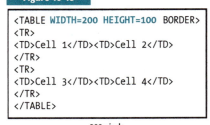

```
<TABLE WIDTH=80% BORDER>
<TR>
<TD>Cell 1</TD><TD>Cell 2</TD>
</TR>
<TR>
<TD>Cell 3</TD><TD>Cell 4</TD>
</TR>
</TABLE>
```

… or as a percentage of the total available width of the window.

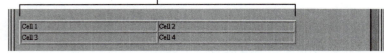

Figure 10-19

```
<TABLE CELLPADDING=15 BORDER>
<TR>
<TD>Cell 1</TD><TD>Cell 2</TD>
</TR>
<TR>
<TD>Cell 3</TD><TD>Cell 4</TD>
</TR>
</TABLE>
```

Cell padding *specifies the margin of space within each cell (between the contents and the cell border).*

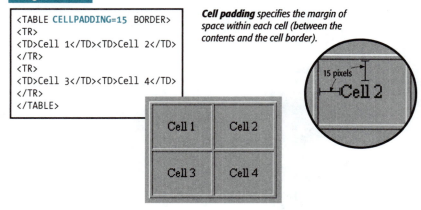

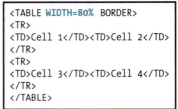

<TABLE WIDTH=*number*
HEIGHT=*number***>**
Table width and height

These attributes are used to specify the table's dimensions (Figure 10-18). You can specify either a pixel dimension or a percentage. For instance, if you set the width to 100%, the table will fill the entire available width of the page. By default, the table will expand to be just wide enough to fit the contents within it.

<TABLE CELLPADDING=*number***>**
Margins around cell content

Cell padding is the amount of space held between the contents of the cell and the cell border (Figure 10-19). Think of it as a margin held within a cell. Because it is specified only at the table level, this setting will apply to all the cells in the table. In other words, you can't specify different amounts of padding for individual cells. If you don't specify anything, the cells will have the default value of one pixel of padding.

<TABLE CELLSPACING=*number*>

Space between cells

Cell spacing is the amount of space held between cells, specified in number of pixels (Figure 10-20). If you don't specify anything, the browser will use the default value of two pixels of space between cells.

<TABLE BGCOLOR=*color*>

Table background color

Use the BGCOLOR attribute to specify the background color applied to the whole table (Figure 10-21). Unfortunately, this will only work in Version 4.0 browsers and higher, so be careful how you implement it. The value is a color name or its numerical equivalent. Specifying colors in HTML is covered in Chapter 12.

Combining table attributes

Of course, it's likely that you'll be using a combination of these settings in a single table, as shown in Figure 10-22.

Figure 10-20

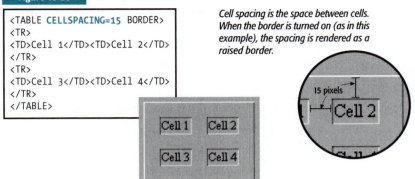

```
<TABLE CELLSPACING=15 BORDER>
<TR>
<TD>Cell 1</TD><TD>Cell 2</TD>
</TR>
<TR>
<TD>Cell 3</TD><TD>Cell 4</TD>
</TR>
</TABLE>
```

Cell spacing is the space between cells. When the border is turned on (as in this example), the spacing is rendered as a raised border.

15 pixels

Figure 10-21

```
<TABLE BGCOLOR="white">
<TR>
<TD>Cell 1</TD><TD>Cell 2</TD>
</TR>
<TR>
<TD>Cell 3</TD><TD>Cell 4</TD>
</TR>
</TABLE>
```

The BGCOLOR attribute assigns a color that fills all the cells in the table. This attribute is implemented differently in Navigator and Internet Explorer, and is not supported at all by pre-4.0 browsers.

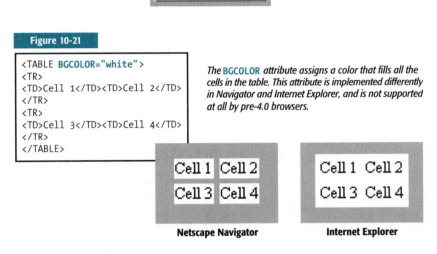

Netscape Navigator　　　**Internet Explorer**

Figure 10-22

```
<CENTER>
<TABLE BORDER=0 CELLPADDING=6 CELLSPACING=6
WIDTH=75% BGCOLOR="yellow">
<TR>
  <TD>Elliott Smith</TD>
  <TD>Supergrass</TD>
  <TD>Wheat</TD>
</TR>
<TR>
  <TD>Cat Power</TD>
  <TD>The Magnetic Fields</TD>
  <TD>Orbit</TD>
</TR>
</TABLE>
</CENTER>
```

In most cases, these attributes are used in combination.

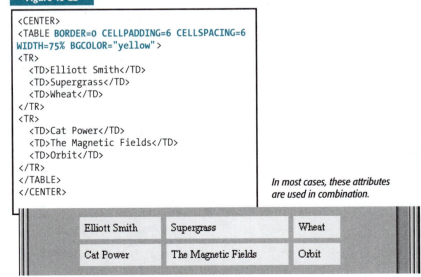

Tables

TOOL TIP

Adding Tables

Here's how you add a table and adjust all table-level settings in three of the more popular authoring programs.

DREAMWEAVER 3

Add a table to the page by dragging the Table icon from the Objects palette into place on the page. A dialog box will open asking you for all table-level specifications.

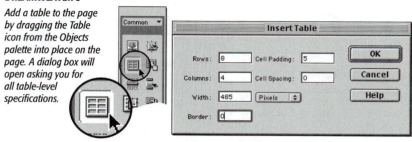

GOLIVE 4

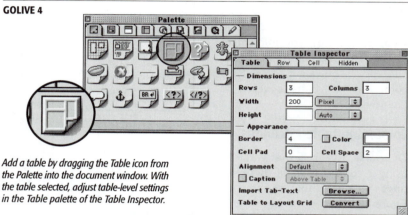

Add a table by dragging the Table icon from the Palette into the document window. With the table selected, adjust table-level settings in the Table palette of the Table Inspector.

FRONTPAGE 2000

The quickest way to insert a table is to use the Table icon in the toolbar. Drag your mouse over the rows and columns to create an instant table.

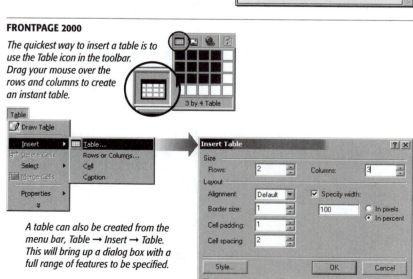

A table can also be created from the menu bar, Table → Insert → Table. This will bring up a dialog box with a full range of features to be specified.

Controlling Individual Cells

Some of the more interesting table settings take place at the cell level. These include:

- Column and row spanning
- Cell dimensions
- Alignment of cell contents
- Background color for the cell

All of these aspects are controlled using attributes within the <TD> tag. Following is a description of each.

<TD COLSPAN=*number*>

Column span

I introduced this design feature earlier in the section Spanning Cells. When you use the COLSPAN attribute in a <TD> tag, it makes that cell expand to the right to span the specified number of columns (Figure 10-23). Be careful with your COLSPAN values; if you specify a number that exceeds the number of columns in the table, most browsers will add columns to the existing table.

Figure 10-23

```
<TABLE BORDER WIDTH=100 HEIGHT=50>
<TR>
<TD COLSPAN=2>Cell 1</TD>
</TR>
<TR>
<TD>Cell 3</TD><TD>Cell 4</TD>
</TR>
</TABLE>
```

The COLSPAN attribute stretches a cell to span the specified number of columns. Note how there is now only one <TD> tag in the first row.

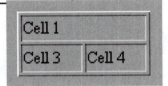

<TD ROWSPAN=*number*>

Row span

When you put the ROWSPAN attribute in a <TD> tag, the cell will expand downward to cover the number of rows you specify (Figure 10-24).

If you specify a ROWSPAN value that is higher than the actual number of rows, extra rows will *not* be added to the table. This means if you have a lot of rows and don't feel like counting them all, aim high with your ROWSPAN value: you'll span all the rows and there won't be any harm done to the table structure.

Figure 10-24

```
<TABLE BORDER WIDTH=100 HEIGHT=50>
<TR>
<TD ROWSPAN=2>Cell 1</TD><TD>Cell 2</TD>
</TR>
<TR>
<TD>Cell 4</TD>
</TR>
</TABLE>
```

The ROWSPAN attribute extends a cell down to span a specified number of rows. Note how there is now only one <TD> in the second row, accounted for by the spanned cell.

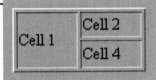

Tables

Header Cells

There is a table cell tag used especially for the headings above each column. These cells are called "headers" and are indicated with `<TH>` tags. They follow the same rules as `<TD>`s, only they display text within them as bold and centered by default:

```
<TABLE CELLPADDING=6
       BORDER=1>
<TR>
  <TH>Name</TH>
  <TH>Occupation</TH>
  <TH>Location</TH>
</TR>
  <TD>Jennifer Niederst</TD>
  <TD>Web Designer</TD>
  <TD>Boston, MA</TD>
</TR>
</TABLE>
```

Name	Occupation	Location
Jennifer Niederst	Web Designer	Boston, MA

When you specify the width of a cell, you are establishing the width of the entire column. Likewise, setting the height of a cell will affect the height of all the cells in that row.

```
<TD WIDTH=number
    HEIGHT=number>
```
Cell width and height

The `WIDTH` and `HEIGHT` attributes are used to specify the dimensions of a particular cell (Figure 10-25). You can specify a pixel measurement or a percentage of the available window.

When you specify the width of a cell, you are establishing the width of the entire column. Likewise, setting the height of a cell will affect the height of all the cells in that row. Be careful you don't have conflicting cell widths within a column (or conflicting heights within a row). The best way to avoid this is to set the widths only once in the table, using a row that has all its cells (i.e., no column spans).

Also, when using specific pixel measurements, take care that the total of your cell measurements is the same as the dimensions set in the `<TABLE>` tag.

Table sizes are unpredictable even when specified. If the content requires more space, the cell will generally resize to accommodate, so cell and table size specifications should be considered minimum values.

Figure 10-25

```
<TR>
<TD WIDTH=200 HEIGHT=50>Cell 1</TD><TD>Cell 2</TD>
</TR>
<TR>
<TD>Cell 3</TD><TD>Cell 4</TD>
</TR>
</TABLE>
```

The dimensions in Cell 1 determine the height of the first row and the width of the first column.

You can specify the width and height of a specific cell. Keep in mind that the specified dimensions will affect all the other cells in the same row and column as that cell.

<TD ALIGN=left|right|center VALIGN=top|center|bottom>

Cell content alignment

The ALIGN and VALIGN attributes control the alignment of elements within cells. By default, the text (or any element) placed in a cell will be positioned flush left and centered vertically within the available height of the cell.

Use the ALIGN attribute to position elements horizontally in a cell. Its values are left, right, or center. VALIGN positions elements vertically in the cell. Its values are top, center, or bottom (Figure 10-26)

<TD BGCOLOR="color name or number">

Cell background color

This specifies the background color to be used in the table cell (Figure 10-27). A cell's background color setting overrides colors set at the table or row level. The system for specifying color is covered in Chapter 12.

Figure 10-26

```
<TABLE BORDER="1" WIDTH="450">
<TR>
    <TD ALIGN=left>flush left</TD>
    <TD ALIGN=center>centered</TD>
    <TD ALIGN=right>flush right</TD>
</TR>
</TABLE>
```

The ALIGN attribute controls the horizontal alignment of the contents in a cell.

flush left	centered	flush right

```
<TABLE BORDER="1" HEIGHT="150">
<TR>
    <TD VALIGN=top>top</TD>
    <TD VALIGN=middle>middle</TD>
    <TD VALIGN=bottom ALIGN="RIGHT">bottom</TD>
</TR>
</TABLE>
```

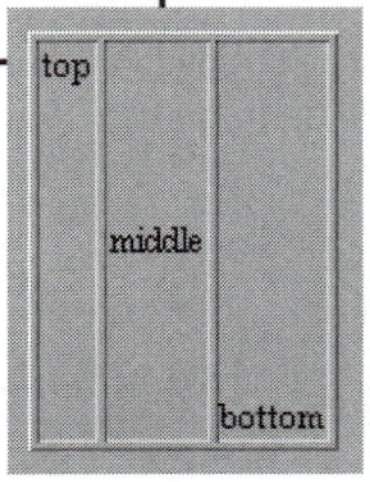

VALIGN controls the vertical alignment of the cell's contents.

Figure 10-27

```
<TABLE BGCOLOR="white" BORDER="1" CELLPADDING="5" >
<TR>
    <TD BGCOLOR="black"><FONT COLOR="white">Cell 1</FONT></TD>
    <TD>Cell 2</TD>
</TR>
<TR>
    <TD>Cell 3</TD>
    <TD>Cell 4</TD>
</TR>
</TABLE>
```

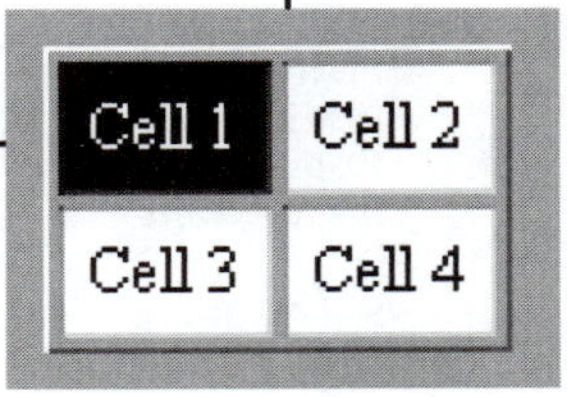

You can set the background color of a cell by using the BGCOLOR attribute in the <TD> tag. Color settings at the cell level will override table color settings.

Tables

Combining cell attributes

As we've seen in other HTML tags, you can put a number of attribute settings in a single `<TD>` tag (Figure 10-28).

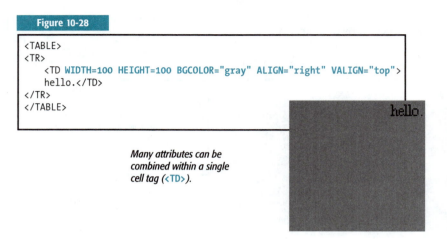

Figure 10-28

```
<TABLE>
<TR>
    <TD WIDTH=100 HEIGHT=100 BGCOLOR="gray" ALIGN="right" VALIGN="top">
    hello.</TD>
</TR>
</TABLE>
```

Many attributes can be combined within a single cell tag (`<TD>`).

Span-o-rama

You can combine ROWSPAN and COLSPAN attributes in a single cell to knock out a whole block of cells:

```
<TABLE WIDTH=200 BORDER=1 CELLPADDING=3>
<TR>
   <TD>one</TD>
   <TD COLSPAN=3 ROWSPAN=2>two</TD>
</TR>
<TR>
   <TD>three</TD>
</TR>
<TR>
   <TD>four</TD>
   <TD>five</TD>
   <TD>six</TD>
   <TD>seven</TD>
</TR>
</TABLE>
```

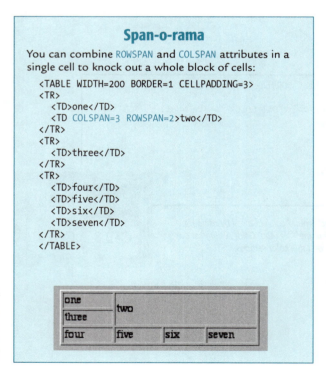

Row Row Row

You can use the ALIGN, VALIGN, and BGCOLOR attributes in the `<TR>` tag to make settings that affect all cells in a table row:

```
<TABLE WIDTH=200 HEIGHT=100 BORDER=1
      BGCOLOR="white">
<TR ALIGN="right" VALIGN="top" BGCOLOR="yellow">
  <TD>Cell 1</TD>
  <TD>Cell 2</TD>
  <TD>Cell 3</TD>
</TR>
<TR>
  <TD>Cell 4</TD>
  <TD>Cell 5</TD>
  <TD>Cell 6</TD>
</TR>
</TABLE>
```

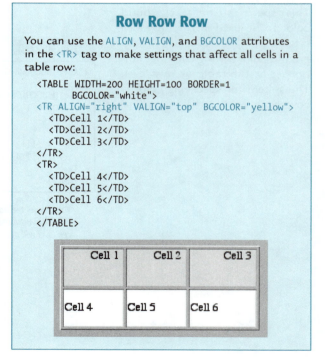

Formatting Table Cells

Here's how you adjust cell-level settings in three of the more popular authoring programs.

DREAMWEAVER 3

When your cursor is in a cell, all cell-level settings can be adjusted in the Properties window (make sure it is fully opened). You can apply settings to several cells at once by dragging and selecting groups of cells.

GOLIVE 4

To make cell settings, select the cell border with the pointer and enter attribute values in the Cell palette of the Table Inspector. You can apply the same settings to several selected cells at once, or use the Rows palette to control the cells in the current row.

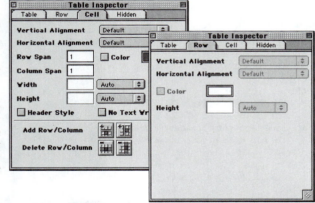

FRONTPAGE 2000

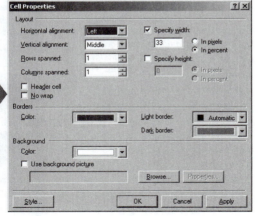

Cell settings can be made when the cursor is in the desired cell(s). Go to the menubar, Table → Properties → Cell. A dialog box to specify cell attributes will appear.

Tables

Where Tables Go Wrong

Tables are known to cause headaches, partly because of the potential for complex code, and partly because of the quirky and inconsistent ways browsers interpret that code. This is especially troublesome for tables that require precise cell dimensions to hold the page together.

Tables can easily go haywire if everything isn't perfectly in place.

Although not every problem can be anticipated, here are a few of the places tables tend to go awry. More table idiosyncracies are discussed in detail in my big book of web design, *Web Design in a Nutshell* (O'Reilly, 1999).

Expanding Text in Cells

Remember that text size varies from user to user. If you are using text in a cell, the cell will expand to accommodate your text, potentially breaking apart a carefully constructed table (Figure 10-29). Make sure there is ample room in the cell for the text, or allow the height of your cell to be flexible.

TIP

Be careful putting text in cells with critical pixel dimensions. Design with room for the text to expand.

Figure 10-29

```
<TABLE BORDER=0 CELLPADDING=0 CELLSPACING=0>
<TR>
    <TD COLSPAN=3><IMG SRC="top.gif"></TD>
</TR>
<TR>
    <TD WIDTH=28 HEIGHT=144><IMG SRC="left.gif"></TD>
    <TD WIDTH=94 HEIGHT=144 BGCOLOR="white">Roses are red, <BR>Violets
are Blue<BR>Sugar is Sweet<BR>And So Are You!</TD>
    <TD WIDTH=28 HEIGHT=144><IMG SRC="right.gif"></TD>
</TR>
<TR>
    <TD COLSPAN=3><IMG SRC="bottom.gif"></TD>
</TR>
</TABLE>
```

I've created a decorative border using four graphics, held together by a table with specific cell measurements.

The effect is great when I view it on my browser with the font size set to 12 pixels.

But if someone has their browser font set larger, the cell expands to fit the larger text, and the decorative border breaks apart.

Collapsing Cells

Netscape Navigator has an annoying habit of collapsing any cell that doesn't contain content: the cell disappears and its cell background color is not displayed (Figure 10-30). If the table border is turned on, the cell will fill in with a solid "raised" area the same color as the page background. For this reason, it is a good idea to make sure there is some minimal content between every set of <TD> tags.

At minimum, you can hold the cell open with a nonbreaking space character, . If precise cell sizing is an issue, try using a transparent graphic that is only 1 pixel wide by 1 pixel tall, then using the WIDTH and HEIGHT attributes in the <IMG> tag to size the graphic to the target cell size.

Figure 10-30

In this table, the second cell is empty
(there is nothing between the <TD> tags).

```
<TABLE BORDER=1 CELLPADDING=0 CELLSPACING=0>
<TR>
    <TD WIDTH=100 HEIGHT=50 BGCOLOR="white"><IMG SRC="leaf.gif"></TD>
    <TD WIDTH=100 HEIGHT=50 BGCOLOR="white"></TD>
</TR>
<TR>
    <TD WIDTH=100 HEIGHT=50 BGCOLOR="white"><IMG SRC="leaf.gif"></TD>
    <TD WIDTH=100 HEIGHT=50 BGCOLOR="white"><IMG SRC="leaf.gif"></TD>
</TR>
</TABLE>
```

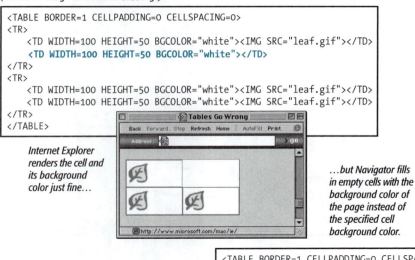

Internet Explorer renders the cell and its background color just fine…

…but Navigator fills in empty cells with the background color of the page instead of the specified cell background color.

To avoid this problem, make sure there is content in every cell—even a non-breaking space ( ) will do.

```
<TABLE BORDER=1 CELLPADDING=0 CELLSPACING=0>
<TR>
    <TD WIDTH=100 HEIGHT=50 BGCOLOR="white"><IMG SRC="leaf.gif"></TD>
    <TD WIDTH=100 HEIGHT=50 BGCOLOR="white"> </TD>
</TR>
<TR>
    <TD WIDTH=100 HEIGHT=50 BGCOLOR="white"><IMG SRC="leaf.gif"></TD>
    <TD WIDTH=100 HEIGHT=50 BGCOLOR="white"><IMG SRC="leaf.gif"></TD>
</TR>
</TABLE>
```

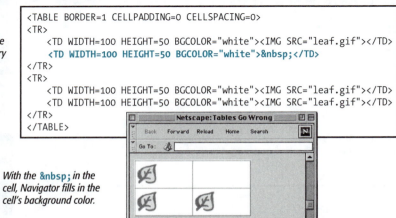

With the   in the cell, Navigator fills in the cell's background color.

Tables

Shifting Columns

Lots of column spans in a table can make your careful column width specifications go haywire. I once wrote the HTML for a table that looked perfect in the source code, but completely fell apart once it hit the browser (Figure 10-31). What I hadn't noticed was that my column spans had left the specific widths of some of my columns unaccounted for. The browser does its best to render the table based on the code you give it.

The trick to getting column widths to behave is to enter the WIDTH values in a row that has all its cells intact, with no COLSPAN settings. If there are no intact rows, create a control row at the top or bottom of the table that has its HEIGHT set to 0 (zero), yet contains all the proper widths for each cell (and therefore, column). The control row won't render in the browser, but it will keep your table in shape, even after lots of spanning.

Many authoring tools will build this control row in automatically, which is why their table code tends to be more reliable across different browsers.

Figure 10-31

```
<TABLE BORDER=0 CELLPADDING=0 CELLSPACING=0 WIDTH=250>
<TR>
    <TD COLSPAN=2><IMG SRC="sweetpea-1.gif" WIDTH=200></TD>
    <TD><IMG SRC="sweetpea-2.gif" WIDTH=50></TD>
</TR>
<TR>
    <TD><IMG SRC="sweetpea-3.gif" WIDTH=50></TD>
    <TD COLSPAN=2><IMG SRC="sweetpea-4.gif" WIDTH=200></TD>
</TR>
</TABLE>
```

This table source code does not contain enough information for the browser to render the table correctly. Both rows span the required center column, so the widths of the columns are never clearly defined.

```
<TABLE BORDER=0 CELLPADDING=0 CELLSPACING=0 WIDTH=250>
<TR>
    <TD WIDTH=50 HEIGHT=0></TD>
    <TD WIDTH=150 HEIGHT=0></TD>
    <TD WIDTH=50 HEIGHT=0></TD>
</TR>
<TR>
    <TD COLSPAN=2><IMG SRC="sweetpea-1.gif" WIDTH=200></TD>
    <TD><IMG SRC="sweetpea-2.gif" WIDTH=50></TD>
</TR>
<TR>
    <TD><IMG SRC="sweetpea-3.gif" WIDTH=50></TD>
    <TD COLSPAN=2><IMG SRC="sweetpea-4.gif" WIDTH=200></TD>
</TR>
</TABLE>
```

To correct the problem, add a control row that explicitly defines the widths for all three columns. Because the cells are empty and the height is set to zero, the row will not display in the browser.

Avoiding Extra Whitespace

It is common for extra whitespace to creep between table cells (or between the cells and the border). When you are trying to create a seamless effect with colored cells or hold together pieces of a larger image, this extra space is unacceptable.

The problem most often lies within the cell (`<TD>`) tag. Some browsers render any extra space within a `<TD>` tag as white space in a table. In the following code, the character space following the `<IMG>` tag introduces extra space within that cell:

```
<TD><IMG SRC="topleft.gif"> </TD>
```

Unwanted whitespace may also occur when there are carriage returns within the cell container tags, as shown here:

```
<TD>
<IMG SRC="topleft.gif">
</TD>
```

If you want a seamless table, begin with the border, cellpadding, and cellspacing all set to zero in the `<TABLE>` tag. Be sure that the enclosing `<TD>` and `</TD>` tags are flush against the content of the cell, with no extra spaces or returns. The safest approach is to keep your cell tags and their contents all on one line, like this:

```
<TD><IMG SRC="topleft.gif"></TD>
```

If you must break the line of code, do so within a tag. It won't hurt the tag, and it won't introduce any extra space to the cell. For example:

```
<TD><IMG
SRC="topleft.gif"></TD>
```

It is worthwhile to note that because `<TABLE>` and `<TR>` tags contain only other tags, not actual content for the table, spaces and returns within these tags are ignored. If you are getting pesky whitespace in your tables, check those `<TD>` tags.

Using Tables for Alignment

As I said earlier in this chapter, tables were *originally* intended to display rows and columns of data. But designers quickly found creative ways to use them to control the display of the page. Here are few popular (albeit renegade) tricks you can do with tables.

Page Structure

Many sites use a two-column table to lay out the structure of the page. The most popular technique is to create a narrow column for links and use the remainder of the page for content.

You have your choice of fixing the width of your table to precise pixel measurements, letting the widths resize relative to the width of the window, or a combination of both (Figure 10-32, following page). The code for each page layout is simple.

Tables

Figure 10-32

Fixed width

In this example, the width of the table and the widths of each column are set to specific pixel measurements.

```
<HTML>
<HEAD>
<TITLE>Page Formatting</TITLE>
</HEAD>

<BODY>

<TABLE BORDER=1 WIDTH=600 HEIGHT=100%>
<TR>
    <TD WIDTH=150>left column</TD>
    <TD WIDTH=450>right column contents here</TD>
</TR>
</TABLE>

</BODY>
</HTML>
```

The columns and table will remain the same width regardless of the size of the browser window.

Relative width

Here, the table always fills the width of the page (its width is set to 100%), and each column is a specified percentage of that width.

```
<TABLE BORDER=1 WIDTH=100% HEIGHT=100%>
<TR>
    <TD WIDTH=15%>left column</TD>
    <TD WIDTH=85%>right column contents here</TD>
</TR>
</TABLE>
```

This layout flexes to fill the width of the window. The columns flex too, but in proportion to each other.

Combination

In this table, the left column stays a fixed width, while the right one is allowed to flex with the page.

```
<TABLE BORDER=1 WIDTH=100% HEIGHT=100%>
<TR>
    <TD WIDTH=150>left column</TD>
    <TD>right column contents here</TD>
</TR>
</TABLE>
```

This table fills the window (its width is set to 100%). Cells with a pixel measurement stay put (this one at 150 pixels), and cells with no measurement expand to fill the remaining space.

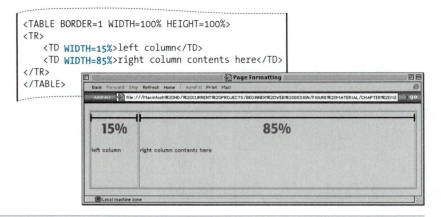

Centering in the Window

Here's a trick that uses a table to keep a page element centered in the browser window. You simply make a table with one cell and set the width and height to 100%. Next, set the alignment to center and the vertical alignment to middle. And *voila*! Your object will be the center of attention! (See Figure 10-33.)

Figure 10-33

```
<HTML>
<HEAD><TITLE>Centered object</TITLE></HEAD>
<BODY>

<TABLE WIDTH=100% HEIGHT=100% BORDER=0>
<TR>
    <TD ALIGN=center VALIGN=middle><IMG SRC="tomato.gif"></TD>
</TR>
</TABLE>

</BODY>
</HTML>
```

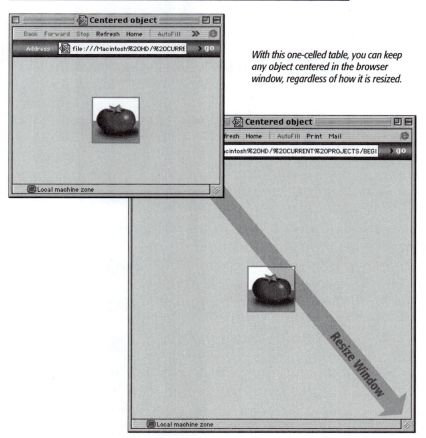

With this one-celled table, you can keep any object centered in the browser window, regardless of how it is resized.

Tables

HTML Review—Table Tags

The following is a summary of the tags we covered in this chapter.

Tag and Attributes	Function
`<TABLE>`	Establishes beginning and end of a table
`BGCOLOR="number"` or `"name"`	Background color for the whole table
`BORDER=number`	Thickness of the border around the table
`CELLPADDING=number`	Space within cells
`CELLSPACING=number`	Space between cells
`HEIGHT=number`	Table height (in pixels or percentage)
`WIDTH=number`	Table width (in pixels or percentage)
`<TD>`	Establishes a cell within a table row
`ALIGN=left|right|center`	Horizontal alignment of cell contents
`BGCOLOR="number"` or `"name"`	Background color for the cell
`COLSPAN=number`	Number of columns the cell should span
`HEIGHT=number`	Cell height (in pixels or percentage)
`ROWSPAN=number`	Number of rows the cell should span
`VALIGN=top|middle|bottom|baseline`	Vertical alignment of cell contents
`WIDTH=number`	Width (in pixels or percentage)
`<TH>`	Table head
(attributes are the same as the `<TD>` tag)	
`<TR>`	Establishes a row within a table
`ALIGN=left|right|center`	Horizontal alignment of cell contents for an entire row
`BGCOLOR="number"` or `"name"`	Background color for the entire row
`VALIGN=top|middle|bottom|baseline`	Vertical alignment of cell contents for the entire row

Frames

Have you ever seen a web page with content that scrolls while the navigation toolbar or an ad stays in the same place? Pages like these are created using a web design feature called frames. Frames divide up a browser window into mini-windows, each displaying a different HTML document (Figure 11-1).

The ability to have one portion of the window always visible while others scroll through longer content is the primary advantage to using frames. Frames open up navigational possibilities, and they can also be used to unify information from several sites onto one page.

However, frames have been controversial from their first introduction in Netscape Navigator 2.0. They cause as many navigational problems as they solve, since some users find it difficult to click through them. It is also difficult for content in frames to be bookmarked or found by search engines. And since each framed page is comprised of several HTML documents, this means more work for developers and a heavier load for the server.

Figure 11-1

Frames divide the browser into separate windows, each displaying its own web page. The windows can scroll independently.

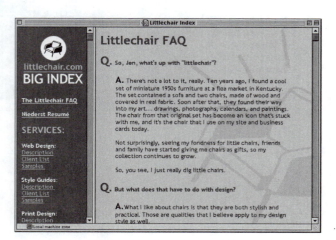

As a result of their numerous disadvantages, frames have become an unspoken "no-no" for big commercial sites.

As a result of their numerous disadvantages, frames have become an unspoken "no-no" for big commercial sites. Don't be surprised if your client declares "no frames" at the very first meeting. But like most things, frames are neither all good nor all bad, so feel free to play around with them and decide for yourself.

How Frames Work

When you view a framed page in a browser, you are actually looking at several HTML documents at once (Figure 11-2). The key to making the page display in frames is the frameset document—an HTML document that contains instructions for how each frame is drawn and which HTML document is displayed in each frame.

Figure 11-2

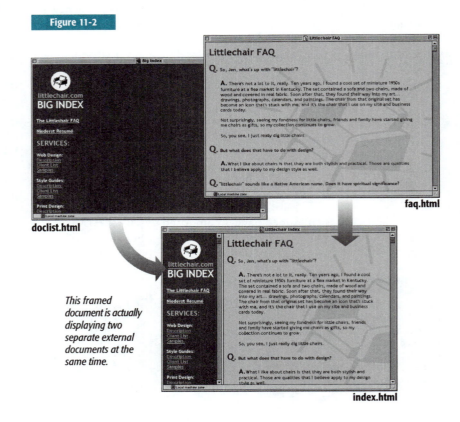

doclist.html

faq.html

This framed document is actually displaying two separate external documents at the same time.

index.html

The primary function of the frameset document is to set up a structure for the page. Let's take a peek at the HTML source for our example framed page (Figure 11-3).

Figure 11-3

```
<HTML>
<HEAD>
<TITLE>Littlechair Index</TITLE>
</HEAD>
<FRAMESET COLS="175,*">

        <FRAME SRC="doc_list.html">
        <FRAME SRC="faq.html">

</FRAMESET>
<NOFRAMES>
You need a frames-enabled browser to view this page.
</NOFRAMES>

</HTML>
```

This is the HTML source for the
*frameset document **index.html***
in our example.

❶ `<FRAMESET>`

We'll talk about creating frameset documents in more detail in the next section, but for now I want to highlight a few points of interest. First, notice that while the frameset document uses the `<HEAD>` structural element, it does not have a `<BODY>`. It uses the `<FRAMESET>` structural tag instead. This sets framesets apart from all other web pages.

❷ `<FRAME>`

Within the `<FRAMESET>` container tags, we see a `<FRAME>` tag for each frame on the page. The primary job of the `<FRAME>` tag is to specify which HTML document to display; however, you can control other features of a frame, as we'll see later in this chapter.

❸ `<NOFRAMES>`

Finally, there's some minimal content within the `<NOFRAMES>` tag. This is what will display if the frames do not work (for instance, if the user is using an ancient browser). It is similar to the alternative text provided in image tags. We'll talk more about "noframes" content at the end of this chapter.

When the browser sees that this is a frameset document, it draws out the frames as instructed in the document, and then pulls the separate HTML documents into the page.

Setting Up a Frameset Document

I'm going to try out a framed interface for the cookbook section of the recipe site I started in earlier chapters. In this section, I'll walk you step by step through the process of writing the HTML for framed documents.

As with any HTML document, the first step is to create the document structure. Let's do that for our new framed document; remember that it will use the <FRAMESET> tag instead of <BODY> (Figure 11-4).

Now we can decide how many rows and/or columns we want the page to have and what size each should be. These settings are all made within the <FRAMESET> tag.

Figure 11-4

```
<HTML>
<HEAD>
<TITLE>From Jen's Cookbook</TITLE>
</HEAD>


<FRAMESET>


</FRAMESET>

</HTML>
```

I begin by adding basic structural tags to a new document.

Frameset documents use a <FRAMESET> *tag instead of* <BODY>*.*

The Finished Product G

The frame demonstration in this section walks you through the creation of this three-framed "Jen's Kitchen" page, shown here and in color in the gallery.

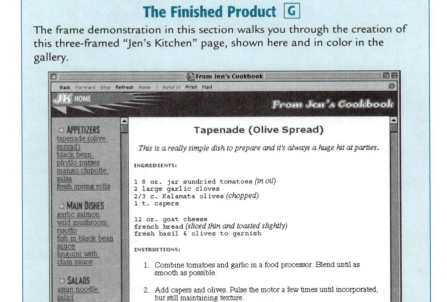

If you want to divide the page into horizontal frames (rows), use the ROWS attribute and specify the height measurement for each row, separated by commas (Figure 11-5). The number of measurements you provide specifies the number of horizontal frames you'll create. Similarly, if you want to create vertical frames (columns), use the COLS attribute, followed by the width measurement for each column (Figure 11-5).

The number of measurements you provide specifies the number of frames you'll create.

Figure 11-5

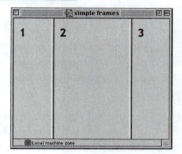

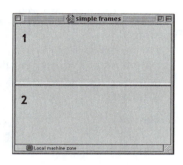

```
<FRAMESET COLS="25%,50%,25%">
```

```
<FRAMESET ROWS="*,*">
```

The COLS attribute creates vertical frames. There are three frames because I provided three measurements after the attribute.

The ROWS attribute creates horizontal frames. Two measurement values after the attribute create two rows.

When it comes to specifying the measurements, you have some options, as the next section explains.

Gridlock

You can combine rows and columns to make a grid of frames. The frames will be filled from left to right, top to bottom:

```
<FRAMESET ROWS="*,*"
          COLS="25%,50%,25%">
    <FRAME SRC="1.html">
    <FRAME SRC="2.html">
    <FRAME SRC="3.html">
    <FRAME SRC="4.html">
    <FRAME SRC="5.html">
    <FRAME SRC="6.html">
</FRAMESET>
```

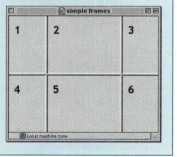

Frame Measurements

There are three ways to specify sizes for frames:

Frame measurements can be specified in pixels, percentages, or relative values.

Absolute pixel values. To make a frame a specific pixel size, enter the number of pixels after the ROWS or COLS attribute. The frameset `<FRAMESET ROWS="100,400">` creates two horizontal frames, one exactly 100 pixels high, the other exactly 400 pixels high. If the browser window is larger than the combined 500 pixels high, it will enlarge each frame proportionally to fill the window.

Percentages. You can also specify sizes as percentages of the browser window. The frameset `<FRAMESET COLS="25%,50%,25%">` creates three columns; the left and right columns always take up 25% of the browser width, and the middle column makes up 50%, regardless of how the window is resized.

Relative values. There's another system that uses asterisks to specify relative values. The best way to explain this is with an example. The frameset `<FRAMESET COLS="100,*">` creates two columns: the left column is exactly 100 pixels wide, and the right column fills whatever portion is left of the window. This combination of fixed-width and flexible-width is one of my personal favorites.

You can also specify relative values in multiples, as in `<FRAMESET COLS="100,2*,*">`, which creates a 100-pixel wide column on the left of the page, then the remainder of the page is divided into two frames; the middle column is always twice the width of the right column.

That said, let's start designing the frames for our new page. I'm going to start with two frames, a narrow one at the top for a banner, and the remainder of the page for my content (Figure 11-6).

Figure 11-6

```
<HTML>
<HEAD>
<TITLE>From Jen's Cookbook</TITLE>
</HEAD>
<FRAMESET ROWS="50,*">


</FRAMESET>
</HTML>
```

I'm designing my cookbook page to have two rows, a narrow one at the top (50 pixels high) for top-level navigation, and a frame that fills the remainder of the window for content.

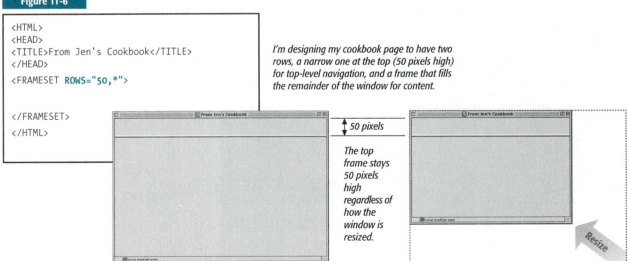

50 pixels

The top frame stays 50 pixels high regardless of how the window is resized.

Resize

Adding and Nesting Frames

Now I need to enter a frame for each row. Frames are added by inserting <FRAME> tags within the <FRAMESET> tags (Figure 11-7). Within each <FRAME> tag, I use the SRC attribute to specify the URL of a document to load into that frame.

Frames

Figure 11-7

```
<HTML>
<HEAD>
<TITLE>From Jen's Cookbook</TITLE>
</HEAD>
<FRAMESET ROWS="50,*">
        <FRAME SRC="header.html">
        <FRAME SRC="tapenade.html">
</FRAMESET>
</HTML>
```

For each frame, I've added a <FRAME> *tag that tells the browser which HTML document to display in that frame.*

Wait, I just had an idea... I'd like to take that large bottom frame and divide it into two vertical frames. I can do that by nesting a second frameset inside my current frameset. Nesting is done by replacing a <FRAME> tag with a complete frameset (a <FRAMESET> tag with its contained <FRAME> tags).

In Figure 11-8, I've swapped out my bottom <FRAME> for a <FRAMESET> containing two vertical frames.

Figure 11-8

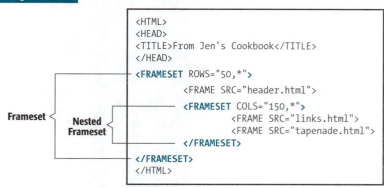

To nest frames (fill one frame with another frameset), simply replace the <FRAME> *tag with a complete* <FRAMESET> *as shown here.*

You can do this as many levels deep as you like. Just be careful to close your <FRAMESET> *tags properly.*

I've already created the HTML documents (*header.html*, *links.html*, and *tapenade.html*) that will be displayed in each frame. Let's take a look at my framed cookbook page in a browser, as it stands so far (Figure 11-9).

Figure 11-9

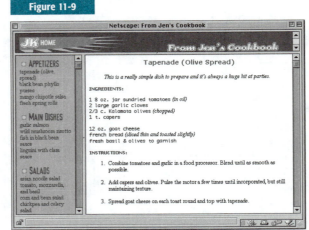

jenscookbook.html

My framed cookbook page as it looks in the browser. Below you can see the separate HTML documents that are held together by the frameset.

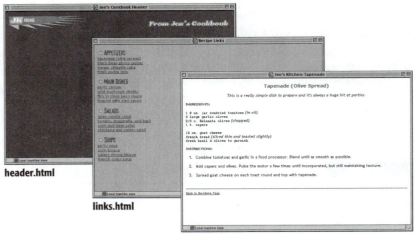

header.html

links.html

tapenade.html

That's a good start, but I can perform some adjustments to make the page less clunky.

Borders

The last decision I can make at the frameset level is whether or not I want borders to appear around my frames. If you don't specify otherwise, frames will be divided by thick, 3-D bars (as shown in Figure 11-9). To control borders for the entire frameset, use the FRAMEBORDER and BORDER attributes in the <FRAMESET> tag.*

To turn the border off completely, making a smooth transition between frames, simply set the BORDER attribute to 0 (zero). This will work for Netscape Navigator and Microsoft Internet Explorer, Versions 4 and higher. If you want to support Navigator 3 and IE 3, set the FRAMEBORDER attribute to 0 (zero, which means "off") as well.

You might want to control just the thickness of the border. If this is the case, set FRAMEBORDER to 1 (which means "on") and use the BORDER attribute to specify a pixel thickness.

I definitely don't want borders around my frames, so I'm turning them off at the frameset level (Figure 11-10).

You can choose whether to have 3-D borders display around your frames.

Figure 11-10

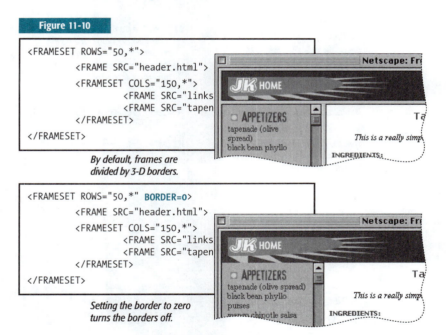

```
<FRAMESET ROWS="50,*">
        <FRAME SRC="header.html">
        <FRAMESET COLS="150,*">
                <FRAME SRC="links
                <FRAME SRC="tapen
        </FRAMESET>
</FRAMESET>
```

By default, frames are divided by 3-D borders.

```
<FRAMESET ROWS="50,*" BORDER=0>
        <FRAME SRC="header.html">
        <FRAMESET COLS="150,*">
                <FRAME SRC="links
                <FRAME SRC="tapen
        </FRAMESET>
</FRAMESET>
```

Setting the border to zero turns the borders off.

We've done everything we can do with the whole frameset. Now let's see the kinds of things we can tweak within each frame.

---

* The BORDER attribute is not part of the standard HTML specification, but it works fine in the current versions of the major browsers.

TOOL TIP

Creating a Frameset

Here's how you create a new frameset in three of the more popular authoring programs.

DREAMWEAVER 3

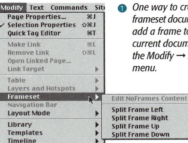

❶ One way to create a frameset document is to add a frame to the current document with the Modify → Frameset menu.

❷ Alternatively, you can click on a predefined frame icon from the Frames panel of the Object window.

❸ The Frames window (accessed from the Windows menu) is used to manage the frameset and its settings.

❹ When you select the whole frameset in the Frames window, you can make frame-level settings in the Properties window.

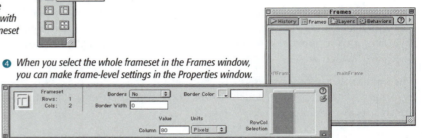

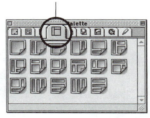

GOLIVE 4

❶ First, select the Frame Editor tab at the top of the document window to switch to the Frames Editor view. This view is used to set up and organize the framed document.

Frame Editor tab

Frames tab

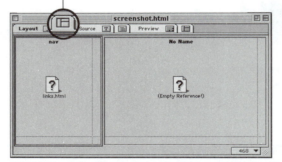

❷ From the Frames tab of the Palette, drag a frame configuration into your document window.

❸ Select the frameset by clicking on any border (you can drag the border to resize the frame) and make your frameset settings in the Frame Inspector.

FRONTPAGE 2000

❶

Create a new document and select the Frames Pages tab. There are a variety of frame templates, each with a short description of suggested use. Choose the frameset closest to the layout you want.

❷

Pages can then be set or created for each frame. The frames can be modified by moving the frame borders.

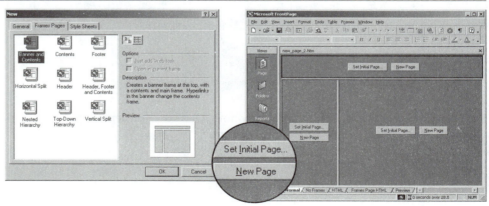

Frame Appearance and Function

At the frame level (that is, within each `<FRAME>` tag), you get to specify three attributes for the frame: whether it has a scrollbar, how wide its margins are, and whether users are able to resize the frame.

That doesn't seem like a lot of control, but remember, everything you see in the frame—the background color or text alignment, for example—is part of the HTML document that is filling the frame.

Scrolling

You control whether the frame has a scrollbar with the SCROLLING attribute in the `<FRAME>` tag. There are three options:

- The default value is auto, which means that scrollbars will only appear if the content of the frame is too big to entirely fit in the window.

- If you want to make sure a scrollbar is always available, regardless of the content, set the SCROLLING value to yes.

- If you want to make sure that scrollbars never appear and clutter up your gorgeous frameset, set the value to no. Be careful with this one, though, particularly if your frame contains text. If the fonts are set large on a viewer's browser, there will be no way for that person to access content that runs out of the frame without a scrollbar.

On my frameset, I'd like the top frame to never scroll, since I'm just using it for a banner (Figure 11-11). Since my other frames contain content that could potentially run out of the user's available browser space, I'll allow them to have scrollbars on an as-needed basis. Because scrolling is set to auto by default, I don't need to add any code to achieve this effect.

TIP

Space for Scrollbars

When scrollbars are visible, they take up some of the width of the frame. So be sure to figure in the width of a scrollbar when calculating frame sizes in precise pixel measurements. On a Macintosh, scrollbars are 15 pixels wide; on a PC, they're 12 pixels wide.

Figure 11-11

```
<FRAME SRC="header.html" SCROLLING=no>
```

I've removed the scrollbar from my top frame by setting the SCROLLING attribute to "no" in the `<FRAME>` tag for that frame.

TIP

Margins Bug in Navigator

There's a weird bug in Netscape Navigator, Versions 4.0 and earlier, that leaves a 1-pixel margin even if the MARGINHEIGHT and MARGINWIDTH attributes are set to zero. There's not much you can do except camouflage it with a matching background color or image. Navigator 6.0 seems to have corrected the problem.

Setting Margins

Browsers automatically add a little space between the edge of the frame and its contents, just as they do for a web page in the browser. You can control the margin amount inside each frame, either adding extra space or setting the contents flush to the frame's edge.

The MARGINHEIGHT attribute controls the pixel width of the margin at the top and bottom edges of the frame. The MARGINWIDTH attribute controls the space on the left and right edges. Figure 11-12 shows examples of these attributes.

Figure 11-12

```
<FRAMESET COLS="*,*">
        <FRAME SRC="sweetpea.html" MARGINHEIGHT=24 MARGINWIDTH=12>
        <FRAME SRC="sweetpea.html" MARGINHEIGHT=0 MARGINWIDTH=0>
</FRAMESET>
```

The MARGINHEIGHT attribute controls the amount of space between the top and bottom edges of the frame and its contents.

MARGINWIDTH controls the space on the left and right edges.

I'm going to set both margins to zero in my top frame, to nestle my banner graphic as close as possible into the top-left corner (Figure 11-13).

Figure 11-13

```
<FRAME SRC="header.html" SCROLLING=no MARGINHEIGHT=0 MARGINWIDTH=0>
```

With MARGINWIDTH and MARGINHEIGHT set to zero, my graphic is positioned flush to the top-left corner of the frame, with no extra space.

Frame Resizing

By default, users can resize your frames, overriding your careful size settings, simply by clicking on and dragging the border between frames. You can prevent them from doing this by plopping the NORESIZE attribute in the <FRAME> tag. I'd like to make that top frame stay put, so I'm adding the NORESIZE attribute there (Figure 11-14). (I had to temporarily turn on my frame borders to demonstrate the NORESIZE trick; I'll turn them off again for the final product.)

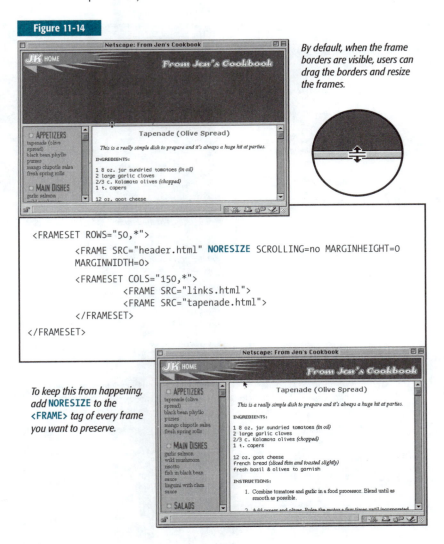

Figure 11-14

By default, when the frame borders are visible, users can drag the borders and resize the frames.

```
<FRAMESET ROWS="50,*">

        <FRAME SRC="header.html" NORESIZE SCROLLING=no MARGINHEIGHT=0
        MARGINWIDTH=0>

        <FRAMESET COLS="150,*">
                <FRAME SRC="links.html">
                <FRAME SRC="tapenade.html">
        </FRAMESET>

</FRAMESET>
```

To keep this from happening, add NORESIZE to the <FRAME> tag of every frame you want to preserve.

Before you go setting all your frames to NORESIZE, consider whether there might be a good reason to allow resizing (such as to view more text in the screen). In my example, users aren't gaining anything by resizing that top frame, so I restricted the ability to change it.

TOOL TIPS

Formatting Frames

Here's how you format individual frames in three of the more popular authoring programs.

DREAMWEAVER 3

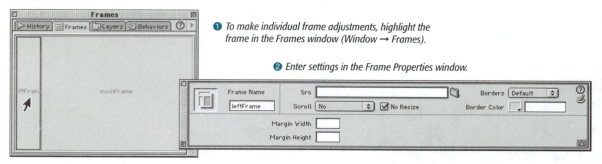

❶ To make individual frame adjustments, highlight the frame in the Frames window (Window → Frames).

❷ Enter settings in the Frame Properties window.

GOLIVE 4

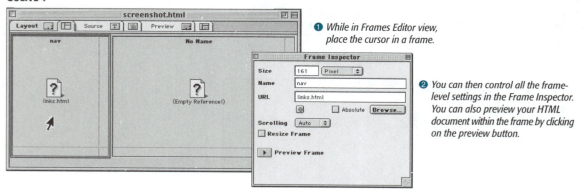

❶ While in Frames Editor view, place the cursor in a frame.

❷ You can then control all the frame-level settings in the Frame Inspector. You can also preview your HTML document within the frame by clicking on the preview button.

FRONTPAGE 2000

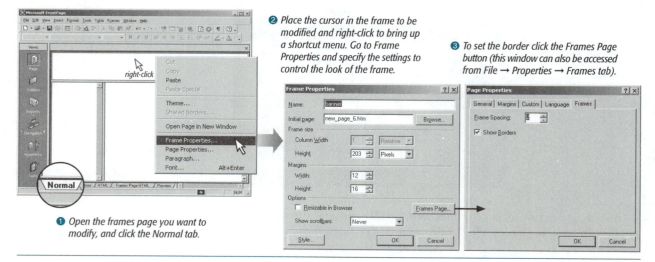

❷ Place the cursor in the frame to be modified and right-click to bring up a shortcut menu. Go to Frame Properties and specify the settings to control the look of the frame.

❸ To set the border click the Frames Page button (this window can also be accessed from File → Properties → Frames tab).

❶ Open the frames page you want to modify, and click the Normal tab.

Targeting Frames

Now that you've gotten the hang of setting up framed documents, it's time to tackle one last aspect of frames: making sure linked documents load into the correct frame.

When you click on a link in an ordinary browser window, the new page replaces the current one in the browser window. The same thing happens by default within a frame. When you click on a link in a frame, the linked document will load in that same frame (a frame is just a mini-browser window).

In many cases, however, you want the linked document to load in a different frame, such as when you have a list of links in one frame and your content in another. In these instances, you need to tell the link which frame to use: in other words, you need to target a specific frame.

Naming the Frame

Before you can target a frame, you need to give it a name using the NAME attribute right in the `<FRAME>` tag ❶ (Figure 11-15, following page). I'd like to load my content documents into the main frame on the page, so I've given that frame the name "main."

Targeting the Frame

Now I can point to that frame from any link ❷. My left frame contains a document (*links.html*) with a list of links. Within *links.html*, I add the TARGET attribute to each of my links and set the value to "main." When someone clicks on that link, the browser will load the new document in the frame called "main."

Reserved Target Names

There are four standardized target names for specific targeting actions. Note that they all begin with an underscore (_). You should avoid giving frames names that begin with an underscore because they will be ignored by the browser. The reserved target names are:

_top
> When you set the target to _top, the new document is loaded in the top level of the browser window, replacing all the frames with a single window. A document that is linked using target="_top" breaks out of its frameset and is displayed in the full browser window.

_parent
> This target name causes the linked document to load into the parent frame (the frameset that is one step up in the nested frame hierarchy). This causes some breaking out as well, but only to the next frame level.

Setting the Target for a Whole Document

If you want all the links on a page to point to the same window, you can specify the target in the header of the document using the `<BASE>` tag as follows:

```
<HEAD>
<BASE TARGET="main">
</HEAD>
```

With this specification in the head of the document, all the links on that page will automatically load in the "main" frame (unless specified otherwise in the link). This technique saves extra typing and keeps the file size down.

Frames

Targeting Frames

Figure 11-15

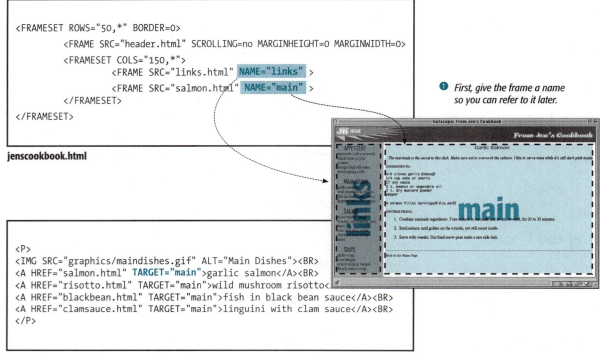

```
<FRAMESET ROWS="50,*" BORDER=0>
        <FRAME SRC="header.html" SCROLLING=no MARGINHEIGHT=0 MARGINWIDTH=0>
        <FRAMESET COLS="150,*">
                <FRAME SRC="links.html" NAME="links" >
                <FRAME SRC="salmon.html" NAME="main" >
        </FRAMESET>
</FRAMESET>
```

jenscookbook.html

❶ *First, give the frame a name so you can refer to it later.*

```
<P>
<IMG SRC="graphics/maindishes.gif" ALT="Main Dishes"><BR>
<A HREF="salmon.html" TARGET="main">garlic salmon</A><BR>
<A HREF="risotto.html" TARGET="main">wild mushroom risotto<
<A HREF="blackbean.html" TARGET="main">fish in black bean sauce</A><BR>
<A HREF="clamsauce.html" TARGET="main">linguini with clam sauce</A><BR>
</P>
```

links.html

❷ *Then, in the HTML document that contains the link, use the TARGET attribute in the anchor tag <A> to call the frame by name.*

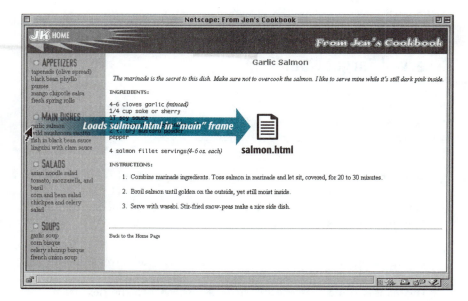

Now, when a user clicks on that link, the linked document will open in the specified frame.

_self

> This causes the document to load in the same frame. Since this action is the default for all frames, you don't need to specify this within the <FRAME> tag. However, it might be useful in the <BASE> tag introduced earlier.

_blank

> A link with target=_blank opens a new browser window to display the linked document. This is not necessarily a frames-related value—you can use it from any web page. Bear in mind, however, that each time a link that targets _blank is clicked, the browser launches a new window, potentially leaving the user with a mess of open browser windows.

I'm going to need to take advantage of the _top value in my documents. The top frame contains a graphic link to the home page. If I leave it as it is, the home page will load in that little sliver of a frame. To break out of the frames and get back to a normal browser window, I'll target the top level in that link (Figure 11-16).

TIP

Linking between frames can be tricky. Pay attention to what you're doing and test all of your links in a browser to make sure they're behaving the way you intend.

Figure 11-16

```
<A HREF="index.html" TARGET="_top"><IMG SRC="graphics/jk-home.gif"
BORDER=0 ALT="HOME"></A>
```

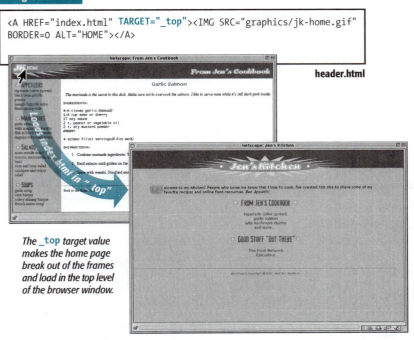

header.html

The _top target value makes the home page break out of the frames and load in the top level of the browser window.

Content for Users Without Frames

The last thing you should add to your frameset document is some content that will display for users without frame-enabled browsers. This benefits people using older browsers (or text-only browsers) that don't support frames, as well as people who have turned frames support off using their browser preferences. You place your alternative content between <NOFRAMES> tags.

NOFRAMES content prevents your framed document from becoming a dead end to search engines and users without frames-enabled browsers.

Many people simply put a message such as "You need a frames-enabled browser to view this page." While this is acceptable, it is preferable to put a full page of content, including links to deeper pages of your site, within the <NOFRAMES> tags.

For one thing, it provides actual content and navigation to users who are using non-frames-enabled browsers (they may be using them for a good reason). In addition, it gives major search engines (such as Lycos, AltaVista, and others) something to index on your page as well as access to content linked to that page. If there are only frameset and frame tags on the page, the page will be ignored.

Between the <NOFRAMES> tags, add everything you would put in an ordinary non-framed document. This includes the <BODY> tag with its attributes for setting background tiles and colors. Figure 11-17 shows the <NOFRAMES> content I've provided for my "From Jen's Cookbook" frameset.

Figure 11-17

```
<HTML>
<HEAD>
<TITLE>From Jen's Cookbook</TITLE>
</HEAD>
<FRAMESET rows="50,*" BORDER=0 FRAMEBORDER=0 FRAMEBORDER=no>
        <FRAME SRC="header.html" MARGINWIDTH=0 MARGINHEIGHT=0 SCROLLING=no>
        <FRAMESET COLS="150,*">
                <FRAME SRC="links.html">
                <FRAME SRC="tapenade.html" NAME="main">
        </FRAMESET>
</FRAMESET>

<NOFRAMES>
<BODY BACKGROUND="graphics/bkgd-grid.gif">
<CENTER>
<IMG SRC="graphics/jensbook.gif">
<P>[NOTE: This page is best viewed with a frames-enabled browser
<P>
<IMG SRC="graphics/appetizers.gif" ALT="Appetizers"><BR>
<A HREF="tapenade.html" TARGET="main">tapenade (olive spread)</A
<A HREF="purses.html" TARGET="main">black bean phyllo purses</A>
<A HREF="mangosalsa.html" TARGET="main">mango chipotle salsa</A>
<A HREF="springroll.html" TARGET="main">fresh spring rolls</A>
```

The content I've provided within <NOFRAMES> tags will appear in any browser that does not support frames. My "noframes" content provides similar functionality and a similar look to the framed document.

HTML Review–Frame Tags

The following is a summary of the tags we covered in this chapter.

Tag and Attributes	Function
`<FRAMESET>`	Indicates the body of a framed document
`BORDER=number`	Border thickness in pixels when border is on
`COLS="measurements"`	Number of columns (vertical frames)
`FRAMEBORDER=1|0`	Specifies whether borders appear between the frames (1 is yes; 0 is no)
`ROWS="measurements"`	Number of rows (horizontal frames)
`<FRAME>`	Adds a frame to a framed document
`MARGINWIDTH=number`	Pixel space held on left edge of the frame
`MARGINHEIGHT=number`	Pixel space held on the top edge of the frame
`NAME="text"`	Name of the frame (for targeting)
`SCROLLING=yes|no|auto`	Specifies whether scrollbars appear in the frame
`SRC="url"`	Name of the file to load in the frame
`<NOFRAMES>`	Content that will display in a non-frames browser

Color on the Web

In past chapters, we've come across several opportunities to specify colors in our HTML code. There are two methods for doing this: by name or by numeric value. Not surprisingly, both methods are quirky. Let's start with the least technical.

Specifying Colors by Name

You can specify a color using one of 140 color names. Some names are normal ("red," "brown," "white") while many of the names are sort of silly (my favorites are "burlywood" and "papayawhip"). The set of names was originally developed for a Unix windowing system and was adopted early on by the creators of the Web.

To use a color name, insert it as the value for any attribute that calls for a color specification (Figure 12-1).

Table 12-1 (next page) lists the complete color name list by hue. To view a sample of each color, see the chart on the web page for this book at *www.learningwebdesign.com*.

IN THIS CHAPTER

Specifying colors by name

Specifying colors by their numeric RGB values

HTML elements you can color

The web palette

Figure 12-1

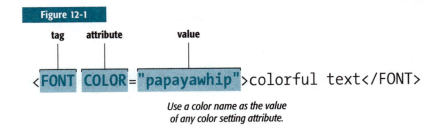

```
<FONT COLOR="papayawhip">colorful text</FONT>
```

Use a color name as the value of any color setting attribute.

WARNING

Bear in mind that the colors you specify will not necessarily look the way they do on your monitor when viewed by your readers. The way the color is rendered is a function of the configuration of the computer monitor it is viewed on—the number of colors it displays as well as its overall brightness (gamma) setting. Colors may be lighter or darker, have a slightly different tint, or even dither.

Table 12-1: Web Color Names by Hue

black
white

Cool Neutrals
darkgray
darkslategray
dimgray
gainsboro
ghostwhite
gray
lightgray
lightslategray
silver
slategray
snow
whitesmoke

Warm Neutrals
antiquewhite
cornsilk
floralwhite
ivory
linen
oldlace
papayawhip
seashell

Browns/Tans
beige
bisque
blanchedalmond
brown
burlywood
chocolate
khaki
moccasin
navahowhite
peru
rosybrown
saddlebrown
sandybrown
sienna
tan
wheat

Oranges
darkorange
orange
orangered
peachpuff

Yellows
darkgoldenrod
gold
goldenrod
lemonchiffon
lightgoldenrod-
  yellow
lightyellow
palegoldenrod
yellow

Greens
aquamarine
chartreuse
darkgreen
darkkhaki
darkolivegreen
darkseagreen
forestgreen
green
greenyellow
honeydew
lawngreen
lightgreen
lime
limegreen
mediumseagreen
mediumspring-
  green
mintcream
olive
olivedrab
palegreen
seagreen
springgreen
yellowgreen

Blue-greens
aqua
cyan
darkcyan
darkturquoise
lightcyan
lightseagreen
mediumaqua-
  marine
mediumturquoise
paleturquoise
teal
turquoise

Blues
aliceblue
azure
blue
cadetblue
cornflowerblue
darkblue
darkslateblue
deepskyblue
dodgerblue
indigo
lightblue
lightskyblue
lightsteelblue
mediumblue
mediumslateblue
midnightblue
navy
powderblue
royalblue
skyblue
slateblue
steelblue

Purples
blueviolet
darkmagenta
darkorchid
darkviolet
fuchsia
lavender
lavenderblush
mediumorchid
mediumpurple
mediumvioletred
orchid
palevioletred
plum
purple
thistle
violet

Pinks
coral
darksalmon
deeppink
hotpink
lightcoral
lightpink
lightsalmon
magenta
mistyrose
pink
salmon

Reds
crimson
darkred
firebrick
indianred
maroon
red
tomato

Specifying Colors by Number

The more precise way to specify color is to provide the numeric description of the color. For those who are not familiar with how computers deal with color, I'm going to start with the basics before jumping into the HTML.

A Word About RGB Color

Computers create the colors you see on a monitor by combining three colors of light: red, green, and blue. This color model is known as RGB color. When you mix full intensities of the three colors, they blend together to create white (Figure 12-2, gallery).

Figure 12-2	G

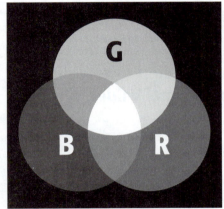

Computer monitors use the RGB color model in which colors are made up of combinations of red, green, and blue light.

If you mix all three colors at full intensity you get white. Another way of saying this is that RGB color is additive.

You can provide recipes (of sorts) for colors by telling the computer how much of each color to mix in. The amount of light in each color "channel" is described on a scale from 0 (none) to 255 (full-blast). The closer the three values get to 255, the closer the resulting color gets to white.

So, any color you see on your monitor can be described by a series of three numbers: the red value, the green value, and the blue value. With the RGB color system, a pleasant lavender can be described as 200, 178, 230.

This is one of the ways that image editors (such as Adobe Photoshop or JASC Paint Shop Pro) keep track of colors. Every pixel in an image is described in terms of its RGB color values. You can use an image editor to find the RGB values for the colors you want to use.

Computers create colors by combining red, green, and blue light (thus "RGB color"). The amount of light in each color "channel" is given a value from 1 to 255. You can specify any RGB color by providing its numeric values.

Color on the Web

Let's say I want to match elements on my web page to a certain yellow-orange that appears in one of my graphics. Using Adobe Photoshop, I can find out the RGB values of any color in my image by positioning the pointer over my chosen color and reading the RGB values in the Info palette (Figure 12-3, gallery).

Figure 12-3 | G

Finding RGB values
In Photoshop, the Info palette provides the RGB values when I pass the eyedropper (or any tool) over the image.

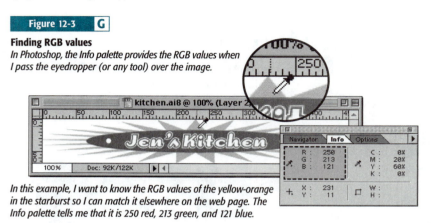

In this example, I want to know the RGB values of the yellow-orange in the starburst so I can match it elsewhere on the web page. The Info palette tells me that it is 250 red, 213 green, and 121 blue.

Hexadecimal Values

Now that I know the RGB values for my yellow-orange color, I should be able to plug them right into my HTML, right? Unfortunately, it's not that straightforward.

In HTML, the RGB values must be provided in hexadecimal (not decimal) numbers.

Browsers want their RGB number values as hexadecimal, not decimal, numbers. The hexadecimal numbering system is base-16 instead of base-10 (base-10 is the decimal system we're used to). Hexadecimal uses 16 digits (0 through 9 and A through F) to make up numbers. Figure 12-4 shows how this works.

Figure 12-4

The hexadecimal numbering system is base-16. It uses the characters 0 through 9 and A through F (for representing the quantities 10 through 15).

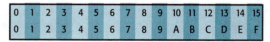

sixteens place

ones place

The decimal number **32** is represented as

20

(2 sixteens and 0 ones)

The decimal number **42** is represented as

2A

(2 sixteens and 10 ones)

The hexadecimal system is used widely in computing to reduce the space it takes to store certain information. For instance, our RGB values are reduced from three to two characters once they are converted to hexadecimal ("hex" for short) values.

You can calculate a hex value by dividing your number by 16 to get the first number, and then using the remainder for the second number. So, 200 equals C8 because 200=(16 × 12) + 8. That's {12,8} in base-16, or C8 in hexadecimal. Whew!

Or, you can use a calculator to do the conversion (much easier). In Windows, the standard calculator has a hexadecimal converter in the "Scientific" view. Mac users can download a copy of Calculator II (*ftp://ftp.amug.org/pub/mirrors/info-mac/sci/calc/calculator-ii-15.hqx*). For your convenience, a decimal to hexadecimal chart is provided in Table 12-2 (following page).

I'll use a calculator to translate my orange-yellow RGB values (R:250, G:213, B:121) into hexadecimal (Figure 12-5).

| TIP |

Handy Hex Values

White = #FFFFFF
(the equivalent of 255,255,255)

Black = #000000
(the equivalent of 0,0,0)

Color on the Web

Figure 12-5

Since I work on a Mac I am using Calculator II to convert my RGB values to hexadecimal.

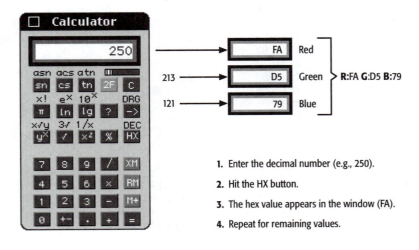

1. Enter the decimal number (e.g., 250).

2. Hit the HX button.

3. The hex value appears in the window (FA).

4. Repeat for remaining values.

Table 12-2: Decimal to Hexadecimal Equivalents

dec = hex	dec = hex	dec = hex	dec = hex	dec = hex	dec = hex
0 = 00	51 = 33	102 = 66	153 = 99	204 = CC	255 = FF
1 = 01	52 = 34	103 = 67	154 = 9A	205 = CD	
2 = 02	53 = 35	104 = 68	155 = 9B	206 = CE	
3 = 03	54 = 36	105 = 69	156 = 9C	207 = CF	
4 = 04	55 = 37	106 = 6A	157 = 9D	208 = D0	
5 = 05	56 = 38	107 = 6B	158 = 9E	209 = D1	
6 = 06	57 = 39	108 = 6C	159 = 9F	210 = D2	
7 = 07	58 = 3A	109 = 6D	160 = A0	211 = D3	
8 = 08	59 = 3B	110 = 6E	161 = A1	212 = D4	
9 = 09	60 = 3C	111 = 6F	162 = A2	213 = D5	
10 = 0A	61 = 3D	112 = 70	163 = A3	214 = D6	
11 = 0B	62 = 3E	113 - 71	164 = A4	215 = D7	
12 = 0C	63 = 3F	114 = 72	165 = A5	216 = D8	
13 = 0D	64 = 40	115 = 73	166 = A6	217 = D9	
14 = 0E	65 = 41	116 = 74	167 = A7	218 = DA	
15 = 0F	66 = 42	117 = 75	168 = A8	219 = DB	
16 = 10	67 = 43	118 = 76	169 = A9	220 = DC	
17 = 11	68 = 44	119 = 77	170 = AA	221 = DD	
18 = 12	69 = 45	120 = 78	171 = AB	222 = DE	
19 = 13	70 = 46	121 = 79	172 = AC	223 = DF	
20 = 14	71 = 47	122 = 7A	173 = AD	224 = E0	
21 = 15	72 = 48	123 = 7B	174 = AE	225 = E1	
22 = 16	73 = 49	124 = 7C	175 = AF	226 = E2	
23 = 17	74 = 4A	125 = 7D	176 = B0	227 = E3	
24 = 18	75 = 4B	126 = 7E	177 = B1	228 = E4	
25 = 19	76 = 4C	127 = 7F	178 = B2	229 = E5	
26 = 1A	77 = 4D	128 = 80	179 = B3	230 = E6	
27 = 1B	78 = 4E	129 = 81	180 = B4	231 = E7	
28 = 1C	79 = 4F	130 = 82	181 = B5	232 = E8	
29 = 1D	80 = 50	131 = 83	182 = B6	233 = E9	
30 = 1E	81 = 51	132 = 84	183 = B7	234 = EA	
31 = 1F	82 = 52	133 = 85	184 = B8	235 = EB	
32 = 20	83 = 53	134 = 86	185 = B9	236 = EC	
33 = 21	84 = 54	135 = 87	186 = BA	237 = ED	
34 = 22	85 = 55	136 = 88	187 = BB	238 = EE	
35 = 23	86 = 56	137 = 89	188 = BC	239 = EF	
36 = 24	87 = 57	138 = 8A	189 = BD	240 = F0	
37 = 25	88 = 58	139 = 8B	190 = BE	241 = F1	
38 = 26	89 = 59	140 = 8C	191 = BF	242 = F2	
39 = 27	90 = 5A	141 = 8D	192 = C0	243 = F3	
40 = 28	91 = 5B	142 = 8E	193 = C1	244 = F4	
41 = 29	92 = 5C	143 = 8F	194 = C2	245 = F5	
42 = 2A	93 = 5D	144 = 90	195 = C3	246 = F6	
43 = 2B	94 = 5E	145 = 91	196 = C4	247 = F7	
44 = 2C	95 = 5F	146 = 92	197 = C5	248 = F8	
45 = 2D	96 = 60	147 = 93	198 = C6	249 = F9	
46 = 2E	97 = 61	148 = 94	199 = C7	250 = FA	
47 = 2F	98 = 62	149 = 95	200 = C8	251 = FB	
48 = 30	99 = 63	150 = 96	201 = C9	252 = FC	
49 = 31	100 = 64	151 = 97	202 = CA	253 = FD	
50 = 32	101 = 65	152 = 98	203 = CB	254 = FE	

Using RGB Values in HTML

Now we are ready to insert the 2-digit, hexadecimal RGB values in our HTML code. Color values are written into HTML in the following syntax: "#RRGGBB" (Figure 12-6).

Color on the Web

Figure 12-6

Putting color values into HTML

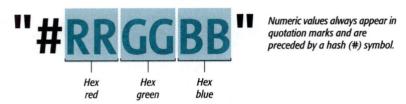

Numeric values always appear in quotation marks and are preceded by a hash (#) symbol.

Hex red   Hex green   Hex blue

For example, if I want to make a table cell the same yellow-orange as my banner graphic, I use the hexadecimal values I calculated in Figure 12-5 after the BGCOLOR attribute, as shown in Figure 12-7.

Figure 12-7

Using my yellow-orange as the background color in a table cell, I get:

```
<TD BGCOLOR="#FAD579">
```

Quick Summary

It took us a few pages to get here, but the process is actually easy: first, find the RGB values of the color you want to use (using an image-editing tool helps), then convert each value to hexadecimal and put it in the tag. Be sure to include the hash (#) mark.

Elements You Can Color with HTML

Now that you know *how* to set colors in HTML, let's look at all the things you *can* color.* We've run across them in past HTML chapters, but it is useful to look at the big picture. Remember, you can use either color names or hexadecimal color descriptions as the values for any of these attributes.

Document-Wide Color Settings

The `<BODY>` tag is primarily used to give structure to an HTML document, but it also has a number of attributes that apply color settings for the entire document. You can use any number and combination of the following attributes in a single `<BODY>` tag:

`<BODY BGCOLOR="`*color name* or *number*`">`
Sets a solid background color for the entire document.

`<BODY TEXT="`*color name* or *number*`">`
Specifies the default text color for the entire document. The default color is black. You can override the default color of any text using the `<FONT COLOR>` tag.

`<BODY LINK="`*color name* or *number*`">`
Specifies the color used for all links in the document. In most browsers, the default color is bright blue. You can override the color of an individual link by using the `<FONT COLOR>` tag, as long as the opening and closing `<FONT>` tags are entirely within the anchor (`<A>`) tags.

`<BODY VLINK="`*color name* or *number*`">`
Sets the color of all visited links in the document. A visited link is one that has already been clicked on and followed. Its default color on most browsers is purple.

`<BODY ALINK="`*color name* or *number*`">`
Sets the color of all active links. The active link color shows up only as the link is in the process of being clicked—so it is a fleeting color, but it does provide useful visual feedback to the user.

AT A GLANCE

The following tags and attributes accept color values:

```
<BODY BGCOLOR>
<BODY TEXT>
<BODY LINK>
<BODY VLINK>
<BODY ALINK>
<FONT COLOR>
<BASEFONT COLOR>
<TABLE BGCOLOR>
<TR BGCOLOR>
<TD BGCOLOR>
<TH BGCOLOR>
```

Coloring Individual Links

Setting the link color in the `<BODY>` tag changes the color for all the links in the document. If you want a link to be different from the global link color, use the `<FONT>` tag with the COLOR attribute. In order for it to work, the opening and closing `<FONT>` tags need to be entirely enclosed within the anchor (`<A>`) tags, as shown here:

```
<A HREF="foo.html"><FONT
COLOR="seagreen">Click
here!</FONT></A>
```

---

* There are more opportunities to specify color using Cascading Style Sheets in addition to HTML; however, it is beyond the scope of this book. An introduction to style sheets is provided in Chapter 20, How'd They Do That?

Coloring Text

You can specify colors for any text selection using the COLOR attribute in the <FONT> tag (see Chapter 7, Formatting Text, for more information about the <FONT> and <BASEFONT> tags):

<FONT COLOR="*color name or number*">

Changes the color of any amount of content between the container tags. Text color set with the <FONT> tag overrides color settings in the <BODY> tag.

<BASEFONT COLOR="*color name or number*">

Changes the color of all the text following the tag (except if it is in a table). BASEFONT can also be used to adjust the size of following text with the SIZE attribute.

Although the COLOR attribute is in the HTML specification and supported by Internet Explorer Version 3 and higher, Netscape Navigator does not support it in the <BASEFONT> tag. For this reason, setting text colors with this method is unreliable.

Table Backgrounds

You can color the backgrounds of cells and tables using the BGCOLOR attribute in the standard table tags (see Chapter 10, Tables, for more information on these tags):

<TABLE BGCOLOR="*color name or number*">

Applies a background color to all the cells in a table. This attribute is implemented differently across browsers. Microsoft Internet Explorer makes the table a solid block of color, while Netscape Navigator only fills the cell space with color, leaving the border and any cell spacing the same color as the background of the page, resulting in a checkered look.

<TR BGCOLOR="*color name or number*">

Applies a background color to every cell in that row. Settings in the row tag will override color settings in the <TABLE> tag.

<TD BGCOLOR="*color name or number*">

Specifies the background color of an individual cell. Color settings in the cell tag will override color settings at the row and table level.

<TH BGCOLOR="*color name or number*">

Specifies the background color of header cells. Like <TD> settings, settings in the header will override row- and table-level settings.

TIP

It is important to note that <FONT> and <BASEFONT> settings do not carry over through tables, so if you want all the text in a table to be a certain color, you'll need to specify the font color for the text in every individual cell.

Color on the Web

The Web Palette

If you spend any time at all in the web biz, you will be sure to hear the term "web palette" sooner or later. It also goes by the names "web-safe colors," "the Netscape palette," and "the browser-safe palette," just to name a few. As a web designer, it is important to understand the web palette concept and its applications.

What It Is

The web palette is a set of 216 predefined colors that will not dither on Macs or PCs.

Before we launch into the web palette, let's talk a little about palettes in general. A palette is just a set of colors. Palettes come in handy for computers that can only display a limited number of colors, such as 8-bit monitors that can display a maximum of 256 colors at a time. PCs with 8-bit color have a palette of 256 system colors that they use to make up images on the screen. Macs have a similar system palette.

The web palette is a specific set of 216 colors that will not dither when viewed in a browser on Macs or PCs. The major browsers use colors from this built-in web palette when they are running on computers with only 8-bit monitors. Because the palette is part of the browser software, this is a way of ensuring that the graphics will look more or less the same on all platforms.

The web palette in its natural habitat can be seen on the web page for this book at *www.learningwebdesign.com*. You can also access the web palette easily in web authoring tools, usually from a pop-up window of color choices (see Tool Tips at the end of this chapter).

You'll probably notice the large percentage of fluorescent shades and otherwise unpleasant colors. Unfortunately, because the colors in the web palette were selected mathematically, not aesthetically, many of the colors wouldn't be your first choice.

TIP

Chapter 14, Creating GIFs, has more information about the web palette as it relates to graphic production, including how to access the web palette swatches in Adobe Photoshop and Macromedia Fireworks.

What Makes Colors "Safe"

It just so happens that the 216 web-palette colors are the colors shared by the Windows and Mac system palettes. This means that colors chosen from the web palette will render accurately on Mac or PC displays without shifting or dithering. That's why they're called web-"safe" colors— they stay true on both platforms. (Unfortunately, the Unix operating system was left out of this equation.)

How It Works

On monitors with millions (24-bit) or thousands (16-bit) of colors, browsers don't need to refer to a palette to render colors accurately. But on 8-bit monitors with only 256 colors available, many colors from the full visual range must be approximated using the colors on hand.

Browsers are stuck using just the 216 colors from the web palette to do this approximating. Most will fill in the extra 40 colors of the possible 256 from the user's system palette.

When a color from the full color space is rendered on an 8-bit monitor, the browser does the best it can to represent the color using colors from the web palette. Depending on the color, it may be shifted to the nearest web-safe equivalent, or it may be approximated by blending two colors from the web palette in a process called dithering (Figure 12-8). The results can be unpredictable and are most undesirable in text and areas of flat color. In continuous tone images, such as photographs, dithering is not as big of a problem; in fact, it can even be beneficial.

The web palette only comes into play on 8-bit monitors.

Figure 12-8

On 8-bit monitors with only 256 colors, browsers need to approximate colors that are not part of the web palette.

Shifting
Some colors will shift to their nearest palette equivalent.

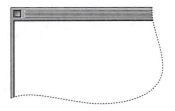

```
<BODY BGCOLOR="#FFAFF0">
```

In the HTML file, I've specified a warm off-white.

In the browser, it shifts to plain old white.

Dithering
Some colors will be dithered (made up by mixing colors from the browser's palette).

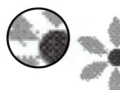

On a monitor with millions of colors, the color is smooth.

For users with 8-bit monitors, the colors are dithered.

Color on the Web

Safe Color Names

Of the 140 color names, only 10 represent colors from the web palette. They are:

aqua	lime
black	magenta
blue	red
cyan	white
fuchsia	yellow

Designing with colors from the web palette ensures your colors are solid and consistent on all displays.

The Web Palette in Numbers

An important way to look at the web palette is by its numeric values. The palette recognizes six shades of red, six shades of green, and six shades of blue, resulting in 216 possible color values (6 × 6 × 6 = 216). That is why it is sometimes called the "6 × 6 × 6 color cube."

Those six shades in decimal values are 0, 51, 102, 153, 204, and 255. These translate to 00, 33, 66, 99, CC, and FF in hexadecimal. It's easy to recognize a web-safe color in HTML code because it is a combination of these six hex values: #6699FF and #0033CC are web-safe, #FAD579 is not.

Table 12-3 shows the decimal, hexadecimal, and percentage values for each of the six component values in the web palette.

Table 12-3: Numerical Values for Web Palette Colors

Decimal	Hexadecimal	Percentage
0 (darkest)	00	0%
51	33	20%
102	66	40%
153	99	60%
204	CC	80%
255 (lightest)	FF	100%

What This Means to You

Now you know that when browsers are running on 8-bit monitors, they use colors from their built-in palette of 216 web-safe colors to approximate the colors on the page. How can this help you?

Since you know *exactly* which color values will not dither, you can use the web palette to your advantage by designing with those colors in the first place. You'll beat the browser to the task. This way, you can ensure that your colors and your graphics look the same to the maximum number of users. You can prevent the color shifts and blotchy dithering that are the result of the browser remapping colors to the web palette.

In addition, you will find that many web design firms and their clients require designers to use colors from the web palette for consistency in quality.

The web palette applies to all colors on the page, whether specified in HTML or as part of a graphic. We'll discuss designing graphics with the web palette in Chapter 14.

TOOL TIPS

Accessing the Web Palette

With so much emphasis placed on the web-safe palette, it is becoming a standard feature of web-authoring software tools. The tools provide an easy visual interface to select web-safe colors for your web page elements, and they take care of filling in the HTML code for you.

Here's how you access the web palette in three of the more popular authoring programs.

DREAMWEAVER 3

Clicking on the Palette icon ( ) in the Properties window or any dialog box pops up a web-safe color palette. Choose a color by clicking on it with the eyedropper pointer (it will even show you the hex values as you pass the cursor over the squares).

#FF3333

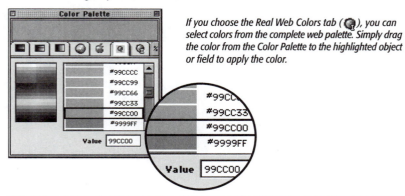

#FF3333

GOLIVE 4

All colors are managed by the Color Palette.

If you choose the Real Web Colors tab ( ), you can select colors from the complete web palette. Simply drag the color from the Color Palette to the highlighted object or field to apply the color.

FRONTPAGE 2000

Color can be applied from the Properties window or most dialog boxes. A few web-safe choices are typically given, with access to a complete web-safe palette. Choose a color by clicking on it with the eyedropper pointer. The hex value will appear as the eyedropper moves over each color.

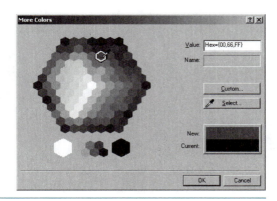

Figure 4-7

The image below shows a graphic as it might appear on a monitor that displays millions or thousands of colors (24-bit or 16-bit monitors). These monitors can smoothly display an enormous range of colors.

8-bit monitors, on the other hand, can display only 256 colors at a time. Within the browser, there are only 216 available colors to choose from.

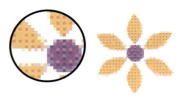

The image above shows what happens to the same graphic when viewed on an 8-bit monitor. The close-up shows how the real color is approximated by mixing colors from the available palette of colors. This effect is called dithering.

Figure 8-11

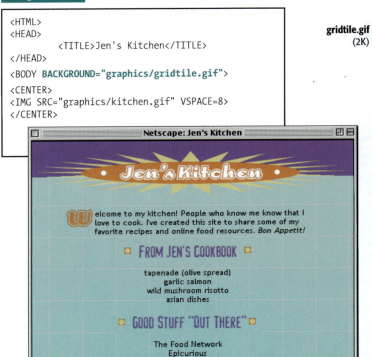

```html
<HTML>
<HEAD>
        <TITLE>Jen's Kitchen</TITLE>
</HEAD>
<BODY BACKGROUND="graphics/gridtile.gif">
<CENTER>
<IMG SRC="graphics/kitchen.gif" VSPACE=8>
</CENTER>
```

gridtile.gif
(2K)

I've added a tiling background image (**gridtile.gif**) to my Jen's Kitchen site. I made the graphic really tall so you can't see the second row of tiles, creating the effect of a band of color at the top of the page.

Figure 4-8

Mac

Windows

Gamma refers to the overall brightness of monitors. Windows machines tend to be darker (the result of higher gamma settings) than Macs.

Chapter 10 Sidebar:
"The Finished Product"

Chapter 11 Sidebar:
"The Finished Product"

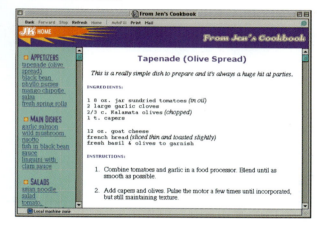

Figure 12-2

Colors on computer monitors use the RGB color model in which colors are made up of combinations of Red, Green, and Blue light.

If you mix all three colors at full intensity you get white. Another way of saying this is that RGB color is additive.

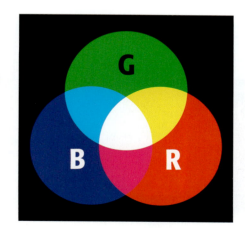

Figure 12-3

Finding RGB values

In Photoshop, the Info palette provides the RGB values when I pass the eyedropper (or any tool) over the image.

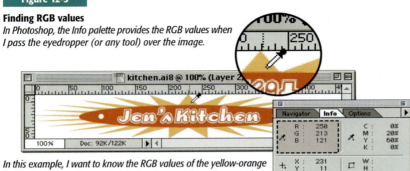

In this example, I want to know the RGB values of the yellow-orange in the starburst so I can match it elsewhere on the web page. The Info palette tells me that it is 250 red, 213 green, and 121 blue.

Figure 13-1

The GIF file format is best for images with sharp lines and areas of flat color.

Figure 13-2

The JPEG file format works best for images with gradient colors, such as photos or paintings.

Figure 13-9

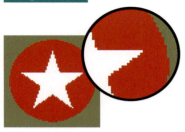

Aliased text and images have stair-stepped edges.

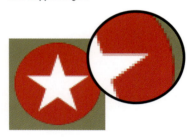

Anti-aliased text and images have blurred edges to make transitions smoother.

Figure 14-1

The GIF format is great for graphical images comprised mainly of flat colors and hard edges.

Figure 14-2

The colors in an indexed color image are stored in and referenced by a color table. The color table (also called a palette) can contain a maximum of 256 colors (8-bit).

In this figure we see the color table for the U.F.O. banner graphic.

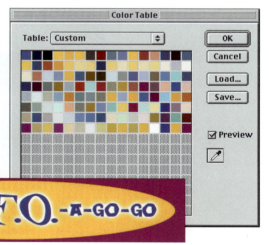

Figure 14-15

"Halos" are the fringe that's left around a transparent image. They happen when anti-aliased edges have been blended with a color that is lighter than the page background.

Halos do not happen around aliased (stair-stepped) text and images because there is a hard edge between colors.

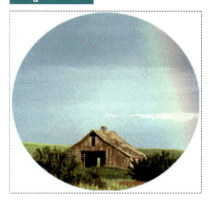

Figure 14-21

256 colors: 21K   **64 colors: 13K**   **8 colors: 8K**

Reducing the number of colors in an image reduces the file size.

Figure 14-22

Dithering: 9.6K   **No dithering: 7.8K**

Turning off or reducing the amount of dithering will reduce the file size.
Both images have 32 pixel colors and use an Adaptive palette.

Figure 14-23

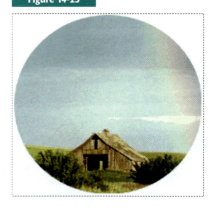

"Lossy" set to 0%: 13.2K   **"Lossy" set to 25%: 7.5K**

Applying a "Lossy" (in Photoshop) or "Loss" (in Fireworks) value removes
pixels from the image and results in smaller file size. Both images shown
here contain 64 colors and use Diffusion dither.

Figure 14-24

You can keep file sizes small by designing in a way that takes advantage of the GIF compression scheme.

This GIF has gradient blends and 256 colors. Its file size is 19K.

Even when I reduce the number of colors to 8, the file size is still 7.6K.

When I create the same image with flat colors instead of blends, the size of the GIF file is only 3.2K.

Figure 14-27

This GIF is designed with non-web-safe colors, resulting in dithering on 8-bit monitors.

On a 24-bit monitor, the solid colors are smooth and accurate.

On an 8-bit monitor, the colors are approximated by dithering colors from the web palette.

If the flat areas are filled with web-safe colors, the photograph still dithers, but the flat colors stay flat.

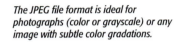

Figure 15-1

The JPEG file format is ideal for photographs (color or grayscale) or any image with subtle color gradations.

Figure 15-2

Original

High compression

JPEG compression discards image detail to achieve smaller file sizes. At very high compression rates, image quality suffers, as shown in the image on the right.

Figure 15-3

gradient.jpg (12K)　　　　**detail.jpg (49K)**

JPEG compression works better on smooth images than images with hard edges and detail. Compare the file sizes of these examples.

Figure 15-4

chair.jpg　　　*The same flat graphical image saved as both a JPEG and a GIF.*　　　**chair.gif**

In the JPEG, the flat color changes and gets blotchy. Detail is lost as a result of JPEG compression.

In the GIF, the flat colors and crisp detail are preserved.

Figure 15-5

Photo courtesy of Liam Lynch

Progressive JPEGs render in a series of passes. The image detail and quality is improved with each pass.

Figure 15-10

A comparison of various compression levels in Adobe Photoshop 5.5 and Macromedia Fireworks 3.

Photoshop 5.5

Photoshop 100% (42.2K) *Photoshop 80% (22.3K)* *Photoshop 60% (13.6K)*

Photoshop 40% (8.2K) *Photoshop 20% (6.0K)* *Photoshop 0% (3.7K)*

Fireworks 3

Fireworks 100% (32.7K) *Fireworks 80% (10K)* *Fireworks 60% (6.8K)*

Fireworks 40% (5.2K) *Fireworks 20% (3.4K)* *Fireworks 0% (0.6K)*

Figure 15-11

Blurring the image slightly before exporting as a JPEG will result in smaller file sizes.

Quality: 20 Blur: 0   (8.7K)

Quality: 20 Blur: .5 (6.9K)

Quality: 20 Blur: 0   (6.6K)
(blur applied manually with Gaussian blur filter)

This JPEG was saved at low quality (20 in Photoshop) with no blurring applied.

In this JPEG, I applied a slight blur to the image (.5 in Photoshop) before exporting it. Although it has the same quality setting (20) the file size is 20% smaller.

In Fireworks, use the "Smoothing" setting to apply a blur.

In this image, I blurred only selected areas of the image. This way, I was able to apply a more aggressive blur to parts of the image while maintaining detail in the face where it is important. The file size is comparable to the blurred example.

Figure 16-1

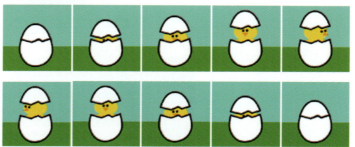

This animated GIF contains all of the images shown above. The images play back in sequence, creating a motion effect. When this GIF is viewed in a browser, the chick pops up, takes a look around, and then goes back in its shell.

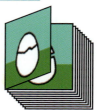

Each frame is similar to a page in a child's flipbook.

Figure 17-12

This decorative element was created with five rows of 1-pixel GIFs of various colors. Each GIF was set to a specific size to form the pattern you see here.

No extra space between `<IMG>` *tags.*

```
<P>
<IMG SRC="1px-blue.gif" WIDTH=200 HEIGHT=2><BR>
<IMG SRC="1px-green.gif" WIDTH=95 HEIGHT=10><IMG SRC="1px-blue.gif"
        WIDTH=10 HEIGHT=10><IMG SRC="1px-green.gif" WIDTH=95 HEIGHT=10><BR>
<IMG SRC="1px-green.gif" WIDTH=85 HEIGHT=10><IMG SRC="1px-blue.gif"
        WIDTH=10 HEIGHT=10><IMG SRC="1px-white.gif"
        WIDTH=10 HEIGHT=10><IMG SRC="1px-blue.gif" WIDTH=10
        HEIGHT=10><IMG SRC="1px-green.gif" WIDTH=85 HEIGHT=10><BR>
<IMG SRC="1px-green.gif" WIDTH=95 HEIGHT=10><IMG SRC="1px-blue.gif"
        WIDTH=10 HEIGHT=10><IMG SRC="1px-green.gif" WIDTH=95 HEIGHT=10><BR>
<IMG SRC="1px-blue.gif" WIDTH=200 HEIGHT=2>
</P>
```

Figure 18-11

Section color-coding is a popular method for orienting users within your site.

Amazon.com

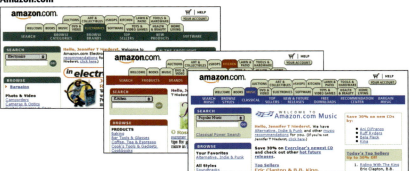

Buy.com

Figure 18-25

The Blue Family
home page.

Figure 18-26

A typical
second-level
page for the
Blue Family site.

Figure 19-2

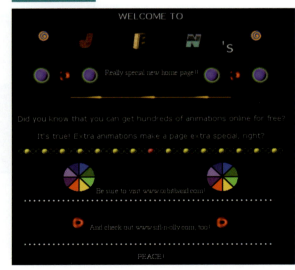

Here's an example of too much
animation! I wish this printed
book could show you the true
"splendor" of my new special
home page, featuring
animated letters, bullets, and
divider bars. Imagine every
graphic spinning, rotating, or
pulsating. This may look like
an exaggeration, but I have
seen pages like this and worse.

Figure 19-4

This excerpt from the Webmonkey home page (**www.webmonkey.com**) uses type treatments effectively to convey the structure of the information. Article listings have the same structure, with the article title given the most visual weight. Section titles are also treated similarly and are given lots of space to set them apart from other listings.

Figure 19-14

This page suffers from color overkill. Making every element a different bright color is a sure way to create visual chaos.

Figure 19-15

Bold background patterns can make the text on the page unreadable.

Figure 19-17

The web page of
my nightmares! This
page has it all:

• Gratuitous black background
• Animated rainbow dividers
• A spinning globe
• An unreadable link color
• Meaningless icons
• Too many colors
• Bad alignment

Figure 20-11

Scenes from a music video for Beck's "Nicotine and Gravy" (created by Fullerene Productions).

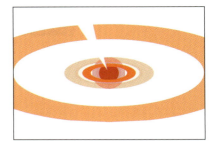

Flash intro and web site interface (screenshots from www.eye4u.com, a web design firm in Munich).

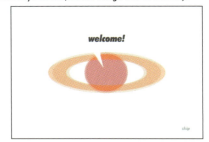

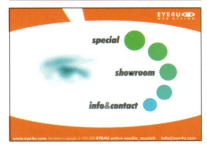

Flash animation. Shots from "A Short Smoke Break" by Rich Oakley and Fawn Scott.
This and other cool animation shorts can be seen at www.animationexpress.com.

Creating Web Graphics

For me—a graphic designer by trade—making the graphics is the fun part of web design. But in the beginning, I needed to learn to adapt my style and process to make graphics that are appropriate for web delivery. The chapters in Part III review the formats and techniques that are part of the web designer's bag of tricks.

The following chapters include step-by-step demonstrations on how to create web graphics in a number of popular graphics programs (Adobe Photoshop 5.5, Macromedia Fireworks 3, and JASC Paint Shop Pro). The examples assume that you have a basic understanding of how to use your image-editing program to create graphics. If you are new to making graphics, I recommend you spend time with the manual or other books about your graphics software. This book will focus on how to make your graphics web-friendly.

All About Web Graphics

Here's what you need to know: web graphics need to be low-resolution graphics saved in GIF or JPEG format.

This tidy sentence basically says it all. Although simple, it touches on some major issues that I'll explore in this and the following chapters. I'll use the above statement as a starting point for discussing the nuts and bolts of web graphics. In addition, I'll share some tips on getting images and creating web graphics.

File Formats

The Web has its own alphabet soup of graphics file formats. Graphics formats that make it on the Internet are those that are easily ported from platform to platform over a network.

Nearly all of the graphics you see on the Web are in one of two formats: GIF (pronounced "jif") and JPEG ("jay-peg"). What follows is a brief introduction to each of these formats.

The Ubiquitous GIF

The GIF (Graphic Interchange Format) file is the traditional favorite of the Internet. GIF files are compressed files that can contain a maximum of 8-bit color information. Compressed means that in turning your graphic into a GIF file, you are running it through a process that squeezes the color information into the smallest file size possible. 8-bit color means that the graphic can contain a maximum of 256 different pixel colors, although it may contain fewer.

The GIF format is most appropriate for images with areas of flat color, such as logos, cartoon-like illustrations, icons, and line art.

The GIF format is most appropriate for images with areas of flat color, such as logos, cartoon-like illustrations, icons, and line art (Figure 13-1, gallery). GIFs are not efficient at saving photographic images.

Figure 13-1   G

The GIF file format is best for images with sharp lines and areas of flat color.

GIFs also have other advantages. You can make parts of a GIF file transparent, allowing your background image or color to show through. They can also contain simple animation effects right in the file. The vast majority of animated ad banners you see on the Web are animated GIFs.

The GIF file format is discussed in detail in Chapter 14, Creating GIFs, and animation is covered in Chapter 16, Animated GIFs.

The Photogenic JPEG

JPEG's full-color capacity and compression scheme make it the ideal choice for photographic images.

The second most popular graphics format on the Web today is the JPEG format. JPEGs are 24-bit color images; they can contain millions of colors. Unlike the GIF format, JPEGs use a compression scheme that loves gradient and blended colors and doesn't work especially well on flat colors or images with hard edges. JPEG's full-color capacity and compression scheme make it the ideal choice for photographic images (Figure 13-2, gallery).

Although the compression scheme is "lossy" (meaning some detail in the image is thrown out to achieve better compression), JPEGs still offer excellent image quality packed into smaller files.

JPEGs are discussed in detail in Chapter 15, Creating JPEGs.

Figure 13-2 **G**

The JPEG file format works best for images with gradient colors, such as photos or paintings.

Choosing the Best File Format

Part of the trick to making quality web graphics that download quickly is choosing the right file format for the job. This chart provides a good starting point:

If your image...	use...	because...
is graphical, with flat colors	GIF	it will compress more efficiently and keep colors flat and crisp, resulting in higher quality images at smaller file sizes.
is photographic or contains gradations of colors, such as a watercolor painting	JPEG	the JPEG compression works best on images with blends of colors, and it can portray images with millions of colors, resulting in better image quality at smaller file sizes.
is a combination of flat and photographic art, such as a banner with text on a flat background and a small photographic image	GIF	in most cases, it is better to preserve your flat colors and crisp edges and to tolerate a little dithering in the photographic edges than to turn the whole image over to JPEG compression.
is a postage stamp– or icon-sized photograph	GIF or JPEG	although JPEG is better suited for photographic images, I have found when the image dimensions are really small, GIF usually creates smaller file sizes with acceptable image quality. It is advisable to try both and find the one that works best for your particular image.
needs a part to be transparent	GIF	it's the only file format that supports transparency.
needs animation	GIF	it's the only format that supports native animation.

Fortunately, the web graphics tools available today allow you to preview your image (and the resulting file sizes) as it would appear in different file formats. You can even view them side by side to choose the format that works the best for your image (Figure 13-3).

Figure 13-3

Photoshop 5.5 and Fireworks 3 allow you to preview the image quality and resulting file sizes for different file formats. This can make choosing the best file format for your image easier.

Adobe Photoshop 5.5
Select File → Save for Web to preview your image and fine-tune its settings before exporting the final file.

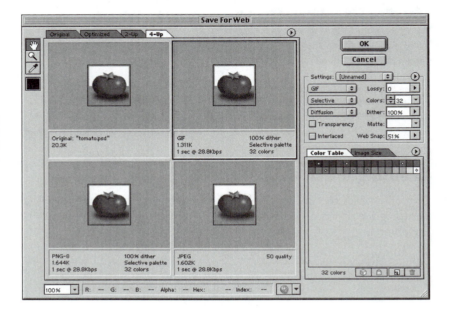

Macromedia Fireworks 3
In Fireworks, you have the opportunity to view the image "4-up" right in the document window. Use the Optimize palette to adjust the settings.

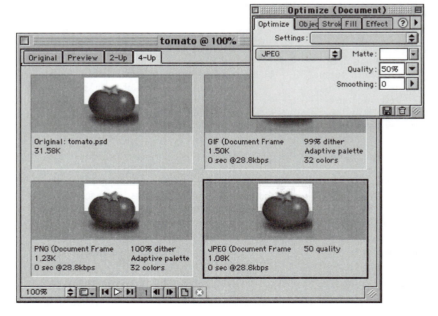

Image Resolution

Both GIFs and JPEGs are pixel-based, or bitmapped (also called raster) images. When you zoom in, you can see the image is like a mosaic made up of many pixels (tiny, single-colored squares). These are different from vector graphics that are made up of smooth lines and filled areas, all based on mathematical formulas (Figure 13-4).

Figure 13-4

Bitmap images are made up of a grid of variously colored pixels, like a mosaic.

Vector images use mathematical equations to define shapes.

Measuring Resolution

Because web graphics exist solely on the screen, it is technically correct to measure their resolution in pixels per inch (ppi). Another resolution measurement, dpi (dots per inch), refers to the resolution of a printed page, dependent on the resolution of the printing device.

In practice, the terms dpi and ppi are used interchangeably (albeit, incorrectly so). It is generally accepted practice to refer to web graphic resolution in terms of dpi.

If you have been using pixel-based images in print design, such as TIFFs, you are familiar with the term resolution, the number of pixels per inch the graphic contains. For print, an image typically has a resolution of 300 dots per inch (or dpi).

Goodbye Inches, Hello Pixels!

On the Web, images need to be created at much lower resolutions; 72 dpi has become the *de facto* standard, but in reality the whole notion of "inches" and even "dots per inch" becomes irrelevant in the web environment. Web graphics are always seen on computer monitors, which have resolutions of their own, as we'll see in a moment. In the end, the only meaningful measurement of a web graphic is its actual number of pixels.

When a graphic is displayed on a web page, the pixels in the image map one-to-one with the display resolution of the monitor, and monitor resolution varies by platform and user. The following example demonstrates the issue.

I have created a graphic that is 72 pixels square (Figure 13-5, following page). Since I set the resolution to be 72 dpi in my image editing program, I expect that graphic to appear about one inch square when I view it on my monitor. And sure enough, on my Mac, that's about right.

But what happens when that same graphic is displayed on another person's monitor—one with a much higher resolution setting? Let's take another look at my "one inch" graphic.

Web graphics need to be low-resolution (typically 72 dpi).

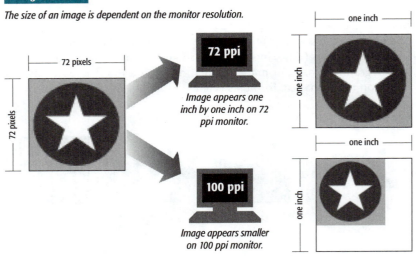

Figure 13-5

The size of an image is dependent on the monitor resolution.

72 pixels

72 pixels

72 ppi

Image appears one inch by one inch on 72 ppi monitor.

100 ppi

Image appears smaller on 100 ppi monitor.

one inch

one inch

one inch

one inch

The only true measurement for web graphics is number of pixels.

Suddenly, my inch-square graphic is less than a three-quarter inch square because the same 72 pixels are mapping one-to-one across a resolution that is closer to 100 pixels per inch. For this reason, it is useless to think of "inches" on the Web. It's all relative. And without inches, the whole notion of dots per inch is basically thrown out the window as well. The only thing we know for sure is that the graphic is 72 pixels across, and that it will be twice as wide as a graphic that is 36 pixels across, for instance.

High-resolution graphics (e.g., 300 dpi) are inappropriate for the Web.

After this example, it should be fairly clear why graphics scanned in or created at higher resolutions (such as 300 dpi) are inappropriate for the Web. At higher resolutions, it's typical for images to be several thousand pixels across. With browser windows as small as 600 pixels wide, all those pixels are unnecessary and will result in graphics that are *huge* once shown in the browser window (Figure 13-6).

Working in Low Resolution

Despite the fact that resolution is irrelevant, nearly everyone creates web graphics at 72 dpi because it gets them in the ballpark for the correct number of pixels. The drawback to working at such a low resolution is that the image quality is lower because there is not as much image information in a given space. This tends to make the image look more grainy or pixelated, and unfortunately, that's just the nature of the Web.

Figure 13-6

*This 3-inch square image fits nicely in
the browser window at 72 dpi…*

*…but at 300 dpi, most of the image falls outside
the visible area of the browser window.*

(photo courtesy of Liam Lynch)

All About Web Graphics

How Long Does It Take?

It's impossible to say exactly how long a graphic will take to download over the Web. It depends on many factors, including the speed of the user's connection, the speed of the user's computer, the amount of activity on the web server, and the general amount of traffic on the Internet itself.

The general rule of thumb is to figure that a graphic will take 1 second per kilobyte (K) on a standard modem connection (say, at 28.8Kbps). That would mean that a 30K graphic would take 30 seconds to download, a long time to be staring at the screen of your home computer. Use this 1 sec/K guideline only to get a ballpark estimate for the lowest common denominator. Actual times may be a lot better, or a lot worse.

File Size Matters

A web page is published over a network, and it will need to zip through the lines as little packets of data in order to reach the end user. It is fairly intuitive, then, that larger amounts of data will require a longer time to arrive. And guess which part of a web page is the greatest hog of bandwidth—that's right, the graphics. Simply put, large graphics mean long download times.

Thus is born the love/hate relationship with graphics on the Web. On one hand, graphics can make a web page look more interesting than a page with text alone. The ability to display graphics is one of the factors that made the Web the first segment of the Internet to explode into mass popularity. On the other hand, graphics can also try the patience of the eager surfer, waiting and waiting for the pictures to download and display on the screen.

The user has three choices: hang in there and wait, turn the graphics-downloading function of the browser off and read the text-only page, or click the "Back" button and surf somewhere else.

Despite the emergence of high-bandwidth connections in the household (such as DSL and cable modems), the 28.8 or 56Kbps dial-up modem connection is far from a thing of the past. The golden rule of web design remains "Keep download times as short as possible."

In fact, many corporate clients will set a kilobyte limit (referred to as the K-limit) that the sum of all the files on a page cannot exceed. I know of one corporate site that set its limit at a scant 15K per page (that includes the HTML file and all the graphics combined!). Similarly, many sites insist that advertising banners be no larger than 6 or 7K. Even if keeping files small is not a priority for you, it may be for your clients.

It is up to web designers to be sensitive to this issue in general, and to mind the graphics files in particular. Here are a few strategies.

Limit the Dimensions

Though fairly obvious, the easiest way to keep file size down is to limit the dimensions of the graphic itself. There aren't any magic numbers; just don't make graphics any larger than they need to be.

By simply eliminating extra space on the graphic in Figure 13-7, I was able to reduce the file size by 3K.

Design for Compression

One of the key ways to make your files as small as possible is to take full advantage of their compression schemes. For instance, since we know that GIF compression likes flat colors, don't design GIF images with gradient

Figure 13-7

You can reduce the size of your files simply by cropping out extra white space.

600 × 200 pixels **(13K)**

500 × 136 pixels **(10K)**

color blends when a flat color will suffice. And since we know that JPEGs like soft transitions and no hard edges, you can try strategically blurring images that will be saved in JPEG format. These techniques are discussed in the Optimizing sections of the GIF and JPEG chapters.

Reuse and Recycle

One way to limit download times is to take advantage of your browser's cache and reuse your graphics. Here's how it works.

When browsing the Web, it's typical to move back and forth between documents, often returning to the same document repeatedly. It doesn't make sense for the browser to ask a server for the same document over and over again; instead, the browser retains a copy of the most recently accessed documents, keeping it handy in the event you return. This is called caching (pronounced "cash-ing"), and the place these files are temporarily stored is called the cache (pronounced "cash").

You can take advantage of the browser's cache by reusing graphics whenever possible on your site. That way, each graphic will only need to download once, speeding up the display of subsequent pages (Figure 13-8).

The only trick is that each instance of the graphic must have the exact same URL in its `<IMG>` tag; that is, it must be a single graphic in a single directory. If you make copies of a graphic and put it in different directories, even though the file has the same name, the browser will do a fresh download when it sees the new pathname.

Figure 13-8

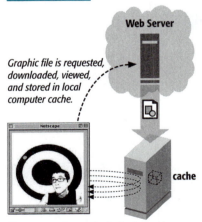

Graphic file is requested, downloaded, viewed, and stored in local computer cache.

You can speed up page display by reusing graphics. The browser only downloads the graphic once and relies on the cache for subsequent instances.

All About Web Graphics

Tools of the Trade

Web graphics tools have come a long way since I started making web graphics in 1993. In those days, we had to make do with tools designed for print graphics, and we relied on one-trick-pony utilities to add web-specific features, such as transparency.

But with the explosion of the Web and the demands it put on designers, software developers have responded quickly and competitively to cater to the specific requirements of web designers.

What follows is a brief introduction to the most popular graphics tools among professional web designers. It is by no means an exhaustive list of the web tools out there. There are many worthy graphics programs that crank out GIF and JPEG files; if you've found one that works for you, that's great.

Adobe Photoshop/ImageReady. Without question, the industry standard for web graphics creation is Adobe Photoshop. It's the tool of choice of every graphic designer I've ever come across. With Version 5.5, Adobe introduced many web-specific features such as a "Save to Web" option that shows previews of your graphic in different file formats and at different compression rates. It also offers advanced palette and dithering control for GIF files.

As of this writing, Photoshop comes bundled with Adobe's Image-Ready software for doing special web tricks, such as animation and rollover effects (the program writes the necessary JavaScript code for you). ImageReady also provides sophisticated tools for optimizing image file size.

Many web development shops actually require their designers and freelancers to create their graphics using Photoshop and ImageReady. If you are interested in making web graphics professionally, I recommend getting up to speed with Photoshop right away.

JASC Paint Shop Pro. If you work on a PC and are on a budget, you might want to try out Paint Shop Pro, which has many of the same features as Photoshop, but at a much lower cost (just U.S. $99 as of this printing). It comes bundled with Animation Shop 2 for creating animated GIFs.

Macromedia Fireworks. This is one of the first graphics programs to be designed from the ground up to address the special requirements of web graphics. It has tools for creating both vector (line-based) and raster (pixel-based) images. Among its many impressive features are editable text, "live" effects that can be edited at any time, side-by-side export previews, animation features, rollover buttons, advanced image-slicing tools, and more, all in one program.

Find It Online

For more information and free downloadable trial versions of the software mentioned here, check these companies' web sites:

Adobe Systems, Inc.
  www.adobe.com

Macromedia, Inc.
  www.macromedia.com

JASC Software
  www.jasc.com

This eliminates the need to switch between a drawing program, a bitmap editing program, and specialized web utilities. The learning curve is rather steep (particularly if you are accustomed to Adobe's interface), but once I got used to it, I found that I could use it for almost all of my web graphics (although, I must admit that it didn't make Photoshop completely obsolete).

Adobe Illustrator; Macromedia Freehand. I list these programs together because they are popular vector drawing programs. Many web designers start their designs in a drawing program because the tools are ideal for creating the flat, graphical images that are well-suited for web delivery. Although these programs have the ability to save directly to GIF format, designers usually open their drawings in a web graphics tool for final processing.

The program you use is a matter of preference; however, it is not uncommon for a client to insist their designers and freelancers use one or the other to ensure consistency in the graphic quality across the site.

Image Sources

We know that graphics need to be either GIF or JPEG, and we've seen some of the tools used to make them, but where to begin? Where do these graphics come from?

Acquiring images to use in web graphics is much the same as finding them for print, with a few extra considerations. Let's look at some possible sources for artwork to jazz up your pages.

Scanning

Scanning is a great way to collect source material for web graphics. You can scan almost anything, from flat art to actual 3-D objects. Beware, however, the temptation to scan and use found images. Keep in mind that most images you find are probably copyright-protected and may not be used without permission, even if you modify them considerably. Remember that millions of people have access to the Web, and using images you do not have permission for can put you and your client at risk.

Digital Cameras

You can capture the world around you and pipe it right into an image editing program with a digital camera. Since the Web is a low-resolution environment, you don't need a fancy high-resolution camera to get the job done. Be aware, however, that digital cameras compress the images (usually using JPEG compression), so you'll be starting out with slightly lower quality originals. Each time you apply JPEG compression to an image, quality suffers.

Scanning Tips

If you are scanning images for use on the Web, these tips will help you to get better quality images:

- Your final images should be at a resolution of 72 dpi. For most images, you can scan directly at 72 dpi. Scanning at a slightly higher resolution (say 100 dpi) may give you more flexibility for resizing (particularly for very small images) because you'll have more pixels to work with. In the end, however, it's the number of pixels that count and 72 dpi is the standard resolution.

- I recommend scanning black and white images in grayscale (8-bit) mode, not in black and white (2-bit, or bitmap) mode. This enables you to make adjustments in the midtone areas once you have sized the image to its final dimensions and resolution. If you really want just black and white pixels, convert the image as the last step.

- If you are scanning an image that has been printed, you will need to eliminate the dot pattern that is a result of the printing process. The best way to do this is to apply a slight blur to the image (in Photoshop, use the Gaussian Blur filter), resize the image slightly smaller, then apply a sharpening filter. This will eliminate the pesky dots.

Stealing Isn't Nice

It's poor form (not to mention illegal) to use copyrighted images that you do not own or have not paid to license. Don't "borrow" graphics from other people's web sites or scan found images and call them your own.

Even if you've bought a photo or clip-art CD collection, be sure to read the licensing information carefully to see if there are additional charges for commercial use.

If you're looking for free image material, use the appropriate resources and look for the magic words "unrestricted" and "royalty-free."

Electronic Illustration

In many cases, you can create your images from scratch in a graphics program such as Illustrator, Fireworks, or Photoshop. Since I enjoy illustrating, I often create my own images in a drawing program using a drawing tablet and stylus. If I'm using a bitmap program (like Photoshop), I create a new file at 72 dpi that is large enough to give me room to play around with adding shapes and text (I can always crop later). I also sometimes use a vector program such as Freehand or Illustrator to create illustrations that I then bring into the bitmap program. These tools make editing and scaling shapes much easier than dealing with pixels. They can also do interesting type effects that can't be done in Photoshop, like editing character shapes and putting type on a curve.

Photo Archives and Clip-Art

If you don't want to generate images from scratch, that's okay, too. There are plenty of collections of ready-made photos, illustrations, and buttons available. Nowadays, there are whole clip-art collections available specifically for web use.

A trip to your local software retail store or a browse through the pages of a software catalog will no doubt turn up royalty-free image collections (many boasting more than 100,000 pieces of art).

There are also a number of great resources online, and the good news is that some of these sites are giving graphics away for *free*. The drawback is that a lot of them are poor quality or kind of hokey (but then, "hokey" is in the eye of the beholder). The following sites are good starting points for accessing thousands of free graphics:

A+ Art
www.aplusart.com
> Icons, backgrounds, buttons, animations and more

Web Clip-Art Links Page (courtesy of The Mining Co.)
webclipart.miningco.com/internet/webclipart/
> Hundreds of clip-art–related links

If you are doing professional work with a professional budget, you should consider these top-notch online resources for images and illustrations:

PictureQuest
www.picturequest.com
> This site features over 100,000 professional-quality images from a variety of stock image companies, including PhotoDisc, Corbis, and many others.

ArtToday
www.arttoday.com
> ArtToday has both free and subscriber libraries of quality images and illustrations.

Graphics Production Tips

I've picked up a few basic tricks for producing web graphics over the years that apply to all file formats. I'll share them with you now. Other format-specific techniques can be found in Chapters 14, 15, and 16.

Work in RGB Mode

You should always do your image-editing work in RGB mode (grayscale is fine for non-color images) regardless of whether the graphic is going to end up a JPEG or a GIF. JPEG files just compress the RGB color image directly. For GIFs, you must convert the RGB color image to Indexed Color first before saving it (we'll discuss this more in Chapter 14).

If you have experience creating graphics for print, you may be accustomed to working in CMYK mode (printed colors are made up of Cyan, Magenta, Yellow, and blacK ink), but ink—and CMYK mode—is irrelevant in web design.

Use Anti-Aliased Text

In general, to create professional-looking graphics for the Web, you should use anti-aliased text and objects. Anti-aliasing is the slight blur used on curved edges to make smoother transitions between colors. Aliased edges, by contrast, are blocky and stair-stepped. Figure 13-9, gallery, shows the effect of aliasing (top) and anti-aliasing (bottom). You will find a control for turning anti-aliasing on and off (or selecting a particular type of anti-aliasing, in the case of Photoshop) with the text tool in your graphics program.

The exception to this guideline is very small text (10 points or smaller), for which anti-aliased edges blur the characters to the point of illegibility. Text at small sizes may fare much better when it is aliased.

The only drawback to anti-aliased edges is that they will add to the number of colors in your image, which can potentially add to the file size. In general, the benefit in the appearance is worth the extra bytes, but you should be aware there is a trade-off.

Save Your Work

Just as you would for any other desktop design, it is a good idea to save your work often. If you are creating your graphic in a layered Photoshop file, be sure to save the layered version separate from the "flattened" GIF or JPEG file. It is much easier to make those inevitable changes to the layered file.

Figure 13-9 G

Aliased text and images have stair-stepped edges.

Anti-aliased text and images have blurred edges to make transitions smoother.

All About Web Graphics

WHERE TO LEARN MORE

Advanced Graphics Techniques

Once you've mastered the basics, you may want to continue learning about advanced graphics techniques. These books are highly recommended.

Photoshop for the Web, Second Edition, by Mikkel Aaland (O'Reilly, 2000)
> This book is loaded with step by step examples and real world examples for making the best web graphics using Adobe Photoshop. The new edition covers Version 5.5 and ImageReady 2.0.

Designing Web Graphics, Third Edition, by Linda Weinman (New Riders Publishing, 1999)
> This is a treasure of web graphics tips and techniques, and includes clear step by step demonstrations.

Name Files Properly

Be sure to use the proper file extensions for your graphics files. All GIF files must be named with the suffix *.gif*. JPEG files must have either *.jpeg* or *.jpg* as a suffix. Even if your files are saved in the correct format, the browser will not recognize them without the proper suffix.

Consider Other End Uses

One of the drawbacks to creating files at low resolution is that they look lousy in print. Normally, resolutions of 300 dpi or higher are required for smooth printing, so the measly 72 dots per inch of a web graphic will make for a blocky and blotchy printed image.

If you anticipate needing images (such as logos or important illustrations) for printed pieces as well as on your web page, it makes sense to create the high resolution image first, save it, and then create a duplicate at a web-appropriate size. Whenever possible, try to take advantage of drawing programs for creating logos in vector format; they can be resized infinitely with no loss of quality, then output at the desired resolution.

Web Graphics Highlights

Here are some of the main points from this chapter that you should keep in mind when creating web graphics:

- Save images with flat areas of color and hard edges in GIF format.

- Save photographic images in JPEG format.

- Images with a combination of flat graphic areas and photographic material are usually best saved in GIF format.

- Web graphics should be low-resolution bitmapped images.

- Web graphics should be created in RGB color mode (not CMYK).

- The only meaningful measurement for web graphics is pixels.

- Images can be created from scratch, scanned in, shot with a digital camera, or taken from a clip-art library.

- The most popular professional tools for creating web graphics are Adobe Photoshop (with ImageReady) and Macromedia Fireworks.

Creating GIFs

If you want to make web pages, plan on becoming handy at making GIFs. Although creating basic GIFs is straightforward, making professional-quality GIFs requires extra attention to matters of transparency, optimization, and the web palette, as we'll see in this chapter. Fortunately, these tasks are made simple with the web-ready graphics tools we have today.

Before we jump into making GIFs, I'll give you a more detailed explanation of how GIFs work and the things you can do with them. In the process, I'll introduce some terminology that will make using your graphics tools easier.

All About GIFs

The vast majority of graphics you see on the web today are GIF (Graphic Interchange Format) files. Although not designed specifically for the Web, the format was quickly adopted for its versatility, small file sizes, and cross-platform compatibility. To this day, it is the only format that is universally supported by all graphical browsers, regardless of version. If you want to make absolutely sure everyone can see your graphic, make it a GIF.

Because the GIF compression scheme excels at compressing flat colors, it is the best file format to use for images with flat areas of color, such as logos, line art, graphics containing text, icons, etc. Although you can save any image as a GIF, you'll find that it is not as efficient at saving photographs or images with a lot of texture. (These are best saved as JPEGs, as discussed in Chapter 15, Creating JPEGs.)

Figure 14-1, gallery and following page, shows a few examples of images that are well suited for the GIF format.

Figure 14-1   G

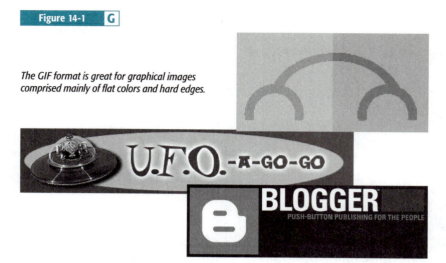

The GIF format is great for graphical images comprised mainly of flat colors and hard edges.

8-Bit, Indexed Color

All GIFs are indexed color images with a maximum of 8-bit color information.

Simply put, all GIFs are indexed color images with a maximum of 8-bit color information. Let's break that statement down.

Indexed color means that all the pixel colors in the image are stored in a color table (also called a palette). The table serves as a numeric index (of sorts) to the colors in the image (Figure 14-2, gallery). Before you can save a graphic as a GIF, you need to convert the RGB image to Indexed Color mode (some tools do this for you automatically when you select "GIF" as the file format).

Figure 14-2   G

The colors in an indexed color image are stored in and referenced by a color table. The color table (also called a palette) can contain a maximum of 256 colors (8-bit).

In this figure we see the color table for the U.F.O. banner graphic.

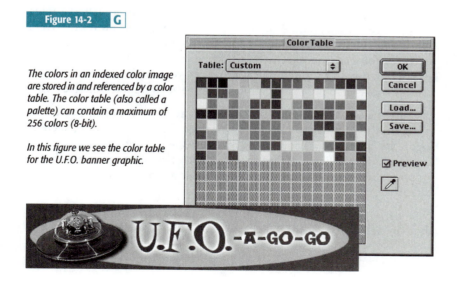

8-bit color means that the image (and its color table) can contain a maximum of 256 colors—the maximum number that 8 bits of information can define ($2^8 = 256$). GIFs can have lower bit-depths as well, resulting in fewer colors and smaller file sizes. This will be discussed later, in the Optimizing GIFs section of this chapter.

When creating GIFs, you often come in direct contact with the color table for that image.

GIF Compression

GIF compression is easy to understand. First, it's "lossless," which means that no image information is sacrificed in order to compress the image. Second, it uses a compression scheme (called "LZW") that compresses the image row by row. When it hits a row of pixels that are the same color, it can compress that into one data description. This is why images with large areas of flat colors condense down more than images with textures (Figure 14-3).

GIFs compress images row by row. Rows of identical pixel colors condense more efficiently and result in a smaller file size.

Figure 14-3

A simple demonstration of GIF compression

The GIF compression scheme condenses pixels in rows. When it hits a long string of pixels of the same color, it can save this information in a single description.

description = "14 teal"

In an image with gradations of color, it has to store information for every pixel in the row. The longer description means a larger file size.

description = "1 teal", "1 light teal", "2 medium teal", etc…

This leads to some interesting design quirks for GIFs. For instance, images with horizontal stripes will be smaller than the same size image with vertical stripes. You can also reduce the size of an image by adding alternating rows of solid color. These techniques are discussed in the Optimizing GIFs section later in this chapter.

Creating GIFs

Figure 14-4

Transparency allows the striped background to show through the graphic. The image on the top uses transparency; the image on the bottom does not.

Transparency

One of the niftiest things about GIFs is that you can make parts of them transparent and allow the background image or color to show through. All bitmapped graphics (including GIFs) are rectangular by nature, but with transparency, you can create the illusion that your graphic has a more interesting shape (Figure 14-4). Transparency is discussed in detail later in this chapter, in the section Adding Transparency.

Interlacing

Interlacing is an effect you can apply to a GIF that makes the image download in a series of passes. Each pass is clearer than the pass before until the GIF is fully rendered in the browser window (Figure 14-5). Without interlacing, some browsers may wait until the entire image is downloaded before displaying the image. Others may display the image a few rows at a time, from top to bottom, until the entire picture is complete.

Over a fast connection, these effects (interlacing or image delays) may not even be perceptible. However, over slow modem connections, interlacing large images may be a way to provide a hint of the image to come while the entire image downloads. If the image is used as an imagemap, the user could even click on part of the image and move on before it's completely downloaded.

Whether you interlace or not is your design decision. My rule of thumb is that for small graphics, it is probably not necessary, but for large images, particularly those used as imagemaps, interlacing is worthwhile.

Figure 14-5

Interlaced GIFs display in a series of passes, each clearer than the pass before.

Animation

Another feature built right into the GIF file format is the ability to display simple animations (Figure 14-6). Once you create all the separate frames of your animation, there are web graphics tools that make it easy to save them as a single animated GIF. We'll explore animated GIFs in Chapter 16, Animated GIFs.

Figure 14-6

All the frames in this simple animation are contained within one GIF file.

Creating a Simple GIF, Step by Step

Now that we know what GIFs can do, let's make one. This first example is going to be very basic; we'll get to the fancy stuff like transparency and optimization later.

When the Web became popular and the demand for GIF graphics sky-rocketed, software companies were quick to respond. Now, virtually every graphics program has some basic GIF-saving functionality. There's no way I can demonstrate them all, so I'm sticking to the most popular tools used by web designers: Adobe Photoshop, Macromedia Fireworks, and JASC Paint Shop Pro (an inexpensive Windows-only image program similar to Photoshop).

Regardless of the tool you use, saving an image as a GIF involves these basic steps:

1. Start with a low-resolution (72 dpi) image in RGB color mode.

2. Do your image editing (resizing, cropping, color correction, etc.) while the image is still in RGB mode.

3. When you have your image looking exactly the way you want it, con-vert it to indexed color (you'll be asked to flatten the image first if it has layers). If you are using a web graphics tool, the image will be converted to indexed color automatically when you select "GIF" from the format options.

   You will be asked to select a palette that will be applied to the image when the colors are reduced. The sidebar Color Palettes describes the various palette options.

4. After you've selected your desired settings, save or export the GIF.

Color Palettes

All 8-bit indexed color images use a palette to define the colors in the image, and there are several standard palettes you can choose from within popular graphics programs:

Exact. Creates a custom palette out of the actual colors in the image if the image already contains fewer than 256 colors.

Adaptive. Creates a custom palette using the most frequently used pixel colors in the image.

Web. Applies the 216-color web palette (discussed later in this chapter) to the image.

Perceptual. "Creates a custom color table by giving priority to colors for which the human eye has greater sensitivity" (Photoshop 5.5 manual).

Selective. "Creates a color table similar to Perceptual color table, but favoring broad areas of color and the preservation of Web colors... usually producing images with the greatest color integrity" (Photoshop 5.5 manual).

Uniform. Creates a palette that contains an evenly stepped sampling of colors from the RGB spectrum.

System (Windows or Macintosh). Uses the colors in the specified system's default palette.

One important note—be sure to hold on to the original RGB image in case you need to make changes later. It is preferable to edit in RGB color mode and then export to GIF as the last step.

In Adobe Photoshop

There are actually a few ways to create a GIF within Photoshop. If you have Version 5.5 or higher, I recommend taking advantage of the versatile "Save for Web" feature (Figure 14-7). In all versions after 3.0, you can do a simple "Save As" and select the GIF format (Figure 14-8). I'll demonstrate both methods here.

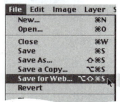

Figure 14-7

Saving a GIF with the "Save For Web" feature in Photoshop 5.5

❶ *Open the file and do any necessary image editing to the original image.*

❷ *When you are ready to save a GIF version of your image, select "Save for Web" from the File menu.*

❸ *In the Save for Web dialog box, first select GIF from the format pull-down menu Ⓐ, then select a palette Ⓑ, the number of colors Ⓒ, the dithering type (diffusion is best) and amount Ⓓ, and whether you'd like the image to be interlaced Ⓔ.*

This dialog box can also be used for setting transparency and carefully controlling web-safe colors.

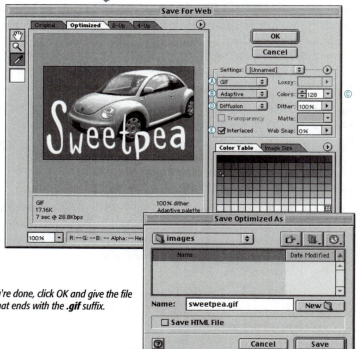

❹ *When you're done, click OK and give the file a name that ends with the .gif suffix.*

Figure 14-8

Saving a simple GIF in Photoshop
(Versions 4 and higher)

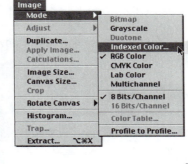

❶ *Open the file and do necessary image editing while still in RGB mode.*

❷ *Convert the image to indexed color by selecting Mode → Indexed Color from the Image menu. You will need to flatten the layers before it can be converted. (It's a good idea to save your layered file before you save as a GIF!)*

❸ *The key decisions you need to make in the Indexed Color dialog box are which palette to use (see the Color Palettes sidebar for palette descriptions) Ⓐ, the number of colors (bit depth) Ⓑ, and whether you want the image to dither Ⓒ. If you have used web-safe colors in your design, select "Preserve Exact Colors" to prevent them from shifting (Version 5 and higher).*

❹ *At this point, you can either Save As or Export.*

Save As
*Select "Save As" from the File menu, then select "CompuServe GIF" from the pull-down menu in the dialog box. Be sure to name the file with the **.gif** suffix. A final options box will ask whether you'd like the image to be interlaced.*

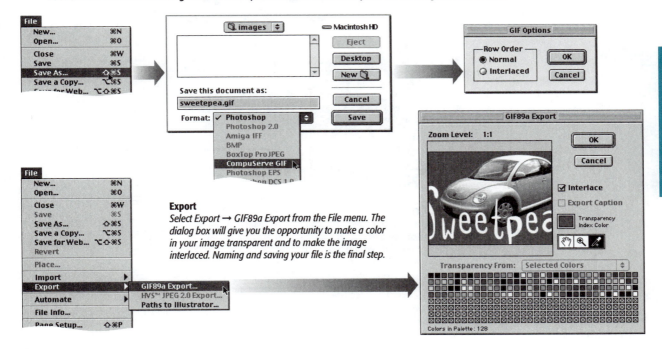

Export
Select Export → GIF89a Export from the File menu. The dialog box will give you the opportunity to make a color in your image transparent and to make the image interlaced. Naming and saving your file is the final step.

Creating GIFs

In Macromedia Fireworks 3

Because Fireworks was designed specifically for web graphics, you'll find its tools are ideal for creating optimized, high-quality GIFs. It gives you very fine-tuned control over many aspects of the image to improve compression rates (Figure 14-9).

> **Figure 14-9**

Exporting a GIF in Fireworks 3

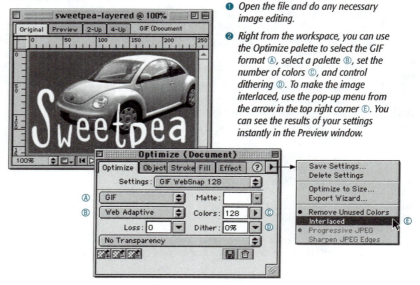

❶ Open the file and do any necessary image editing.

❷ Right from the workspace, you can use the Optimize palette to select the GIF format Ⓐ, select a palette Ⓑ, set the number of colors Ⓒ, and control dithering Ⓓ. To make the image interlaced, use the pop-up menu from the arrow in the top right corner Ⓔ. You can see the results of your settings instantly in the Preview window.

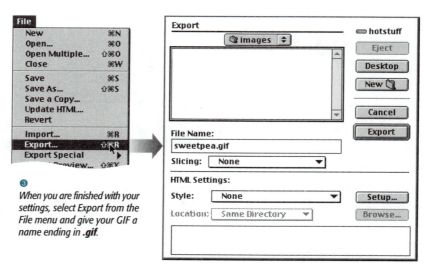

❸

When you are finished with your settings, select Export from the File menu and give your GIF a name ending in *.gif*.

In JASC Paint Shop Pro 6

As with Photoshop, it is easy to create GIFs in Paint Shop Pro. Version 6 introduces a new GIF optimization tool as well (Figure 14-10).

Figure 14-10

Saving a GIF file in Paint Shop Pro 6 and higher

❶ Open the file and do necessary image editing while in RGB mode. When you are ready to save the image as a GIF file, choose File → Save As.

❷ In the Save As dialog box, type a filename for the image and choose "CompuServe Graphics Interchange (*.gif)" from the pull-down menu.

❸ Click the Options button. In the Save Options dialog box, you can select the GIF version (89a supports transparency and animation) and whether you want the image to be interlaced. At this point, you can click OK to save the GIF, or Run Optimizer for more options.

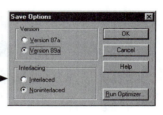

❹ Use the Colors panel of the GIF Optimizer to set the bit-depth, dither amount, and palette for the image. The "method of color selection" choices refer to the palette. Use Existing if you are starting with an Indexed Color image. Use "Standard/Web-safe" to apply the web palette to the image. Optimized Median Cut reduces the image to a few colors using something similar to an adaptive palette. Use Optimized Octree if the original image has just a few colors and you want to keep those exact colors.

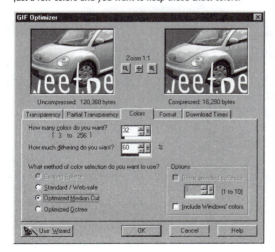

❺ Use the Transparency panel if you'd like portions of your GIF to be transparent. If you are starting with a layered image with transparent areas, select "Existing image or layer transparency". If you would like to make a specific pixel color in the image transparent, select "Areas that match this color".

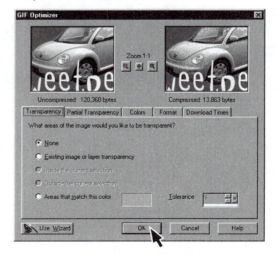

❻ When you have made your adjustments in the GIF Optimizer, click OK to save the file.

Creating GIFs

Adding Transparency

Another feature of the GIF format is that you can set parts of the image to be transparent. Whatever is behind the transparent area (most likely the background color or pattern) will show through.

The way it works is that one slot in the color table is designated as "transparent"—you simply select the color you'd like to turn transparent and the tool takes care of the rest. Be aware, however, that *all* instances of that color will turn transparent when you select a color. See Preventing Unwanted Transparency later in this chapter for more on this topic.

The method you use to add transparency to your image depends upon whether your source image is layered (in native Photoshop or Fireworks format) or flat (such as a pre-existing GIF file). Let's look at both techniques, starting with the layered file.

Preserving Transparency in Layered Images

If you are starting with a layered image that already has transparent areas (you can tell because the gray and white checker-board shows through, then keeping those areas transparent is a no-brainer with Photoshop 5.5 (or higher) or Fireworks 3.

In both tools, when you choose Transparency from the "Save for Web" (Photoshop) or Optimize (Fireworks) palette, the transparent areas in your layered graphic will stay transparent in the final GIF (Figure 14-11). Both tools allow you to specify a "Matte" color, which is the color that will fill in the transparent areas of your image if GIF transparency is *not* selected.

TIP

The Matte color is useful for transparent images, too. When you are exporting a transparent image, setting the Matte color to match the color of your web page will make the graphic blend into the background better. (We'll discuss this further in Avoiding Halos coming up later in this chapter.)

Figure 14-11

Preserving transparency in layered documents

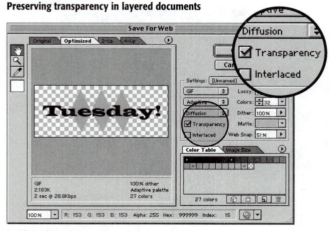

In Photoshop 5.5
Select "Save for Web" from the File menu. Check the box next to Transparency to preserve the transparent areas when you save.

In Fireworks 3
Use the Optimize palette to select "Index Transparency" from the Transparency pull-down menu.

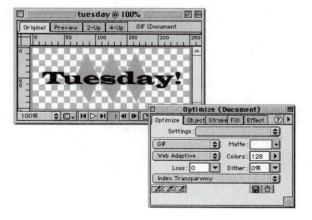

Index Versus Alpha Transparency

The most straightforward method for adding transparency to an image is via index transparency—assigning one pixel in the color table to be transparent. This is what you are doing by selecting a color to be transparent with an eyedropper tool.

Photoshop offers an advanced method for dealing with transparency called alpha transparency. Alpha transparency is a method for saving a map of the transparent areas of a GIF in a separate channel (called an alpha channel) of the document. The areas of the image corresponding to the black pixels in the alpha channel will be transparent, regardless of their pixel colors. Areas corresponding to white pixel areas in the alpha channel display as opaque.

By editing the alpha channel (located in Photoshop's Channels palette), you can paint transparency into the image, as shown below, regardless of the pixel colors in the image.

Manipulating transparency directly with an alpha channel is an advanced and somewhat esoteric technique that even professional web designers rarely resort to. Therefore, in this chapter, we'll focus primarily on index transparency.

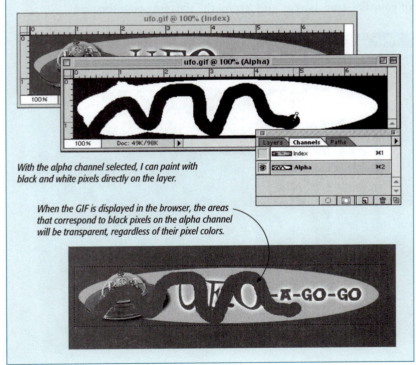

With the alpha channel selected, I can paint with black and white pixels directly on the layer.

When the GIF is displayed in the browser, the areas that correspond to black pixels on the alpha channel will be transparent, regardless of their pixel colors.

Creating GIFs

Adding Transparency to a Flattened Image

Adding transparency to a flattened image (like an existing GIF) is easy to do, but you may run into problems with quality.

What if you are starting with an image that has already been flattened, such as a pre-existing GIF file? The good news is that adding transparent areas to an existing file is simple in Photoshop and Fireworks. The bad news is that depending on your image, you may run into problems with quality. If the image was flattened to a background color that is different from the background color of your web page, you may see a fringy outline of different color pixels (called a "halo") around the transparent image when it is displayed. We will discuss halos in detail in the next section, Avoiding Halos.

In the meantime, let's add transparency to a flattened image under the best possible circumstances, in which the solid background color of the GIF matches the patterned background of the web page.

Say you've got a GIF file filled with a green that perfectly matches the green background of your page. But now, you've decided to jazz up the page by changing the solid green background to a subtle tiled pattern. That nice GIF file is suddenly a big green rectangle floating like a raft on a sea of pattern (Figure 14-12). You can fix that by making the green areas of your GIF transparent and letting the pattern show through.

Figure 14-12

The flat GIF on the top looks awkward in front of a patterned background.
We can fix this by making the flat green areas transparent as shown in the bottom example.

In Adobe Photoshop 4 (or higher)

The only way to change solid pixel colors to transparent in Photoshop is to use the Export → GIF89a Export function, as shown in Figure 14-13.

The fancier "Save for Web" function requires that the original image contain transparent pixels (see Figure 14-11). If you want to take advantage of the "Save for Web" options, you can copy the flattened image to a new document and use the Magic Wand to select pixels and delete them. Then your image will have transparent pixels to preserve.

Figure 14-13

Making a color transparent using Photoshop
(Versions 4 and higher)

❶ *Open the image and convert it to indexed color (if it isn't already), then select Export → GIF89a Export from the File menu.*

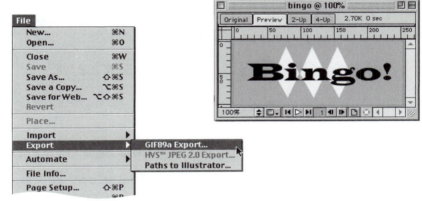

❷ *Use the eyedropper tool to select the color you'd like to turn transparent. Select multiple colors for transparency by holding the Shift key while selecting. When you click, all pixels of that color are filled with the "Transparency Index Color." This indicates which areas of the image are transparent, and it is also the color that will fill the transparent areas if for some reason the transparency does not work. The default is gray, but you can change it to whatever you like.*

❸ *Click OK when you are finished.*

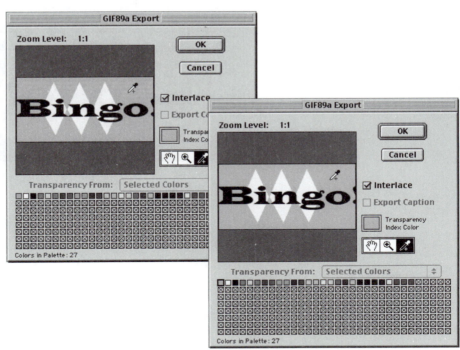

Creating GIFs

In Macromedia Fireworks 3

In Fireworks, you can make colors in a flattened graphic transparent right from the workspace using the Optimize palette, as shown in Figure 14-14.

Figure 14-14

Adding transparency to a flat graphic in Fireworks 3

❶ *With the graphic open, use the Optimize palette to select "Index Transparency" from the Transparency pull-down menu.*

❷ *Using the "Set Transparency" eyedropper tool Ⓐ, click on the color in the image that you'd like to be transparent.*

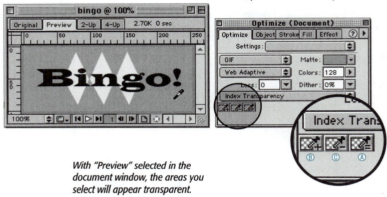

With "Preview" selected in the document window, the areas you select will appear transparent.

❸
To make additional colors transparent, use the "Add to Transparency" eyedropper Ⓑ. To turn a transparent color opaque again, use the "Subtract from Transparency" eyedropper Ⓒ.

❹
When you are finished, export the graphic (File → Export).

Avoiding Halos

Ever see a transparent graphic that has a fringe of pixels that doesn't blend in with the background color of the page? That's what's commonly known as a halo, and it's easy to prevent, especially with the aid of the web graphics tools we've been using in this chapter.

Halos are the result of anti-aliased edges (the slight blur around a graphic or text that creates smoother transitions between colors) that have been blended with a color other than the background color of the page (Figure 14-15, gallery). When the color around an anti-aliased edge is made transparent, the blur along the edge is still intact, and all those shades will be visible against the new background color. This ruins the transparency effect.

Figure 14-15

"Halos" are the fringe that's left around a transparent image. They happen when anti-aliased edges have been blended with a color that is lighter than the page background.

Halos do not happen around aliased (stair-stepped) text and images because there is a hard edge between colors.

One way to prevent halos is simply to avoid using anti-aliased edges in the first place. In aliased images, there is a hard edge between colors. When there is no blur, there are no halos! Unfortunately, the jagged, stair-stepped effect of aliased edges usually looks just as bad.

But in the more likely event that your image does have anti-aliased edges, there are two ways to prevent halos, both requiring that you start with a layered Photoshop or Fireworks file. The parts of your graphic must be on transparent layers without any surrounding pixels. In other words, the image must not have already been "flattened."

TIP

Fixing Halos in Flattened Images

Unfortunately, the only way to fix a halo in an image that has already been flattened is to get in there and erase the anti-aliased edges, pixel by pixel. You need to get as close to the image area as possible to get rid of the blended edge, making sure not to erase parts of the image itself. Even if you get rid of all the edges, you'll be left with aliased (stair-stepped) edges, and the quality of the image will suffer.

If you're concerned with the professional appearance of your site, I'd say it's better to recreate the graphic from scratch, taking care to prevent halos, than to waste time trying to fix them. This is another good reason to always save your layered files.

If you are working in Photoshop 5.5 or Fireworks 3, the best way to prevent the halo is to set the Matte color to the same color as the background for your page (Figure 14-16). When you export the GIF with Transparency selected, the anti-aliased edges in your image will be blended with the specified Matte color. No more halos!

Figure 14-16

Using the Matte feature to prevent halos

In Photoshop 5.5
Select "Save for Web" from the File menu. Click Matte to launch a color picker where you can specify the background color of your web page.

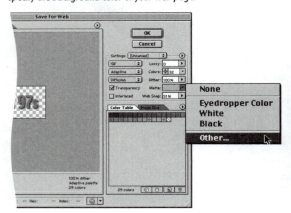

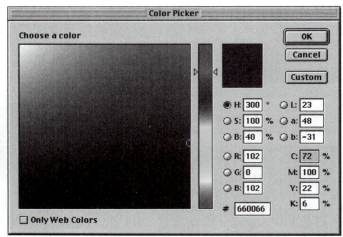

In Fireworks 3
The Matte option is available on the Optimize palette. Clicking it pops up a palette of web-safe colors (or you can click the color picker button to choose an alternate color).

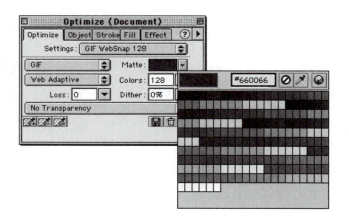

Results
Now the anti-aliased edges blend with the specified Matte color and the effect will be seamless when the graphic appears on the page.

Layered graphic with Matte color selected.

Transparent GIF as it appears on the page.

If you are working with an earlier version of Photoshop or JASC Paint Shop Pro, the trick is to create a new layer at the bottom of the layer "stack" and fill it with the background color of your page. When the image is flattened (as a result of changing it to Indexed Color), the anti-aliased edges will blend with the proper background color (Figure 14-17). Next, just select the background color to be transparent during export and your halo problems should be over.

Preventing Unwanted Transparency

In some instances, you'll find that the color around the edge of your image also appears *within* your image. In these cases, if you use an eyedropper tool to select the edge color for transparency, parts of your image will disappear as well, as in Figure 14-18.

Figure 14-18

If I use an eyedropper tool to make the white background transparent, all the whites within my image will turn transparent too Ⓐ! The goal is to make the background transparent while keeping the interior whites opaque Ⓑ.

overeasy.gif

Ⓐ

Ⓑ

This won't be a problem if you are using Photoshop 5.5 or Fireworks 3 because the Matte feature will allow you to blend to a specific color while keeping it opaque within the image. By now, the benefits of these web-ready tools should be evident.

However, if you are using more traditional tools, the solution to preserving the opaque color within your image is as simple as changing the border color to something else. The trick is to do the color swap after the image has been flattened (so that the anti-aliased edges blend to the desired color) and to make sure that you do not select any of those anti-aliased edges when you fill with the new color. Figure 14-19 (following page) shows this technique step by step.

Figure 14-17

If your tool does not have a Matte function, simply create a new layer behind the image and fill it with the background color of your web page. When the image is merged to create a GIF, the anti-aliased edges will blend with the background color.

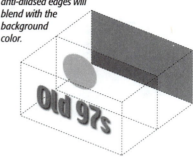

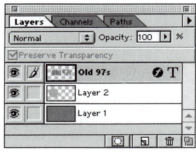

TIP

If your page background is a multi-colored pattern or is otherwise difficult to match with the Matte color, opt for a color that is slightly darker than the dominant web page color.

Creating GIFs

Figure 14-19

Preventing unwanted transparency in Photoshop 4 and 5

❶ If you are starting with a layered image, save it, then flatten the layers. The bottom layer should be filled with the background color of your web page to prevent a "halo."

❷ Use the Magic Wand tool to select the color on the outside of the image that you'd like to be transparent.

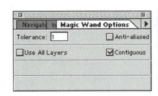

NOTE: *It is very important that the Magic Wand tolerance be set to "1" and the anti-aliasing turned OFF. Make sure that no pixels within your image are selected.*

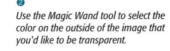

❸ Fill the selected area with a color that you are certain does not appear anywhere else in your image. I've set mine to a bright, obnoxious yellow.

❹ Convert the image to Indexed Color, and Export to GIF89a. In the Export dialog box, select your new color to make it transparent.

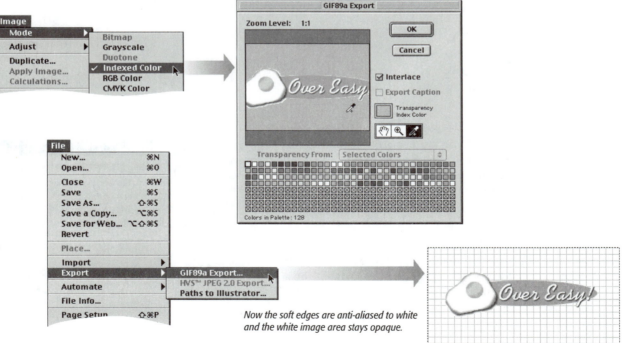

Now the soft edges are anti-aliased to white and the white image area stays opaque.

Optimizing GIFs

Do you remember the Golden Rule of Web Design, "Keep your files as small as possible"? That especially applies to graphic files, since they are typically the biggest files on the page. For this reason, it is certainly worth the extra effort to optimize your GIFs.

When optimizing GIF files, it is useful to keep in mind that GIF compression works by condensing rows of identical pixel colors. In most of these optimization strategies, the net result is that you are creating more areas of solid color in the image for the compression to sink its teeth into.

Again, if you're using Photoshop 5.5 (or higher) or Fireworks, you'll find a number of tools that make the job of optimization simple, such as the ability to see the effects of your settings instantly and even do side-by-side comparisons (Figure 14-20).

"Optimizing" refers to measures taken to make files as small as possible.

Figure 14-20

New web tools such as Fireworks and Photoshop 5.5 allow you to preview up to four variations of your image at once. This allows you to try out a number of settings to get the best image quality at the smallest file size.

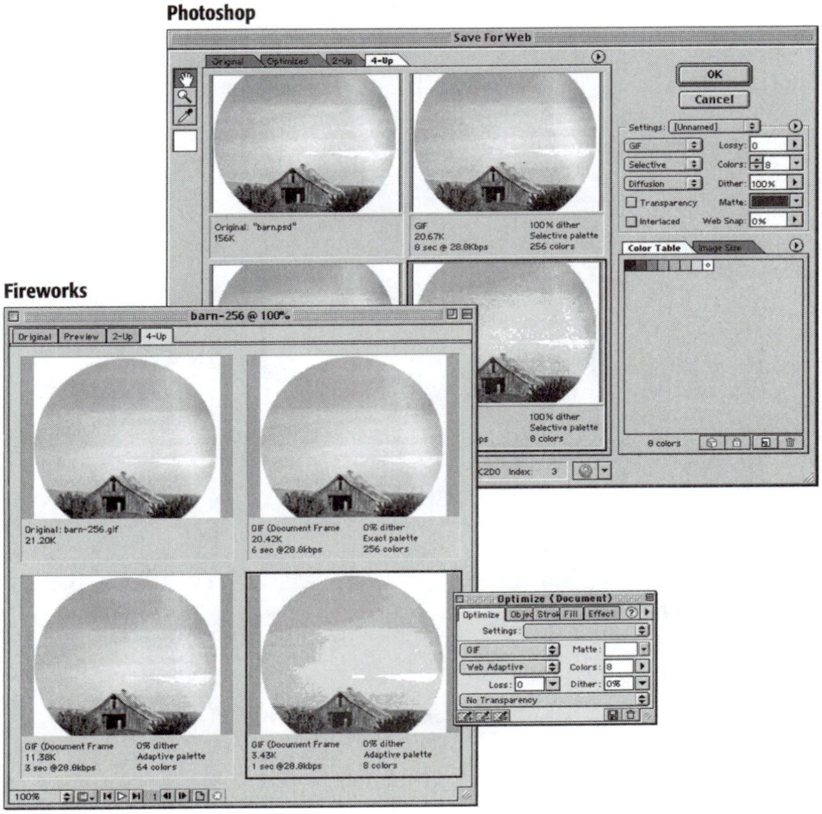

Creating GIFs

Bit Depth

"Bit depth" is a way to refer to the maximum number of colors a graphic can contain. This chart shows the number of colors each bit depth can represent:

1-bit	2 colors
2-bit	4 colors
3-bit	8 colors
4-bit	16 colors
5-bit	32 colors
6-bit	64 colors
7-bit	128 colors
8-bit	256 colors
16-bit	65,536 colors
24-bit	16,777,216 colors (usually referred to as "millions")

Newer web tools allow you to select the number of colors. In some graphic tools (such as older versions of Photoshop), you can select the number of colors indirectly by choosing the bit-depth from a pop-up menu.

Reduce the Number of Colors

Although GIFs can contain up to 256 colors, there's no rule that says they have to. In fact, by reducing the number of colors in the image (i.e., reducing its bit-depth), you can significantly reduce its file size (Figure 14-21, gallery). One reason is that files with lower bit-depths contain less data. Another by-product of the color reduction is that more areas of flat color are created by combining similar, abutting pixel colors. More flat color, more efficient compression.

Nearly all graphics programs that allow you to save or export to GIF format will also allow you to specify the number of colors (or bit-depth).

At a certain point, of course, if you reduce the number of colors too far, the image will begin to fall apart or will cease to communicate the effect you are after. For instance, in Figure 14-21, once I reduced the number of colors to eight, I lost the rainbow, along with the whole point of the image. This "meltdown" point is different from image to image.

You'll be surprised to find how many images look perfectly fine at 5-bit with only 32 pixel colors (that's usually my starting point for color reduction, and I go higher only if needed). Some image types fare better than others with reduced color palettes, but as a general rule, the fewer the colors, the smaller the file.

The real size savings kicks in when there are large areas of flat color. Keep in mind that even if your image only has eight pixel colors, if it has a lot of blends and gradients, you won't see the kind of file size savings you might expect with that kind of severe color reduction.

Figure 14-21

| 256 colors: 21K | 64 colors: 13K | 8 colors: 8K |

Reducing the number of colors in an image reduces the file size.

Reduce Dithering

When the colors in an image are reduced to a specific palette, the colors that are not in the palette are approximated by dithering. Dithering is the speckle pattern you see in images when palette colors are combined to simulate unavailable colors.

In photographic images, dithering is not a problem and can even be beneficial; however, dithering in flat areas is usually distracting and undesirable. Beyond aesthetic reasons, dithering is undesirable because the speckles disrupt otherwise smooth areas of color. Those stray speckles stand in the way of GIF compression and result in larger files.

One way to shave extra bytes off a GIF is to limit the amount of dithering. Again, nearly all GIF-creation tools will allow you to turn dithering on and off. Photoshop (5.5 and higher) and Fireworks go one step further by allowing you to set the specific amount of dithering on a sliding scale. You can even view the results of the dither setting, so you can decide at which point the degradation in image quality is not worth the file size savings (Figure 14-22, gallery). In images with smooth color gradients, turning dithering off results in unacceptable banding and blotches.

Dithering is the speckle pattern you see in images when palette colors are combined to simulate unavailable colors.

Figure 14-22 G

Dithering: 9.6K   **No dithering: 7.8K**

Turning off or reducing the amount of dithering will reduce the file size. Both images have 32 pixel colors and use an Adaptive palette.

Creating GIFs

Lossy GIFs

As we discussed earlier, GIF compression is "lossless," which means every pixel in the image is preserved during compression. But you can force some pixels to be thrown out using the "Lossy" or "Loss" setting in Photoshop 5.5 and Fireworks, respectively (Figure 14-23, gallery). Again, throwing out stray pixels is all in the name of maximizing the number of uninterrupted rows of pixel color, thus allowing the GIF compression to do its stuff. Depending on the image, you can apply a lossy/loss value of 5–30% without seriously degrading the image. This technique works best for continuous tone art (however, images that are all continuous tone should probably be saved as JPEGs anyway). You might try it on an image with a combination of flat and photographic content.

Figure 14-23 **G**

"Lossy" set to 0%: 13.2K   "Lossy" set to 25%: 7.5K

Applying a "Lossy" (in Photoshop) or "Loss" (in Fireworks) value removes pixels from the image and results in smaller file size. Both images shown here contain 64 colors and use Diffusion dither.

Design for Compression

We've looked at several ways you can use the settings in your tools to reduce the size of your GIFs. But even before you get to that point, you can be proactive about optimizing your graphics by designing them to compress well in the first place.

You can be proactive about optimizing your graphics by designing them to compress well in the first place.

Keep it flat

I've found that, as a web designer, I've changed my illustration style to match the medium. In instances where I might have used a gradient blend, I now opt for a flat color. In most cases, it works just as well, and it doesn't introduce unflattering banding and dithering or drive up the file size (Figure 14-24, gallery).

Figure 14-24 G

You can keep file sizes small by designing in a way that takes advantage of the GIF compression scheme.

This GIF has gradient blends and 256 colors. Its file size is 19K.

Even when I reduce the number of colors to 8, the file size is still 7.6K.

When I create the same image with flat colors instead of blends, the size of the GIF file is only 3.2K.

Play with horizontal stripes

When you are designing your web graphics, keep in mind that the compression works best on horizontal bands of colors. If you want to make something striped, better to make the stripes horizontal than vertical (Figure 14-25). Silly, but true.

Figure 14-25

GIFs designed with horizontal bands of color will compress more efficiently than with vertical bands.

280 bytes

585 bytes

Figure 14-26

13K

10K

Adding a 1-pixel striped pattern over a photographic image is one design technique for reducing file size.

One technique that is commonly used in web design is to apply 1-pixel wide horizontal lines over a photographic image. The image still shows through the horizontal lines, but the GIF compression can work its magic on a significant portion of the image area (Figure 14-26).

Creating GIFs

What Does the Web Palette Look Like?

The colors in the web palette were not chosen because of the way they look; they are just the results of combining amounts of red, green, and blue light at even 20% increments. Because web colors are light-based, it is impossible to get even a decent representation of them in print (especially the more fluorescent tones), so they are not reproduced in this book.

To see samples of all the colors in the web palette, load them into your Photoshop swatches palette (see Figure 14-28 for a demonstration) or view the web palette chart available at *www.learningwebdesign.com*.

TIP

To see how your image will look in the 8-bit environment, try using Photoshop 5.5's "Browser Dither" preview (accessed in the "Save for Web" dialog box). This may help you make decisions regarding optimization.

Designing with the Web Palette

Another big part of designing GIFs for the Web is whether and how to use the web palette. The web palette is a set of 216 colors that will not dither on PCs or Macs, and is built into all the major browsers. When a browser is running on a computer with an 8-bit monitor (capable of displaying only 256 colors at a time), it refers to its internal web palette to make up the colors on the page. The colors in the images are re-mapped to the colors in the web palette.

We've seen several examples already of what happens when colors are mapped to a smaller palette—shifting and dithering. But at least we have the advantage of knowing exactly which colors the browser will use, and if we use those "web-safe" colors in the first place, we can prevent unpredictable results on 8-bit monitors (Figure 14-27, gallery). Our graphics will look consistent from platform to platform, user to user.

Figure 14-27 G

This GIF is designed with non-web-safe colors, resulting in dithering on 8-bit monitors.

On a 24-bit monitor, the solid colors are smooth and accurate.

On an 8-bit monitor, the colors are approximated by dithering colors from the web palette.

If the flat areas are filled with web-safe colors, the photograph still dithers, but the flat colors stay flat.

In Chapter 12, Color on the Web, there is a more technical explanation of how the web palette was devised and how it is applied in HTML documents. But the web palette comes into play when you are designing and creating GIF graphics as well. It is particularly useful for images with flat colors, since those suffer the most from unwanted dithering.

When You Don't Need to Worry About the Web Palette

There are some instances when you don't need to be concerned with the web palette:

If you don't care about performance on 8-bit monitors. Remember, the web palette only comes into play on 8-bit monitors. 16- and 24-bit monitors can accurately display just about any image. So if you are not concerned with your site's performance on low-end systems, you don't need to worry about the web palette.

However, in the interest of designing democratically and keeping an eye on the "lowest common denominator," most web designers take the extra step of making sure their GIFs use colors from the web palette. You may even find that your clients insist upon it to maintain consistent quality on their sites.

If your image is primarily photographic. First, I should say, if you're starting with a purely photographic image, you should save it in JPEG format (see Chapter 15 for more information).

But say you have a photographic image that you want to save as a GIF. Because the image is going to dither somewhat anyway when you reduce its colors, and because dithering can actually be beneficial in photographic images, you do not need to apply the web palette. Selecting an adaptive palette (a customized palette based on the colors most used in the image) is a better choice during the conversion process.

If your image is in JPEG format. The web palette is irrelevant for JPEG images. For one thing, JPEGs don't use palettes to keep track of colors. But more importantly, even if you have flat areas of web-safe colors in your original image, they will get shifted and distorted during the JPEG compression process. Designing with the web palette is a GIF-specific issue.

Starting with Web-Safe Colors

If you are creating images from scratch, you have the perfect opportunity to use web-safe colors in your design. The benefit is knowing that your graphics will look the same for all users. The main drawback is that the color selection is very limited. Not only is 216 not many colors to choose from, but a good percentage of them are colors you'd never be caught dead using for anything (the web palette was generated mathematically, not aesthetically!).

The trick is to have the colors of the web palette available in a Swatches palette (or in whatever device your graphics program uses to make colors handy). Fortunately, with the great demand for web graphics, the web

If you are creating images from scratch, you have the perfect opportunity to use web-safe colors in your design.

Creating GIFs

palette has been integrated in to the majority of graphics related programs, including, but not limited to:

Adobe Photoshop (5.0 and higher)
Macromedia Fireworks (1.0 and higher)
JASC Paint Shop Pro (5 and higher)
Adobe Illustrator (7.0 and higher)
Corel (previously MetaCreations) Painter (6 and higher)
Macromedia Freehand (7.0 and higher)
Macromedia Director (5.0 and higher)
Macintosh System Color Picker OS8

The web palette may be called by one of its many names, such as the Netscape Palette, Web 216, Browser-safe Palette, Non-dithering Palette, the 6×6×6 Cube, and so on—but you should recognize it when you see it.

Photoshop and other graphics tools save palettes in files called CLUTs (Color Look-Up Tables). Some tools, such as Fireworks, offer the web palette by default. In others, you may need to load the appropriate web CLUT file into the program to make it available. Figure 14-28 shows how that works in Adobe Photoshop.

Figure 14-28

Loading the web palette into Photoshop

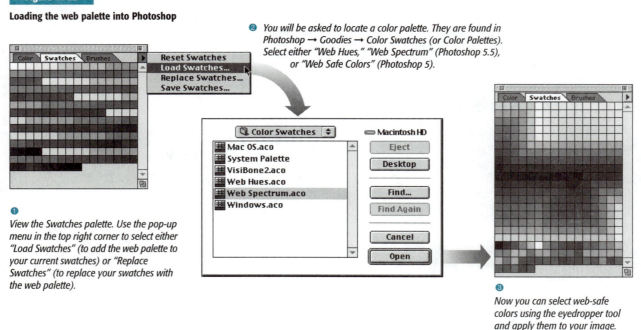

❷ You will be asked to locate a color palette. They are found in Photoshop → Goodies → Color Swatches (or Color Palettes). Select either "Web Hues," "Web Spectrum" (Photoshop 5.5), or "Web Safe Colors" (Photoshop 5).

❶ View the Swatches palette. Use the pop-up menu in the top right corner to select either "Load Swatches" (to add the web palette to your current swatches) or "Replace Swatches" (to replace your swatches with the web palette).

❸ Now you can select web-safe colors using the eyedropper tool and apply them to your image.

Applying the Web Palette

Another way to make sure your image uses web-safe colors is to apply the web palette in the conversion process from RGB to Indexed Color. In any tool, once you have chosen to make your image into a GIF or to convert it to Indexed Color, you will be asked to select a palette for the image.

The simplest and crudest method is to select the "Web" palette option when you are asked for the palette. The color table for the resulting GIF will contain colors from the web palette exclusively, regardless of the colors in the source image (Figure 14-29).

Figure 14-29

Many tools allow you to select the web palette during the process of converting to indexed color. If you view the Color Table for the image (shown here in Photoshop), you will see the web palette colors.

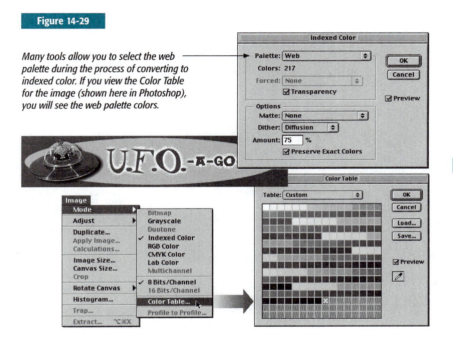

The newer web graphics tools offer a more sophisticated method for applying and preserving web-safe colors in the conversion process. These are especially useful for images that contain a combination of full-color photographic images and flat, web-safe colors.

Fireworks 3 gives the option of saving with the "Web Adaptive" palette. It is an adaptive palette, so the palette will be customized for the image, but any colors that are near in value to web palette colors will "snap" to the closest web palette colors (Figure 14-30).

Figure 14-30

Fireworks 3 offers a Web Adaptive palette.

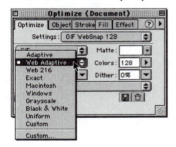

You can view the color table for the image in the Color Table palette.

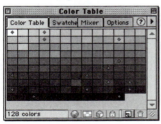

Creating GIFs

In Photoshop 5.5, you can control how many colors shift to their nearest web-safe equivalents by selecting an adaptive palette (Adaptive, Perceptual, or Selective) and using the "Web Snap" slider tool (Figure 14-31). The higher you set the slider, the more colors will shift. This allows Photoshop to construct a custom color table for the image while keeping areas of the image web-safe.

Figure 14-31

Use Photoshop 5.5's Web Snap slider to control precisely how many colors snap to their nearest web-safe equivalents. In the Color Table, the swatches with dots are web-safe.

You can see the results of your settings immediately in the preview window.

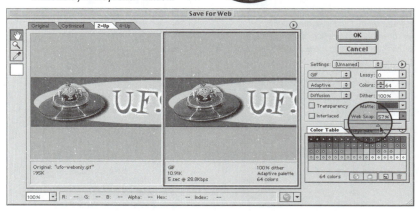

Web Palette Strategies for Graphics

Many beginners make the mistake of applying the web palette to every graphic they produce. After all, they're "web" graphics, right? Wrong! The web palette isn't appropriate for all image types, and can actually reduce potential quality. In fact, I almost never apply the straight Web palette to an image, particularly now that web graphics tools provide more sophisticated options.

There are no hard and fast rules, since every image has its own requirements. The following are some basic guidelines for using—and resisting—the web palette.

Flat graphical images

GOAL: Keep flat color areas from dithering while maintaining smoothness in the anti-aliased edges.

STRATEGY: Use colors from the web palette to fill flat color areas when you are designing the image. Do not apply the simple Web palette option when saving or exporting because you'll lose the gradations of color in the anti-aliasing. It is better to choose an Adaptive palette with a "Web Snap" option, if it is available. In Photoshop, set the amount of "Web Snap" with the slider scale. In Fireworks, apply the "Web Adaptive" palette. This will maintain the web colors in your flat areas, but allow some of the colors in the anti-aliasing to remain.

The web palette isn't appropriate for all image types, and can actually reduce potential quality.

Photographic images

GOAL: To maintain clarity and color fidelity for the maximum number of users.

STRATEGY: First, if it's an entirely photographic image, consider saving it in JPEG format. Otherwise, choose an Adaptive palette (or Selective in Photoshop 5.5 and up) when converting the image to GIF format. Any time you reduce the colors in a photographic image you'll get some dithering, so choose a palette that best matches the colors in the image. That way, the image will look the best it possibly can for users with 24-bit monitors. For users with 8-bit monitors, the image will map again to the web palette, but dithering is usually not detrimental in photographic images. The only advantage to applying the web palette to a continuous-tone image is that you'll know it will look equally bad to everyone.

Combination images (both flat and photographic areas)

GOAL: To keep the flat areas from dithering while allowing the continuous tone areas to dither with an adaptive palette.

STRATEGY: Use web-safe colors in the flat areas when you are designing the image. When it's time to save or export to GIF format, choose an Adaptive palette with a "Web Snap" option if it is available. The Adaptive palette preserves the color fidelity in the photographic areas while the "Web Snap" option preserves the web-safe colors in the flat areas.

Some Things to Remember About GIFs

In closing, I'd like to round up some of the major points from this lengthy but important chapter:

- GIF is the best file format for images with flat areas of color, such as logos, line art, text graphics, etc. The GIF compression scheme works by finding and condensing rows of identically colored pixels.

- GIFs can be interlaced, transparent, and/or animated.

- A GIF uses a color palette that can contain up to 256 colors. When you save an image as a GIF, you need to convert it to Indexed Color and select an appropriate color palette.

- You can make parts of a GIF transparent either by preserving the transparent areas in a layered document (in Photoshop and Fireworks), or by selecting a color in a flattened image with the proper transparency tool.

- Halos occur when an image is anti-aliased to a color other than the background color of the page, causing a fringe of pixels around the image. Halos are easier to prevent than correct.

- Some strategies for keeping GIF file sizes small are: design with flat areas of colors, reduce the number of colors when converting to Indexed Color, limit dithering, and take advantage of lossy GIF compression if available.

- The web palette is a set of 216 colors that will not dither in browsers on 8-bit monitors. Choosing colors from the web palette when designing GIF images prevents flat areas of color from dithering.

Chapter 15

Creating JPEGs

If you have a photograph or any other image with blended color (such as a painting or realistic digital illustration), JPEG is the file format to use. It's perfect for compressing continuous-tone color and even grayscale images (Figure 15-1, gallery).

IN THIS CHAPTER

Characteristics of JPEG compression

Making JPEGs, step by step

Optimizing JPEGs

Figure 15-1

The JPEG file format is ideal for photographs (color or grayscale) or any image with subtle color gradations.

Compared to GIFs, saving your images in JPEG format is a walk in the park. Before we get into the JPEG creation process, there are a few things you should know about the file format that will help you decide when to use JPEG and how to make the best possible JPEG images.

More About JPEGs

JPEG (Joint Photographic Experts Group, the standards body that created it) is a compression algorithm especially developed for photographic images. By understanding JPEG terminology and the nature of JPEG compression, you'll be able to use your graphics tools efficiently to make the highest-quality JPEGs at the smallest size.

24-Bit Color

The nice thing about JPEGs is that they can contain 24-bit RGB color information; that's millions of colors! This is one aspect that makes them ideal for photographs—they have all the colors you'll ever need. With JPEGs, you don't have to worry about color palettes or limiting yourself to 256 colors the way you do with GIFs. JPEGs are much more straightforward.

Lossy Compression

The JPEG compression scheme is lossy, which means that some of the image information is thrown out in the compression process. Fortunately, this loss is not discernable for most images at most compression levels. When an image is compressed with high levels of JPEG compression, you begin to see color blotches and squares (usually referred to as "artifacts") that result from the way the compression scheme samples the image (Figure 15-2, gallery).

Figure 15-2 **G**

Original

High compression

JPEG compression discards image detail to achieve smaller file sizes. At very high compression rates, image quality suffers, as shown in the image on the right.

Cumulative Image Loss

Be aware that once image quality is lost in JPEG compression, you can never get it back again. For this reason, you should avoid resaving a JPEG as a JPEG: you lose image quality every time.

It is better to hang on to the original image. That way, if you need to make a change to the JPEG version, you can go back to the original and do a fresh save or export. Fortunately, today's web-specific graphics tools make this easy.

As an added bonus, you get to control how aggressively you want the image to be compressed. This involves a trade-off between compression level and quality. The more you compress the image (for a smaller file size), the more the image suffers. Conversely, when you maximize quality, you also end up with larger files. You'll need to set your levels based on the particular image and your objectives for the site. We'll talk more about this in the Optimizing JPEGs section later in this chapter.

JPEGs Love Smooth Colors

JPEGs compress areas of smooth, blended colors much more efficiently than areas with high contrast and sharp detail (Figure 15-3, gallery). In fact, the blurrier your image, the smaller the resulting JPEG. Later in this chapter, we'll look at how you can use this to your advantage when optimizing JPEGs.

Figure 15-3 | G

gradient.jpg (12K)   detail.jpg (49K)

JPEG compression works better on smooth images than images with hard edges and detail. Compare the file sizes of these examples.

Totally flat colors don't do well in JPEG format because the colors may shift and get mottled (Figure 15-4, gallery). (Flat graphical images should be saved as GIFs.)

Figure 15-4 | G

chair.jpg

The same flat graphical image saved as both a JPEG and a GIF.

chair.gif

In the JPEG, the flat color changes and gets blotchy. Detail is lost as a result of JPEG compression.

In the GIF, the flat colors and crisp detail are preserved.

What About the Web Palette?

When you're working with JPEGs, you don't need to worry about the web palette. JPEGs don't have color tables like GIFs: they just try to stay true to the original RGB colors in the image.

When a JPEG appears on an 8-bit monitor, the browser will apply its internal web palette to the image and, as a result, the image will dither. Fortunately, while dithering is distracting on areas of flat color, it is usually not a problem in photographic images with smooth transitions.

JPEGs and GIFs Don't Match

In GIF files, you have total control over the colors that appear in the image, making it easy to match colors in adjoining GIFs, or in an inline GIF and a tiled background image.

Unfortunately, flat colors will shift around and get somewhat blotchy with JPEG compression, so there is no way to control the colors precisely. Even pure white will be distorted in a JPEG.

This makes it nearly impossible to create a perfect, seamless match between a JPEG and a GIF with its pure flat colors. If you are planning on matching a graphic in the foreground to a tiling background graphic, don't mix formats. You will have the best results in matching GIF to GIF because of the unpredictability of JPEG color.

Creating JPEGs

Progressive JPEGs

Progressive JPEGs are just ordinary JPEGs that display in a series of passes (like interlaced GIFs), starting with a low-resolution version that gets clearer with each pass (Figure 15-5, gallery). In some graphics programs, you can specify the number of passes it takes to fill in the final image (3, 4, or 5). The advantage of using Progressive JPEGs is that viewers can get an idea of the image before it downloads completely. The disadvantage is that they take more processing power to display and are not supported in very early browser versions.

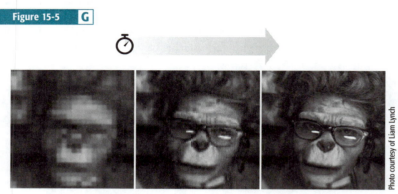

Figure 15-5   G

Progressive JPEGs render in a series of passes. The image detail and quality is improved with each pass.

Photo courtesy of Liam Lynch

Decompression

JPEGs need to be decompressed before they can be displayed; therefore, it takes a browser longer to decode and assemble a JPEG than a GIF of the same file size. It's not a big difference, though, and is not a reason to avoid the JPEG format.

Naming JPEGs

JPEGs must be named with the *.jpg* or *.jpeg* suffix in order to be used on a web page. Even if the graphic is in JPEG format, the browser relies on the proper suffix to recognize the file as a JPEG and to place it on the page.

Making JPEGs, Step by Step

Regardless of the tool you use, the process for creating a JPEG is about the same. You'll begin by opening your image in an image editing program and performing any necessary edits such as resizing, cropping, color adjustments, etc. Always save your original in case you need to make changes to the image later.

In the process of saving or exporting the JPEG, you will be asked to make the following decisions:

Image quality. The quality setting tells the program how aggressively to compress the image. Image quality is generally tracked on a scale from 1 to 10 or from 0 to 100%. Higher numbers correspond to better image quality and therefore, larger file sizes. Lower numbers correspond to worse image quality with smaller file sizes. In most cases, "medium," or approximately 50%, produces an acceptable JPEG image; however, you may be able to go even lower.

Progressive. Decide whether you want the JPEG to be progressive (see the section Progressive JPEGs earlier in this chapter).

Optimized. Decide whether you want the JPEG to be optimized. This results in a slightly smaller JPEG, but it may not display in early browser versions.

Matte. If you are working with a layered image or one that contains transparent areas, the matte color you specify will be used to fill in the transparent areas of the image. Generally, you'd want to select a color that matches the background color of the page to simulate transparency (JPEGs can't have real transparent areas like GIFs.)

Blur or smoothing. Some tools let you blur your image slightly to improve the compression and reduce file size. If you choose to do this, it is important to preview your image to make sure the image quality is still acceptable. The setting, of course, will depend on your image.

Once you have made all your settings, export or save the file as a JPEG. Be sure to name it with the *.jpg* or *.jpeg* suffix.

Now let's take a look at how these steps are worked out in several popular image creation tools.

IMPORTANT

Be sure that your image is in RGB or grayscale color mode (not CMYK) and that the resolution is set at 72 dpi.

WARNING

Some really old browsers (Version 2 and earlier) do not support optimized and progressive JPEGs, so if you are concerned with 100% browser support, choose "Baseline (Standard)" and avoid the special options.

Creating JPEGs

In Adobe Photoshop 5.5 (and Higher)

Adobe Photoshop 5.5 introduced the handy "Save for Web" feature. Selecting "Save for Web" is essentially the same as doing a "Save As," since your original is preserved and a separate JPEG document is created. Figure 15-6 shows the steps for creating a JPEG using the File → Save for Web option.

Figure 15-6

Saving a JPEG with Photoshop 5.5's (and higher) "Save for Web" feature

❶ *Open the image and do any necessary editing.*

❷ *Make sure the image is flattened,*

❸ *...is at a low resolution (72 dpi),*

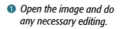

❹ *... and in RGB or grayscale color mode.*

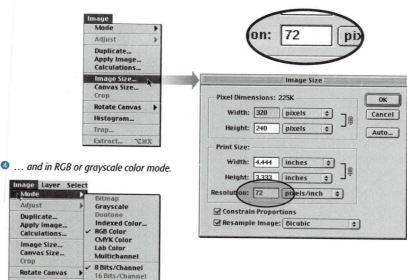

Figure 15-6 (cont.)

Saving a JPEG with Photoshop 5.5's (and higher) "Save for Web" feature

⑤ *Select File → Save For Web.*

⑥ *Select JPEG from the pull-down menu ⓐ. Use the controls to manipulate the compression as indicated.*

The Save for Web dialog box features the ability to view your compressed JPEG side by side with your original.

ⓐ *Selects file format.*

ⓑ *Makes the JPEG Optimized when checked.*

ⓒ *Image quality is set with the pull-down menu or the numeric slider (they work in tandem).*

ⓓ *Makes the JPEG Progressive when checked.*

ⓔ *Applies a slight blur to the image to improve compression rates.*

ⓕ *ICC Profile contains precise color information for the file, but it usually results in unacceptably large file sizes.*

ⓖ *Any transparent areas in the image will be filled in by the color specified in the Matte box.*

ⓗ *The Color Table will be empty because JPEGs don't use color tables.*

ⓘ *Use this palette to resize the saved image while maintaining the size of the original. Be sure to hit the Apply button before you hit OK.*

⑦ *When you are done click the OK button. In the "Saved Optimized As" dialog box, give the file a name ending with **.jpg** or **.jpeg**.*

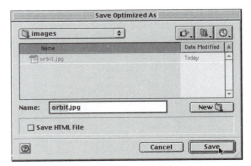

If you check "Save HTML File", Photoshop will generate the HTML tag containing information about the graphic. This can be cut and pasted into your HTML document.

⑧ *Click Save to save the file.*

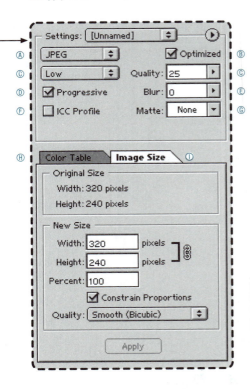

Creating JPEGs

In Earlier Photoshop Versions

If you are working with an earlier version of Photoshop, you can still save your files in JPEG format by using the File → Save As or Save option. JPEG is one of the standard file formats that Photoshop saves to.

If you are working with a layered original, you must flatten the image (Layer → Flatten) in order for the JPEG option to be available in the Format pull-down menu. Figure 15-7 shows how to save an image as a JPEG in all versions of Photoshop.

Figure 15-7

Saving an image as a JPEG in Adobe Photoshop
(Versions 4 and higher)

❶ *Open image and do any necessary editing.*

❷ *Make sure the image is flattened, is at a low resolution (72 dpi), and is in RGB or grayscale color mode (see previous figure).*

❸ *Select File → Save As.*

❹ *Select JPEG from the pull-down menu. Give the file a name ending in either .jpg or .jpeg and choose the file location. Click Save.*

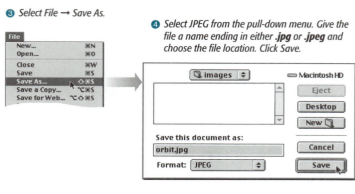

❺ *Set the compression rate Ⓐ and the format Ⓑ. The file size and approximate download time are provided at the bottom of the window Ⓒ.*

When you are finished, click OK.

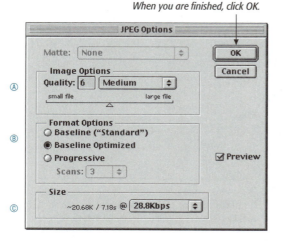

In Macromedia Fireworks 3

It's easy to make JPEGs in Fireworks because you can do all your compression settings right in the workspace using the Optimize palette and the Preview option in the document window. You also have access to the same settings during the export process when you select File → Export Preview. Figure 15-8 shows the JPEG controls in Fireworks 3.

Figure 15-8

Exporting a JPEG in Macromedia Fireworks 3

❶

Open the image in Fireworks. Do any necessary image editing such as cropping, resizing, etc. Make sure the image is at low resolution. In Fireworks, images are in RGB mode by default and it is not necessary to flatten an image prior to export.

Ⓐ *Selects the file format.*

Ⓑ *Any transparent areas in the image will be filled with the matte color.*

Ⓒ *Select the quality on a scale from 0 to 100%.*

Ⓓ *Smoothing will blur the image slightly to improve compression rates.*

❷

You can optimize and export the JPEG right from the workspace. Use the Optimize palette to make your JPEG settings. The document window can show side-by-side previews of your settings.

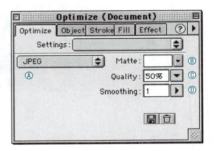

❸ *When you are finished, select Export from the File menu. Give your file a name ending in .jpg or .jpeg and choose its location.*

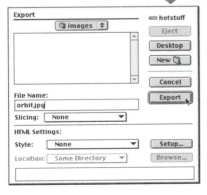

Another Approach
You can access the same JPEG settings directly in the Export Preview dialog box (under the File menu). When you've made all your settings, hit the Export button.

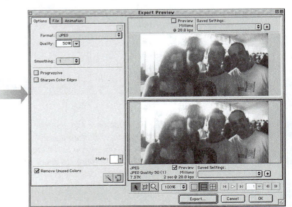

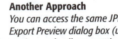

Creating JPEGs

In JASC Paint Shop Pro 6

Paint Shop Pro works similarly to early versions of Photoshop, but is a less expensive alternative. The downside is that it only works on the Windows operating system, so you Mac users are out of luck. Figure 15-9 shows the steps for saving a graphic as a JPEG in Paint Shop Pro 6.

Figure 15-9

Saving a JPEG in JASC Paint Shop Pro 6 and higher

❶
Open the image and do any necessary image editing. When you are ready to save it as a JPEG, select File → Save As.

❷
In the Save As dialog box, give the file a filename and select "JPEG - JFIF Compliant (.jpg, *.jif, *.jpeg,)".*

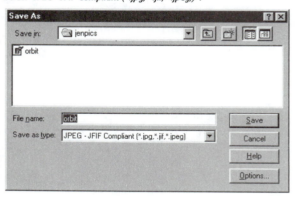

❸
Click the Options button. In the Save Options dialog box, you can specify whether you want the JPEG to be progressive and set the compression rate.

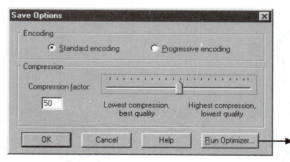

❹
The JPEG Optimizer (accessed by clicking the "Run Optimizer" button) gives you the same options, but allows you to see the results of your settings compared to the original. When you are finished, click OK to save the file.

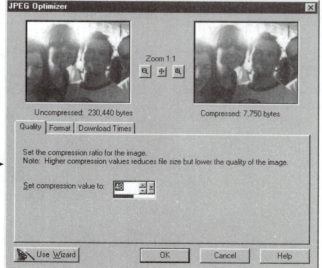

Optimizing JPEGs

I've said it before and I'll say it again—when you're producing graphics for the Web, it is crucial to keep file sizes as small as possible. Using the tools and settings we've seen above, there are basic strategies you can take to make sure your JPEGs are lean and mean.

Be Aggressive with Compression

The easiest and most straightforward way to reduce the file size of a JPEG is to opt for a higher compression rate. Of course, this comes with the sacrifice of some image quality, but you'll be surprised how far you can compress a JPEG while maintaining an acceptable image. Figure 15-10 (gallery, following page) shows the results of different quality (compression) rates as applied in Macromedia Fireworks 3 and Adobe Photoshop 5.5.

Notice that the image holds up well, even at very low quality (high compression) rates. Every image is different, so where you draw the line between file size and image quality will vary. But unless you are publishing works of art or other types of images in which detail is important, feel free to be aggressive with compression.

Try Different Tools

Another interesting aspect of Figure 15-10 is that the same settings in each program produce different results. That's because the quality rating scale is not objective—it varies from program to program. For instance, a quality of 0% in Photoshop is similar to 30% in Fireworks and other programs. JPEG compression can actually go further than Photoshop allows, but you probably don't want to go there. (Take a look at the mess that happens at the 0% rating in Fireworks!)

It's better to go by the way the image looks rather than a specific number setting.

In my personal testing, I've found that Fireworks produces smaller JPEGs at a similar visible quality than Photoshop 5.5. However, there are third-party JPEG plug-ins that work within Photoshop and other image-editing programs that make the smallest JPEGs of all. See the sidebar JPEG Optimization Tools for details.

> ### JPEG Optimization Tools
>
> If you are really concerned with making the smallest JPEGs possible while maximizing image quality, I recommend checking out third-party Photoshop plug-ins. These tools have been programmed specifically to work with JPEGs, so they've got fancy algorithms that can work magic:
>
> ProJPEG by BoxTop Software
> *www.boxtopsoft.com*
>
> HVS JPEG by Digital Frontiers
> *www.digfrontiers.com*

Choose Optimized

Optimized JPEGs have slightly smaller file sizes and better color fidelity than standard JPEGs. For this reason, you might select the Optimized option if your image software offers it.

The drawback is that the optimized JPEG format is not supported in some older browsers (Versions 2 and earlier). If you don't want to risk broken image icons, stay away from the Optimized option.

Creating JPEGs

Figure 15-10 **G**

A comparison of various compression levels in Adobe Photoshop 5.5 and Macromedia Fireworks 3.

Photoshop 5.5

Photoshop 100% (42.2K) *Photoshop 80% (22.3K)* *Photoshop 60% (13.6K)*

Photoshop 40% (8.2K) *Photoshop 20% (6.0K)* *Photoshop 0% (3.7K)*

Fireworks 3

Fireworks 100% (32.7K) *Fireworks 80% (10K)* *Fireworks 60% (6.8K)*

Fireworks 40% (5.2K) *Fireworks 20% (3.4K)* *Fireworks 0% (0.6K)*

Soften the Image

As I mentioned earlier, the JPEG compression scheme loves images with subtle gradations, fewer details, and no hard edges. One way you can take advantage of that compression is to start by softening the image prior to compression.

If you are using one of the newer web graphics tools, you will find a setting with the optimization options that softens the image. In Photoshop 5.5 and higher, the tool is called "Blur"; in Fireworks 3, it's "Smoothing". If you apply a soft blur, the JPEG compression works better, resulting in a smaller file (Figure 15-11, gallery). If you don't have these tools, you can soften the whole image by applying a slight blur to the image with the "Gaussian Blur" filter (or similar).

A more sophisticated, albeit labor-intensive, approach is to apply aggressive blurs to areas that are not important and to leave areas of detail alone. For instance, if you are working with a portrait, you could apply a rigorous blur to the background while maintaining detail in the face. I've done this in the image on the right in Figure 15-11.

You can help JPEG compression by applying a slight blur to your image or parts of it.

Figure 15-11 G

Blurring the image slightly before exporting as a JPEG will result in smaller file sizes.

Quality: 20 Blur: 0   (8.7K)

This JPEG was saved at low quality (20 in Photoshop) with no blurring applied.

Quality: 20 Blur: .5 (6.9K)

In this JPEG, I applied a slight blur to the image (.5 in Photoshop) before exporting it. Although it has the same quality setting (20) the file size is 20% smaller.

In Fireworks, use the "Smoothing" setting to apply a blur.

Quality: 20 Blur: 0   (6.6K)
(blur applied manually with Gaussian blur filter)

In this image, I blurred only selected areas of the image. This way, I was able to apply a more aggressive blur to parts of the image while maintaining detail in the face where it is important. The file size is comparable to the blurred example.

Creating JPEGs

Some Things to Remember About JPEGs

JPEGs are simpler to use than their GIF counterparts. Still, there are a few points from this chapter you might want to keep in mind:

- JPEG compression works best on continuous-tone images such as photographs or illustrations with smooth colors (like a watercolor). It loves smooth colors and blurry areas. It doesn't like hard edges and fine detail.

- JPEGs can contain millions of colors (24-bit color).

- JPEG is a "lossy" compression scheme, meaning small parts of the image are actually thrown away upon compression.

- Each time you open and resave a JPEG, you throw away more data. The loss in image quality is cumulative. For this reason, it is best to save the originals of your images and do fresh exports when you need to make changes.

- You can be fairly aggressive with the quality setting for JPEGs in order to reduce file size.

- Another way to reduce the file size of JPEGs is to apply a slight blur to all or part of the image.

Animated GIFs

When you see a web graphic spinning, blinking, pulsating, fading in and out, or otherwise putting on a little show, chances are it's an animated GIF. These days, they're *everywhere*—most notably in the advertising banners that crown nearly every page on the Web.

This chapter provides a basic introduction to how animated GIFs work and how to create them. Like so many web techniques, it's not difficult to start making simple animations, but it takes time and dedication to really master the art. This chapter is the first step.

Animated GIFs have a lot going for them—they're easy to make, and because they are just ordinary GIF files, they will work on virtually any browser without the need for plug-ins. Adding simple animation to a web page is an effective way to attract attention (those advertisers are no dummies). This makes using GIF animation tempting indeed!

However, be forewarned that it's easy to end up with too much of a good thing. Many users complain that animation is distracting and even downright annoying, especially when trying to read content on the page. So if you choose to use it, use it wisely (see the sidebar Responsible Animation on the following page).

How They Work

Basic animation is one of the features built into the "GIF89a" graphic file format. It allows one graphic to contain a number of animation "frames"—separate images that, when viewed quickly together, give the illusion of motion or change over time (Figure 16-1, gallery, following page). All of those images are stored within a single GIF file, along with settings that describe how they should be played in the browser window.

Within the GIF, you can control whether and how many times the sequence repeats, how long each frame stays visible (frame delay), the manner in which one frame replaces another (disposal method), whether the image is transparent, and whether it is interlaced. We'll discuss each of these settings later in this chapter.

Responsible Animation

If you don't want to annoy your audience, follow these recommendations for animation moderation:

• Avoid more than one animation on a page.

• Use the animation to communicate something in a clever way (not just gratuitous flashing lights).

• Avoid animation on text-heavy pages that require concentration to read.

• Consider whether the extra bandwidth to make a graphic "spin" is really adding value to your page.

• Decide if your animation really needs to loop continuously.

• Experiment with timing. Sometimes a long pause between loops can make an animation less distracting.

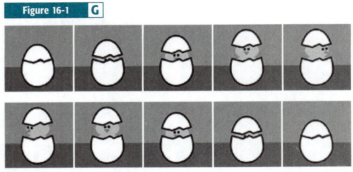

Figure 16-1 G

This animated GIF contains all of the images shown above. The images play back in sequence, creating a motion effect. When this GIF is viewed in a browser, the chick pops up, takes a look around, and then goes back in its shell.

Each frame is similar to a page in a child's flipbook.

GIF Animation Tools

To make an animated GIF, all you need is an animated GIF–making tool. These tools fall roughly into two categories.

The first are standalone GIF-animation utilities. These take a pre-existing group of GIF files (one for each frame in the animation sequence) and turn them into a single animated GIF. They provide a simple interface for entering the animation settings (speed, looping, etc.). Some also provide excellent optimization options and even transition effects. The good news is that animation utilities are inexpensive (even free) and available for download (see the sidebar GIF Utilities, facing page).

Other animation utilities are built into web graphics tools such as Adobe ImageReady and Macromedia Fireworks. If you already have one of these tools, you won't need additional software to make animations. The nice thing about built-in tools is that they allow you to create and save your animations all in one place. Another advantage is that they have advanced features that can do automatic frame generation.

Creating a Simple Animated GIF

Let's begin with the most straightforward method for creating an animated GIF—starting with a directory of separate GIF files and a standalone animation utility.

First things first: you have to create the GIFs. Fortunately, you can do this in any graphics program you have handy that supports the GIF format. Simply draw each frame of the animation and save it as a GIF. It makes things easier if you make all of the GIFs the same pixel dimensions.

I like creating my animations in a graphics tool that supports layers (Photoshop comes to mind). I use each layer to represent a frame in the animation. Then I make each layer visible—one at a time—and export each in GIF format (Figure 16-2).

Photoshop's layers are useful for creating animation frames by hand.

Figure 16-2

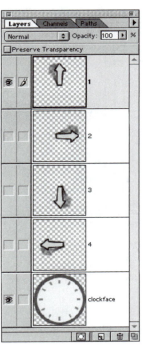

1.gif

2.gif

3.gif

4.gif

Layers are useful for designing animation frames. I've built my image in a single layered file, then exported each frame to GIF format.

As you can see in this example, I used the background to contain the unchanging parts of the animation (the clockface) and used the layers to manipulate the parts I want to move (the hands). You can use all the editing features in your drawing program to make changes from frame to frame, including color, position, and opacity changes.

Animated GIF Utilities

These tools are inexpensive, and useful for creating animated GIFs:

GifBuilder 0.5

(Mac only)
GifBuilder, developed by Yves Piguet, is the old standby for creating animated GIFs. It's freeware that is easy and intuitive to use. It is available for download at *www.mac.org/ graphics/gifbuilder/*.

Ulead GIF Animator 4.0

(Windows only)
Ulead's GIF Animator features wizards for quickly and easily constructing animations. Download a preview copy at *www.ulead.com*. Registration is $39.95 as of this writing.

GIFmation 2.3

(Mac and Windows)
This commercial software from BoxTop Software comes highly recommended by web developers for its visual interface, efficient compression methods, and sophisticated palette handling. GIFmation costs $49.95 (as of this writing). It is available at *www.boxtopsoft.com*.

Using a GIF Animation Utility

Next, I load the GIF files into a GIF animation tool. I am using BoxTop Software's GIFmation in this demonstration, but you'll find that other animation utilities work basically the same way.

GIF animation utilities take a set of individual GIF frames and turn them into a single animated GIF file.

I begin by loading my GIF files into the Frames palette. I can do this either by dragging the files right from my desktop into the window, or by using the File → Import menu item. When my GIFs are loaded, the Frames palette allows me to view the frame sequence as well as the settings for each individual frame (Figure 16-3).

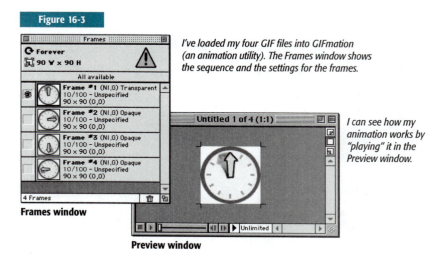

Figure 16-3

I've loaded my four GIF files into GIFmation (an animation utility). The Frames window shows the sequence and the settings for the frames.

I can see how my animation works by "playing" it in the Preview window.

Frames window

Preview window

The Preview window allows me to view the animation based on the current settings. I can "play" the animation and tweak my settings until I get the results I'm after.

Animation Settings

The real heart of the process is the settings. There are standard settings in every GIF animation tool (including those built into Fireworks and Image-Ready) that affect the behavior of the animation. Some of these settings will be familiar and intuitive; some you will be encountering for the first time. Different tools provide access to these settings in different places, but they'll be there.

Frame delay

Also called "interframe delay," this setting adjusts the amount of time between frames. Frame delays are measured in 1/100ths of a second. Theoretically, a setting of 100 would create a one-second delay, but in reality, this is a loose estimate and depends on the processor speed of the user's computer.

You can apply a uniform delay across all the frames in your animation, or apply delay amounts to individual frames. With custom frame delays, you can create pauses and other timing effects. You can set the frame delay to zero (or "as fast as possible"), but I find that a setting of 10 (that's 10/100ths, or .1 second) gives a smoother result for most continuous-motion animations.

Transparency

Like their static cousins, animated GIFs can contain areas of transparency. You can set transparency for each frame within an animation. Previous frames will show through the transparent area of a later frame. If the background frame is made transparent, the browser background color will show through. You need to properly coordinate frame transparency with the disposal method.

Don't be surprised if the transparent areas you specified in your original GIFs are made opaque when you open the files in a GIF animation utility. You may need to set the transparency again in the animation package.

Transparency can generally be set to black, white, "first color" (the top left pixel color), or a color chosen from within the image with an eyedropper tool.

Looping

You can specify the number of times an animation repeats: "none," "forever," or a specific number. Early browsers do not consistently support a specific number of loops. Some will show the first frame, others the last. One workaround is to build the looping into the file by repeating the frame sequence a number of times. Of course, this increases the file size.

Color palette

Animated GIFs use a palette of up to 256 colors that are used in the image. Although each frame can have its own palette, it is recommended that you use a global palette for the whole animation for smoother display (especially on older browsers).

Interlacing

Like ordinary GIFs, animated GIFs can be set to be interlaced, which causes them to display in a series of passes (starting blocky, finishing clear). It is recommended that you leave the interlacing option set to "no" or "off" because each frame is on the screen for a short amount of time.

Like their static cousins, animated GIFs can contain areas of transparency.

TIP
Starting Points

These settings are a good starting point for creating full-frame animations:

Color palette:	Global, adaptive palette
Interlacing:	Off
Dithering:	On for photos, off for drawings with few colors
Image size:	Minimum size
Background color:	Black or white
Looping:	None or forever
Transparency:	Off
Disposal method:	Do Not Dispose

Disposal method

The disposal method gives instructions on what to do with the previous frame once a new frame is displayed (Figure 16-4). The options are:

Unspecified (Nothing). Use this option to replace one full-size, non-transparent frame with another.

Do Not Dispose (Leave As Is). In this option, any pixels not covered by the next frame continue to display. Use this method if you are using transparency within frames.

Restore to Background. The background color or background tile shows through the transparent pixels of the new frame (replacing the image areas of the previous frame).

Restore to Previous. This option restores to the state of the previous, undisposed frame. This method is not well supported and is best avoided.

TIP

Most GIF animation utilities offer "optimization," a file-size reducing process that takes advantage of the fact that previous frames will "show through" transparent areas of a latter frame. In order for the optimization process to work, the disposal method must be set to "Do Not Dispose" (or "Leave As Is").

Figure 16-4

Disposal Methods

Unspecified

frame 1   frame 2   frame 2 - result

Replaces entire non-transparent frame with another

Do Not Dispose

light gray is not transparent

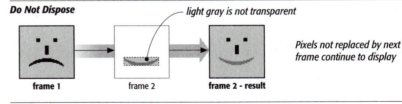

frame 1   frame 2   frame 2 - result

Pixels not replaced by next frame continue to display

Restore to Background

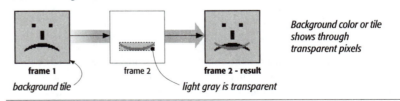

frame 1   frame 2   frame 2 - result

background tile   *light gray is transparent*

Background color or tile shows through transparent pixels

Restore to Previous (supported by Microsoft Internet Explorer 3.0 or greater)

restore previous

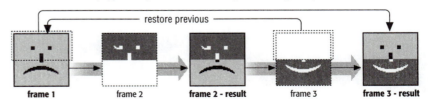

frame 1   frame 2   frame 2 - result   frame 3   frame 3 - result

---

Putting It Together

Back to that clock animation. I need to get all my settings in order (Figure 16-5). Because I want it to appear as though the hand is spinning around and around, I'll set looping to "forever" **Ⓐ** and the frame delay to 10/100ths of a second on all frames for a smooth, visible motion **Ⓑ**. And since the animation is made up of four solid frames (with no transparency), I've selected the "Unspecified" disposal method **Ⓒ**. I also want to make sure that interlacing is turned off **Ⓓ**.

Figure 16-5

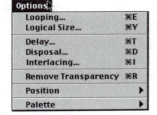

Using GIFmation's Options menu, I set the looping Ⓐ, frame delay Ⓑ, disposal method Ⓒ, and interlacing Ⓓ for my clock animation.

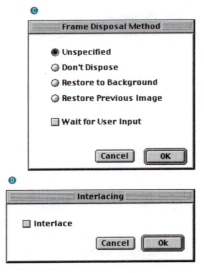

Figure 16-6

Optimized frames contain just the pixels that change from frame to frame. The result is a smaller file size than if you stored complete image information in every frame.

Frame 1 **Frame 2**

Frame 3 **Frame 4**

When I have everything working the way I want in the Preview menu, I save the graphic. GIFmation offers an "Export Optimized" option under the File menu. This optimization process saves only the pixels that change from frame to frame and throws out redundant image areas (Figure 16-6). The result is a big savings in file size with no change in the animation's appearance.

A Cool Shortcut (Tweening)

If you've invested in the latest and greatest web graphics creation tools (such as Macromedia Fireworks or Adobe ImageReady), you're in luck, because creating animations is easier than ever. The real advantage to these tools is that they will do some of the frame generation for you.

If you want an image to move from one side of the graphic to another, or you want a graphic to fade in from light to dark, you just need to provide the beginning frame and the end frame, and the tool generates all the frames in between (Figure 16-7). This process is known as tweening, and it is a great timesaver.

Figure 16-7

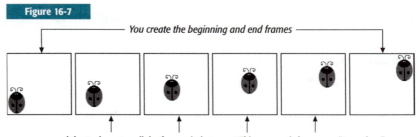

You create the beginning and end frames

…and the tool creates all the frames in between! This process is known as "tweening."

Adobe ImageReady (which comes bundled with Adobe Photoshop 5.5 and higher) makes this process easy. In ImageReady, animations are managed in the Animations window, which provides a representation of all the frames in the sequence. When you select a frame, it becomes "active" in the document window where you can edit the frame's contents just as you would any other graphic.

To create a smooth motion effect, I create a frame with my object (a ladybug) in the starting position and another frame with the same object in the final position. Selecting Tween from the Animations pop-up menu will fill in the motion in between, in as many steps as I specify. Let's take a look at this process step by step (Figure 16-8).

Figure 16-8

Using Adobe ImageReady 2 to create transitions

❶
With the first (and only) frame of my animation selected, I've drawn the element that I'd like to animate.

Original window
(Where you edit the content of each frame)

❷ I add a new frame to the animation by using the pull-down menu in the top right corner of the animation window.

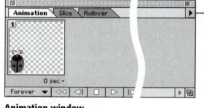

Animation window
(Where you manage frames and their settings)

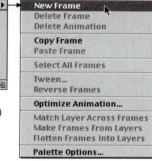

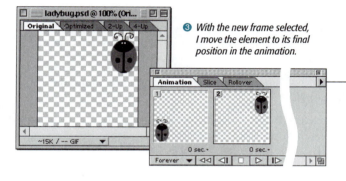

❸ With the new frame selected, I move the element to its final position in the animation.

❹ Now I can use ImageReady's "tween" function to generate the frames in between. I select Tween from the Animation window pop-up menu.

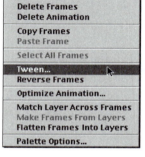

❺
In the dialog box, I specify that I want to vary the position of the selected layer. I can also specify how many steps I want the transition to take.

❻
When I click OK, the new frames are automatically inserted.

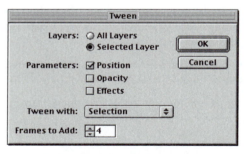

❼
When I am done, I select "Save Optimized" from the File menu to create the animated GIF. I can save my layered file in case I want to edit it later.

When the graphic is viewed in a browser, the ladybug will move from corner to corner.

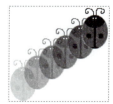

Beyond Beginner

In this chapter, I've barely scratched the surface of GIF animation. If you are using a graphics tool such as Fireworks or ImageReady for animation, I recommend reading the manuals provided to gain a better understanding of how the tool works and the interesting effects you can create with it.

You also might want to check out the list of GIF animation resource links gathered by WebReference.com available at *www.webreference.com/authoring/graphics/animation.html*. They have an amazing article about animated GIF optimization, which you will find at *www.webreference.com/dev/gifanim/*.

Some Things to Remember About Animated GIFs

Animated GIFs are quite popular on the Web today, particularly in banner advertising. With the proper tool, they are simple to create and they are added to the web page just like any other graphic. Here are the major points about animated GIFs we covered in this chapter:

- The ability to contain many frames of animation is a characteristic of the GIF file format.

- It's extremely easy to overdo animation on a web page. Consider carefully whether animation is adding or detracting from the success of your web page.

- In order to create an animated GIF, you need an animation utility. There are inexpensive (and even free) programs that do nothing but create GIF animations. In addition, animation tools are built into popular web graphics tools such as Adobe ImageReady and Macromedia Fireworks.

- When you create an animated GIF, you need to set the frame delay, disposal method, transparency, looping, color palette, and interlacing.

- Advanced animation tools will create frames for you automatically in a process called "tweening."

Form and Function

Now that we've covered the nuts and bolts, it's time to get back to some big-picture issues. We begin by combining our new HTML and graphics skills to create some of the most common web design tricks and special elements.

Chapter 18, Building Usable Web Sites, is an overview one of the most important and easily overlooked aspects of web design—usability. If users can't find what they're looking for on your site, or they get lost and frustrated trying, the snazziest graphics in the world aren't going to save the day.

Of course, appearance counts, too, so I've provided a rapid-fire list of web design do's and don'ts in Chapter 19, Web Design Dos and Don'ts. They should help you avoid the tell-tale signs of amateur web design.

The book closes with a glimpse of some exciting web design topics that are just beyond the scope of this book. I want you to be familiar with advanced techniques so you can recognize them when you see them and decide for yourself if you'd like to explore further. Consider it a look at the web design horizon.

Web Design Techniques

Parts II and III of this book cover the nuts and bolts of creating HTML documents and web graphics. In this chapter, we'll put these skills together to create some of the common design elements that you see on professional web pages.

You'll find that a significant number of these techniques rely on HTML tables, which is why, as a web designer, you'll want to have a good command of table creation. Chapter 10, Tables, is an in-depth exploration of table creation, including table-related HTML tags, the ways tables tend to go haywire, and how they are used to format whole pages. Now let's look at some tricks of the trade!

Fancy Bulleted Lists

In Chapter 7, Formatting Text, we saw how you can make a bulleted list using the "unordered list" tag (`<UL>`). This works just fine if you are happy with the browser's automatically-inserted bullet styles, but what if you want a bullet with more character—such as a daisy, or a little skull? In this case, you'll need to abandon the `<UL>` tag and create the list manually, using your own custom graphics as bullets.

The first step is to create the bullet graphic. If you want the bullet to fit into the flow of text seamlessly without adding any extra space, you should keep the height of the graphic to 10 or 12 pixels. Bullet graphics are best saved in the GIF format. See the sidebar Creating Bullets and Icons, later in this chapter, for more tips.

Next, create the list in HTML. If the list consists of short entries (just a few words), you can probably separate each entry with line or paragraph breaks, depending on how much space you want between lines (Figure 17-1, following page). I'm not using any list tags here because I don't want any bullets or numbers inserted automatically. Notice also how I've added space to the left and right of the graphic using the HSPACE attribute in the `<IMG>` tag in order to create an indent.

IN THIS CHAPTER

- Fancy bulleted lists
- Tables as sidebars and decorative elements
- The 1-pixel square graphic trick
- Vertical rules
- Background tile tricks
- Multi-part (sliced) images
- Pop-up windows

Keep the height of bullet graphics to 10 or 12 pixels.

Figure 17-1

🌼 puppy dogs

🌼 sugar frogs

🌼 kittens' baby teeth

The bulleted list was created by placing individual bullet graphics before each line.

```
<P><IMG SRC="daisy.gif" HSPACE=12>puppy dogs</P>
<P><IMG SRC="daisy.gif" HSPACE=12>sugar frogs</P>
<P><IMG SRC="daisy.gif" HSPACE=12>kittens' baby teeth</P>
```

If your list consists of longer entries, you'll need to use a table to control the alignment of the entry paragraphs (Figure 17-2). Use the width setting of the first table column for precise control over the amount of indentation. I've centered the bullets in their column to keep them from bumping up against the text. You can adjust the column width and horizontal alignment to achieve the look you want. Remember to set the vertical alignment (VALIGN) in each bullet cell to top to position the bullet next to the first line of text.

Figure 17-2

Long list entries require a table to maintain an indent after the bullets.

💀 **Avoid character spaces** in filenames. Although this is acceptable for local files on a Mac or Windows 95/98/NT machine, character spaces are not recognized by other systems.

💀 **Avoid special characters** such as ?, %, #, etc. in filenames. It is best to limit filenames to letters, numbers, underscores (in place of character spaces), hyphens, and periods.

```
<TABLE BORDER=0 WIDTH=400>
<TR>
<TD WIDTH=30 VALIGN=top ALIGN=center><IMG SRC="skull.gif"></TD>
<TD><B>Avoid character spaces</B> in filenames. Although this is acceptable
for local files on a Mac or Windows 95/98/NT machine, character spaces are
not recognized by other systems.</TD>
</TR>

<TR>
<TD VALIGN=top ALIGN=center><IMG SRC="skull.gif"></TD>
<TD><B>Avoid special characters</B> such as ?, %, #, etc. in filenames.
It is best to limit filenames to letters, numbers, underscores (in place
of character spaces), hyphens, and periods.</TD>
</TR>
```

Creating Bullets and Icons

There are many approaches to creating small graphic images. These are my personal techniques.

For bullets (images 12 pixels square or smaller), I usually create the graphic at actual size and draw the image, pixel by pixel, using the pencil tool in my image program. The process involves a lot of zooming in (to make the drawing process easier) and zooming out (to see the results at actual size). I find this method works well for tiny pictures because the sharp edges between colors help readability.

Actual size (11×11 pixels)

Zoomed in for editing

For icon-sized images, I usually create the image at twice or three times the final size of the graphic, then shrink the image to its final size once I'm happy with it. Working at a larger size gives me more room to play around and to take advantage of layers and image-editing tools. When the image is reduced to the smaller size, the aliased edges often help the overall quality. Sometimes I find that adding a "sharpen" filter as the final step tidies things up nicely.

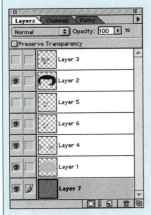

Original working file (60×60 pixels)

Final image size (30×30 pixels)

Web Design Techniques

Fun with Boxes

A table can be used as an attention-getting device for special announcements, pull-quotes, or sidebars.

A table can be used as an attention-getting device for special announcements, pull-quotes, or sidebars. You can have fun with the background color and make the box a decorative element. Once you've got the table made, just place it on a page as you would a graphic (see the sidebar Text Wrap Around Tables).

Simple Announcement Box

A single-celled table with some text centered in it can be used for a special announcement (Figure 17-3). I've adjusted the space within the cell with the CELLPADDING attribute in the <TABLE> tag. You can also control the size of the box precisely using WIDTH and HEIGHT. Try playing with the table background color and text color to create a box that is eye-catching yet is still in harmony with the color scheme of your page. The 3-D border can be set as thick as you like, or it can be turned off completely (BORDER=0).

Figure 17-3

Sale ends this week!

A one-celled table can be used for eye-catching announcements.

```
<TABLE BORDER=1 BGCOLOR="#CC0066" CELLPADDING=10>
<TR>
<TD ALIGN=center><FONT COLOR="white">Sale ends this week!</FONT></TD>
</TR>
</TABLE>
```

Text Wrap Around Tables

You can wrap text around a table just as you would an image by using the ALIGN=left or right attribute in the <TABLE> tag. You can also use the HSPACE and VSPACE attributes to adjust the space around the table. This is a nice technique for adding sidebars or call-outs to a long page of text:

```
<TABLE ALIGN=right
HSPACE=9 WIDTH=100
BORDER=1
BGCOLOR="#003399"
CELLPADDING=4>
```

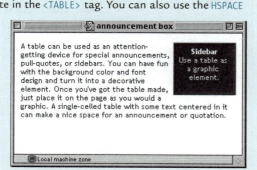

Boxes with Borders

If you don't like the browser's 3-D border effect, you can create a colored rule around a box of text by placing one table within another (Figure 17-4). The outer table should be slightly larger than the inner table, and it should be a different color (the color of the outer table forms the border around the box). To nest the tables, place the entire contents of one table within the <TD> of the other.

Web Design Techniques

Figure 17-4

The rule around this box is created by filling a table with another table that is a different color and slightly smaller.

```
<TABLE WIDTH=200 HEIGHT=200 CELLPADDING=0 BORDER=0>
<TR>
<TD BGCOLOR="#333333" ALIGN=center VALIGN=center>
        <TABLE WIDTH=198 HEIGHT=198 BORDER=0 CELLPADDING=10>
        <TR><TD BGCOLOR="#999999">Your content here!</TD></TR>
        </TABLE>
</TD>
</TR>
</TABLE>
```

To make the border wider, make the inside table smaller (or the exterior table larger).

```
<TABLE WIDTH=200 HEIGHT=200 CELLPADDING=0 BORDER=0>
<TR>
<TD BGCOLOR="#333333" ALIGN=center VALIGN=center>
        <TABLE WIDTH=180 HEIGHT=180 BORDER=0 CELLPADDING=10>
        <TR><TD BGCOLOR="#999999">Your content here!</TD></TR>
        </TABLE>
</TD>
</TR>
</TABLE>
```

In Figure 17-4, I've created a table and restricted its size to 200 pixels square. Since I want the color of my box rule to be dark gray, I set the background color of this table to dark gray (#333333).

Within that table's cell, I inserted another single-celled table of a lighter gray (#999999). The thickness of the border will be one-half the difference in size between the two boxes. This is easier to explain using examples.

In the top example of Figure 17-4, I wanted the border to be just one pixel thick, so I set the interior box two pixels smaller in both width and height (198 by 198), allowing one pixel of the exterior table to show on the left, right, top, and bottom. If I want a 10-pixel border, I'd make the interior box 20 pixels smaller than the exterior (180 by 180), as shown in the bottom example.

Rounded Corners

Any time you see rounded edges on a web page, you know it's been done with graphics.

There is currently no way to make rounded corners using HTML alone, so any time you see rounded edges on a web page, you know it's been done with graphics. In most cases, rounded elements rely on tables to hold the pieces together. When you deconstruct the rounded box in Figure 17-5, you see that it is actually made of a 9-cell table and four graphic files. The side and center cells are filled with a color that exactly matches the corner graphics.

Figure 17-5

This rounded box is made of a 9-cell table with four graphics for corners.

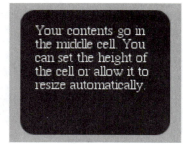
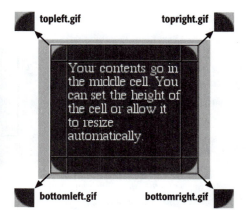

It's not hard to create a box with rounded corners like this one. First, decide what colors you want for the page background and for the table itself (you'll need the precise RGB values for both the graphics creation and the HTML file). I find that sticking to colors from the web palette (see Chapter 12, Color on the Web) gives you better results in matching the graphic color to the HTML color in the table cells. In Figure 17-5, I've chosen a light gray for the background color (#CCCCCC) and a dark blue for the box (#003399).

Next, create the graphics for the corners. I make mine by taking a circle and cutting it into four pieces (see the sidebar later in this chapter, Tips on Corner Creation) and saving each piece with a descriptive name that helps me keep track of it later (e.g., *topleft.gif*, *topright.gif*, *bottomleft.gif*, and *bottomright.gif*).

The final step is writing the code for the table. If you use a web-authoring tool, you may need to tweak the generated code to make the table behave properly. Following is the code for the example in Figure 17-5:

```
①—  <TABLE WIDTH=150 BGCOLOR="#003399" CELLSPACING=0 CELLPADDING=0
     BORDER=0>
      <TR>
②————     <TD WIDTH=15 HEIGHT=15><IMG SRC="topleft.gif"></TD>
         <TD WIDTH=120 HEIGHT=15 BGCOLOR="#003399"><FONT
         SIZE=-2> </FONT></TD>
         <TD WIDTH=15 HEIGHT=15><IMG SRC="topright.gif"></TD>
      </TR>
      <TR>
③————     <TD BGCOLOR="#003399"><FONT SIZE=-2> </FONT></TD>
④————     <TD ALIGN=left VALIGN=top HEIGHT=100 BGCOLOR="#003399"><FONT
         COLOR="white"> Your contents go in the middle cell. You can
      set the height of the cell or allow it to resize
      automatically.</FONT></TD>
         <TD BGCOLOR="#003399"><FONT SIZE=-2> </FONT></TD>
      </TR>
      <TR>
         <TD><IMG SRC="bottomleft.gif"></TD>
         <TD BGCOLOR="#003399"><FONT SIZE=-2> </FONT></TD>
         <TD><IMG SRC="bottomright.gif"></TD>
      </TR>
      </TABLE>
```

You can see that the table consists of three rows and three columns. In addition, there are some things about the code that I'd like to point out:

❶ Note that I've set the cell padding, cell spacing, and border to zero (0); this is crucial for creating a seamless effect between the cells. I've also used the `<TABLE>` tag to specify the background color for the box with the `BGCOLOR` attribute. The page background color is set in the `<BODY>` tag for the document (not shown).

❷ The corner cells of the table are filled with the image files. I've set the width and height of the cells containing graphics to match the graphic dimensions exactly (15 pixels square). I've also set the width of the center column to 120 pixels wide. Setting the cell widths in this first row establishes the column widths for the whole table, so I don't need to set them in subsequent rows. (When setting cell dimensions, be sure that the total width of the cells matches the width set for the whole table.)

❸ The cells that make up the edges of the box are set dark blue and are essentially empty. I have added a nonbreaking space (` `) to ensure the cells won't collapse in Netscape Navigator. (These principles are described in detail in Chapter 10.) In this instance, I found that the height of the nonbreaking space (the same as a line of text) was too tall for the narrow top row and it was adding space within the table, so I set the font size of the space to –2. This is typical of the kind of tweaks you may need to use to get your table to look right in most browsers.

❹ The content for the box goes in the center cell. You can set a specific height for this cell, as I did, or omit the height attribute and allow the table to size to fit the contents automatically.

Tips on Corner Creation

This is my preferred method for creating curved corner graphics (I'm using Photoshop 5.5 in this example):

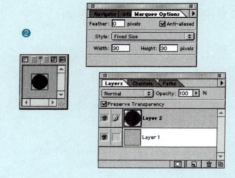

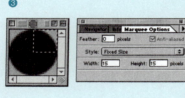

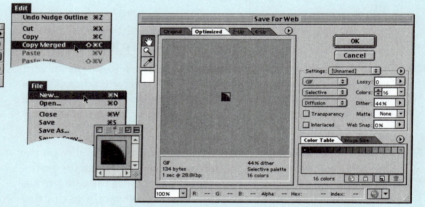

❶ Create a square layered file with an even pixel measurement (so it can be divided in half easily later). My graphic is 30 pixels square.

❷ Fill the background layer with the page's background color (in the example, it's light gray with an RGB value of #CCCCCC, or decimal 204, 204, 204). On a new layer, use the circle marquee to select a circle that is the same dimensions as the graphic file (30 pixels). I find it useful to use the "Fixed Size" style in the "Marquee Options" box to get a perfect fit. Fill the circle with the color you've chosen for the box (in our case, dark blue with the values #003399, or decimal 0, 53, 153). I always save my layered file, in case I need to make color changes later.

❸ Divide the image into four equal parts. I do this by selecting each quarter of the image (I restricted the marquee selection tool to 15 pixels square) and copying the selection using the "Copy Merged" method. This will grab both the circle and the background layers. Then, each corner gets pasted into a new graphic file, and is saved as a GIF and named using "Save for Web". Now they are ready for placement in the table.

Using 1-Pixel Square Graphics

Very early on, designers realized that HTML did not offer the kind of layout control they were accustomed to in print. Almost immediately, a system of "cheats" developed that used existing HTML tags in ways never intended by its developers.

One of the classic workarounds is the 1-pixel-GIF trick. This technique involves placing a transparent GIF file that is just one pixel square on the page, then stretching it to the desired size using the WIDTH and HEIGHT attributes in the <IMG> tag. These invisible graphics can be used to nudge text and other page elements around on the page in specific pixel increments (Figure 17-6).

1-pixel square graphics can be used to nudge text and other page elements in specific pixel increments.

Figure 17-6

This text is positioned using 1-pixel square transparent GIFs that have been set to various sizes.

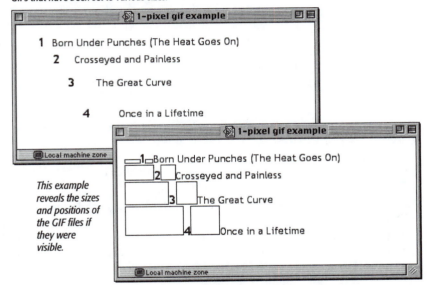

This example reveals the sizes and positions of the GIF files if they were visible.

Of course, this technique has both advantages and disadvantages. On the good side, adding graphics to the page does not interrupt the structure of the HTML document (in other words, you aren't using a "definition list" just to get an indent for a paragraph that isn't really a list). And since the graphic is only one pixel, it's just a few bytes of extra download (and once it is in the browser's cache, it can be used over and over with no load on the server).

On the bad side, using 1-pixel GIFs all over the place adds extra junk to your document and can add to the size of your HTML file. Furthermore, this junk is apparent and distracting for users without graphical browsers or with the graphics turned off (Figure 17-7).

Figure 17-7

This is how 1-pixel graphics look when graphics are not available in the browser.

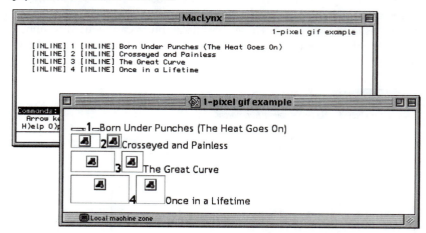

That said, let's look at a few ways in which 1-pixel graphics can be put to work.

Paragraph Indents

As we've seen, there is no way to make a standard paragraph indent using HTML alone. However, by inserting a 1-pixel GIF of the beginning at the paragraph, you can use the WIDTH and HEIGHT attributes to stretch the graphic to a specific pixel width and push the text to the right (Figure 17-8).

Figure 17-8

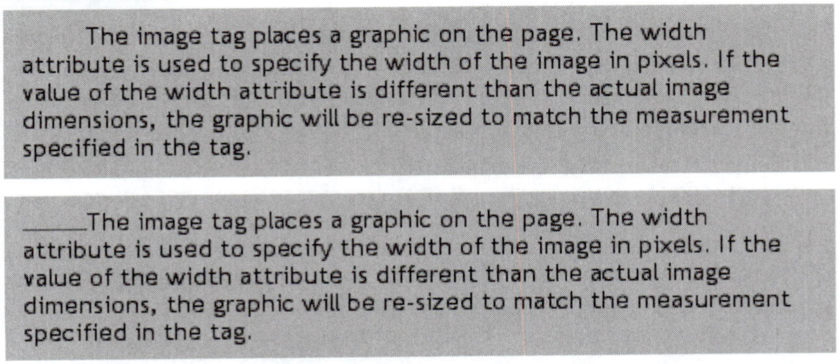

> The image tag places a graphic on the page. The width attribute is used to specify the width of the image in pixels. If the value of the width attribute is different than the actual image dimensions, the graphic will be re-sized to match the measurement specified in the tag.

A 1-pixel transparent GIF creates a paragraph indent.

> _____The image tag places a graphic on the page. The width attribute is used to specify the width of the image in pixels. If the value of the width attribute is different than the actual image dimensions, the graphic will be re-sized to match the measurement specified in the tag.

This non-transparent 1-pixel GIF reveals the shape of the graphic in the example above.

```
<P>
<IMG SRC=1px.gif WIDTH=36 HEIGHT=1>The image tag places a graphic on the
page. The width attribute is used to specify the width of the image in
pixels. If the value...
</P>
```

Spacers

The graphic can be stretched in both directions, giving you the ability to clear larger areas of the page. In Figure 17-9, I've used a 1-pixel graphic to indent a paragraph of text. One downside to this technique is that it is difficult to know how large to size the graphic since there is no way of knowing how many lines of text there will be when your page is viewed on other users' machines.

Figure 17-9

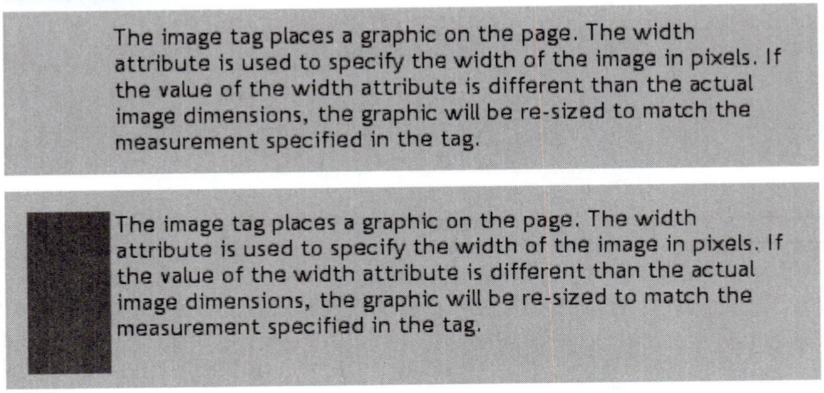

> The image tag places a graphic on the page. The width attribute is used to specify the width of the image in pixels. If the value of the width attribute is different than the actual image dimensions, the graphic will be re-sized to match the measurement specified in the tag.

In this example, the 1-pixel trick is used to clear a larger space on the left edge of the page.

> The image tag places a graphic on the page. The width attribute is used to specify the width of the image in pixels. If the value of the width attribute is different than the actual image dimensions, the graphic will be re-sized to match the measurement specified in the tag.

This shows how the graphic would look if it weren't transparent.

```
<P>
<IMG SRC=1px.gif WIDTH=50 HEIGHT=100 ALIGN=LEFT>The image tag places a
graphic on the page. The width attribute is used to specify the width of
the image in pixels. If the value...
</P>
```

Table Cell Fillers

There is a bug in Navigator that causes cells to collapse if they are left empty. Some designers use 1-pixel GIFs to fill otherwise empty table cells (Figure 17-10). By setting the specific width and height of the graphic the same as the specified dimensions of the cell, you can ensure that the cell will not shrink smaller than your intended size (although, if the table is constructed incorrectly, it may still stretch larger than your specifications).

Figure 17-10

1-pixel GIFs can be used to prevent table cells from collapsing in Netscape Navigator.

When the table cell is left empty ⒶＡ, the specified cell color doesn't render.

By adding transparent GIFs to the blank cells Ⓑ, this problem is fixed.

Ⓐ

Empty table cells

```
<TABLE WIDTH=100 HEIGHT=100 BORDER=1 CELLPADDING=0 CELLSPACING=0>
<TR>
<TD WIDTH=50 HEIGHT=50 BGCOLOR="#333399"></TD>
<TD WIDTH=50 HEIGHT=50 BGCOLOR="#333399" ALIGN=center><FONT SIZE=7>2</FONT></TD>
</TR>
<TR>
<TD WIDTH=50 HEIGHT=50 BGCOLOR="#333399" ALIGN=center><FONT SIZE=7>3</FONT></TD>
<TD WIDTH=50 HEIGHT=50 BGCOLOR="#333399"></TD>
</TR>
</TABLE>
```

Ⓑ

Cells held open with graphics

```
<TABLE WIDTH=100 HEIGHT=100 BORDER=1 CELLPADDING=0 CELLSPACING=0>
<TR>
<TD WIDTH=50 HEIGHT=50 BGCOLOR="#333399"><IMG SRC="1px.gif" WIDTH=50 HEIGHT=50></TD>
<TD WIDTH=50 HEIGHT=50 BGCOLOR="#333399" ALIGN=center><FONT SIZE=7>2</FONT></TD>
</TR>
<TR>
<TD WIDTH=50 HEIGHT=50 BGCOLOR="#333399" ALIGN=center><FONT SIZE=7>3</FONT></TD>
<TD WIDTH=50 HEIGHT=50 BGCOLOR="#333399"><IMG SRC="1px.gif" WIDTH=50 HEIGHT=50></TD>
</TR>
</TABLE>
```

Rules and Boxes

Colored pixels can be used to create rules and boxes of solid color. Again, the advantage is that a 1-pixel graphic will download in an instant. You can use the same graphic over and over (taking advantage of the browser cache) and just change its dimensions with the WIDTH and HEIGHT attributes, rather than downloading separate solid graphics at the various sizes.

For instance, I can make a colored horizontal rule with a 1-pixel graphic (only a few bytes) and set its dimensions easily in the HTML. The length can either be set as a specific pixel measurement (as shown in Figure 17-11) or as a percentage of the width of the page (for example, WIDTH=80%).

Figure 17-11

A colored 1-pixel GIF file can be stretched to make a horizontal rule.

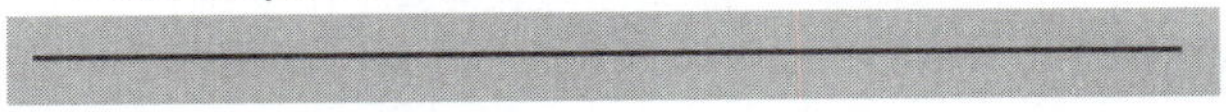

```
<P>
<IMG SRC="1px-blue.gif" WIDTH=400 HEIGHT=2>
</P>
```

With a little planning, you can combine single-pixel GIFs into decorative elements (Figure 17-12, gallery) or, if you're really clever and patient, even whole illustrations. There are a few tricks to making the graphics stay together with no whitespace between them. First, separate each row with a <BR>, and second, make sure there are no returns or character spaces between neighboring <IMG> tags. Either keep all the images in each row in one line of code, or if that is unwieldy, make sure that you break code lines somewhere within the <IMG> tag (as shown in the code).

Figure 17-12 **G**

This decorative element was created with five rows of 1-pixel GIFs of various colors. Each GIF was set to a specific size to form the pattern you see here.

No extra space between <IMG> tags.

```
<P>
<IMG SRC="1px-blue.gif" WIDTH=200 HEIGHT=2><BR>
<IMG SRC="1px-green.gif" WIDTH=95 HEIGHT=10><IMG SRC="1px-blue.gif"
      WIDTH=10 HEIGHT=10><IMG SRC="1px-green.gif" WIDTH=95 HEIGHT=10><BR>
<IMG SRC="1px-green.gif" WIDTH=85 HEIGHT=10><IMG SRC="1px-blue.gif"
      WIDTH=10 HEIGHT=10><IMG SRC="1px-white.gif"
      WIDTH=10 HEIGHT=10><IMG SRC="1px-blue.gif" WIDTH=10
      HEIGHT=10><IMG SRC="1px-green.gif" WIDTH=85 HEIGHT=10><BR>
<IMG SRC="1px-green.gif" WIDTH=95 HEIGHT=10><IMG SRC="1px-blue.gif"
      WIDTH=10 HEIGHT=10><IMG SRC="1px-green.gif" WIDTH=95 HEIGHT=10><BR>
<IMG SRC="1px-blue.gif" WIDTH=200 HEIGHT=2>
</P>
```

Vertical Rules

As we saw in Chapter 8, Adding Graphic Elements, there is a tag that creates an automatic horizontal rule (`<HR>`), but in order to get a vertical rule, you need to resort to some clever workarounds. Following are several techniques that may fit your needs.

Stretching an <HR>

Say you really like the look of the browser's built-in 3-D horizontal rule, but you'd just like it to be vertical. While you can't actually make a horizontal rule run vertically, you can make a rule that is extremely thick (e.g., `SIZE=150` pixels) and extremely short (e.g., `WIDTH=6` pixels). This gives the appearance of a vertical rule (Figure 17-13).

Figure 17-13

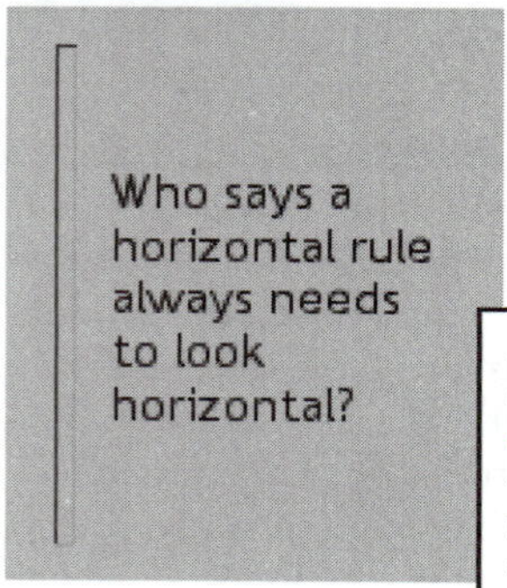

Who says a horizontal rule always needs to look horizontal?

This "vertical" rule is actually a very thick and short horizontal rule created with the `<HR>` tag and extreme `SIZE` and `WIDTH` settings.

```
<TABLE>
<TR>
<TD WIDTH=20><HR SIZE=150 WIDTH=6></TD>
<TD WIDTH=100>Who says a horizontal rule always
needs to look horizontal?</TD>
</TR>
</TABLE>
```

One drawback to this approach is that because the `<HR>` tag is a block element, you can't position any text next to it. Placing the `<HR>` and the text in separate table cells (as shown in Figure 17-13) solves this problem.

Again, it's tricky to try to match the pixel height for the rule (using the `SIZE` attribute) to nearby text since the final size of the text is always an unknown.

Stretching a Graphic

This is another application of the 1-pixel GIF trick we learned earlier. You can set the height of the graphic to any pixel measurement or percentage, then use the `ALIGN=left` or `right` attribute to cause the text to wrap around it (Figure 17-14).

Figure 17-14

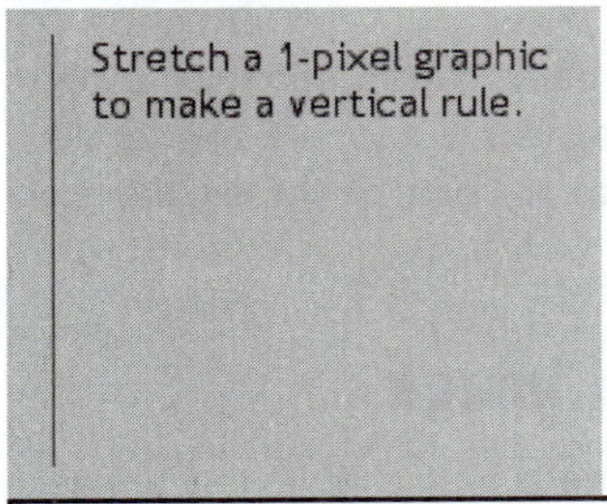

Stretch a 1-pixel graphic to make a vertical rule.

A vertical rule can be created out of a 1-pixel colored GIF.

```
<IMG SRC="1px-red.gif" WIDTH=1 HEIGHT=150 ALIGN=left HSPACE=12>Stretch a
1-pixel graphic <BR>to make a vertical rule.
```

Using a Table Cell

If you want to be sure that the height of your vertical rule always matches the surrounding contents, you may consider creating it with a table cell that is set to just one pixel wide, or whatever width you choose (Figure 17-15). That way, when the contents of the neighboring cell expand or contract, the height of the "rule" cell will expand or contract along with it. Set the color of the rule by specifying the background color (BGCOLOR) of the cell. Remember that the cell needs to have something in it so that it doesn't collapse in Netscape Navigator. I've used a simple line break (<BR>) tag because it doesn't take up any space and won't expand the cell. I could also have used a 1-pixel graphic.

Figure 17-15

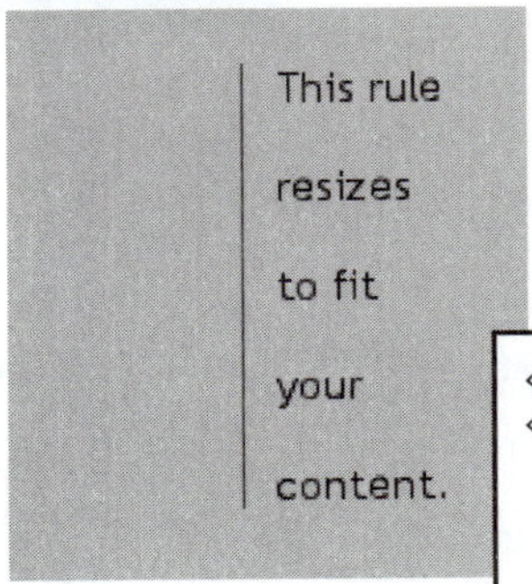

This rule

resizes

to fit

your

content.

This rule is just the background color of a 1-pixel wide table cell.

```
<TABLE BORDER=0 CELLPADDING=0 CELLSPACING=10>
<TR ALIGN=left VALIGN=top>
        <TD WIDTH=50><BR></TD>
        <TD BGCOLOR="darkred" WIDTH=1><BR></TD>
        <TD>
                <P>This rule</P>
                <P>resizes</P>
                <P>to fit</P>
                <P>your</P>
                <P>content.</P>
        </TD>
</TR>
</TABLE>
```

Background Tile Tricks

There's nothing simpler than adding a tiling background image to a page using the BACKGROUND attribute in the <BODY> tag (see Chapter 8 for details). Once you've mastered that, you may want to try one of these advanced tiling techniques.

A "Non-Repeating" Background Image

Unfortunately, HTML alone does not provide a way to prevent a background image from repeating.

Unfortunately, HTML alone does not provide a way to prevent a background image from repeating, so if you want an image to appear only once, you need to fudge it. If you make the dimensions of the background image very large—say, larger than most monitors—then even though it repeats, there will be no way for users to open their browser windows wide enough to see the repeated images. The effect will be a single background image.

I did this for a previous version of my personal home page, as shown in Figure 17-16. My background image is a whopping 1200 × 800 pixels! This ensures that the image will only be seen once on most monitors.

If you use this technique, be careful that the file size of the graphic doesn't get out of control at such large pixel dimensions. The last thing you want is a 30 second wait just for your background to appear. Because my graphic only has four pixel colors and lots of flat, solid areas, it compresses down to just 9K.

Figure 17-16

You can't prevent a background image from tiling, but you can make it so big that the repeated pattern will not be visible in even the largest of monitors.

One word of warning: be sure to monitor the file size of that graphic! By using a few flat colors in my "littlechair" background, I was able to keep the image size to 9K.

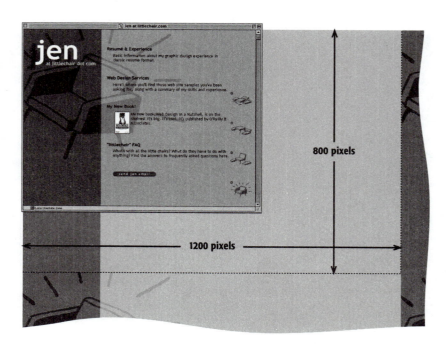

Stripes

Another neat trick using the "make-it-so-wide-they-won't-see-the-repeat" technique is to create stripes with a graphic that is just one pixel thick but very long. If it's wide enough (greater than 1200 pixels or so), the next band of color won't be visible for most users. When this graphic "tiles" in the browser, the little 1-pixel graphics stack up to form solid bands of color (Figure 17-17).

The advantage of this trick is that, at only one pixel in height, the file size of the background image is extremely small. It's a big bang for a small byte investment.

You could also do this with a very tall graphic that is only one pixel wide to create horizontal stripes (Figure 17-18). The only drawback here is that because the graphic is tiling, the next row will be visible again if the page is long enough to scroll that far. So make sure the graphic is tall enough to span your entire page contents, or only use this approach for short pages when you know users won't be able to scroll.

Figure 17-17

```
<BODY BACKGROUND="stripetile.gif">
```

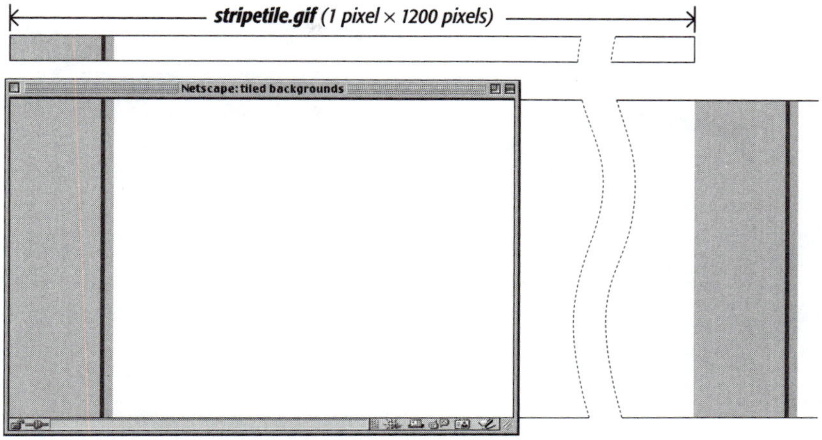

stripetile.gif (1 pixel × 1200 pixels)

You can create a stripe effect by tiling a very long graphic just one pixel high. The real advantage is that at only one pixel in height, the graphic file is tiny and downloads quickly.

Figure 17-18

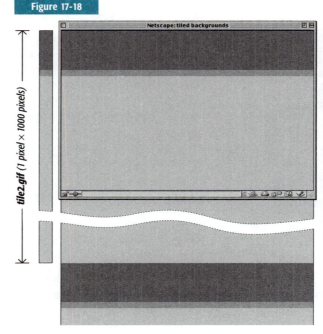

This horizontal band of color was created by tiling a very tall, skinny graphic. If you don't want the repeated tile to show, be sure that the graphic is at least taller than the contents of your page (so it won't be seen when the user scrolls), and tall enough that it won't be seen on really large monitors (approx. 1000 pixels).

tile2.gif (1 pixel × 1000 pixels)

Web Design Techniques

Figure 17-19

I've used this technique so I can automatically change the center image when a user points to each numbered button (also known as a "rollover" effect).

Drawings by Liam Lynch

`border=0`

This image is actually made up of separate graphics held together by a table. The pieces are evident when the table border is turned on.

`border=1`

Multipart (Sliced) Images

A common, slightly more complex web design technique is using a table to hold together a multipart image (Figure 17-19). There are a number of reasons you might want to use this technique:

- If you have a large image and you want to animate just one area of it. Instead of making the whole thing an animated GIF (with the resulting hefty file size), you can break up the image into pieces and animate just the necessary parts. The remaining pieces will be ordinary GIFs.

- If you are doing a fancy rollover effect where you want a part of the image to change when you roll the mouse over another part of the image. Instead of swapping out the whole image, you can swap out just the necessary section—again, saving the amount of data that needs to be downloaded.

- If you have a large, complex image with both flat color areas and photographic areas. When you break up the image, you can save each piece in the most appropriate file format (GIF and JPEG, respectively).

The process for creating a multipart image involves creating the image and dividing it into separate graphic files (noting the specific dimensions of each graphic), then building a table to hold the pieces together. The table needs to be constructed carefully so that no extra space creeps into the cells, spoiling the illusion of a seamless graphic.

While it is certainly possible to do this manually (I explain how in the section Producing Images in Tables by Hand, later in this chapter), it can be cumbersome and time-consuming work. Fortunately, Macromedia Fireworks and Adobe ImageReady come with slicing and dicing tools built right in. Whichever tool you use, the process involves creating slicing objects or dragging rules where you want the divisions to occur. The program exports the individual graphics, names them, and writes the table code for you. It's super!

Using Macromedia Fireworks

Fireworks makes its slicing tool handy right in the Toolbox. Figure 17-20 shows the basic steps for creating a sliced image and its accompanying HTML file:

❶ First, create or open your image. Using the Slice tool from the Toolbox palette, define rectangular segments of the image. Note, if you place a rectangular slice in the middle of a graphic, Fireworks will automatically slice the remainder of the image into the fewest number of segments to contain the specified slice.

❷ In order to set the default export settings (file format, bit-depth, dithering, etc.) for the entire image, you must be sure that no slicing objects are selected, then adjust the settings in the Optimize palette.

Figure 17-20

① Create slice objects in the image with the Slice tool. I will create slice objects for the screen area and each of the numbered buttons.

② To set the global optimization settings, be sure nothing is selected and use the Optimize (Document) dialog box.

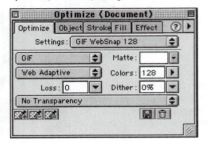

③ If you want to override the settings for a particular slice, select the slice object, and make settings for it in the Optimize (Slice) dialog box.

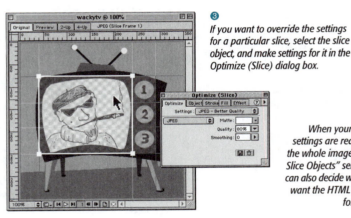

④ When your slices and settings are ready, export the whole image with "Use Slice Objects" selected. You can also decide whether you want the HTML generated for the table.

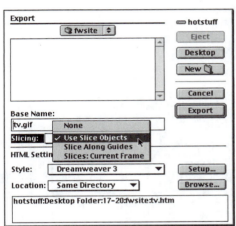

Web Design Techniques

These settings will be applied to each resulting slice after exporting (all slices will share the same color palette and settings).

③ You can override the default export settings for an individual slice—for instance, to reduce its palette, or to make it a different file format. Just select the slice object, then adjust its properties in the Optimize palette (the word "slice" appears in the top bar when a slice is selected).

④ Once you have your slices chosen and configured, export the file by selecting File → Export. In the Export dialog box, select "Use Slice Objects" from the Slicing pop-up menu and set a base name for the graphics (Fireworks will name them automatically based on the name you provide). You can also set a target directory for the files.

When you click Export, Fireworks creates all the graphic files and the HTML file for the sliced image. You can now copy the table code from the generated HTML file and paste it into your final document (be sure that the pathnames of all your graphics are still correct once you paste it into the final file).

TIP

If your image is to be divided into a simple grid (with no row or column spans), you can just drag guides into the image where you want the slices to occur, then select "Slice Along Guides" from the Slicing pop-up menu when exporting.

Figure 17-21

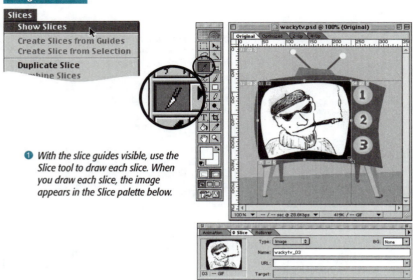

❶ *With the slice guides visible, use the Slice tool to draw each slice. When you draw each slice, the image appears in the Slice palette below.*

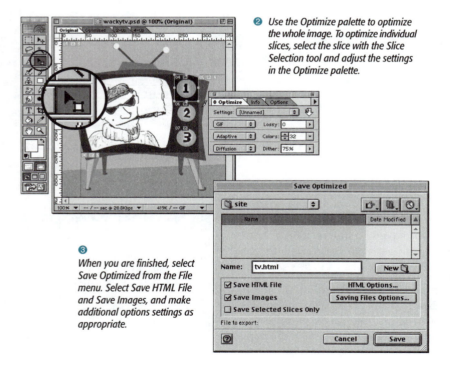

❷ *Use the Optimize palette to optimize the whole image. To optimize individual slices, select the slice with the Slice Selection tool and adjust the settings in the Optimize palette.*

❸
When you are finished, select Save Optimized from the File menu. Select Save HTML File and Save Images, and make additional options settings as appropriate.

Using Adobe ImageReady 2.0

The process for creating a sliced image in ImageReady is nearly the same as the one we've just seen (Figure 17-21):

❶ Open the source image. Select Slices → Show Slices to make the Slices layer visible. You may also want to use guidelines to help control your selections. Use the Slice tool (it looks like a little knife) to outline the important elements in your design. When a slice is selected, its image appears in the Slice palette.

❷ With the Slices layer turned off, you can use the Optimize palette to make export settings (file format, number of colors, etc.) for the entire image. You can override these settings for a particular slice by selecting it with the "Slice Selection" tool, then making adjustments in the Optimize palette.

❸ When you are ready, save the file using File → Save Optimized. This gives you a dialog box where you can choose to have ImageReady save the images and the HTML file. Click the Options buttons next to each selection to access other relative options. For an explanation of these options, see the ImageReady manual. When you are ready, click Save.

Producing Images in Tables by Hand

If you don't have Fireworks or ImageReady, don't fear! You can still put one of these together using your image-editing tool, an HTML editor, and a little patience. Because I use Adobe Photoshop for almost all my graphic needs, I refer to it in the following explanation; however, you can use the same approach for other full-featured image editing programs.

Planning the structure

The first step is to plan out the divisions of the image and establish the structure of the table (Figure 17-22). This process is reviewed in Chapter 10. The goal is to make the table as simple as possible, with as few pieces as possible, so take advantage of any column span and row span opportunities. At this point, you can also begin to plan widths and heights for your cells, although they may shift slightly once you've created the actual graphics.

Figure 17-22

Begin by planning the structure of the table, paying attention to the total number of rows and columns, their pixel dimensions, and the possibility for column spans and row spans.

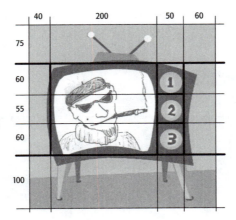

With that done, you are ready to begin graphic production.

Dividing the image

Assuming you're starting with a whole image, you'll need to select each fragment and copy it to a separate graphic file by hand, then save it as a GIF. When I am working with a layered image, I like to save the whole thing as a GIF first; this takes care of flattening the image and reducing the colors so all the fragments have colors from the same palette.

Web Design Techniques

With the flattened image open, make sure the rulers are visible by select-ing View → Show Rulers, then drag guidelines into place at the points you want the image to be divided. You can use your table structure sketch as a reference.

Now, begin selecting parts of the image. When dividing an image with Photoshop, it is important to set the guide preferences in a way that enables easy and accurate selections without redundant or overlapping pixels between image sections. Set your preferences to use pixels as the unit of measurement by selecting File → Preferences → Units & Rulers. Select "pixels" from the pop-up menu and hit OK. Select View → Snap to Guides. This will snap your selection to the precise location of the guide.

Use the rectangle marquee (make sure feathering and anti-aliasing options are turned off) to select each area of the image (Figure 17-23). You can use the Info palette (Window → Show Info) to get accurate pixel measurements for each section as you select it. This information will be needed when you create the HTML file, so it is a good idea to jot down the numbers as you go along.

Copy and paste each selection into a new file. If the image is to be a GIF, convert it to Indexed Color using the Exact palette and export to GIF. If it is a JPEG, flatten the image and save it in JPEG format.

Figure 17-23

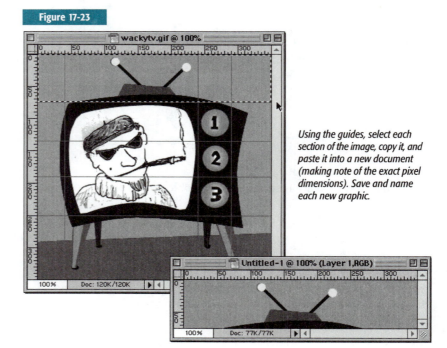

Using the guides, select each section of the image, copy it, and paste it into a new document (making note of the exact pixel dimensions). Save and name each new graphic.

Creating the HTML table

Like any complex table, tables that hold together multi-part images can be tricky to construct, so it is best to do things one step at a time.

Using my table sketch (from Figure 17-22), I create the skeleton of the table, focusing on getting the `<TR>` and `<TD>` tags in order. The table in the example has five rows and four columns:

```
<TABLE>
<TR>
    <TD COLSPAN=4></TD>
</TR>
<TR>
    <TD ROWSPAN=3></TD><TD ROWSPAN=3></TD><TD></TD><TD ROWSPAN=3></TD>
</TR>
<TR>
    <TD></TD>
</TR>
<TR>
    <TD></TD>
</TR>
<TR>
    <TD COLSPAN=4></TD>
</TR>
</TABLE>
```

TIP

Some rows seem to be missing cells, but that is because the cells are included in column spans or row spans earlier in the table.

With the structure established, I can add the image tags within each cell and set both the cell and image dimensions using WIDTH and HEIGHT attributes. The code below looks complicated, but follow along and see how the table is constructed:

```
<TABLE WIDTH=350 HEIGHT=350 CELLSPACING=0 CELLPADDING=0 BORDER=0>
<TR>
    <TD COLSPAN=4 WIDTH=350 HEIGHT=175><IMG SRC="top.gif" WIDTH=350
      HEIGHT=75 BORDER=0></TD>
</TR>
<TR>
    <TD ROWSPAN=3 WIDTH=40 HEIGHT=175><IMG SRC="leftside.gif" WIDTH=40
      HEIGHT=175 BORDER=0></TD>
    <TD ROWSPAN=3 WIDTH=200 HEIGHT=175><IMG SRC="beatnik.gif" WIDTH=200
      HEIGHT=175 BORDER=0></TD>
    <TD WIDTH=50 HEIGHT=60><IMG SRC="1.gif" WIDTH=50 HEIGHT=60
      BORDER=0></TD>
    <TD ROWSPAN=3 WIDTH=60 HEIGHT=175><IMG SRC="rightside.gif" WIDTH=60
      HEIGHT=175 BORDER=0></TD>
</TR>
<TR>
    <TD WIDTH=50 HEIGHT=55><IMG SRC="2.gif" WIDTH=50 HEIGHT=55
      BORDER=0></TD>
</TR>
<TR>
    <TD WIDTH=50 HEIGHT=60><IMG SRC="3.gif" WIDTH=50 HEIGHT=60
      BORDER=0></TD>
</TR>
<TR>
    <TD COLSPAN=4 WIDTH=350 HEIGHT=100><IMG SRC="bottom.gif" WIDTH=350
      HEIGHT=100 BORDER=0></TD>
</TR>
</TABLE>
```

Web Design Techniques

The most common problem with creating tables to hold together graphics is the ease with which extra space creeps in and prevents it from piecing together seamlessly on all browsers. The following are some tips for avoiding that problem:

- In the `<TABLE>` tag, set the following attributes to zero: `BORDER`, `CELLPADDING`, `CELLSPACING`.

- In the `<TABLE>` tag, specify the width of the table with an absolute pixel value. Be sure that the value is exactly the total of the widths of the component images. You may also add the height attribute for thoroughness's sake, but it is not required.

- Don't put extra spaces or line returns between the `<TD>`, `<IMG>`, and `</TD>` tags (extra space within `<TD>`s causes extra space to appear when the image is rendered). Keep them flush together on one line. If you must break the line, break it somewhere within the `<IMG>` tag.

- Set the `WIDTH` and `HEIGHT` values in pixels for every image. Be sure that the measurements are accurate.

- Set `BORDER=0` for every image. Then you can make any image a link and not worry about a visible border.

- Specify the `WIDTH` and `HEIGHT` pixel values for every cell in the table, particularly if it contains column spans (`COLSPAN`) or row spans (`ROWSPAN`). Be sure they match the pixel values set in the `<IMG>` tag and the actual pixel dimensions of the graphic. If you have a lot of column spans, you may consider setting up an extra row in the table with zero height that contains the exact measurement of every column.

  For simple grid-like tables (like the one in the previous example), you may not need to give individual cell dimensions; the enclosed images will force each cell to the proper dimensions.

Pop-Up Windows

One problem with putting links on your page is that when people click on them, they may never come back! One popular solution to this dilemma is to have the linked page open in a new browser window. That way, users can check out the link and still have your content available right where they left it.

The method you use for opening a new browser window depends on whether you want to control its size. If the size doesn't matter, you can use standard HTML. However, if you want to open a window of a particular size (say, to display an image or a small amount of text), you'll need to use JavaScript. Let's look at both of these techniques.

Targeting a New Window with HTML

To open a new window using HTML, use the TARGET attribute in the anchor tag (Figure 17-24). This attribute tells the browser that you want the linked document to open in a window other than the one in which the current document is displayed. You won't have any control over the size of the new window, although you can assume that it will be similar to the window size the user already has open. You have a choice of using the standard _blank value or giving the new window a specific name (of your choosing).

Web Design Techniques

Figure 17-24

The TARGET attribute opens a new window, but at an unknown size.

Setting TARGET="_blank" always causes the browser to open a fresh window. For example:

```
<A HREF="http://www.oreilly.com/" TARGET="_blank">...</A>
```

If you use this for every link, every link will open a new window, potentially leaving your user with a mess of open windows.

A better method, especially if you have more than one link, is to give the targeted window a name, which can then be reused by subsequent links. The following link will open a new window called display:

```
<A HREF="http://www.oreilly.com" TARGET="display">...</A>
```

If you target every link on that page to the display window, each targeted document will open in the same second window.

Opening a Window of a Specific Size

Opening a new window at a specific size requires JavaScript.

If you want to control the dimensions of your new window, you'll need to take advantage of some simple JavaScript commands. JavaScript is a web-specific scripting language that adds interactivity and conditional behaviors to web pages. It is discussed further in Chapter 20, How'd They Do That?

In the following example, we will open a new window that is 300 pixels wide by 400 pixels high (Figure 17-25). There are two parts to the JavaScript for this trick. The first is the script itself, which we will place in the <HEAD> of the document Ⓐ. The second is a reference to the script within the link Ⓑ. The comment tags (<-- and //-->) hide the script from browsers that do not support JavaScript.

```
<HTML>

<HEAD>
Ⓐ <SCRIPT LANGUAGE="JavaScript">
<!--
function openWin(URL) {
aWindow=window.open (URL,"thewindow","width=300,height=400,
toolbar=no,status=no,scrollbar=yes,resize=no,menubar=no");
}
//-->
</SCRIPT>

</HEAD>

<BODY>
Ⓑ <P><A HREF="javascript:openWin('waits.html');">Tom Waits</A></P>
<P><A HREF="javascript:openWin('eno.html');">Brian Eno</A></P>
</BODY>
</HTML>
```

Notice in the script Ⓐ that you are given the opportunity to specify the width and height of the new window in pixels. You can also decide which parts of the browser window (toolbar, status bar, scrollbar, and menubar) you want to display and whether you want the user to be able to resize the window. The values for each of these are either yes or no.

The link Ⓑ uses a regular <A HREF> tag, but the value of the HREF is not a standard URL, it is a call to the JavaScript function. The word javascript tells the browser that this will be a JavaScript link. Next, the openWin() function, which was defined in the script, is called. The URL of the linked document is placed within parentheses.

TIP

The easiest way to make a sized pop-up window is to use a web-authoring program to generate the code for you automatically. But it doesn't hurt to learn how it works.

Figure 17-25

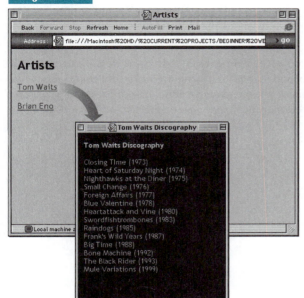

The `openWin()` *JavaScript function allows you to open a window at specific pixel dimensions. You can also choose which elements of the browser window you want to display.*

This JavaScript example is easy to copy and use on your own web pages. The parts of the code that are in bold text within the second color indicate the parts you should replace with your own information. The rest needs to be copied exactly. Be sure not to put any spaces or hard carriage returns within the function code in the script (soft text wrap is acceptable, but technically, the code needs to be on one line).

A Closing Word on Web Design Techniques

The true art of web design lies in the clever combination of the skills covered in this book. For instance, even a simple element such as a box with rounded corners involves the following skills:

- Writing HTML for table creation, table placement, text formatting, and color specification

- Understanding the web palette, both in HTML and in graphics

- Graphic production, including optimization techniques

- Knowledge of typical browser bugs (like collapsing tables) so you can avoid them

In web design, there are often several methods for accomplishing the same task, so consider the directions in this chapter as a starting point. You can learn other techniques by viewing the HTML source of page elements you come across on the Web.

By all means, go out and experiment on your own. Be sure to test your results on different browsers and platforms to make sure things are working the way you planned. In time, your personal bag of tricks will grow and you will be creating cool and original web elements and page designs on your own!

Building Usable Web Sites

Looks are important, but the real key to a web site's success is how well it *works*. You might have fabulous graphics and solidly coded pages, but if your users can't find the information they need or figure out how to buy your products, all of your efforts have been for nothing. Shoddy interfaces have been known to send commercial web sites right down the tubes.

Building a site that works involves attention to how the information is organized (information design) and how users get to that information (interface design and navigation systems). This planning needs to take place before you type your first HTML tag or create a single GIF.

Don't skimp on this planning phase, regardless of the scale or purpose of your site. Even a personal web site will benefit from logical organization and good navigation (Figure 18-1, following page).

In this chapter, I'll introduce the basic principles of information design, interface design, and navigation. Each of these topics is rich enough to warrant further study (see the sidebar later in this chapter, For Further Reading); in fact, some designers choose to become specialists in these fields. But even if you're just starting out, it's important to keep these issues in mind.

Focus on the User

All design shapes a user's experience. Print designers can affect how information is perceived on a page and in what order. An architect designs not just the building, but the visitor's experience walking through it. Similarly, a web designer needs to consider the user's experience of "moving through" the site.

In web design, it's all about the user. Terms like "user experience" and "user-centric design" are used frequently and taken seriously. Formal studies abound, but in essence, it's about getting into the heads of your users in order to create a design that meets their needs and expectations.

Simply throwing all your information on the home page does not create a good user experience.

Interviewing users early on can give you a better idea of what they're look-ing for on a particular site and where they expect to find it. Later in the design process, user testing is an important step in finding out if your solutions are working.

Here are some common frustrations that can kill a good user experience:

- Not being able to find the information they are looking for
- Hitting dead ends
- Not being able to get back to where they started
- Having to click through too many pages to get to the information

Many of these can be avoided by setting up a logical structure and pro-viding clear and appropriate tools for navigating it.

The family web site pictured in Figure 18-1 needs serious help. Throughout this chapter, I'll apply principles of information and interface design to whip the site into shape and make it more usable.

Information Design

Information design involves both organizing information and planning how users will find it. Designers who specialize in this discipline are often called "information architects" because, like traditional architects, they are concerned with designing structures and access to areas within those structures.

Information design, whether highly structured or completely informal, is the first step in any web site–creation process. Your exact process will cer-tainly depend on the scale and goals of your site. A large commercial site may require months of research and model building before production can begin. For a personal site, a quick list of the contents and a site sketch may suffice. Either way, there are a number of standard steps and exer-cises that make up the information design process:

1. Take an inventory of the information you want to include on the site.

2. Organize the information.

3. Give it shape by designing the overall structure of the site.

Taking Inventory

A good first step is to make a list of *everything* you'd like the site to include. This is often referred to as the site inventory, or asset list. The list should include not only the information you want to make available, but also the things your visitors can do on the site. Remember that some content comes in the form of functionality, such as shopping, chat rooms, research tools, etc.

Once you've determined what you want (or your client wants) to publish, you also need to give careful thought to the types of information and functionality that your *users* want and expect. This is a good time to do research on your site's audience and their needs.

The information-gathering process will vary from site to site. For a personal web site, it might just be some time spent considering the options and making a list in a notebook. For instance, the site inventory for the Blue Family site is a manageable list of information about the family and each of its members (Figure 18-2).

At the other end of the scale, large commercial sites benefit from more in-depth research. Web development firms often spend months identifying the most effective content for a site through a process of market research and interviews, both with the client and potential users.

Figure 18-2

Start by making a simple list of everything that should go in the site.

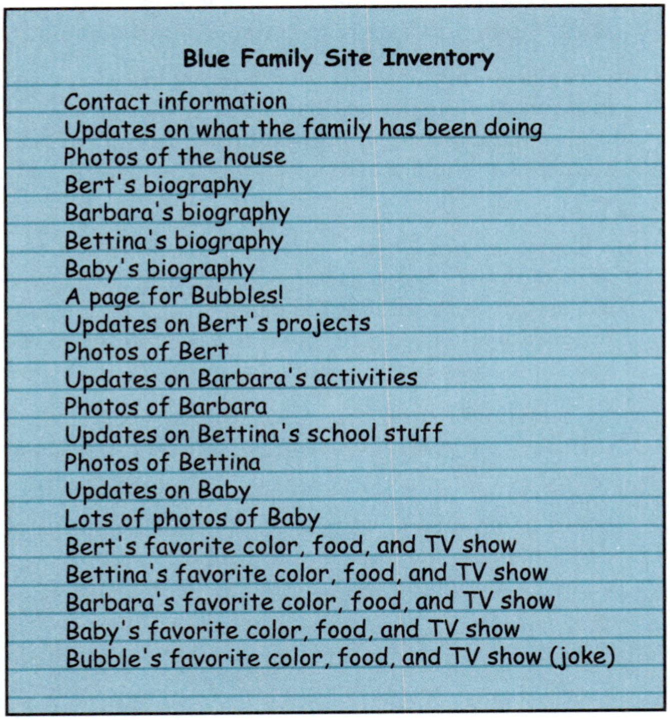

Blue Family Site Inventory

Contact information
Updates on what the family has been doing
Photos of the house
Bert's biography
Barbara's biography
Bettina's biography
Baby's biography
A page for Bubbles!
Updates on Bert's projects
Photos of Bert
Updates on Barbara's activities
Photos of Barbara
Updates on Bettina's school stuff
Photos of Bettina
Updates on Baby
Lots of photos of Baby
Bert's favorite color, food, and TV show
Bettina's favorite color, food, and TV show
Barbara's favorite color, food, and TV show
Baby's favorite color, food, and TV show
Bubble's favorite color, food, and TV show (joke)

WHERE TO LEARN MORE

Information Design

The following books are excellent resources on information design and usability:

Web Navigation: Designing the User Experience, by Jen Fleming (O'Reilly, 1998)

Information Architecture for the World Wide Web, by Lou Rosenfeld and Peter Morville (O'Reilly, 1998)

Web Site Usability: A Designer's Guide, by Jared M. Spool, Tara Scanlon, Will Shroeder, Carolyn Snyder, and Terri DeAngelo (Morgan Kaufmann Publishers, 1998)

Designing Large-Scale Web Sites: A Visual Design Methodology, by Darrell Sano (John Wiley & Sons, 1996)

Designing Web Usability, by Jakob Nielsen (New Riders Publishing, 1999)

The Art & Science of Web Design, by Jeffrey Veen (New Riders Publishing, 2001)

Building Usable Web Sites

Organizing Information

The next step is to organize your site's assets. Organizing information can be a complex business. Information is highly subjective in that the same set of elements can be organized in different ways, depending on the organizer's perspective.

Sorting strategies

TIP

The sorting strategies listed here are not web-specific—they are useful for any instance when information needs to be organized.

There are standard approaches to bringing logical order to information. The method you choose will depend on the type of information you have. However, even the same set of data can be organized differently. For instance, a list of national sales data can be sorted a number of ways, as listed in the examples for each approach:

Alphabetical. Putting elements in a list from A to Z is one of the most fundamental approaches to information organization. An example is sorting sales by customer name.

Chronological. You can organize sequential events or step-by-step information according to a timeline, usually from earliest to latest. Sorting sales by purchase date is an example of this method.

Class (or type). This approach organizes information into logical groupings based on similarities. See the section Information clumping later in this chapter. An example is sorting sales by product lines (office supplies, art supplies, etc.).

Hierarchical. This takes organizing by class to the next level by breaking information into large sections, then each section into sub-sections, and so on. It is a popular organizational strategy for web sites; we'll discuss this method in more detail later. Examples include breaking product line sales (art supplies) down by sub-groups (brushes), and sub-sub-groups (sable watercolor brushes).

Spatial. Some information can be organized geographically or spatially, such as room-by-room. Organizing sales by state is one example.

By order of magnitude. You can organize some sorts of information according to a continuum, such as from largest to smallest, or lightest to darkest, etc. An example of this method is sorting sales from smallest purchase amount to largest purchase amount.

Information clumping

People tend to get overwhelmed by large numbers of options. In fact, it is our nature to search for similarities among individual items and begin to divide them into fewer, more manageable groups. In information design, this is sometimes referred to as clumping. Instead of making all of your site offerings available in a big list on the home page, I recommend that you divide them into logical groupings.

Again, there is usually more than one way to slice up the same set of information, so you may need to move things around a few times until you find the solution that works best. Even simple lists, such as the Blue Family's site inventory, present more than one option for organization by class (Figure 18-3).

TIP

The Sticky-Note Trick

One tool web developers commonly use is the old "sticky-note on the wall" trick. Each sticky-note represents a chunk of information that needs to go into the site. Sometimes different colored stickies are used to differentiate types of information. With all the sticky-notes on the wall, they can be grouped and regrouped easily until the structure of the site begins to emerge.

Figure 18-3

There are usually many ways to organize the same information. Here the items from the Blue Family site inventory are arranged two different ways.

BERT:
    email address
    birthday information
    current projects
    favorite color
    favorite food
    favorite TV show
    photos

BARBARA:
    email address
    birthday information
    current projects
    favorite color
    favorite food
    favorite TV show
    photos

BETTINA:
    email address
    birthday information
    current projects
    favorite color
    favorite food
    favorite TV show
    photos

BABY:
    email address
    birthday information
    current projects
    favorite color
    favorite food
    favorite TV show
    photos

BUBBLES:
    email address
    favorite color
    favorite food
    favorite TV show

Email addresses:
    Bert
    Barbara
    Bettina
    Baby
    Bubbles

Photographs:
    Bert
    Barbara
    Bettina
    Baby

Current events:
    Bert
    Barbara
    Bettina
    Baby

Favorite lists:
    Bert
    Barbara
    Bettina
    Baby
    Bubbles

Birthday information:
    Bert
    Barbara
    Bettina
    Baby

Building Usable Web Sites

Remember the user

While you're organizing, be sure to keep the users' perspective in mind. One of the most common mistakes that companies make is to organize their corporate web sites to match their internal department structure. While someone who works for XYZ Corporation may know which department handles special promotions, chances are that the average user will not know to look there.

A good example of designing for the user is the FedEx site (Figure 18-4). They know a significant percentage of people visiting their site are there to track a package. Although this activity makes up a small part of the functions of FedEx as a whole, it is given a prominent space on the home page of the site.

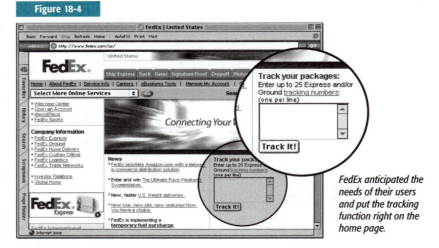

Figure 18-4

FedEx anticipated the needs of their users and put the tracking function right on the home page.

Do your research up front to learn what your users expect to find at your site and what you can do to meet their needs. Remember that the way you perceive your own information may be confusing and useless to others.

After examining the possibilities, I've decided to divide the information for the Blue Family site into sections by family member. In addition, I've added three special pages that are updated frequently (Figure 18-5).

Giving It a Shape: Site Structure

Once you've identified the contents of your site and given it a basic organization, it is helpful to create a diagram of your site. Professional information architects use site diagrams as tools for communicating the structure of the site to clients, and as a road map for providing guidance throughout the web production process.

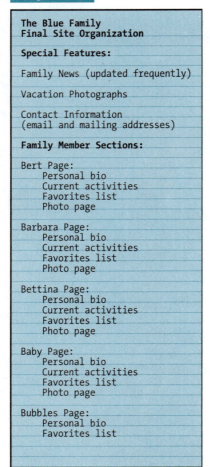

Figure 18-5

**The Blue Family
Final Site Organization**

Special Features:

Family News (updated frequently)

Vacation Photographs

Contact Information
(email and mailing addresses)

Family Member Sections:

Bert Page:
    Personal bio
    Current activities
    Favorites list
    Photo page

Barbara Page:
    Personal bio
    Current activities
    Favorites list
    Photo page

Bettina Page:
    Personal bio
    Current activities
    Favorites list
    Photo page

Baby Page:
    Personal bio
    Current activities
    Favorites list
    Photo page

Bubbles Page:
    Personal bio
    Favorites list

Site diagrams use boxes to represent pages with lines and/or arrows to represent the relationships (links) between pages (Figure 18-6). It's nice to have a mental model for the overall shape of the site; it creates a sense of space and begins to suggest a system for navigation.

Figure 18-6

A sample site plan

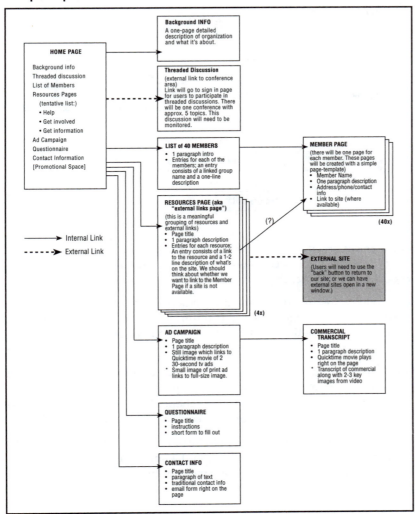

Professional information architects use site diagrams as tools for communicating the structure of the site.

Building Usable Web Sites

Hierarchical structure

Most sites are organized hierarchically, starting with a top page that offers several choices and then successive layers of choices branching out below, so that a "tree" is formed (Figure 18-7).

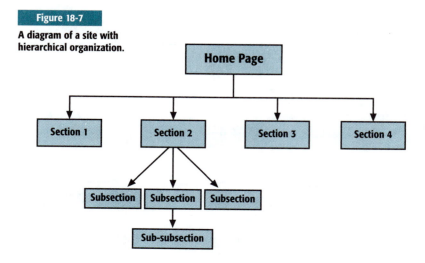

Figure 18-7

A diagram of a site with hierarchical organization.

Hierarchical organization is a tried-and-true method.

Hierarchical organization is a tried and true method, and if done well, it offers the user clear, step-by-step access to material on the site. If you choose this structure, there are a few guidelines you should follow.

First, make sure that important information doesn't get buried down too deeply. With each required click, you run the risk of losing a few readers who may only have time to skip through the top layers of a site.

Also, make sure that the branches of the hierarchy "tree" are generally balanced. For example, if the majority of the categories are shallow (only a few levels deep), avoid having one category drill down through lots of levels of information. If this is the case, chances are you can organize the information better to create consistency throughout the site.

Our family site is based on a simple hierarchical structure (Figure 18-8) with the addition of special sections on the home page. The family member sections are available from every page on the site.

Figure 18-8

The Blue Family site diagram
The site is divided into sections by family member. There are three additional special features.

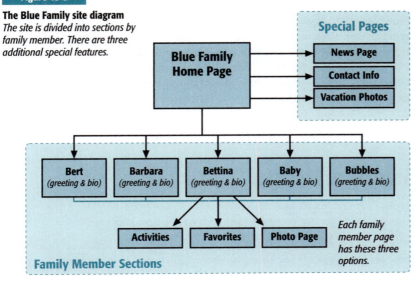

NAVIGATION TIP

How Far Do I Have to Go?

When you're driving down a highway, you see mile markers and signs telling you how many miles it is to the next city. This is an important type of feedback for knowing where you are and planning your trip.

Likewise, when users are clicking through a series, such as a multipart article, they need some feedback as to the total length of the trip (total number of pages) and where they are in the flow (the current page number).

Each page in a linear arrangement should be clearly labeled with this status information. There are several common approaches:

1 of 5
 Lists the current page number (1) and the total number of pages (5).

1, 2, 3, 4, 5
 Lists each page number individually with the current page somehow highlighted. Each page number serves as a link to that page.

Intro
 Information Design
 Interface Design
 Navigation Design
 Conclusion
 Instead of just numbers, it is more informative to provide actual titles for each page so users can make a better decision whether they want to continue or skip ahead.

Linear arrangement

Although tree-style structure is the most popular and multipurpose, it is by no means your only option, and may not be the best suited for your type of information. You may consider organizing your site (or a part of it) linearly. In a linear arrangement, the user is guided from page to page in a particular order. This is appropriate for narratives or any information that must be viewed in sequence.

In the Blue Family site, I've chosen a linear arrangement for the vacation photographs, which have been arranged in chronological order (Figure 18-9). Notice that I've also planned for access to the home page from any page in the photo sequence, so the user never gets stuck in the flow.

Figure 18-9

A linear site diagram

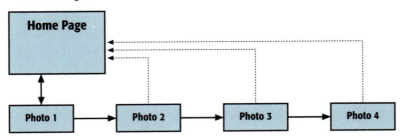

Building Usable Web Sites

Planning Server Structure

If you are building a web site that has more than a dozen or so pages, you'll probably want to divide your files into subdirectories on the server. In general, it is most convenient when the organization of your files on the server matches the structure of your site. Therefore, the information-design phase of a web design project is also a good time to set up a directory structure on the server.

There are many approaches to server management, but in general, a single directory contains all the files for a site. That directory is divided into subdirectories that reflect the site's major sections. It is common to keep all of the graphics in a directory called *graphics* or *images*. I keep an *images* directory in each of my section subdirectories so all the common information sticks together.

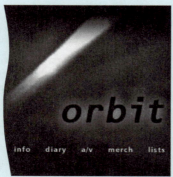

www.orbitband.com

Complex structures

Not every site is going to fit nicely into a tree or a straight line. Most commercial web sites today offer so much information and functionality that the site diagrams can become enormous and quite complex. I've seen a site diagram for one popular media site that used postage-stamp sized boxes to represent pages, and the overall site diagram sprawled the length of the hallway!

But that's just the point of using a site diagram. It enables you to get a handle on the site as a whole and to keep track of its farthest corners.

Interface Design

Now that we've got our content in shape, we need to give our visitors a way to get to it. We're entering the interface design phase.

The interface design determines how a site's logical structure appears visually on the page. It includes all the visual cues to understanding what information is available as well as navigational tools for moving through the site.

Because the interface works visually, it is closely integrated with the graphic design of the site. For instance, the interface designer might say, "This information will be accessed via a button on the home page," while the graphic designer says, "Our buttons will be blue with yellow outlines and white type." In the real world, however, it is quite common for both of these roles to be performed by the same person or department.

Let's look at some of the visual cues and conceptual models that you can use to make the structure of your information more apparent and understandable.

Grouping Like Elements

Long lists of choices can be overwhelming and discourage browsing. If there are a large number of items available on a page (and there often are), it is a good idea to break them into a small number of major groups and to indicate these groups visually (Figure 18-10).

The magic number in interface design is seven. The theory is that the human brain tends to short-circuit when faced with more than seven options at a time. So when designing interfaces, choices are often limited to seven, plus or minus two. While it's unlikely that you'll have just seven elements on a page, you can break your longer list into seven or fewer groups.

For instance, you may put all of your navigational buttons in a row across the top of the page. By using a colored background for that area or similar graphical treatments for each button, the buttons will work together as one visual unit. Likewise, you may put links to archived material in a shaded table to set them apart from the main content areas of the site.

Figure 18-10

These sites do a good job of dividing a large number of page elements into manageable groups through the use of tables and color.

Building Usable Web Sites

Color Coding

Color, when used deliberately and thoughtfully, is a powerful visual cue with many applications.

Color, when used deliberately and thoughtfully, is a powerful visual cue with many applications. A bright color calls attention to an element on a page. Coloring individual items with similar colors causes them to be perceived as a group. Assigning colors to each section of a site can help orient the user.

Keep in mind that the key to effective color usage is restraint and control. Too many amateur web sites make the mistake of using every available color on a single page, resulting in visual chaos. Choose a few colors, and stick with them.

I'll address a few specific examples of color use on the Web.

Link colors

The very first graphical browsers were designed to display hypertext links in bright blue, underlined text. This initial decision to assign a link color distinct from the text color was an effective method for indicating that linked text was somehow different from ordinary text. It has become the primary visual cue for "click here."

Since then, browser manufacturers have stuck with blue text as the default link color, and it is the closest thing we have to a true interface convention on the Web. Want to get to another page? Click on the blue text!

Lately, there's been some controversy over whether designers should use HTML and Cascading Style Sheets to override the default link colors. Some more conservative designers feel that it requires more work if the user has to learn a new link color for every web site. The more popular opinion is that it is fine to change the color of links on a site as long as it is done consistently within that site. If you prefer red links, that's fine; just keep them red throughout the whole site.

Another consideration in coloring links is the difference between regular links and visited links (links that have already been followed). In general, you should set the link color to be somehow brighter or bolder than the visited link color. A toned-back visited link color better communicates a "less active" state.

TIP

For information on how to set link colors, see the sidebar, Coloring Your Links in Chapter 9, Adding Links. Specifying colors in HTML is covered in Chapter 12, Color on the Web.

Section color-coding

If you have just a few major sections in your site, you might consider assigning each section a different color (Figure 18-11, gallery). This can be a useful method for orienting your user in the site, and is particularly helpful if you anticipate linking from section to section. The shift in overall color scheme is an instant indication that you've arrived in a new "place."

This advice comes with a word of caution, however. Do not rely on color alone to communicate the current section. The color-coding system should be secondary to clear labeling of the sections. Users can't be expected to memorize that corporate information is blue and small business information is green. Furthermore, they may not see the colors at all! Make sure that color is used only as a reinforcement.

Section color-coding should be secondary to clear labeling of sections.

Figure 18-11 **G**

Section color-coding is a popular method for orienting users within your site.

Amazon.com

Buy.com

Building Usable Web Sites

Metaphors

Another way to make the information on a site more accessible and understandable is to use a metaphor. A metaphor associates a new concept (such as a site organization or navigational tool) with a familiar model or idea. The knowledge the user has of the familiar setting will provide a head start to understanding the new environment.

Site-wide metaphors

Some web sites use a metaphor as the top-level interface for the site. So instead of arriving at a home "page," you arrive in a town square or walk into a kitchen. Objects in that space correlate with sections of the site (Figure 18-12).

Site-wide metaphors were extremely popular when the Web first started because it was easy to assume that everyone was new to the Web and needed a little hand-holding. Since then, metaphors have fallen out of fashion, and for good reason. It's all too easy for the metaphor to break down—not every section in your site is going to have a logical association with something in the metaphorical scene. It becomes confusing quickly, and at times, even trite. In addition, it often requires a graphics-heavy design to set the stage, which can slow down performance. If you must use a site-wide metaphor, be sure it makes perfect sense and adds to the content of the site.

Tool metaphors

Metaphors are more effective when they are used to explain specific concepts or tools. I think the best example of this is the online "shopping cart." People know what you do with a shopping cart in the real world: you load it up with the things you want to buy and then take them to the cash register for purchase. Shopping sites quickly adopted the shopping cart metaphor for online shopping functionality.

PhotoDisc, a company that licenses digital photography, has a function for saving selected images that can be looked at later and shared with a group. They call this feature the "lightbox," referring to the backlit table that traditional designers use to view transparent artwork. The activities that take place around a traditional lightbox are a good match for what takes place on PhotoDisc's virtual photo-viewing area, making the lightbox an effective metaphor.

Again, I urge you to use any metaphor with caution. When the symbol misses its mark, it's not only confusing, it can be comical.

It's all too easy for the metaphor to break down—not every section in your site is going to have a logical association with something in the metaphorical scene.

Figure 18-12

Examples of site-wide metaphors

www.lsjcc.org
This Jewish Community Center site uses a neighborhood metaphor. The assignment of topic to building is somewhat arbitrary since the drawing is not of the Center itself.

www.kraft.com
The Kraft food company's site is called the "Interactive Kitchen." Can you guess how to access the "New This Month" section? Curiously, it's the flag-shaped cake on the table. This shows how metaphors can stand in the way of information.

Just for you

Food & Family in July
Hot and Humid, hammocks and hot dogs, all are part of these easy-livin' long summer days. Time to get out of the kitchen and into the backyard to BBQ.

www.irs.gov
The Internal Revenue Service has been stuck on this newspaper metaphor for nearly five years. If any organization should cut the cute stuff and dole out the information quick, it should be the IRS.

Building Usable Web Sites

Interface Design Methods

Diagrams show how pages work, and are generally devoid of graphic design.

Like information architects, interface designers use diagrams and flow-charts to work out the functionality of their designs. Diagrams show how pages work, and are generally devoid of graphic design. You can even use them to do a round of user testing to make sure your site works before the time is spent developing the prototype.

Page diagrams

One type of diagram used in the interface-building process is a wireframe page layout of typical pages in the site. In most cases, large web sites use a limited number of page templates that can be reused for common page functions (such as login pages, top-level section pages, etc.).

I developed the interface for a site that allowed members to search through a large database of public records. In the early design process, I created diagrams of each page type to communicate the functionality of the site to the client and to give the graphic designer a basic structure for the page design (Figure 18-13).

Figure 18-13

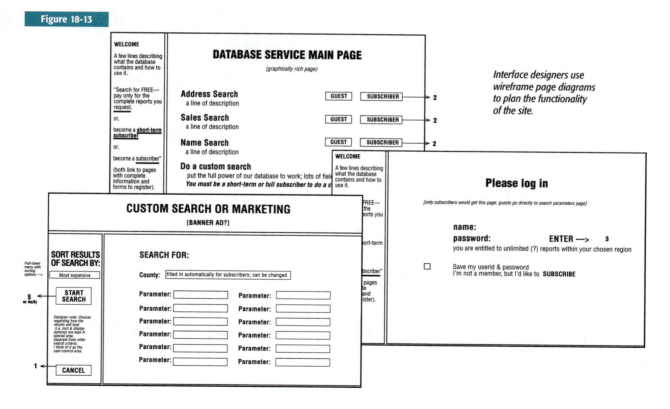

Interface designers use wireframe page diagrams to plan the functionality of the site.

Even if you are just working on a web site for yourself, you might find that sketching out the home page and representative pages within your site is a useful step before you dig into writing the HTML and developing the look and feel for the page. It helps you make sure that all the pieces are there. Page diagrams for the Blue Family site might look like Figure 18-14.

Figure 18-14

Page diagrams for the Blue Family site

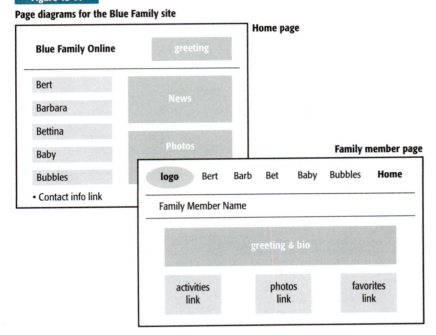

User scenarios

For complex commercial sites, particularly those with interactive functionality and step-based features such as shopping, personalized content (accessed by logging in), and so on, the interface designer might also produce typical user-scenario flowcharts. These flowcharts show how one typical user might click through the various levels and features of the site. It's a diagram of one possible pathway through the site.

The database site I mentioned earlier had a complicated interface that changed depending on the level of membership the user signed up for and the number of records that were retrieved. The development team and I used flowcharts to anticipate and plan for each of these variations (Figure 18-15, following page). Flowcharts may be accompanied by a more descriptive narrative of the action, as shown in the flowchart sample.

Figure 18-15

A sample user-scenario flowchart

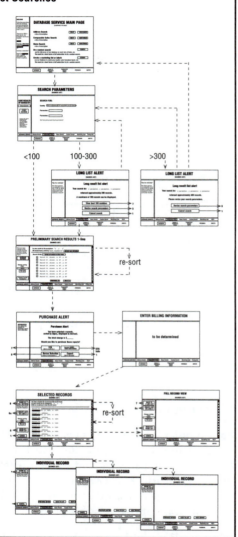

Guest Searches

A. User enters "NAME SEARCH," "ADDRESS SEARCH," or "SALES SEARCH" as a GUEST from the database main menu.)

B. User enters his or her search parameters.

C. If search returns fewer than 100 records, user goes directly to preliminary results screen.

If search returns between 100 and 300 records, user is given the choice to refine the search or just see 100 records.

If search returns more than 300 records, the user is sent back to either refine or cancel the search.

D. Preliminary results are displayed in a 1-line format, in one long scroll, with "AV" or "N/A" tags in place of actual information. The user selects records for viewing using checkboxes. He or she can also re-sort the list or go back and change the search parameters.

E. A purchase notification appears with the option to buy the individual records, become a short-term subscriber, revise the request, or cancel the search. If the guest chooses to purchase something, he or she will go to a page to enter credit card information.

F. The user's chosen records are displayed in a 2-line format (with the information fields filled in), in one long scroll.

G. It is possible to view them all as full-screen reports in a long scroll, or click on a hyperlink to see an individual full-screen record.

H. The user can click forward and backwards through the individual records.

Navigation Design

Navigation is a subset of the site's interface, but since it's an important topic, I'll give it a little extra attention.

The information in a web site is often perceived as occupying a physical space. Like a real physical space, such as a city or airport, a web site requires a system of signage to help visitors find their way around. On web sites, this takes the form of logos, labels, buttons, links, and other shortcuts. These elements make up the navigational system for the site.

Where Am I?

One of the main duties of a navigation system is to let users know where they are. Remember that users can enter your site at any point if they have the right URL or if they are clicking on a link from a list of search engine results. There's no guarantee that they will have the benefit of the home page to tell them where they've landed, so it is important that every page on your site contains some label that identifies the site.

Nordstrom's web site (*www.nordstrom.com*) uses an effective global navigation bar at the top of every page (Figure 18-16). The Nordstrom logo on the left clearly identifies the site.

In addition, if your site has different sections or levels, it is a good idea to orient the reader within the site's structure. As you can see in the Nordstrom navigational toolbar, the subsection is also identified by highlighting its name in the toolbar.

Like a real physical space, such as a city or airport, a web site requires a system of signage to help visitors find their way around.

Figure 18-16

Nordstrom's global navigation toolbar clearly identifies the site and is used on every page.

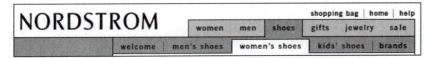

Where Can I Go?

The other responsibility of a navigation system is to clearly present the options for where users can go (or what they can do) next. I usually ask myself two questions in deciding exactly what navigational buttons to add. The first question is user-based: where might this person want to go next? For the second question, I play the role of the client or web site publisher: where do *we* want that person to go next?

Building Usable Web Sites

It is impractical to provide a link to every page on a site from every other page, so you need to choose your links wisely. By limiting choices, you can help to shape the users' experience of your site while providing the flexibility they need to get around.

The navigational options for every site will be different, but there are a few standards. An expanded view of the Nordstrom site shows how it employs some standard navigational systems (Figure 18-17).

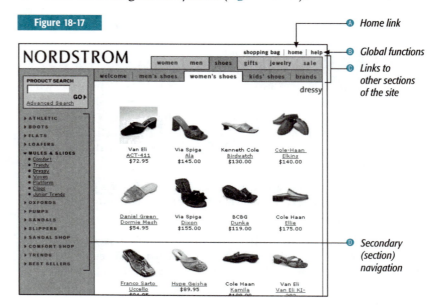

Figure 18-17

- Ⓐ Home link
- Ⓑ Global functions
- Ⓒ Links to other sections of the site
- Ⓓ Secondary (section) navigation

Ⓐ First, a link back to the home page from every page in the site is usually expected. If the reader ever gets lost in the maze, this provides a way to get back to the beginning with one click.

Ⓑ There might also be a set of links that should be accessible site-wide, regardless of the current section. These include links to a help section, personalized information, search capabilities, and other general information that you want to have always handy. These can be incorporated into the global navigation system, but usually with less visual weight.

Ⓒ If your site is divided into sections, you might choose to provide links to the main pages of the other sections as part of the navigation system on every page.

Ⓓ You may also have options that are specific to a particular section of the site. This is called secondary navigation or section navigation. On Nordstrom.com, the secondary navigation is in a column on the left and appears in the section color. Each section has its own set of section-specific navigational options as well as the global navigation system.

Fundamentals of Good Navigation

Navigation systems are highly site-specific. The list of choices that are perfect for one site could totally bomb on another. However, there are a few guiding principles that apply regardless of the type of site you're building. The key characteristics of a successful navigation system are clarity, consistency, and efficiency. Let's look at what each of these means in practical terms.

Clarity

In order for navigation to work, it must be easily learned. One of the main gripes about surfing the Web is that you have to learn how to use every new site you visit. It is in your interest to make the learning process as quick and painless as possible by making your navigational tools intuitive and easily understood at a glance.

Try following these guidelines for keeping your navigation system clear and user-friendly:

Navigation should look like navigation. Your navigational tools (such as links to the home page and other parts of the site) should somehow stand out on the page. This can be accomplished by grouping them together and applying some sort of visual treatment that sets them apart from ordinary content. Buttons don't necessarily need to be in 3-D to look "clickable," but they should still read as navigation at a glance.

Label everything clearly. I can't emphasize this point strongly enough. Despite the fact that the Web is a visual medium and we've been discussing visual cues for interface design, people still find their way around with words. Nothing stands in the way of finding information more than labels that are vague or too cute to be understood. Don't call a section "A Light in the Darkness" when it's really just "Help."

User testing shows that longer, more descriptive link text is more effective in getting people where they want to go. Make sure your section names and all links are labeled in a way that everyone will understand.

Use icons with caution. Although there are a few icons that have taken on standardized meanings (such as a small house picture as a link to the "home" page), for the most part, icons are difficult to decipher and can stand in the way of usability. Can you tell what each of the icons in Figure 18-18 do?

NAVIGATION TIP

List Navigation

Here's a simple tip to save your users some clicks. If you have a number of items in a list of links, be sure that each page has a link to the next item in the list. This prevents users from needing to click back to the list page each time they want to get to the next item.

Of course, you need to provide a link back to the list as well, in case the viewer does not want to view the list in order. You might add a link to the previous item in the list as well (not shown below) to allow movement through the list both backward and forward.

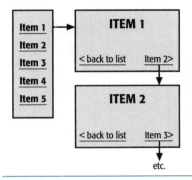

Figure 18-18

 A
 B
 C

Building Usable Web Sites

Did you guess "align elements" **A**, "expand window" **B**, and "News" **C**?* This shows how, in general, icons alone do a poor job of communicating. Some icons, such as a globe, are so overused that they mean absolutely nothing. If you choose to use icons, it is best to reinforce them with clear labels in every instance. If you have just one or two carefully-chosen icons, you may get away with defining them once on the home page and using the icons alone throughout the site. Either way, you should carefully consider whether icons are really aiding your navigation.

Consistency

It's important that navigational options be consistent throughout the site, in availability as well as in appearance.

Providing navigational options is not enough if they aren't predictable or dependable. It's important that navigational options be consistent throughout the site, in availability as well as in appearance.

Pages that are alike should have the same navigational options. If I could get back to the home page directly from one second-level page, I'd expect to be able to get back from all the others as well. Third-level pages might have a different set of options, but those options need to be consistent among all third-level pages, and so on.

Furthermore, it helps usability to present the options in the same fashion every time they are presented. If your home page button appears in blue at the top right-hand corner of one page, don't put it at the bottom in red on another page. If you offer a list of options, such as in a toolbar, keep the selections in the same order on each page, so users don't have to spend time hunting around for the option they just used. Navigation options should stay put.

Efficiency

With every click into a site's hierarchy, you run the risk that the user will lose interest and leave. When you are designing the structure and navigation of a site, be mindful of how many clicks it takes to get to a piece of content or to get a task done (such as filling out a form, or purchasing something). The goal is to get users to the information they want efficiently and keep them engaged in the process.

The navigation system for a site should alleviate extra clicking, not add to it. Your navigation should include shortcuts to information—it can be as simple as providing links to other major sections of the site. You might want to supplement the global site-navigation system with specialized shortcuts such as a site map or search function.

---

* Icons were taken from Macromedia Freehand 8, RealPlayer 7, and *www.k10k.com*, respectively.

Navigational Elements

There are many tools that you can use to help users move around a site. Here are some of the most popular.

Toolbars and panels

The majority of web sites group their navigational options (whether graphical buttons or text links) into some sort of horizontal toolbar or vertical panel. Toolbars are generally placed along the top of the page (sometimes below an advertising banner). The left edge of the page is another convenient location for navigation options and lists of related links (Figure 18-19).

Most web sites group their navigational options into a vertical or horizontal toolbar.

Building Usable Web Sites

Figure 18-19

Navigational toolbars and panels

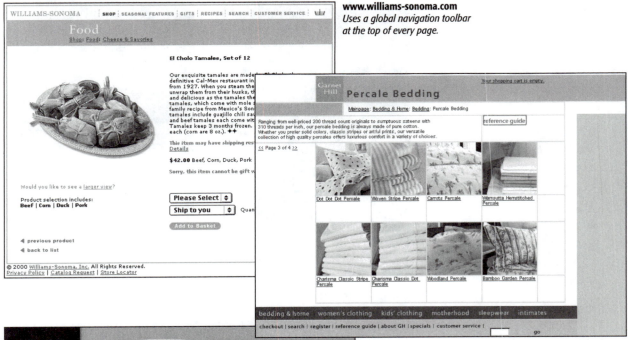

www.williams-sonoma.com
Uses a global navigation toolbar at the top of every page.

www.garnethill.com
Places their global toolbar in a frame at the bottom of the page.

www.sifl-n-olly.com
Uses the left side of the page for main site navigation.

Pull-down menus

A great space-saving method for adding a large number of links on a page is to put them in a pull-down menu form element (Figure 18-20). That way, all the links are readily available but don't require much precious screen real estate. Form elements require some scripts on the server in order to function, so you may need some assistance from a programmer to implement this shortcut.

Figure 18-20

Pull-down menus are a great way to add shortcuts to a page without taking up much screen real estate.

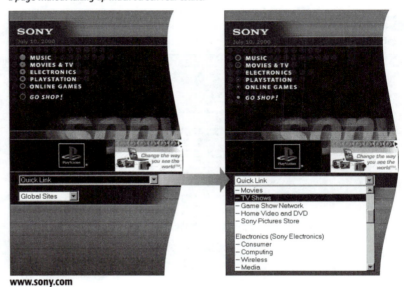

www.sony.com

Tabs

Navigational tabs across the top of the page are all the rage as I write in the summer of 2000. They are everywhere! While they serve as a compact and fairly intuitive device for allowing access to different sections of a site, I find that they are often applied inappropriately or gratuitously.

Ideally, tabs should be used to indicate similar functionality across a number of categories (Figure 18-21). Amazon.com (one of the early tab adopters) uses them correctly in this case—whether you've selected books or movies, you have the same basic options for viewing specials, reading reviews, and shopping.

Figure 18-21

Tabs are appropriate for indicating similar functionality across a number of categories.

In many cases tabs are just used arbitrarily.

All too often, tabs are used arbitrarily for access to divisions of the site. While there's nothing inherently wrong with this, the tabs aren't communicating functionality... they're just tabs for tabs' sake.

One drawback to tabs, which Amazon.com is currently facing, is that graphical tabs stack up pretty quickly, and you may end up with an unwieldy mountain of tabs.

As the Web continues to evolve, navigational approaches come and go like any fad. Buy.com, another formerly tab-reliant site, ditched its tabs altogether and now just presents options in a navigational panel. If you choose to use tabs, be sure that they are a logical metaphor for the task.

"Breadcrumb" navigation

One of my favorite navigational elements is what's become known as the "breadcrumb trail." It's so useful and economical. As you click through the site's hierarchy, each successive level is indicated as a text link (Figure 18-22). Eventually, you end up with a string of section and subsection names that show exactly where you are and where you've been (like Hansel and Gretel's breadcrumb trail through the forest). The trail also allows users to return to the higher levels they've passed through with just one click.

Perhaps the best feature is that, because they are only HTML text links, this form of navigation barely adds to the file size. That's a lot of communication and functionality packed into a few bytes.

Figure 18-22

Examples of "breadcrumb trail" navigation

Site maps

Site maps provide an overhead view of the site's logic as well as instant access to information via links.

If your site is large and complex, you may want to supplement the navigational system on each page by providing shortcuts to your information. One approach is to provide a site map, a list of the contents of the site, organized to reflect the structure of the site by section and subsection (Figure 18-23). By providing an overhead view of the site's logic, you may help the user feel better oriented when travelling through the site. Each topic in the site map is also a handy link directly to that page.

As an alternative, smaller sites may be represented with a graphical site map. It is generally more difficult to do this effectively. In addition, because it is a graphic, it will take longer to download than text.

You might also choose to provide a site index, which is an alphabetical listing (like a book index) of all the topics available on your site.

Site map examples

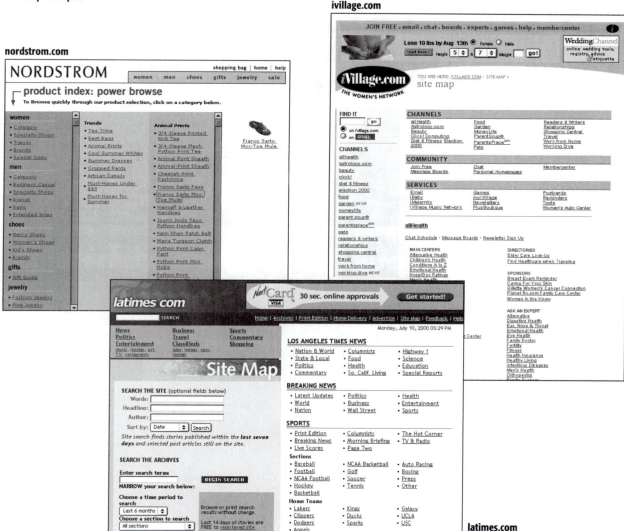

*Search functions may offer a
false sense of security.*

Search functionality

One of the most widely used shortcuts for finding information on a web site is the search box (Figure 18-24). While it's tempting to assume that a search engine is the answer to everybody's information-seeking problems, in reality, most search functions offer a false sense of security. Search engines require special scripting on the server side, and although that can be simple to do, it's not so easy to do well. It requires careful site indexing for it to work efficiently.

Figure 18-24

Search boxes are ubiquitous, but unless the technology behind them is well-designed, they may offer a false sense of navigational security.

The unfortunate truth about many search engines is that they may turn up irrelevant links, or too many links to sort through. Some search engines do not provide enough description of each listing for users to make an informed choice. This can cause wasted time following links that *seem* useful, but actually aren't.

There's nothing wrong with supplementing your navigation system with search capabilities, as long as you actually take the time (and spend the money) to do it right, and don't rely on it too strongly.

Bringing It All Home

Let's wrap up the interface and navigation design for the Blue Family site. On the home page, I've grouped the links to the family member sections and given them a similar graphical treatment to imply that they have similar content and functionality (Figure 18-25, gallery). The news and photo page areas are given special visual treatments that are appropriate for features that will be updated frequently.

Figure 18-25 **G**

The Blue Family home page.

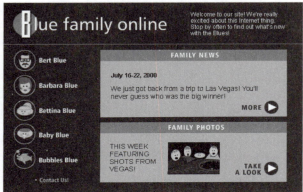

I've designed a navigational toolbar that will be used on every page of the site (Figure 18-26, gallery). It features the Blue Family "logo" in the left corner to identify what site it is from any point of entry. It also provides links to each family member section as well as the home page. The current section is identified both by the labeled area below the toolbar and by the orange dot behind the member's name in the toolbar itself.

Figure 18-26 **G**

A typical second-level page for the Blue Family site.

Building Usable Web Sites: In Review

There are a lot of big, meaty topics in this chapter—all warranting further study and experimentation. Here are a few of the highlights:

- A successful web site requires attention to how the information is organized (its information design) and how users get to that information (its interface design and navigation system).

- Users' top frustrations in browsing the Web include not being able to find information, hitting dead ends, not being able to get back to where they started, and having to click through too many pages to get to the information they want.

- Information design involves organizing information and planning how users will find it. It requires taking an inventory of all the information on the site, organizing it, and giving it structure.

- Interface design determines how a site's structure is represented visually on the page. It includes all the visual cues to understanding what information is available, as well as how to get to it. It includes how items are grouped, color-coding systems, metaphors, and all the buttons and tools for navigating the site.

- Site diagrams are useful for communicating the structure of the site and developing its navigational system.

- A good navigation system must answer the questions "Where am I?" and "Where can I go from here?"

- The key characteristics of a successful navigation system are clarity, consistency, and efficiency.

- The most common navigation tool is the navigational toolbar, usually at the top (but sometimes along the side or bottom) of every page.

- You may choose to supplement the navigation system with a search function or a site map.

Web Design Dos and Don'ts

There is no absolute right or wrong way to design a web site. When people ask me about the best way to design a site, it always seems to come down to "It depends."

Your design decisions depend on the type of site you're publishing. Personal sites, entertainment sites, and corporate e-commerce sites all have different priorities and abide by different guidelines, both in terms of content and how that content is presented. And, as you might have already guessed, it depends a lot on your audience—the hardware and software they're using, their reason for visiting your site, etc.

Good and bad design decisions are always relative. There are no "nevers"—there's always a site out there for which a web design "don't" makes perfect sense and is really the best solution.

Consider the contents of this chapter to be general guidelines. These are some pointers to possible improvements and some red flags for common beginner traps that can be easily avoided. In the end, you'll need to decide what works best for your site.

General Page Design Advice

The following dos and don'ts apply to the formatting and structure of the whole page.

DO...
Keep all file sizes as small as possible for quick downloads.

Because...
Quick downloads are crucial for a successful user experience. If your pages take forever to download, your visitors may grow impatient and go surf elsewhere. At the very least, they'll get cranky.

DO...

Design for a screen size of 640 × 480 pixels, unless you are certain that your audience will be viewing your pages with a different configuration.

Because...

When you design larger page sizes, you risk parts not being visible for users with older, smaller monitors or WebTV. For some target audiences, it is now considered "safe" to design for an 800 × 600 monitor size. But if you want to be absolutely sure your whole page will be visible, stick with the 640 × 480 lowest common denominator. For more information, see Chapter 4, Why Web Design Isn't Like Print Design.

Put your most important messages in the first screenful.

DO...

Put your most important messages (who you are, what you do, etc.) in the first screenful (the top 350 pixels of the page).

Because...

Most users make judgments about a site based on that first impression, without taking the time to scroll down for more information. For details, see the sidebar Designing 'Above the Fold' in Chapter 4.

DO...

Limit the length of your pages to two or three "screenfuls."

Because...

Longer pages that require lots of scrolling are unmanageable for online reading and make it more difficult for readers to find their place. For some reason, users do not like to scroll; they'd rather keep moving forward. It is better to break long flows of text into a few separate pages and link them together (Figure 19-1).

DON'T...

Design specifically for one browser or platform (unless you are 100% certain your audience will be viewing your pages under that configuration).

Because...

You never want to alienate your visitors. Nothing is more off-putting than arriving at a site only to find a sign that says, "You must have X browser running on X platform with X, Y, Z plug-ins to use this site." The only thing worse is just to find that nothing works!

DON'T...

Use too many animations, especially on pages with content you want people to read.

Because...

While animations are effective in drawing attention, users find them annoying and distracting when they are trying to read the text on the page. Even one looping animation can be an annoyance to some people. A whole page of spinning and flashing is a disaster (Figure 19-2, gallery).

Figure 19-1

Typical "screenful"

Avoid long scrolling pages. Webmonkey (**www.webmonkey.com**) does a good job of dividing their long articles into smaller, more manageable pieces that are linked together with a clear navigational system.

Figure 19-2 G

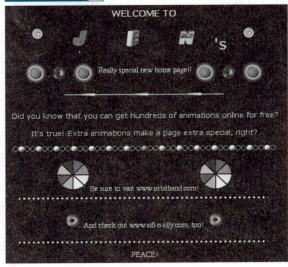

Here's an example of too much animation! I wish this printed book could show you the true "splendor" of my new special home page, featuring animated letters, bullets, and divider bars. Imagine every graphic spinning, rotating, or pulsating. This may look like an exaggeration, but I have seen pages like this and worse.

DON'T...

Use "under construction" signs. In particular, don't make "under construction" pages that appear after a user clicks on the link. If your site or section isn't ready, simply don't post it.

Because...

While you may intend to show that you have information that will be available soon, "under construction" signs and other placeholders just make it look like you don't have your act together. I especially hate it when I end up on a "construction" page after I've taken the time to follow a link from the home page (Figure 19-3). Providing links that go nowhere is a waste of your visitors' time and patience.

Figure 19-3

"Under construction" pages like this are annoying. If the section is not available, don't provide a link to it.

Thanks for visiting!

This page is currently UNDER CONSTRUCTION!

`UNDER CONSTRUCTION`

Please stop by another time to see if we got around to putting anything up here.

< Back to HOME PAGE

Text Formatting Tips

These tidbits of wisdom pertain to the formatting of text. In many cases, text on web pages follows the same design guidelines as text on a printed page. Some of these recommendations are particular to the special requirements of the web medium.

DO...

Take the time to proofread your site.

Because...

Typos and bad grammar reflect badly on your site and your business. If your authoring tool does not have a built-in spellchecker, be sure to have another person carefully review your content.

DO...

Make the structure of your information clear by giving similar elements the same design and important elements more visual weight (using size, space, or color) (Figure 19-4, gallery).

Because...

It enables your readers to understand your content at a glance and speeds up the process of finding what they need.

Figure 19-4 **G**

This excerpt from the Webmonkey home page (www.webmonkey.com) uses type treatments effectively to convey the structure of the information. Article listings have the same structure, with the article title given the most visual weight. Section titles are also treated similarly and are given lots of space to set them apart from other listings.

DON'T...

Change the size setting for all the text on a page.

Because...

You should respect the fact that each user has his default font set at a size that is most comfortable for him to read. If you feel your page would look better with all the type set one size smaller, be sure to test the page on a Mac and with various browser text settings.

Respect the fact that many users have set their browser's default font to a size that is comfortable to read.

Web Design Dos and Don'ts

DON'T...

Set type in all capital letters.

Because...

All capital letters are harder to read than upper- and lowercase letters (Figure 19-5). In addition, it makes it look like you're shouting your message, which is just rude!

DON'T...

Set more than a few words in italics.

Because...

Most browsers just slant the regular text font to achieve an "italic" (Figure 19-5). The result is often nearly unreadable, especially for large quantities of text at small sizes.

DON'T...

Set text in all capital, bold, and italics (Figure 19-5).

Because...

Three wrongs don't make a right! This is just overkill, but I see it all the time.

Figure 19-5

Avoid setting large amounts of text in all capital letters or all italic text, because it makes it more difficult to read. A combination of capitals, italic, and bold styles is overkill.

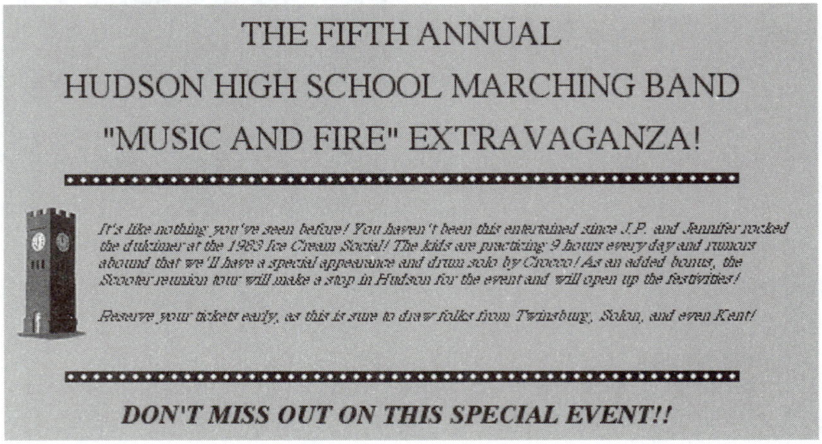

THE FIFTH ANNUAL
HUDSON HIGH SCHOOL MARCHING BAND
"MUSIC AND FIRE" EXTRAVAGANZA!

It's like nothing you've seen before! You haven't been this entertained since J.P. and Jennifer rocked the dulcimer at the 1983 Ice Cream Social! The kids are practicing 9 hours every day and rumors abound that we'll have a special appearance and drum solo by Chocco! As an added bonus, the Scooter reunion tour will make a stop in Hudson for the event and will open up the festivities!

Reserve your tickets early, as this is sure to draw folks from Twinsburg, Solon, and even Kent!

DON'T MISS OUT ON THIS SPECIAL EVENT!!

DON'T...

Insert line breaks unless you really mean them.

Because...

Text will wrap differently for each user, depending on the default text size setting in her browser and the width of the browser window. If you've inserted hard line breaks (`<BR>`) to format lines of text, you run the risk of the text re-wrapping in an awkward way (Figure 19-6).

Figure 19-6

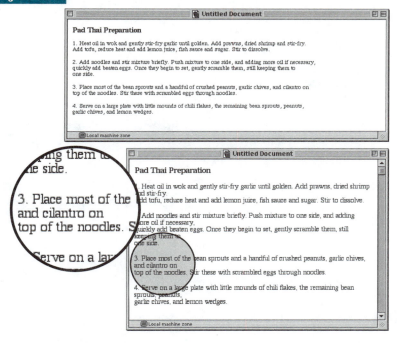

Figure 19-7

`<FONT SIZE=-2>`

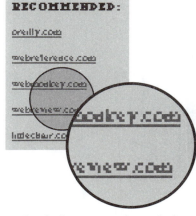

Type that is set to –2 may be completely unreadable depending on the user's browser setup and platform (Macs tend to display text smaller than PCs).

DON'T...

Set type at `SIZE=-2` or smaller.

Because...

Type that is set to `SIZE=-2`, while it may look tidy on your Windows machine, will be downright unreadable on a Mac or even on a Windows machine with its browser type set to a smaller size (Figure 19-7).

DON'T...

Use `<H5>` or `<H6>`

Because...

In most browsers, these headings are displayed at a size even smaller than the default text. The small size along with the bold formatting makes these elements difficult to read.

Web Design Dos and Don'ts

Graphics Advice

These dos and don'ts apply to both graphic production and placing graphics on the page using HTML.

DO...

Use anti-aliasing for most text in graphics (except for fonts under 10 points).

Because...

Smooth anti-aliased edges will make your graphics look more polished and professional. For type under 10 points, however, anti-aliasing can blur the whole letter shape and make the text less readable. It is usually best to turn anti-aliasing off for small text (Figure 19-8).

Figure 19-8

Anti-aliasing smooths out the jagged edges between colors and makes your text look better. In most cases, turn anti-aliasing on for text in graphics.

The exception is small type, which gets blurry when it's anti-aliased. Depending on the font face, you will get better results turning anti-aliasing off for type under 10 points.

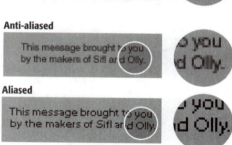

DO...

Keep graphic files under 30K (unless an exception is absolutely necessary).

Because...

A 30K graphic could take approximately 30 seconds to download over a modem Internet connection, and that's a long time to wait for something to appear on the screen. Of course, you should keep all graphic file sizes as small as possible (aim for under 10K). If you want a maximum guideline, use the 30K-rule.

DO...

Take the time to prevent halos around transparent graphics.

Because...

They make your graphics look sloppy and unprofessional (Figure 19-9). For detailed instructions on preventing halos, see Chapter 14, Creating GIFs.

Figure 19-9

Halos (the ugly fringe around transparent graphics) are easily preventable.

Graphic with a halo

Clean and well-produced graphics help make your site look professional.

Graphic that blends well with background

DO...

Turn off the blue border around linked graphics.

Because...

Blue boxes around all your linked graphics detract from the design of the page (Figure 19-10). To turn the border off, set BORDER=0 within the <IMG> tag. Your graphics will blend more smoothly into the page.

Figure 19-10

Linked graphics look much better with borders turned off.

DO...

Provide alternate text for every graphic. Alternate text displays in the event that the graphic doesn't.

Because...

This is the easiest way to make the content of your site accessible to a wider audience, including people with text-only browsers and users who have their graphics turned off for faster page downloading. Specify alternative text using the ALT attribute in the <IMG> tag (for more information, see Chapter 8, Adding Graphic Elements).

DON'T...

Make graphics that look like buttons but don't link to anything (Figure 19-11).

Because...

A 3-D beveling effect is a strong visual cue for "click here." I've seen some sites that used this visual effect on ordinary graphical labels. I was duped into clicking on them, and nothing happened.

Figure 19-11

These section header graphics beg to be clicked because of the 3-D bevel effect. Contrary to appearances, they are not buttons and don't do anything.

Aesthetic Suggestions

The way your site looks communicates a certain level of professionalism. A cluttered and chaotic web site tend to reflect badly on the company the site represents. Even if corporate image isn't one of your priorities, basic readability is important for any site. Here are a few suggestions that pertain to that all-important first impression.

DON'T...

Center everything on the page.

Because...

Centering the whole page makes the content difficult to read (Figure 19-12). This is not to say that you should never center anything. For some types of information, particularly when the page contains just a few elements or when you want a formal tone, center alignment is the best choice, both logically and aesthetically.

In general, it is best to stick with left justification for pages with a significant amount of content. I also recommend using a table to establish one or two strong lines of alignment and stick with them. This creates a solid and clean first impression and makes it easier to find information.

> *Cluttered and chaotic web sites tend to reflect badly on the company the site represents.*

Figure 19-12

Avoid centering all the content on a page. Not only are the edges ragged and untidy, it is more difficult to read since each line starts in a different position. Notice how much clearer the page is when I use a table to create strong left alignments.

Web Design Dos and Don'ts

DON'T...

Mix alignments. In other words, avoid combinations of left-justified, centered, and right-justified elements on the same page (Figure 19-13).

Because...

Not only is it less elegant than a page with a single alignment, it also hinders clear communication because the readers' eyes need to jump all over the page.

Figure 19-13

The messy-looking page on the left suffers from the combination of too many text alignments. The page on the right takes all the same elements but gives the page a cleaner (and more usable!) look by sticking with a consistent alignment.

DON'T...

Use too many colors.

Because...

It's visually chaotic and makes it difficult to prioritize the information (Figure 19-14, gallery). Better to choose one or two dominant colors and one highlight color, then stick with them throughout the site.

Figure 19-14 G

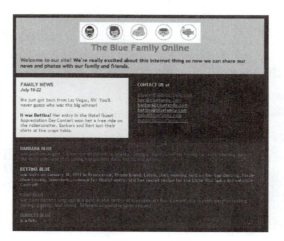

This page suffers from color overkill. Making every element a different bright color is a sure way to create visual chaos.

DON'T...

Use wild background tile patterns (Figure 19-15, gallery).

Because...

It makes it difficult to read the text of the page. Background patterns should be as subtle as possible. (Background tiles are discussed in more detail in Chapter 8.)

Figure 19-15 **G**

Bold background patterns can make the text on the page unreadable.

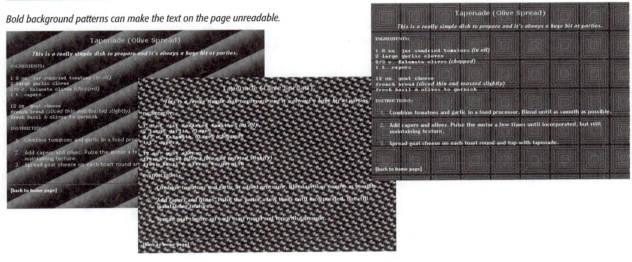

DON'T...

Automatically use white type on dark backgrounds, particularly for large amounts of small text.

Because...

The contrast is too high and it can be uncomfortable to read (Figure 19-16). Better to choose a very light pastel shade instead, such as light gray against black, or very pale blue against dark blue. The text will still be clear, and the slightly lower contrast is more gentle on the eyes, making your page look less glaring overall.

Figure 19-16

In this line, the type is white. The contrast is as high as it can get, which is a strain on the eyes.

In this type, the type is light gray. The eye still perceives the type as white, but it is easier to read.

Lots of white type on a dark background can be uncomfortable to read. Try using a light tint of the background color instead.

DESIGN TIP

Consider the Existing Corporate Image

Tie the look and feel of your site into your existing corporate identity (if one exists).

Web sites should be considered part of a unified identity package. Your audience should be able to recognize your company whether they see it in print, on television, or online. Too often, web designers take the look and feel of a web site in their own direction, which foils any attempt to build a coherent and recognizable corporate image or brand.

Web Design Dos and Don'ts

Jen's Personal Pet Peeves

Granted, these recommendations may come down to personal taste, but I would be shirking my responsibilities if I didn't at least mention them.

DO...

Change your link and visited link colors when using a dark background color or pattern (Figure 19-17, gallery).

Because...

The default dark blue link color is only readable against light colors.

DON'T...

Assume a black background will automatically make your site "cool" (Figure 19-17).

Because...

If it isn't done right, the effect can be overly dramatic and "heavy metal." Of course, it can be handled very elegantly. But for the average site (especially a small business site), black backgrounds are inappropriate.

DON'T...

Use a globe, especially a spinning globe (Figure 19-17).

Because...

Globes as icons have been so overused that they no longer carry any meaning at all. This is just a visual cliché.

DON'T...

Use rainbow dividers, especially animated rainbow dividers.

Because...

They are sure-fire indication of amateur web design and have been since the very beginning. Not cool, just tacky (Figure 19-17).

Figure 19-17 **G**

The web page of my nightmares! This page has it all:

- Gratuitous black background
- Animated rainbow dividers
- A spinning globe
- An unreadable link color
- Meaningless icons
- Too many colors
- Bad alignment

How'd They Do That?
An Introduction to Advanced Techniques

This book has covered quite a bit of territory—enough to get you up and running with creating web pages and linking them together in well-organized sites. But if you spend any time browsing the Web, you're sure to come across pages with special effects and interactivity that will make you say, "How'd they *do* that?!"

While it is beyond the scope of this book to teach you everything, I do want you to be able to recognize certain techniques and technologies when you see them. In this chapter, I'll zero in on some common web tricks, tell you how they're done, and provide some pointers for further learning. Bear in mind, however, that most of these topics are vast. While I'll do my best to give you the highlights, you'll need to take it from there.

Remember that you don't need to learn how to do everything yourself, so don't feel overwhelmed. The important part is knowing what *can* be done so you can speak intelligently with the folks who will be responsible for actually creating it.

Forms

How do I put a text entry field and a button on my page so people can send me messages?

Adding form elements to a web page is simple: they are created using a set of HTML form tags that define menus, text fields, buttons, and so on (Figure 20-1, following page). These elements make up an interface for the collection of information.

However, making a nice-looking form on a web page is only part of the story. Getting the form to actually *work* requires a script or a small program on the server that knows how to process the information the form collects. The program that does the work behind the scenes is often a CGI (Common Gateway Interface) script. CGI scripts are generally written in the Perl programming language (although C and C++ are also used). Form-processing programs can also be implemented as PHP scripts, Java servlets, or ASP scripts, to name a few other technologies.

WHERE TO LEARN MORE

Forms

Web Design in a Nutshell, by Jennifer Niederst (O'Reilly, 1999)

Features a chapter with detailed information on creating form elements with HTML and adapting existing CGI scripts.

HTML and XHTML: The Definitive Guide, Fourth Edition, by Chuck Musciano and Bill Kennedy (O'Reilly, 2000)

Features a chapter with detailed information on HTML form elements.

Forms: Interactivity for the World Wide Web, by Malcolm Guthrie (Adobe Press, 1998)

A whole book about creating visually effective forms for the Web.

Figure 20-1

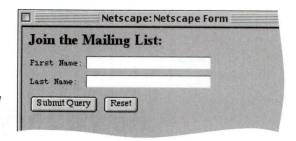

You can get a general idea of how forms are created by looking at this simple example. The whole form is indicated by the `<FORM>...</FORM>` *tags. Each element in the form is placed with an* `<INPUT>` *tag. The* `TYPE` *attribute specifies which form element to display.*

```
<H2>Join the Mailing List:</H2>
<FORM ACTION="/cgi-bin/mailform.p1" METHOD=GET>
<PRE>
First Name: <INPUT TYPE="text" NAME="first">
Last Name: <INPUT TYPE="text" NAME="last">
<INPUT TYPE="SUBMIT"> <INPUT TYPE="RESET">
</PRE>
</FORM>
```

If you want your site to have forms, you need to find a programmer. The scripts need to be set up on the server and you will need to include key bits of information in the forms' HTML code that feed the scripts information. Be sure to communicate your goals clearly to the person assisting you with the technical aspects.

For basic form functionality, such as a form that sends a piece of email, you may find that your hosting service provides a few canned CGI scripts that you can personalize and use for free. Be sure to ask whether these services are available.

Audio

How do I add music to a web page?

There are many options for adding music and other sound files to a web page. Of course, you'll need to start with some audio files. If you want to generate your audio files yourself, you need to make sure that your computer is equipped with the proper sound card and input device (such as a microphone or CD player). You also need audio-editing software that saves the audio information to a file format that can be transferred over the Web. Some popular tools for web audio include Macromedia's SoundEdit 16, Apple's QuickTime Pro, and Terran MediaCleaner Pro.

Audio Downloads

The most straightforward approach to adding sound to a web site is simply making the audio file available for download. Put the file on the server and make a link to it as you would to any other file (Figure 20-2). When the users click on the link, the file is downloaded to their desktops and is played with a sound application such as QuickTime (which comes built into recent browsers). In general, it is necessary for the whole file to download before it can start playing.

Figure 20-2

```
<A HREF="http://www.ora.com/audio/song.mp3">Play the song.</A>
```

Linking to a sound file is the same as linking to another document. When the user clicks the link, the sound file is downloaded from the server and plays with a helper application or audio browser plug-in.

The file format you use is important. Today, the most popular format is the MP3 (you can recognize it by the *.mp3* suffix). You may also hear them referred to as MPEGs (pronounced "EM-peg") because they use the MPEG compression scheme. MP3s are able to maintain excellent audio quality even at relatively small file sizes, making them ideal for music. All of the online "jukebox" type services use MP3s to store and transfer songs.

Other common formats for web audio are WAVE (*.wav*), AIFF (*.aif*), and QuickTime Audio (*.mov*). All sacrifice sound quality in favor of smaller files. There's also MIDI (*.mid*) format, which stores synthesized musical tones in a numerical format, resulting in extremely small file sizes.

Streaming Audio

Another method for delivering audio over the Web is called "streaming" audio. It differs from simple downloading in that the audio files start playing almost immediately and continue playing as the server delivers the file. This alleviates long waits for the files to download completely and begin playing. You can even deliver live broadcasts. The other significant difference is that the file is never actually downloaded to the user's machine, which alleviates some copyright concerns.

The most popular streaming audio format is RealAudio format (*.ra*), created by Real Networks, Inc. Although you can put RealAudio files on any server, you get true streaming performance by serving it from a machine using the RealServer software. For more information on streaming media and how to add them to your pages, see Real Network's web site at *www.realnetworks.com*.

"Streaming" Downloads

When played with the QuickTime audio player, both MP3s and QuickTime audio files will begin playing before they are completely downloaded, simulating a streaming effect. The QuickTime audio player comes built into Netscape Navigator and Internet Explorer.

How'd They Do That?

WHERE TO LEARN MORE

Web Audio

Designing Web Audio, by Josh Beggs and Dylan Thede (O'Reilly, 2001)
Everything you'd ever want to know about Internet audio, including case studies and step-by-step instructions.

MP3: The Definitive Guide, by Scot Hacker (O'Reilly, 2000)
A whole book devoted to the creation and serving of MP3 audio files.

Background Sound

Sometimes when you arrive at a web page, music starts playing automatically, like a soundtrack to the page. In general, you should never force something as intrusive as an audio file on a user unless they ask for it. In fact, I almost always hit the "back" button immediately on any site that serves up an uninvited sound file. First it startles me when it comes blasting out of my speakers, then it just annoys me with its constant looping. But if you still think you have a *really* good reason for doing it, I'll show you how it's done.

To set a background sound that will work with both Microsoft Internet Explorer and Netscape Navigator, you need to use both the <BGSOUND> tag (for IE) and the <EMBED> tag (for Navigator) in the beginning of the document (Figure 20-3).

Figure 20-3

```
<EMBED SRC="audio/song.mid" autostart=true hidden=true></EMBED>
<NOEMBED><BGSOUND="audio/song.mid"></NOEMBED>
```

The <BGSOUND> tag works only in Internet Explorer. To make audio play automatically for Navigator users, I've added the <EMBED> tag. The <NOEMBED> tag ensures that Navigator ignores the <BGSOUND> element.

Video

How did they get a little movie to play right on their page?

When you see a video playing right on a web page, chances are it's a QuickTime movie that has been placed on the page with an <OBJECT> tag (the W3C's preferred method) or an <EMBED> tag (Apple's recommended method). In order for the movie to display on the page, the QuickTime plug-in must be installed on the user's browser. Fortunately, this plug-in is included in current browsers' installation packages.

Placing a movie on a page is a lot like placing an image on the page (Figure 20-4). You must specify the SRC, WIDTH, and HEIGHT attributes. In order for the controller to display properly, you must add 16 pixels to the height of the movie.

Figure 20-4

```
<TD VALIGN=top ROWSPAN=20><EMBED SRC="moon.mov" width="160" height="136"></TD>
```

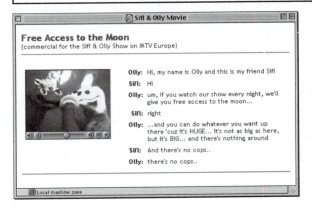

Use the `<EMBED>` tag to place a movie and its player right on the page like an image. Note that I've added 16 pixels to the actual movie height (120 pixels) to accommodate the player controls.

As an alternative, you can provide a link to the movie file and let the user download it whenever they want (Figure 20-5). When the movie downloads, it can be viewed in the browser window with the QuickTime plugin or it can be played with another movie-playing helper application.

Figure 20-5

```
<A HREF="moon.mov">Play the movie (906K)</A>
```

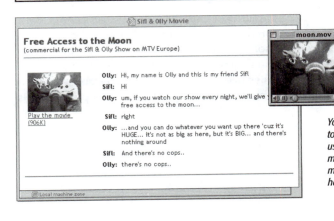

You can also simply link to a movie file. When the user clicks the link, the movie opens in whatever movie player the browser has configured.

TIP

When linking to an audio or video file, always provide the file size so users can make an informed decision about whether they want to commit to clicking the link.

How'd They Do That?

Movie Files

Let's talk a little more about movie files. The QuickTime Movie format (*.mov*) is ideal for delivering movies over the Web because it is a highly condensed format supported on both PCs and Macs. Movies can also be saved in MPEG (*.mpg* or *.mp2*) format or as Windows-only AVI files (*.avi*).

Making movies is easier than ever with digital video recorders that can be plugged directly into your computer. You'll need to start with some sort of video source (whether out of your camera or from videotape). You'll also need video-editing software, such as QuickTime by Apple, Media Cleaner Pro (by Terran Interactive, *www.terran.com*), or Adobe Premier if you want to go for professional-level editing (*www.adobe.com*). If you work on a newer Macintosh, you can take advantage of Apple's iMovie technology, which puts basic movie-making abilities in the hands of consumers (see *www.apple.com/imovie/* for more information).

Because video and audio information can be huge, the trick to making web-appropriate movies is optimization—the frame rate, the image compression, and the sound compression. All video-editing packages will provide the tools you need for compressing your video as small as possible.

Streaming Video

Like audio, video source can be streamed so that it starts playing quickly after the "click" and continues playing as the data is transferred. There are several options for doing this, but I recommend the Real Networks system for its popularity and cross-platform capabilities (*www.realnetworks.com*). Streaming movies are saved in the RealMovie format (*.rm*) and can be created with the RealProducer software by Real Networks or with some other video software such as Media Cleaner Pro. Again, for true streaming performance, your RealMovie files need to reside on a server outfitted with the RealServer software, so make sure your hosting service provides this option.

Cascading Style Sheets

Is there a way to get better control over typography?

Throughout this book, I've been singing the praises of Cascading Style Sheets. So what are they, exactly? A style sheet, like it sounds, is a set of instructions that control the appearance of a web page. Style sheets offer more sophisticated control over typographic style and placement than HTML (which was never designed to be used that way in the first place).

Some Good Points; Some Bad Points

Style sheets have a number of tempting advantages:

Greater typography and page layout control. With style sheets, you can specify traditional typography attributes such as font size, line spacing, letter spacing, indents, and margins.

Easier site maintenance. I think my favorite thing about style sheets is that you can apply one style sheet to all the pages in a site. Then if you want to change the appearance of your headings, you only have to make the change once (in the style sheet) instead of for each and every document in the site.

Style information is kept separate from structure. In the HTML section of this book, I explained that HTML was only intended to mark up the structure of a document, not the way it looks. With style sheets, you can affect the appearance of a file without disturbing its structure.

Cascading Style Sheets offer superior control over presentation, but they are poorly and inconsistently supported by browsers.

But of course, there's always a downside. The major drawback to Cascading Style Sheets is that they have yet to be fully implemented in any browser. Style sheets won't work at all on Netscape Navigator 3.0 and Microsoft Internet Explorer 2.0 or earlier. Even the browsers that do support style sheets do so inconsistently and erratically.

Unfortunately, this means that while style sheets offer great solutions to many of our HTML woes in theory, they cannot be relied upon for crucial display instructions for web sites with a general audience likely to still be using older browsers. Hopefully one day, we'll be able to use style sheets without a second thought to browser performance, but we aren't there yet.

How Style Sheets Work

Although I can't give you a thorough tutorial on style sheets in this chapter, I'd at least like to give you a taste for how they work.

Style sheets are made up of one or more style instructions (called rules) for how a page element should be displayed. The following sample contains

How'd They Do That?

two rules. The first makes all the H1s in a document red; the second spec-ifies that the paragraphs should be set in 12 point Verdana or some sans-serif font:

```
H1 { color: red; }
P  { font-size: 12pt;
     font-family: Verdana, sans-serif;
   }
```

A rule says how a particular page element (whether it is a heading, a para-graph, or a blockquote) should be displayed. The two main sections of a rule are the selector (which identifies the element to be affected) and the declaration (the style or display instructions to be applied to that element) (Figure 20-6). The declaration is made up of a property and a value (sim-ilar to an attribute in an HTML tag). You can list several properties in a single declaration, separated by semicolons (as shown in the second rule in the sample code above).

Figure 20-6

The parts of a style sheet rule.

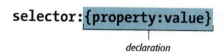

selector:{property:value}

declaration

Style sheets can be more complex than I have described here. For instance, there are interesting things you can do with selectors beyond simply point-ing to a specific HTML tag. In addition, there are dozens of properties to play with, each with its own set of values. Regardless, the basic rule struc-ture is always the same.

Applying Style Sheets to a Web Page

There are three ways to add style sheet information to a web page: right in the tag itself, embedded at the top of the document, and as an external link. I'll give you a quick introduction to all three.

Inline styles

Style information can be added to an individual element by adding the STYLE attribute within the HTML tag for that element:

```
<H1 STYLE="color: red">This Heading will be Red</H1>
<P STYLE="font-size: 12pt; font-family: Verdana, sans-serif">This is the
content of the paragraph.</P>
```

Although this is a valid application of style information, applying a style attribute to every tag in the file does not yield the time and file size savings that style sheets offer.

Embedded style sheets

A more compact method for adding a style sheet is to embed a style block at the top of the HTML document using the `<STYLE>` tag. Here's how our sample code would look as an embedded style sheet:

```
<HTML>
<HEAD>
<STYLE TYPE="text/css">
<!--
    H1 { color: red ;}
    P  { font-size: 12pt;
         font-family: Verdana, sans-serif;
       }
-->
</STYLE>
<TITLE>Document Title</TITLE>
</HEAD>
…
</HTML>
```

Make sure that the `<STYLE>` tag contains the `TYPE="text/css"` attribute and is contained within the `<HEAD>` of the document. You need to place HTML comment tags (`<!--` and `-->`) around the `<STYLE>` contents to hide the code from browsers that don't understand style sheet information.

External style sheets

If you are applying one set of style instructions to a number of pages in a site, an external style sheet is the best method. It is powerful because you can change the appearance of an entire site by making one change in the external style sheet document.

First, put your style sheet rules in a separate document and save the document in a file with the *.css* suffix. This document contains only the rules for your style sheet; it should not include any HTML structural tags.

Next, create a link to the style sheet document from within your web page (or pages). The best way to do that is with a `<LINK>` tag, as shown below:

```
<HEAD>
<LINK REL="STYLESHEET" HREF="pathname/stylesheet.css" TYPE="text/css">
</HEAD>
```

The `REL` attribute defines the linked document's relation to the current document—a "stylesheet." The `HREF` attribute (as always) provides the URL to the style sheet document.

Positioning

In addition to type styles, you can also use style sheets to position elements on the page. Style sheets treat each text element as though it were in a little box. You can use style sheets to position the box a specific number of pixels from the corner of the browser window. You can also place one box in front of another.

Why "Cascading"?

You can actually apply several style sheets to the same document. The word cascading refers to what happens when several style sheets vie for control of the same element on a page. The W3C anticipated this situation and assigned different weights to each type of style information (or a "cascading" order). Styles with more weight (those defined at a more specific level) will take precedence over styles set in a higher-level style sheet. So, for instance, a style rule appled within a tag will override a conflicting rule in an external style sheet.

WARNING

Unfortunately, the positioning aspects of style sheets are poorly and inconsistently supported by the major browsers. That's why technologies that rely on style sheets and their positioning properties (such as DHTML, described later in this chapter) are so tricky to implement successfully.

WHERE TO LEARN MORE

Cascading Style Sheets

Webmonkey's Style Sheet Resources
hotwired.lycos.com/webmonkey/
reference/stylesheet_guide/
  WebMonkey has a style sheet reference section with clearly written articles about style sheets and how they work.

Cascading Style Sheets: The Definitive Guide, by Eric Meyer (O'Reilly, 2000)
  A thorough review of all aspects of CSS1 and a comprehensive guide to CSS implementation for both advanced and novice web authors.

Trying Your Hand at Cascading Style Sheets

If you have Macromedia Dreamweaver or Adobe GoLive, you can take advantage of style sheets right away. In addition to generating the style sheet code, these tools will keep track of browser compatibility.

However, basic style sheets are so simple to create, you could write one yourself following the examples in this chapter. Start simply by using HTML tags as your selectors. Then change their appearance using the text-formatting properties listed below.

These properties work with all browsers that support style sheets (Netscape Navigator 4 and up and Microsoft Internet Explorer 3 and up, unless otherwise noted). There may be additional values for some properties, but I've only listed the ones that work reliably.

Font and text properties

You can add more than one property in the declaration portion of the rule:

font-family	Name of the font (or fonts, separated by a comma) *Values:* font name, generic font name (e.g., sans-serif) *Example:* P {font-family: Verdana, Arial, sans-serif;}
font-weight	Weight of the font *Values:* bold (there are others in the specification, such as light and medium, but only bold is universally supported) *Example:* P {font-weight: bold;}
font-size	Size of the text *Values:* number measurement (in any of the units in the sidebar) *Example:* P {font-size: 12 pt;} P {font-size: 1 in;}
color	Color of the text *Values:* color name or hexadecimal RGB value *Example:* P {color: #330099;}
text-align	Text alignment *Values:* left | right | center *Example:* P {text-align: center;}
text-indent	Amount of indent for the first line of text *Values:* number measurement (in specific units) *Example:* P {text-indent: .5 in;}
line-height	Adjusts the height of the line of type (similar to leading) *Values:* number measurement (in specific units); not supported by IE 3.0, but still worth mentioning *Example:* P {line-height: 24 pt; font-size: 12 pt;}
margin-left	Sets the left margin for the element. *Values:* number measurement (in specific units) *Example:* BODY {margin-left: .5 in;}
margin-right	Sets the right margin for the element. *Values:* number measurement (in specific units) *Example:* BODY {margin-right: .5 in;}

Style Sheet Units

Use these abbreviations when a value calls for a measurement:

cm	centimeters
in	inches
mm	millimeters
pc	picas
pt	points
px	pixels

JavaScript
How do I make a graphic change when the mouse pointer touches it?

The effect of making a graphic change when the mouse pointer touches it (Figure 20-7), also known as a rollover, is one of the things you can do with JavaScript. JavaScript (not related to the powerful programming language Java) is a scripting language that works specifically on web pages in web browsers. It adds interactivity and conditional behavior (as in, "when this happens, do this") to web pages. The script for a rollover instructs, "When the mouse is over graphic X, replace it with graphic Y."

JavaScript adds interactivity and conditional behavior (as in, "when this happens, do this") to web pages.

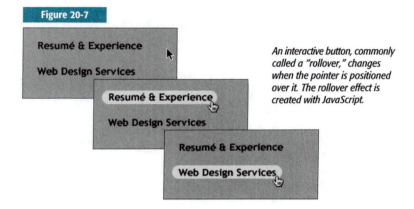

Figure 20-7

An interactive button, commonly called a "rollover," changes when the pointer is positioned over it. The rollover effect is created with JavaScript.

JavaScript is also responsible for these common web tricks (and many more):

- Displaying notes in the status bar of the browser based on mouse position

- Opening links in "pop-up" browser windows

- Changing the content of the page based on certain conditions (such as browser version)

Learning to write JavaScript from scratch is tricky, particularly if you have no prior programming experience. Unfortunately, a tutorial on how to write JavaScript is beyond the scope of this book. However, if you'd like to see a simple example of JavaScript in action, see the "Pop-up Windows" section in Chapter 17, Web Design Techniques.

The good news is you don't need to learn to write JavaScript to implement it on your pages. You can use professional-level web authoring tools such as Macromedia Dreamweaver 3 and Adobe GoLive 2 to write the JavaScript for basic tasks (such as pop-up windows and rollovers). If it's just rollover effects you're after, they can also be easily generated using web graphics tools such as Macromedia Fireworks 3 and Adobe ImageReady 2 (included with Photoshop 5.5).

How'd They Do That?

A rollover consists of two images of the same size. The original image is what displays when the page loads. The rollover image is what displays when the user's pointer passes over the original image. Let's look at how you'd use Dreamweaver 3 to add a rollover to a web page (Figure 20-8).

Figure 20-8

❶ *With a document open, place an insertion point where you want to place the rollover then select Rollover Image from the Insert menu.*

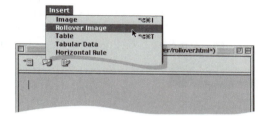

❷ *In the dialog box, give the rollover a name, then use the Browse button to select a graphic for the Original Image field. This is the image that appears when the page first loads.*

Browse again to select a graphic for the Rollover Image field. This is the image that appears when the pointer passes over the original image.

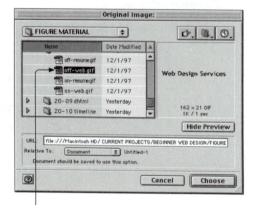

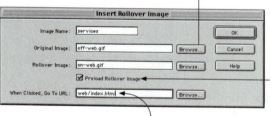

Finally, if the image is to be a link, enter the URL for the link in the "When Clicked…" field.

In most cases, you will want to have the images preloaded into the browser's cache so they are ready to go when the user touches the image.

❸ *Click OK when you're finished. To test your rollover, save the Dreamweaver document and preview the page in a browser.*

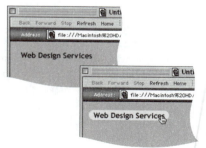

DHTML

I saw a site that had a menu panel that slid into view when I clicked on its edge. How did they do that?

Most likely, that sliding panel was done with DHTML (Dynamic HTML). DHTML is not a programming language in itself, but rather a clever combination of HTML, JavaScript, and Cascading Style Sheets.

The HTML source controls the content of the page and its elements; JavaScript is used to control the functionality of the elements—the causes and effects; and Cascading Style Sheets are used for controlling the appearance and positioning of objects on the page. Together, they can be used to orchestrate cool effects (Figure 20-9) like expanding menus Ⓐ, sliding panels Ⓑ, and animated objects that float around in the browser window Ⓒ. This is by no means a complete list... DHTML can be used to many creative and practical ends.

DHTML is a combination of HTML, Cascading Style Sheets, and JavaScript.

Figure 20-9

Common DHTML tricks

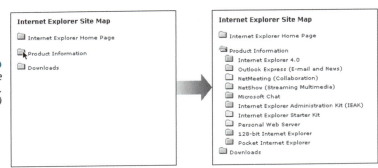

Ⓐ *In this expanding menu, you can view the contents of a folder by clicking on the icon. (Sample taken from www.microsoft.com.)*

Ⓑ *The panel on the left slides out when you click on the tab.*

Ⓒ *DHTML can be used for basic animation, such as making an object float around the browser window. (Sample taken from www.dhtmlzone.com/tutorials/.)*

WHERE TO LEARN MORE

DHTML

A good place to start your exploration of DHTML is with online resources. Many provide good overviews and beginner-level tutorials:

Webmonkey
hotwired.lycos.com/webmonkey/
authoring/dynamic_html/

CNET's Builder.com
www.builder.com

Macromedia's DHTML Zone
www.dhtmlzone.com

When you're ready for the more technical stuff, try this book:

Dynamic HTML: The Definitive Reference,
by Danny Goodman (O'Reilly, 1998)
A comprehensive guide for those serious about learning to code DHTML.

The downside to DHTML is that it is difficult to learn and implement successfully. First of all, creating DHTML effects from scratch requires an adept hand at both Cascading Style Sheets and JavaScript. But the thing that makes it a real monster is that browsers are notoriously inconsistent in the way they support DHTML objects and commands, so it is difficult to create an effect that will work for all users. In many cases, developers create several versions of a page and serve the appropriate version based on the browser making the request. Overall, DHTML is a lot of effort for questionable rewards (for instance, does the menu panel *really* need to slide out, or is that just an effect for effect's sake?).

For non-programming types who just want a basic DHTML trick (such as animation), once again, web-authoring tools come to the rescue. Macromedia Dreamweaver 3 provides a timeline and set of tools that allow you to create the effect visually and it takes care of the coding for you (Figure 20-10). You can even specify which browsers you are targeting and let the tool worry about creating compatible code. Adobe GoLive 4 also offers DHTML animation features. Even with the tools, however, it is important to test pages with DHTML effects thoroughly in a variety of browser environments.

Figure 20-10

Macromedia Dreamweaver's uses a timeline interface for creating DHTML animation effects.

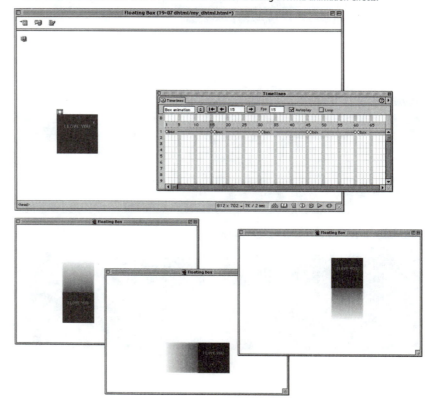

Flash

I saw this really cool page! It had music, animation, and buttons that did stuff when I touched them. How did they do that?

This sounds like a Flash page to me. Flash is a multimedia format developed by Macromedia especially for the Web (although it's now being used for other purposes as well). Flash gives you the ability to create full-screen animation, interactive graphics, and integrated audio clips, all at remarkably small file sizes.

Flash is great for putting animation and interactive elements (such as games) on web sites (Figure 20-11, gallery and following page). Some sites are using Flash for their entire site interface and content, instead of HTML (like the example in the center).

There are a number of advantages to the Flash format:

- Because it uses vector graphics, the files are small and download quickly.

- Vector graphics also allow Flash animations to be rescaled to any size without loss of detail. Real-time anti-aliasing keeps the edges smooth.

- It is a streaming format, which means the files start playing quickly and continue to play as they download.

- You can integrate sound files as either a background soundtrack (Flash developers seem to be partial to techno music, but that's certainly not required) or as user-triggered sound effects. By compressing, looping, and reusing sound files, you can keep the file sizes in check.

But of course, no technology is ideal. Here's the downside:

- Flash files require a plug-in to play in the browser. Many developers and clients are squeamish about sinking important navigation or content into a format that will require the user to go out and download a plug-in. But keep in mind that the Flash player plug-in is extremely popular, and as of this writing, Macromedia estimates that almost 92% of web users can view Flash content (see *www.macromedia.com/ software/player_census/*).

- Content is lost for non-graphical browsers. Any time you take content out of HTML text and put it in a picture, it is no longer available to text-only browsers. In addition, information in a Flash movie cannot be indexed or searched.

- You need specific software to create Flash content, and it isn't cheap! Both Macromedia Flash 5 and Adobe LiveMotion 1.0 retail for $299.

Flash animations are saved in the *.swf* (ShockWave Flash) format and can be embedded right into a web page. To create a Flash file, the most obvious choice is to use Macromedia's new and improved Flash 5 software. You can download a free demo from the Macromedia site at *www.flash.com*.

Flash is a multimedia format developed by Macromedia especially for the Web. It is great for adding animation, sound effects, and interactive elements to a web page.

How'd They Do That?

Figure 20-11 **G**

Scenes from a music video for Beck's "Nicotine and Gravy" (created by Fullerene Productions).

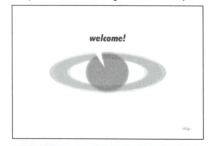

Flash intro and web site interface (screenshots from www.eye4u.com, a web design firm in Munich).

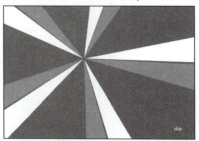

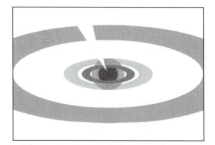

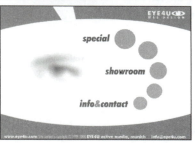

Flash animation. Shots from "A Short Smoke Break" by Rich Oakley and Fawn Scott.
This and other cool animation shorts can be seen at www.animationexpress.com.

You may also want to check out Adobe's LiveMotion 1.0 software, which can also save interactive animations in the *.swf* format. It is nicely integrated with other Adobe products such as Photoshop and Illustrator. For more information, see Adobe's web site: *www.adobe.com/products/livemotion/main.html*.

Before you jump on the Flash bandwagon, I want to make it clear that Flash is not appropriate for every web site, and it is certainly not going to make HTML obsolete (as some Flash enthusiasts may claim). While it is a wonderful medium for putting animations and interactive elements on web pages, it is generally less successful as the navigational interface for a whole site. For every user out there who thinks Flash sites are the best, there's someone else who finds them plain annoying and not worth the download. Ever notice all the "Skip Intro" links on Flash sites? Even the pros tread softly.

Consider whether Flash is appropriate for your site and avoid Flash for Flash's sake. If your site is about self-expression and entertainment, go nuts! But if you are trying to serve large amounts of information to people who need that information in a straightforward and timely fashion, stick to good old HTML.

Advanced Techniques in Review

There is a world of web design beyond simple HTML and graphics. The Web is always growing and evolving. You may choose to become proficient at advanced skills such as Cascading Style Sheets or JavaScript yourself, or you may use tools to create the basic effects. You may even choose to hire a specialist to add advanced functionality for you. Whatever your strategy, if you are in the world of web design, it is crucial that you at the very least have a familiarity with the more technical aspects. Following are a few tidbits from this chapter that you might keep in mind:

Forms. Forms are created with a set of form-related HTML tags. In order to be functional, they require a script or program running on the server to process the information they collect.

Audio. The most popular audio file format on the web is MP3 (*.mp3*). Other appropriate file formats include WAVE (*.wav*), AIFF (*.aif*), MIDI (*.mid*), and QuickTime Audio (*.mov*).

Audio can be made available from a web page via a link. When the user clicks the link, the audio file downloads and plays with an audio player.

Streaming audio is a method for delivering audio on a web page in which the file starts playing immediately after the user clicks. The file is never downloaded to the user's machine, rather, it is served in a stream, similar to radio. RealAudio (*.ra*) is one popular streaming media solution (however, there are others worth researching).

WHERE TO LEARN MORE
Flash

Try these online resources first:

Shockwave.com
www.shockwave.com
This site is a showcase of the latest and greatest shows, games, videos, etc. created in Flash. It's a good place to see what can be done.

"Starting Point" for Flash users
flash.start4all.com
This is a big page o' links to everything Flash-related.

Macromedia's Flash site
www.flash.com
For information about Macromedia Flash software, including technical support and tutorials.

There are quite a few books on Flash available. For a good beginner-level introduction, try:

Flash 4 for Windows and Macintosh: Visual QuickStart Guide, by Katherine Ulrich (Peachpit Press, 1999)
Like all QuickStart Guides, this provides a no-nonsense and pictorial overview of Flash basics. As of this writing, only Flash 4 is covered, but I expect this title to be updated soon once Flash 5 is widely available.

Video. The most popular web video format is the QuickTime Movie (*.mov*). Other formats include MPEG video (*.mpg*) and Windows-only AVI (*.avi*).

Like audio, video material can be made available for download or via streaming.

Cascading Style Sheets. Cascading Style Sheets give you advanced control over typography and page layout. A style sheet is made up of one or more rules (an instruction for how an element should be displayed).

One of the biggest advantages to style sheets is that you can control the display of a whole site with one style sheet document, making global changes a snap.

The biggest disadvantage is that style sheets are not supported universally nor consistently by popular browsers.

JavaScript. JavaScript is a web-specific scripting language that adds interactivity and conditional behavior to web pages. It is responsible for common tricks such as rollovers, pop-up windows, and status bar messages.

DHTML. DHTML is not a language in itself, but rather a combination of HTML, Cascading Style Sheets, and JavaScript. The main drawback to DHTML effects is inconsistent browser support. There is also a steep learning curve.

Flash. Flash is a multimedia format developed by Macromedia that gives you the ability to create full-screen animation, interactive graphics, and integrated sound effects for web delivery.

To make Flash files (*.swf*), you need a tool such as Macromedia Flash or Adobe LiveMotion.

Glossary

24-bit color
A color model capable of displaying approximately 16,777,216 colors.

8-bit color
A color model capable of displaying a maximum of 256 colors, the maximum number that 8 bits of information can define.

absolute pathname
Directions to a file's location on the server, starting at the topmost level of the server. An absolute URL begins by defining the HTTP protocol, followed by the name of the server and the complete pathname.

aliasing
The jagged, "stair-stepped" edges that can appear between colors in a bitmapped graphic.

alternative text
Text that is provided within an image tag that will display in the browser window if the image is not visible. It is specified using the `ALT` attribute within the `<IMG>` tag.

anchor
Another word for a link.

anti-aliasing
A slight blur added to the edges of objects and type in bitmapped graphics to smooth out the edges.

applet
A self-contained, mini-executable program, such as one written in the Java programming language.

attribute
Parameters added within an HTML tag to extend or modify its actions.

bit-depth
In web design, a measurement of the number of colors based on the number of bits (1s and 0s) allotted by the file or the system. A bit is the smallest unit of information on a computer (one bit can define 2 colors). Strung together, they can represent more values (8 bits can represent 256 values).

bitmapped image
A graphic that is made up of a grid of colored pixels, like a tiny mosiac. See also vector graphic.

block element
In HTML, a distinct unit of text that is automatically displayed with space above and below.

browser

A piece of software that displays web pages.

Cascading Style Sheets

An addition to HTML for controlling presentation of a document, including color, typography, alignment of text and images, etc.

CGI

Common Gateway Interface; a mechanism for communication between the web server and other programs (CGI scripts) running on the server.

character entity

A string of characters used to specify characters not found in the normal alphanumeric character set in HTML documents.

container tag

An HTML tag that has both an opening tag (e.g., <H1>) and a closing tag (e.g, </H1>).

CSS

See Cascading Style Sheets.

DHTML

Dynamic HTML; an integration of JavaScript, HTML, and Cascading Style Sheets. DHTML can be used to make content respond to user input or for adding simple animation effects.

dithering

The approximation of a color by mixing pixels of similar colors that are available in the image or system palette. The result of dithering is a random dot-pattern or noise in the image.

domain name

A name that corresponds to a specific IP address. It is easier for humans to remember than a 12-digit IP address.

Flash

A multimedia format developed by Macromedia for the delivery of animation, interactivity, and audio clips over the Web.

frames

A method for dividing the browser window into smaller subwindows, each displaying a different HTML document.

FTP

File Transfer Protocol; a system for moving files over the Internet from one computer to another.

gamma

Refers to the overall brightness of a computer monitor's display.

GIF

Graphic Interchange Format; common file format of web graphic images. GIF is a palette-based, 8-bit format. It is most appropriate for images with areas of flat color and sharp contrast.

hexadecimal

A base-16 numbering system consisting of the characters 0, 1, 2, 3, 4, 5, 6, 7, 8, 9, A, B, C, D, E, and F (where A through F represent the decimal values 10 through 15). It is used in HTML for specifying color values.

HTML

HyperText Markup Language; the format of web documents.

HTTP

Hypertext Transfer Protocol; the system that defines how web pages and media are requested and transferred between servers and browsers.

host

Another term for a server. Hosting services are companies that provide server space for web sites. See also ISP.

imagemap

A single image that contains multiple hypertext links.

IP address

A numeric identifier for a computer or device on a network. An IP address has four numbers (from 0 to 255) separated by periods (.).

ISP

Internet Service Provider; the company that sells access to the Internet computer network, whether through a dial-up modem connection, DSL, ISDN, cable, or other connection.

Java

A cross-platform, object-oriented programming language developed by Sun Microsystems. It is typically used for developing large, enterprise-scale applications, but it can also be used for creating small applications for the Web in the form of applets.

JavaScript

A scripting language developed by Netscape that adds interactivity and conditional behavior to web pages.

JPEG

A lossy graphics compression scheme developed by the Joint Photographic Experts Group. JPEG is most efficient at compressing images with gradations in tone and no sharp edge contrasts, such as photographs.

MP3

A popular file format for high-quality audio that uses MPEG compression.

MPEG

A family of multimedia standards created by the Motion Picture Experts Group, commonly used to refer to audio and video files saved using one of the MPEG compression schemes.

nesting

Placing one set of HTML tags within another tag pair, usually resulting in a combination of styles or a hierarchical display (as in lists).

optimizing

Reducing file size. Optimizing is an important step in web development, where file size and transfer time are critical.

palette

A table in an 8-bit indexed color file (such as a GIF) that provides color information for the pixels in the image.

pathname

Directions to a file using a nomenclature in which directory hierarchies and filenames are separated by slashes (/).

pixel

A single square in a graphic image (short for Picture Element).

PNG

Portable Network Graphic; a versatile graphics file format that features support for both 8-bit (PNG8) indexed images and 24-bit images (PNG24). PNGs also feature variable transparency levels, automatic color correction controls, and a lossless, yet highly efficient, compression scheme.

QuickTime

A system extension that makes it possible to view audio and video information on a computer. It was originally developed for the Macintosh, but is now available for Windows as well. The term also refers to the file format.

relative pathname

Directions to a file based on the location of the current file.

resolution

The number of pixels per inch (ppi) in an online graphic. In print, resolution is measured in dots per inch (dpi).

RGB color

A color system that describes colors based on combinations of red, green, and blue light.

rollover

The act of passing the mouse pointer over an element's space, or the events triggered by that action (such as a changing graphic or pop-up message).

server

A networked computer that provides some kind of service or information.

Shockwave

Proprietary technology from Macromedia for the web delivery of multimedia content

standalone tag

An HTML tag (e.g., `<IMG>`) that places an object on the page and does not use a closing tag (`</>`).

Unix

A multiuser, multitasking operating system developed by Bell Laboratories. It also provides programs for editing text, sending email, preparing tables, performing calculations, and many other specialized functions that normally require separate applications.

URL

Universal Resource Locator; the address of a site or document on the Web.

vector image

A graphic that uses mathematical equations to define shapes and fills. Vector images can be resized without change in quality. See also bitmapped image.

W3C

The World Wide Web Consortium; a consortium of many companies and organizations that "exists to develop common standards for the evolution of the World Wide Web." It is run by a joint effort between the Laboratory for Computer Science at the Massachusetts Institute of Technology and CERN, the European Particle Physics Laboratory, where the WWW was first developed.

web palette

The set of 216 colors that will not dither or shift when viewed with browsers on 8-bit monitors.

XML

eXtensible Markup Language; a new standard for marking up documents and data. XML allows authors to create customized tag sets that make content perform as databases and provide functionality not available with HTML.

Index

X

Jennifer Niederst was one of the first designers for the Web. As the designer of O'Reilly's Global Network Navigator (GNN), the first commercial web site, she has been designing for the Web since 1993. Since then, she has been working almost exclusively on the Web, first as Creative Director of Songline Studios (a subsidiary of O'Reilly), where she designed the original interface for WebReview (*webreview.com*), and as a freelance designer and consultant since 1996. She is the author of the best-selling *Web Design in a Nutshell* (O'Reilly, 1999), and has taught web design at the Massachusetts College of Art and the Interactive Factory in Boston, MA. She has spoken at major design and Internet events including the GRAFILL conference (Geilo, Norway), Seybold Seminars, and the W3C International Expo. In addition to designing, Jennifer enjoys cooking, travel, indie-rock, and making stuff. You can visit her site at *www.littlechair.com* or send her email at *jen@oreilly.com*.

Colophon

Our look is the result of reader comments, our own experimentation, and feedback from distribution channels. Distinctive covers complement our distinctive approach to technical topics, breathing personality and life into potentially dry subjects.

The cover image on *Learning Web Design* is a spiral. Spirals have been a part of the human experience as early as ancient Greece, and possibly since pre-history, fascinating the human imagination. In ancient times spirals were often used to represent what people believed to be portals between the present world and the world of their ancestors. In the Minoan civilization, spirals were commonly used in art and as decoration. In modern times, millions have been entertained by the spiral known as Slinky®.

The spiral shape is found throughout the natural world, most notably in the shell of the nautilus, the design of many spider webs, and the blooms of certain flowers. Another form of spiral is the double helix of DNA. In weather patterns, the spiral can be found in hurricanes, tornadoes, and the isobars surrounding high and low pressure centers. Of the known galaxies, the spiral is the most common shape.

The spiral can also be found in architecture. It tops Ionic columns, and from ancient to modern, the spiral staircase is a common architectural form. The helical spiral is the central structure of Frank Lloyd Wright's design of the Guggenheim Museum.

Mathematically speaking, spirals are planar curves, circling outward from a central point at a regular ratio. Archimedes discovered the first mathematical representation of a spiral: $r = a^\theta$, where r is the radius, a is any constant, and θ is the angle of rotation from the axis. This spiral is known as the Spiral of Archimedes. Many other, more complex, spirals have been found and described by mathemeticians since. Spirals can also be non-planar; these three-dimensional spirals either maintain a constant radius as the central point shifts along the third axis (a helical spiral, as in the thread of a screw), or travel outward from the central point as it moves along the third axis (as in the thread of a cone-shaped drill).

Colleen Gorman was the production editor and copyeditor for *Learning Web Design*. David Futato did the typesetting and page makeup, with assistance from Pam Spremulli. Rachel Wheeler proofread the manuscript. Linley Dolby, Nicole Arigo, Jane Ellin, Edie Freedman, Hanna Dyer, and Melanie Wang provided quality control. Bruce Tracy and Joe Wizda wrote the index.

Edie Freedman designed the cover of this book, with help from the O'Reilly Design team, using Photoshop 5.5 and QuarkXPress 4.1. Emma Colby produced the cover layout with QuarkXPress 4.1 using Adobe's version of Berthold Formata Condensed font.

David Futato designed and implemented the interior layout using QuarkXPress 4.1. The text and heading fonts are ITC Legacy Sans Book and Formata Condensed; the code font is TheSans Mono Condensed from LucasFont. The illustrations and screenshots that appear in the book were produced by Chris Reilley using Macromedia Freehand 8 and Adobe Photoshop 5.5. This colophon was written by David Futato.

Whenever possible, our books use a durable and flexible lay-flat binding. If the page count exceeds this binding's limit, perfect binding is used.

the Web Studio series

Learning Web Design: A Beginner's Guide to HTML, Graphics, and Beyond

By Jennifer Niederst
March 2001
418 pages, $34.95
ISBN 0-596-00036-7

In *Learning Web Design*, Jennifer Niederst shares the knowledge she's gained from years of experience as both web designer and teacher. She starts from the very beginning—defining the Internet, the Web, browsers, and URLs—assuming no previous knowledge of how the Web works. Jennifer helps you build the solid foundation in HTML, graphics, and design principles that you need for crafting effective web pages.

Designing Web Audio: RealAudio, MP3, Flash, Beatnik

By Josh Beggs & Dylan Thede
January 2001
395 pages, $34.95
ISBN 1-56592-353-7

Designing Web Audio is the most complete Internet audio guide on the market, loaded with informative real-world case studies and interviews with some of the world's leading audio and web producers. Its step-by-step instructions on how to use the most popular web audio formats to stream music make it an invaluable resource for web developers and web music enthusiasts.

Designing with JavaScript, 2nd Edition

By Nick Heinle & Martin Webb
June 2001 (est.)
350 pages (est.), $34.95
ISBN 1-56592-360-X

Completely rewritten, the second edition of this popular book is a true introduction to JavaScript™ for the designer. By teaching JavaScript in the context of its most powerful capability—document manipulation through the DOM—*Designing with JavaScript*, 2nd Edition, not only teaches the language, object, library, and DOM concepts, it also delivers useful strategies and techniques from the first page to the last.

Web Navigation: Designing the User Experience

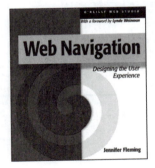

By Jennifer Fleming
September 1998
268 pages, $34.95
ISBN 1-56592-351-0

This book takes the first in-depth look at designing web site navigation using design strategies that help you uncover solutions that work for your site and audience. It focuses on designing by purpose, with chapters on entertainment, shopping, identity, learning, information, and community sites. Comes with a CD-ROM containing software demos and a "netography" of related web resources.

O'REILLY®

To Order: **800-998-9938** · **order@oreilly.com** · **www.oreilly.com**
OUR PRODUCTS ARE AVAILABLE AT A BOOKSTORE OR SOFTWARE STORE NEAR YOU.
For information: **800-998-9938** · **707-829-0515** · **info@oreilly.com**

Web Design in a Nutshell

By Jennifer Niederst
1st Edition November 1998
578 pages, $29.95
ISBN 1-56592-515-7

Web Design in a Nutshell contains the nitty-gritty on everything you need to know to design web pages. It's the good stuff, without the fluff, written and organized so that answers can be found quickly. Written by veteran web designer Jennifer Niederst, this book provides quick access to the wide range of front-end technologies and techniques from which web designers and authors must draw.

It is an excellent reference for HTML 4.0 tags (including tables, frames, and Cascading Style Sheets) with special attention given to browser support and platform idiosyncrasies. The HTML section is more than a reference work, though. It details strange behavior in tables, for instance, and gives ideas and workarounds for using tables and frames on your site. *Web Design in a Nutshell* also covers multimedia and interactivity, audio and video, and emerging technologies like Dynamic HTML, XML, embedded fonts, and internationalization.

The book includes:

- Discussions of the web environment, monitors, and browsers

- A complete reference to HTML and Server Side Includes, including browser support for every tag and attribute

- Chapters on creating GIF, JPEG, and PNG graphics, including designing with the Web Palette

- Information on multimedia and interactivity, including audio, video, Flash, Shockwave, and JavaScript™

- Detailed tutorial and reference on Cascading Style Sheets, including an appendix of browser compatibility information

- Appendices detailing HTML tags, attributes, deprecated tags, proprietary tags, and CSS compatibility

O'REILLY™

To Order: **800-998-9938** · **order@oreilly.com** · **www.oreilly.com**
OUR PRODUCTS ARE AVAILABLE AT A BOOKSTORE OR SOFTWARE STORE NEAR YOU.
For information: **800-998-9938** · **707-829-0515** · **info@oreilly.com**

Web Authoring and Design

Cascading Style Sheets: The Definitive Guide

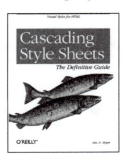

By Eric A. Meyer
May 2000
467 pages, $34.95
ISBN: 1-56592-622-6

Cascading Style Sheets (CSS) is the HTML 4.0-approved method for controlling visual presentation on web pages. This comprehensive guide to CSS and CSS1 explores in detail each property, how individual properties interact, how to avoid common mistakes in interpretation. For both beginning and advanced web authors, this is the first major CSS title to address actual current browser support, rather than the way things work in theory.

CSS Pocket Reference

By Eric A. Meyer
May 2001 (est.)
112 pages (est.), $9.95
ISBN: 0-596-00120-7

The *CSS Pocket Reference* introduces CSS and lists all CSS1 properties, plus the CSS1 pseudo-elements and pseudo-classes. To help overcome the obstacle of browser incompatibility, we've included a comprehensive guide to how each browser supports CSS1. For anyone who wants to correctly implement CSS, this is a handy condensed reference to all the details in the larger volume, *Cascading Style Sheets: The Definitive Guide.*

HTML Pocket Reference

By Jennifer Niederst
December 1999
95 pages, $9.95
ISBN: 1-56592-579-3

This pocket reference by Jennifer Niederst, author of the bestselling *Web Design in a Nutshell*, delivers a concise guide to every HTML tag. You'll find detailed information on each tag's attributes, as well as browser support information. This is likely to be the most dog-eared book on every web professional's desk.

HTML & XHTML: The Definitive Guide, 4th Edition

By Chuck Musciano & Bill Kennedy
August 2000
677 pages, $34.95
ISBN: 0-596-00026-X

This complete guide is full of examples, sample code, and practical hands-on advice for creating truly effective web pages and mastering advanced features. Web authors learn how to insert images, create useful links and searchable documents, use Netscape extensions, design great forms, and much more. The fourth edition covers XHTML 1.0, HTML 4.01, Netscape 6.0, and Internet Explorer 5.0, plus all the common extensions.

Information Architecture for the World Wide Web

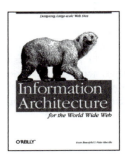

By Louis Rosenfeld & Peter Morville
February 1998
221 pages, $29.95
ISBN: 1-56592-282-4

Learn how to merge aesthetics and mechanics to design web sites that "work." This book shows how to apply principles of architecture and library science to design cohesive web sites and intranets that are easy to use, manage, and expand. Covers building complex sites, hierarchy design and organization, and techniques to make your site easier to search. For webmasters, designers, and administrators.

O'REILLY

*To Order: **800-998-9938** · **order@oreilly.com** · **www.oreilly.com***
OUR PRODUCTS ARE AVAILABLE AT A BOOKSTORE OR SOFTWARE STORE NEAR YOU.
*For information: **800-998-9938** · **707-829-0515** · **info@oreilly.com***

The Missing Manuals

Mac OS 9: The Missing Manual

By David Pogue
March 2000
472 pages, $19.95
ISBN: 1-56592-857-1

Mac OS 9: The Missing Manual is a warm, witty, jargon-free guide to the Macintosh platform's latest system software. Written with enough patience for the novice and enough depth for the power user, the book includes the short-cuts, surprises, and design touches that make the Mac the most passionately championed computer in the world.

AppleWorks 6: The Missing Manual

By Jim Elferdink & David Reynolds
May 2000
450 pages, $19.95
ISBN: 1-56592-858-X

AppleWorks 6: The Missing Manual guides readers through both the basics and the hidden talents of the new version of AppleWorks. With over 250 illustrations, a 2,000-entry index, and a menu-by-menu explanation of every command, AppleWorks 6: The Missing Manual is as smoothly put together as AppleWorks itself.

Windows 2000 Pro: The Missing Manual

By Sharon Crawford
November 2000
450 pages, $19.95
ISBN: 0-596-00010-3

In Windows 2000 Pro: The Missing Manual, bestselling Windows NT author Sharon Crawford provides the friendly, authoritative book that should have been in the box. It's the ideal (and desperately needed) user's guide for the world's most popular corporate operating system.

iMovie 2: The Missing Manual

By David Pogue
December 2000
408 pages, $19.95
ISBN: 0-596-00104-5

iMovie 2: The Missing Manual covers every step of iMovie video production, from choosing and using a digital camcorder to burning the finished work onto CDs. Far deeper and more detailed than the meager set of online help screens included with iMovie, the book helps iMovie 2 users realize the software's potential as a breakthrough in the cost, complexity, and difficulty of desktop video production.

Windows ME: The Missing Manual

By David Pogue
September 2000
423 pages, $19.95
ISBN: 0-596-00009-X

In Windows Me: The Missing Manual, author David Pogue provides the friendly, authoritative book that should have been in the box. It's the ideal user's guide for the world's most popular operating system.

POGUE PRESS™
O'REILLY®

To Order: **800-998-9938** • **order@oreilly.com** • **www.oreilly.com**
OUR PRODUCTS ARE AVAILABLE AT A BOOKSTORE OR SOFTWARE STORE NEAR YOU.
For information: **800-998-9938** • **707-829-0515** • **info@oreilly.com**

O'REILLY BOOKS ONLINE

Safari is a web-based subscription service that lets you read and search an online collection of O'Reilly titles. You can preview every section of every book in the collection so you'll instantly know which titles will help you through your project or answer your technical questions. You decide what information you need and when you need it—and the best part is that Safari finds it for you!

A subscription evolves along with your need for technical information. Every month you can swap out some (or all) of your titles and swap in replacements, or you can just add more and increase your subscription level.

Even if you don't subscribe, you can still search the Safari library—at no cost. As a non-subscriber, you can use Safari to help you decide which O'Reilly book to buy, or where to find information in the O'Reilly books you already own.

We've never seen anything like it and we're sure you haven't either. Subscribing is quick, easy, and offers the flexibility you need to keep up in today's fast-paced world.

Photoshop for the Web

Designing Web Audio

MP3: The Definitive Guide

Cascading Style Sheets

Information Architecture
for the World Wide Web

Web Design in a Nutshell

If you've never been on a Safari before, now is the time.

SAFARI.OREILLY.COM

How to stay in touch with O'Reilly

1. Visit Our Award-Winning Web Site

http://www.oreilly.com/

★ "Top 100 Sites on the Web" —*PC Magazine*
★ "Top 5% Web sites" —*Point Communications*
★ "3-Star site" — *The McKinley Group*

Our Web site contains a library of comprehensive product information (including book excerpts and tables of contents), downloadable software, background articles, interviews with technology leaders, links to relevant sites, book cover art, and more. File us in your Bookmarks or Hotlist!

2. Join Our Email Mailing Lists

New Product Releases

To receive automatic email with brief descriptions of all new O'Reilly products as they are released, send email to:
ora-news-subscribe@lists.oreilly.com
Put the following information in the first line of your message (*not* in the Subject field):
subscribe ora-news

O'Reilly Events

If you'd also like us to send information about trade show events, special promotions, and other O'Reilly events, send email to:
ora-news-subscribe@lists.oreilly.com
Put the following information in the first line of your message (*not* in the Subject field):
subscribe ora-events

3. Get Examples from Our Books via FTP

There are two ways to access an archive of example files from our books:

Regular FTP

- FTP to:
  ftp.oreilly.com
  (login: anonymous
  password: your email address)
- Point your web browser to:
  ftp://ftp.oreilly.com/

FTPMAIL

- Send an email message to:
  ftpmail@online.oreilly.com
  (Write "help" in the message body)

4. Contact Us via Email

order@oreilly.com
To place a book or software order online. Good for North American and international customers.

subscriptions@oreilly.com
To place an order for any of our newsletters or periodicals.

books@oreilly.com
General questions about any of our books.

software@oreilly.com
For general questions and product information about our software. Check out O'Reilly Software Online at http://software.oreilly.com/ for software and technical support information. Registered O'Reilly software users send your questions to: website-support@oreilly.com

cs@oreilly.com
For answers to problems regarding your order or our products.

booktech@oreilly.com
For book content technical questions or corrections.

proposals@oreilly.com
To submit new book or software proposals to our editors and product managers.

international@oreilly.com
For information about our international distributors or translation queries. For a list of our distributors outside of North America check out:
http://www.oreilly.com/distributors.html

5. Work with Us

Check out our website for current employment opportunites:
http://jobs.oreilly.com/

O'Reilly & Associates, Inc.

101 Morris Street, Sebastopol, CA 95472 USA
TEL 707-829-0515 or 800-998-9938
      (6am to 5pm PST)
FAX 707-829-0104

O'REILLY

To Order: **800-998-9938** • **order@oreilly.com** • **www.oreilly.com**
OUR PRODUCTS ARE AVAILABLE AT A BOOKSTORE OR SOFTWARE STORE NEAR YOU.
For information: **800-998-9938** • **707-829-0515** • **info@oreilly.com**

Titles from O'Reilly

O'REILLY

To Order: **800-998-9938** · **order@oreilly.com** · **www.oreilly.com**
OUR PRODUCTS ARE AVAILABLE AT A BOOKSTORE OR SOFTWARE STORE NEAR YOU.
For information: **800-998-9938** · **707-829-0515** · **info@oreilly.com**

International Distributors

http://international.oreilly.com/distributors.html

UK, Europe, Middle East and Africa
(except France, Germany, Austria, Switzerland, Luxembourg, and Liechtenstein)

INQUIRIES
O'Reilly UK Limited
4 Castle Street
Farnham
Surrey, GU9 7HS
United Kingdom
Telephone: 44-1252-711776
Fax: 44-1252-734211
Email: information@oreilly.co.uk

ORDERS
Wiley Distribution Services Ltd.
1 Oldlands Way
Bognor Regis
West Sussex PO22 9SA
United Kingdom
Telephone: 44-1243-843294
UK Freephone: 0800-243207
Fax: 44-1243-843302 (Europe/EU orders)
or 44-1243-843274 (Middle East/Africa)
Email: cs-books@wiley.co.uk

Germany, Switzerland, Austria, Luxembourg, and Liechtenstein

INQUIRIES & ORDERS
O'Reilly Verlag
Balthasarstr. 81
D-50670 Köln
Germany
Telephone: 49-221-973160-91
Fax: 49-221-973160-8
Email: anfragen@oreilly.de (inquiries)
Email: order@oreilly.de (orders)

France

INQUIRIES & ORDERS
Éditions O'Reilly
18 rue Séguier
75006 Paris, France
Tel: 1-40-51-71-89
Fax: 1-40-51-72-26
Email: france@editions-oreilly.fr

Canada (French language books)
Les Éditions Flammarion ltée
375, Avenue Laurier Ouest
Montréal (Québec) H2V 2K3
Tel: 00-1-514-277-8807
Fax: 00-1-514-278-2085
Email: info@flammarion.qc.ca

Hong Kong
City Discount Subscription Service, Ltd.
Unit A, 6th Floor, Yan's Tower
27 Wong Chuk Hang Road
Aberdeen, Hong Kong
Tel: 852-2580-3539
Fax: 852-2580-6463
Email: citydis@ppn.com.hk

Korea
Hanbit Media, Inc.
Chungmu Bldg. 210
Yonnam-dong 568-33
Mapo-gu
Seoul, Korea
Tel: 822-325-0397
Fax: 822-325-9697
Email: hant93@chollian.dacom.co.kr

Philippines
Global Publishing
G/F Benavides Garden
1186 Benavides Street
Manila, Philippines
Tel: 632-254-8949/632-252-2582
Fax: 632-734-5060/632-252-2733
Email: globalp@pacific.net.ph

Taiwan
O'Reilly Taiwan
First Floor, No.21, Lane 295
Section 1, Fu-Shing South Road
Taipei, 106 Taiwan
Tel: 886-2-27099669
Fax: 886-2-27038802
Email: taiwan@oreilly.com

India
Shroff Publishers & Distributors Pvt. Ltd.
12, "Roseland", 2nd Floor
Mumbai 400 050
Tel: 91-22-641-1800/643-9910
Fax: 91-22-643-2422
Email: spd@vsnl.com

China
O'Reilly Beijing
SIGMA Building, Suite B809
No. 49 Zhichun Road
Haidian District
Beijing, China PR 100080
Tel: 86-10-8809-7475
Fax: 86-10-8809-7463
Email: beijing@oreilly.com

Japan
O'Reilly Japan, Inc.
Yotsuya Y's Building
7 Banch 6, Honshio-cho
Shinjuku-ku
Tokyo 160-0003 Japan
Tel: 81-3-3356-5227
Fax: 81-3-3356-5261
Email: japan@oreilly.com

Singapore, Indonesia, Malaysia and Thailand
TransQuest Publishers Pte Ltd
30 Old Toh Tuck Road #05-02
Sembawang Kimtrans Logistics Centre
Singapore 597654
Tel: 65-4623112
Fax: 65-4625761
Email: wendiw@transquest.com.sg

All Other Asian Countries
O'Reilly & Associates, Inc.
101 Morris Street
Sebastopol, CA 95472 USA
Tel: 707-829-0515
Fax: 707-829-0104
Email: order@oreilly.com

Australia
Woodslane Pty., Ltd.
7/5 Vuko Place
Warriewood NSW 2102
Australia
Tel: 61-2-9970-5111
Fax: 61-2-9970-5002
Email: info@woodslane.com.au

New Zealand
Woodslane New Zealand, Ltd.
21 Cooks Street (P.O. Box 575)
Waganui, New Zealand
Tel: 64-6-347-6543
Fax: 64-6-345-4840
Email: info@woodslane.com.au

Argentina
Distribuidora Cuspide
Suipacha 764
1008 Buenos Aires
Argentina
Phone: 5411-4322-8868
Fax: 5411-4322-3456
Email: libros@cuspide.com

O'REILLY

To Order: **800-998-9938** · **order@oreilly.com** · **www.oreilly.com**
OUR PRODUCTS ARE AVAILABLE AT A BOOKSTORE OR SOFTWARE STORE NEAR YOU.
For information: **800-998-9938** · **707-829-0515** · **info@oreilly.com**